THE LIFE

OF

MAJOR JOHN ANDRÉ.

The Life of Major John André
Adjutant-General of the British Army in America

Winthrop Sargent

HERITAGE BOOKS
2008

HERITAGE BOOKS
AN IMPRINT OF HERITAGE BOOKS, INC.

Books, CDs, and more—Worldwide

For our listing of thousands of titles see our website at
www.HeritageBooks.com

Published 2008 by
HERITAGE BOOKS, INC.
Publishing Division
100 Railroad Ave. #104
Westminster, Maryland 21157

Copyright © 1871 Winthrop Sargent

All rights reserved. No part of this book may be reproduced or transmitted in any form or by any means, electronic or mechanical, including photocopying, recording or by any information storage and retrieval system without written permission from the author, except for the inclusion of brief quotations in a review.

International Standard Book Numbers
Paperbound: 978-0-7884-2176-1
Clothbound: 978-0-7884-7128-5

TO THE

HONORABLE JARED SPARKS,

AS A MEMORIAL OF

PUBLIC ADMIRATION AND PERSONAL FRIENDSHIP,

THIS VOLUME

IS RESPECTFULLY DEDICATED.

THE present edition of Winthrop Sargent's "Memoirs of Major André" is published, as the most fitting memorial which those who loved him best can make of a life now ended. For, although this work, which is but one of many historical essays that were the fruit of his studious youth, would alone suffice to guard their author's name " against the tooth of time and razure of oblivion," none the less do it and all his other writings seem, to those who knew him well, but the vernal promise of an autumn which never came. Yet, in what he accomplished, is so much knowledge, so correct a judgment of men and things, such graceful power of thought and style, that this promise may stand beside the riper work of others; but

"Lycidas is dead, dead ere his prime."

PREFACE.

The romantic nature of the circumstances which connect the name of Major André with the history of our Revolution induced me some time ago to inquire more closely into the details of a character that seems to have inspired so warm an interest in the minds of all who have had occasion to observe it. In this undertaking, I am free to confess that my success in obtaining information has been commensurate neither with my labors nor desires. No pains indeed were spared to procure intelligence concerning André himself. Every repository that could be heard of was examined; and the old-world tales of those who "mumble their wisdom o'er the gossip's bowl" have been carefully gathered and sifted. Thus, much curious matter more or less relevant to his story has been brought together from one quarter or another; and by joining what has hitherto scarcely been known at all with what every one knows, something like a connected sketch of his career has been compiled. Several of the manuscript authorities that I have made use of (such as the Notes of Sir Henry Clinton on a copy of Stedman's American War, and the original Journals and papers of members of either party in our Revolution) appeared to me to possess no light value, and I thought it well to take advantage of an opportunity to set their contents before the world ere the documents themselves should perish ; for, as honest old Aubrey says — " 'tis pitie that they should fall into the merciless hands of women, and be put under pies." This consideration may perhaps apologize for the insertion of more than one paragraph whose direct connection with the subject of this volume might not otherwise be very manifest. With these acquisitions, however, in hand, and with such sketches of the political and social condition of affairs during the period as naturally followed the thread of the story, the preparation of the following pages gave me a very pleasant employment for some leisure country weeks. Whether they will prove as easy in the reading as they were in the writing is another question. If I have not entirely pursued the plan commemorated by Miguel Cervantes, and eked out my task with profuse histories of every giant or river which crosses its path, I have at least avoided pestering the reader with a myriad of references and authorities. There are indeed vouchers for the facts put forward : but to drag them all in on every occasion great or small, would too much cumber my text. As it is, I fear that the critical reader will find the book amenable to the censure of the nobleman in Guzman D'Alfarache, who, having ordered a picture of his horse, complained that though indeed his steed was faithfully enough drawn, the canvas was so loaded with other objects — temples, trees, and the setting sun — that poor Bavieca was the least prominent part of the production. This is a fault of which no one is more conscious than myself; yet there is room for a hope that it may still find pardon, since many of the passages which are not immediately personal to André himself are nevertheless more or less involved with the mighty events in which he was concerned, and often are compiled from sources hitherto unexplored. For access to many of these I am especially indebted to the kindness of Mr. Sparks, Mr. Bancroft, and Mr. John Carter Brown, whose American library is the most admirable collection of the kind that I have ever seen in private hands. To Mr. Tefft of Savannah, Mr. Cope, Mr. Townsend Ward, and Mr. Penington of Philadelphia, and to several others, I am under obligations for valuable aid and friendly suggestions.

The map that accompanies this volume is engraved from a number of original military drawings by Villefranche and other engineers, and preserved by Major Sargent of the American Army, who was stationed at West Point as aide to General Howe until that officer was relieved by Arnold.

WINTHROP SARGENT.

CONTENTS.

CHAPTER I.
André's Parentage, Birth, and Early Life. — Nicholas St. André. — Miss Seward. — His Courtship. — Letters to Miss Seward, . . 1

CHAPTER II.
Failure of André's Courtship. — Richard Lovell Edgeworth. — Thomas Day. — Marriage and Death of Miss Sneyd, ... 29

CHAPTER III.
André joins the Army. — Visits Germany. — Condition of the Service. — He comes to America. — State of American Affairs, . . . 39

CHAPTER IV.
Political Condition of Massachusetts in 1774. — State of Affairs at Boston, ... 57

CHAPTER V.
Condition of Canada in 1775. — Operations on Lake Champlain and the Sorel. — Fall of Fort St. John, and Capture of André, . . 71

CHAPTER VI.
André's Captivity. — Detained in Pennsylvania. — Treatment of Prisoners. — André's Relations with the Americans. — His Letters to Mr. Cope. — Exchange and Promotion. — Sir Charles Grey. — Sir Henry Clinton and the Operations on the Hudson, ... 83

CONTENTS.

CHAPTER VII.

The British embark for Philadelphia. — Brandywine, the Paoli, and Germantown. — André's Humanity. — Occupation and Fortification of Philadelphia. — Character of the City in 1777, ... 106

CHAPTER VIII.

Affairs at Philadelphia. — Disorders and Discontents. — Fall of Red Bank. — André follows Grey with Howe to Whitemarsh. — Character of Sir William Howe, ... 123

CHAPTER IX.

The British Army in Philadelphia. — Features of the Occupation. — Sir William Erskine. — Abercrombie. — Simcoe. — Lord Cathcart. — Tarleton. — André's Social Relations in the City. — Verses composed by him. — Amateur Theatricals. — Misconduct of the Royal Arms. — The Mischianza. — André's Account of it. — Howe removed from the Command, ... 143

CHAPTER X.

Evacuation of Philadelphia. — Battle of Monmouth. — D'Estaing's Arrival. — André accompanies Grey against New Bedford. — His Satirical Verses on the Investment of Newport. — Aide to Clinton. — Character of this General. — André's Verses upon an American Duel, 182

CHAPTER XI.

New York in 1778. — André's Political Essay. — His Favor with Clinton. — Receives the Surrender of Fort La Fayette. — Letter to Mrs. Arnold. — Commencement of Arnold's Intrigue. — Appointed Deputy Adjutant-General. — Siege of Charleston. — Letter to Savannah. — Accused of entering Charleston as a Spy, ... 206

CHAPTER XII.

Clinton returns to New York. — Proposed Attack on Rochambeau. — Plans for a Loyal Uprising. — Anecdotes of André. — The Cow-Chase, 230

CHAPTER XIII.

Progress of Arnold's Treason. — Condition of American Affairs in 1780. — Plans for Surrendering West Point. — Letters between André and Arnold. — An Interview Concerted. — André's Last Hours in New York, ... 250

CHAPTER XXII.

Considerations upon the Justice of André's Sentence. — Conflicting Opinions. — Character of our Generals. — Reflections on André's Fate, ... 413

APPENDIX.

No. I. Benedict Arnold, ... 447
No. II. The Captors, ... 461
No. III. Verses connected with André's Execution, ... 464
No. IV. Colonel Benjamin Tallmadge to General Heath, . . 469

INDEX. 473

Major André

LIFE OF MAJOR ANDRÉ.

CHAPTER I.

André's Parentage, Birth, and Early Life.—Nicholas St. André.—Miss Seward.—His Courtship.—Letters to Miss Seward.

ACCORDING to Debrett, Burke, and other genealogical authorities, John André was descended from a French refugee family, settled in England, at Southampton, in the county of Hants; but whether this descent was by the paternal or the maternal line, does not appear. His mother, whose family name was Girardot, though of French parentage, was born at London. His father was a native of Geneva in Switzerland; but it would seem that a very considerable portion of his life must have been passed in London, where he carried on an extensive business in the Levant trade, and where also, in 1780, several of his brothers had their abode. Of these, Dr. Andrée, of Hatton Gardens, was apparently the only one who preserved what is said to have been an earlier method of spelling the family name.

Notwithstanding the establishment of a part of the André family in England, its connections upon the continent would appear to have been the most numerous and the most permanent. Indeed, the name is not an uncommon one, and the biographical dictionaries supply a numerous list of persons bearing it, and distinguished in various lines. Of course it is impossible to trace any relationship between the majority of these and the subject of this memoir. During her sojourn at Naples, not long after Major André's death, Mrs. Piozzi relates that she became acquainted with "the Swedish minister, Monsieur André, uncle to the lamented officer who perished in our sovereign's service in America:" but the only result of recent inquiries, set on foot in Sweden and carried as far as the isle of Gottland, in the Baltic, is to discredit her assertion. There exist, indeed, in that kingdom, the families of André and Andrée, which have given to the state men of high official rank; yet there is no reason to suppose that Major André was of the same blood. Turning to Germany, however, we are more successful. Branches of the stock from which he sprung have long been seated at Frankfort-on-the-Maine and at Offenbach; some of the members of which are very well known to the world as publishers and editors of numerous musical works, and especially of Mozart's. The most celebrated of these was Johann André, author of the opera of The Potter, who was born at Offenbach in 1741, and who died in 1799.

Though as yet opportunity is wanting to verify the supposition, there is strong reason to believe that a near connection existed between the immediate family of Major André and the once celebrated Nicholas St. André of Southampton; — a character whose career is scarcely to be paralleled even in the pages of Gil Blas. This person came over to England, from his native Switzerland, at a very early age, and, probably, towards the close of the seventeenth century. By his own account, his origin was perfectly respectable, and even distinguished; and in his later days he would assert that by right he was possessed of a title. Yet he arrived in England in the train of a Jewish family, and, it is said, in a menial position. He was related to a famous dancing-master of the same name who is mentioned in Dryden's Mac Flecknoe, published in 1682:

"St. André's feet ne'er kept more equal time;"

and was himself originally destined for a fencing or a dancing master. His knowledge of the French tongue extended to all the provincial dialects, and it is conjectured that he was, for a time, a teacher of that language; his sister certainly followed this occupation at a Chelsea boarding-school. But being early placed with a surgeon, he rapidly acquired such a considerable, though perhaps superficial, knowledge in that science, that he soon rose to a conspicuous position, and was among the first to deliver public lectures upon surgery. To an invincible assurance he united such a variety of accomplishments that we need not wonder at his receiving the appointment of Anatomist to the Royal Household, and being presented by George I. with the King's own sword. He was singularly expert not only in manly exercises, such as fencing, running, jumping, or riding the great horse, but also in pursuits that involve the employment of mental ingenuity. At chess he was an adept; and his pretensions in botany, architecture, and music, were very respectable. Indeed, his skill with the viol de gambo was something remarkable. In 1723, he printed an account of a mysterious adventure that had nearly cost him his life. His story made a great sensation at the time, and the Privy Council offered a reward for the detection of his assailants; but it has not always encountered implicit confidence. A little later, however, he became involved in another affair by which his professional reputation was hopelessly damaged. It seems that when the impostor Mary Tofts, the rabbit-breeder of Godalming, came forth with her wonderful tale, St. André was among the readiest of her believers. He professed to have examined carefully into the matter, and that the story she told was entirely faithful. It is difficult at this day to rightly estimate the credulity of the English people on that occasion. High and low were infected with the absurd conviction that the race of rabbits were of the children of men. "The public horror was so great that the rent of rabbit-warrens sank to nothing; and nobody, till the delusion was over, presumed to eat a rabbit." The learned Whiston not only devoutly believed in the fable, but wrote a pamphlet to prove, in its occurrence, the fulfilment of a prophecy in Esdras. In short, as Lord Onslow wrote to the great naturalist, Sir Hans Sloane, (Dec. 4, 1726,) all England was disturbed by this story. But Queen Caroline having charged Dr. Cheselden to investigate the matter, the imposture was speedily exposed, and they whose countenance had given it all its weight were now visited with a full measure of public opprobrium. Swift, and perhaps Arbuthnot, had already taken up the pen against St. André, and now Hogarth seized on him. In the print of Mary Tofts, he is introduced; and in another entitled The Wise Men of Godliman, the figure marked A is designed for the court anatomist. Again, in the print of The Doctors in Labor, he figures as a merry-andrew; and by a host of coarse caricatures and doggerel ballads his weakness was stigmatized and made yet more ridiculous. In December, 1726, the affair was burlesqued upon the stage, — a new rabbit-scene being added to the play of The Necromancer; and in 1727, the ballad of St. André's Miscarriage was sung through the streets:

> " He dissected, compared, and distinguish'd likewise,
> The make of these rabbits, their growth and their size;
> He preserv'd them in spirits and — a little too late,
> Preserv'd (*Vertue sculpsit*) a neat copperplate."

The consequence was, that on his return to Court he was so coldly treated that he would never reappear; nor, though continuing to hold his appointment till his death, would he touch the official salary. A more amusing circumstance was his testiness for the future upon the subject of rabbits; absolutely forbidding any allusion, even to their name, being ever again made in his presence.

On the 27th of May, 1730, St. André married Lady Betty Molyneux, the childless widow of Samuel Molyneux, M. P., who brought him, it was said, £30,000. The lady's conduct was so imprudent that she was forthwith dismissed by the Queen from her service. Mr. Molyneux was but recently dead, and whispers named her as his murderer: nor did her second husband escape a share of the imputation. The Rev. Dr. Madden, of Dublin, however, having made use of this scandal in a pamphlet, St. André at once prosecuted him successfully for defamation. But the accusation has been immortalized by Pope, in the second dialogue of the Epilogue to his Satires, where "the poisoning dame" is brought into discussion. St. André had once the good fortune to attend the poet when he was upset in Lord Bolingbroke's coach as it returned from Dawley. His fingers were incurably wounded, and this being the nearest surgeon, was called in.* About 1755, he took up his permanent abode at Southampton. The greater part of the property that came with Lady Betty passed on her death to Sir Capel Molyneux; and St. André's expensive tastes dissipated much of what remained. Architecture was one of his hobbies; and large sums were squandered on a house at Chepstow. About a mile's distance from Southampton, he erected a thoroughly inconvenient dwelling, which he called Belle-Vue, and boasted it as constructed "on the true principles of anatomy." He had, however, another dwelling within the town, with a large and valuable library; and here he died in March, 1776, being then upwards of ninety-six years of age.

St. André is represented as having been loose in religion and in morals; of a vivacious and agreeable manner in conversation; his speech abounding in foreign idioms; his countenance fierce and muscular. In earlier life his manners must have been polite and graceful, from the social positions to which he rose; but Nichols, who wrote of him after death, and who characterizes him as "a profligate man of an amo-

---

* St. André is also, truly or falsely, reported as having had a share in a strange rencontre between the Earl of Peterborough and his guest, the famous Voltaire, on occasion of the detection of the latter in a piece of pecuniary dishonesty. The earl would have slain him but for the presence of St. André, who held him tightly while Voltaire fled — not only from the house, but from the kingdom. — *Gent. Mag.*, 1797.

rous constitution," declares that "no man will be hardy enough to assert that the figure, manners, and language of St. André were those of a gentleman."

Such was the character with whom, as has already been observed, John André was probably nearly allied by blood as well as by name; though why the latter was altered to André or Andrée, we do not know. It is not likely that any of the lineage now reside in England. About 1820 or 1825, when a young French gentleman, M. Ernest André, came over from Paris on a visit to the surviving sisters of Major André, he was declared by those ladies to be their nearest living relative.

Where John André was born, cannot with certainty be stated. It may have occurred at London, where his father, after the fashion of those days, had long had his dwelling and his place of business under one roof, in Warnford Court, Throgmorton Street. Or it may have been at Southampton, since in 1780 we find his mother, then a widow and chiefly residing with her brother, Mr. Girardot, in Old Broad Street, London, yet still possessing a house there. We are able to fix the date of his birth with more accuracy; although, even on this head, the contemporaneous accounts are conflicting: one pointing to the year 1749, and another to 1752; while Rose puts it at London, in 1750. But the monumental inscription in Westminster Abbey that says "he fell a sacrifice to his zeal for his king and country, on the 2d of October, 1780, aged twenty-nine," and which is followed by Lord Mahon, is borne out by a letter of André's own, written in October, 1769, in which he speaks of himself as "a poor novice of eighteen." Hence we may fairly ascribe the period of his birth to the year 1751.

The very little that is known respecting André's earlier years, renders it proper to be particular in presenting to the reader such details, naked though they be, as can now be laid hold of; and even these do not always agree, as they come to us from his contemporaries. One story gives Westminster as the scene of his education, and with a particularity that brings to mind the circumstantial evidence of Sheridan's double-letter scene, even fixes the date "near the latter end of Dr. Markham's time, now Archbishop of York." In this case, he might have had for school-mates Thomas and Charles Cotesworth Pinckney, so renowned afterwards in the service of their country in the war that cost André his life; while for a master he would have had a man whom Gibbon distinguished, among the whole bench of English bishops, for eminent scholarship and skill in the instruction of youth. This was the prelate, too, whose feelings towards insurgent America are thus alluded to by Lord John Townshend:

> "To Cramner's stake be Adams ty'd;
> Mild Markham preaching by his side
> The traitor's heart will gain:
> For if he sees the blaze expire,
> Locke's works he'll fling to wake the fire,
> And put him out of pain."

Another account, however, says that he was first placed at Hackney, under a Mr. Newcombe; whence he was after a time withdrawn, and sent for several years to Geneva to complete his education. It may be that both of these stories are correct; that from Hackney he went to St. Paul's, and thence to Geneva; but wherever he was taught, his acquirements were such as to reflect honor alike on the teacher and the pupil. He was master of many things that in those days very rarely constituted a part of a gentleman's education, and which, indeed, even in these are to be found rather in exceptions than the rule. The modern European languages — French, German, Italian, &c. — are said to have been possessed by him in singular perfection; while in music, painting, drawing, and dancing, he particularly excelled. When we consider that with these accomplishments was joined a nature always ambitious of distinction, a mind stored with the *belles lettres* of the day, and endowed not only with a taste for poetry, but with considerable readiness in its composition ; and a person which, though slender, was remarkably active and graceful, we need not wonder that his attractions were such as to win the favor of all with whom he came in contact. At the university of Geneva, he was remarked for a diligent student, and for an active and inquiring mind; and in especial was distinguished by his proficiency in the schools of mathematics and of military drawings. To his skill in this last branch, his subsequent rapid advancement in the army was in great part attributable.

André's father was a respectable merchant, whose success had been sufficiently great to convince him that his own profession was the very best his son could embrace ; yet not sufficient to enable him to give that son a fortune which would permit him to follow the bent of his own inclinations. In this relation, it would seem as though the old gentleman had pursued very much the same course as that adopted by the elder Osbaldistone, in Rob Roy ; and to a certain extent the consequences were alike. Summoned home from the continent, young André found a place assigned him in his father's counting-house, where for some time he appears to have undergone that training which it was hoped and expected would enable him to carry on successfully the business that had already afforded a competency to its founder. For, in the process of time, his father had found himself in condition to withdraw from at least the more laborious cares of his affairs, and, abandoning the residence in Throgmorton Street, had removed his household to a country-seat at Clapton, called The Manor House. This building, now used for a school, is still standing opposite to Brook House, Clapton Gate ; and the graves of several of its former occupants are to be seen in Hackney churchyard, hard by the old tower.

Although at this stage in his career there is no evidence that John André's conduct was that of

> "A clerk condemned his father's soul to cross,
> Who penned a stanza when he should engross;"

yet we may fairly infer, from his own language, that the commercial line of life chalked out for him was less to his taste than the profession of arms; that, like young Frank Osbaldistone, in preference to any other active pursuit, he would choose the army; and that the desk and stool " by a small coalfire in a gloomy compting-house in Warnford Court," would have been joyfully exchanged for the sash and gorget, and any barrack-yard in the United Kingdom. The bent of his studies at Geneva must have satisfied his judgment as to the sphere in which he was best calculated to attain success. But his years were too few to enable him to oppose his father's wishes; and in 1767 or 1768, when about sixteen or seventeen years of age, he entered the counting-house. Nor did the death of his father, which occurred at the house in Clapton, in April, 1769, make at the time any material difference in the nature of his avocations.

What family was left by the elder André can only be gathered from the fact that in 1780, besides his widow, there still remained a second son, William Lewis, who was eight years behind his brother; and three daughters, Louisa Catherine, Mary Hannah, and Anne. The last is said to have been distinguished for a poetical talent. In her Monody, Miss Seward thus makes her hero address this little domestic band on his departure for America:

> "Dim clouds of Woe! ye veil each sprightly grace
> That us'd to sparkle in MARIA's face.
> My tuneful ANNA to her lute complains,
> But Grief's fond throbs arrest the parting strains.
> Fair as the silver blossom on the thorn,
> Soft as the spirit of the vernal morn,
> LOUISA, chase those trembling fears, that prove
> Th' ungovern'd terror's of a sister's love;
> They bend thy sweet head, like yon lucid flow'r
> That shrinks and fades beneath the summer's show'r.
> Oh! smile, my sisters, on this destin'd day,
> And with the radiant omen gild my way!"

Of these sisters, Louisa Catherine was born about 1754, and Mary Hannah about 1752, according to the inscriptions in the churchyard at Bath-Hampton, where they are buried;—the last of these two dates going far to fix that of Major André's birth as of 1751.

In 1780 also there were yet living at London two brothers of the elder André: Mr. David André of New Broad Street, and Mr. John Lewis André, of Warnford Court, Throgmorton Street; who were known to the community as respectable Turkey merchants, and who doubtless still carried on at the old place the business in which their brother had prospered well, but which their nephews had declined. For it was not John alone who renounced the ledger for the spontoon. Not very long after he entered the army he was followed by his only brother, whose years forbid the supposition that he could ever have had any prolonged experience in the mysteries of trade.

During some months after his father's death, John André was probably sufficiently occupied with new and urgent cares, to prevent his taking any active step towards freeing himself from the chains of business. From circumstances we may conclude that the summer of 1769 — the year in which he became the head of his mother's house — was passed by the family at Buxton, Matlock, and other places in the interior of England, whither it was customary for invalids, and persons whose health was impaired by affliction, to resort for relief and change of scene: and if it was not now that he first became acquainted with Miss Seward, it is at least almost certain that he formed with another lady a friendship that left its coloring on the whole of his future life.

Anna Seward, the eulogist of Major André, was born at Eyam, in Derbyshire, in 1747. The bishop's palace at Lichfield, in which her father — who was a canon of the cathedral there — resided, was the head-quarters of the literary world of that region, and of the better classes of society generally; and we are told, by one well fitted to judge, that at this period Miss Seward, by grace and beauty of person, and by conversational skill, was amply qualified to maintain the attractions of the house. She was besides of an enthusiastic, not to say romantic disposition, and not a little addicted to the perpetration of a sort of poetry, " most of which," says her friend and biographer, Sir Walter Scott, " is absolutely execrable." With many virtues she appears to have possessed a certain spice of that self-conceit which results from an exaggerated opinion of one's own capacity, and in the writings of her contemporaries occurs more than one sarcastic allusion, that savors rather of personal than of literary animadversion. But between André and herself no other feeling than of delicate and tender friendship seems ever to have subsisted; and the lines in which she bewailed his unhappy fate, were evidently the genuine expression of her sorrow and regret.

The character of the society at Lichfield has already been referred to. The little circle that was accustomed to pay its homage to Miss Seward and to receive her smiles and praises in return, if not a constellation of the first magnitude, comprised at least many names which in those days occupied a respectable rank in the republic of letters. Foremost among them was Dr. Darwin, the author of The Botanic Garden, but, unless we except the lines —

" Soon shall thy arm, unconquered steam, afar
Drag the slow barge, or drive the rapid car,"

better known to this generation by Canning's sarcastic parody, The Loves of the Triangles, than by anything of his own. Then follow Hayley, the author of the Triumphs of Temper; Sir Brooke Boothby; Richard Lovell Edgeworth; the eccentric Thomas Day, whose story of Sandford and Merton for a time rivalled even Robinson Crusoe in popularity; and others, either residents of Lichfield or sojourners who had been attracted thither by " its good report." Thus established the magnates of a provincial town sufficiently remote from London to be beyond many of the terrors of its superior authority, the cathedral critics of Lichfield lived, and wrote, and praised each other for great authors, and were we may suppose as happy as this belief could make them.

A traveller in England, shortly after Major André's death, relates that being in 1782 at Hagley, the seat of Earl Ferrers and the scene of many of the younger Lyttleton's extraordinary exploits, he was assured by his lordship's brother-in-law, Mr. Green, of Portugal House, Birmingham, that at the very mansion they were then in he had introduced the unfortunate Major André to Miss Seward, afterwards so well known for her genius, her connection with André, and her sorrows. We may presume that this introduction occurred in the summer of 1769.

At this time the family of Mr. Thomas Seward comprised not only his wife and his daughter Anna, but also a young lady, Miss Honora Sneyd, a daughter of Edward, the youngest son of Ralph Sneyd, Esq., of Bishton, in Staffordshire. Mrs. Sneyd dying at an early period, the daughters were kindly taken in charge by her friends and kindred, and the care of Honora fell to the faithful hands of Mrs. Seward. As nearer her own age, a greater intimacy than with Anna naturally grew up between the orphan and Miss Sally Seward, a younger sister; but she dying when Honora was thirteen, the latter was left to the immediate companionship of the elder daughter, from whom she derived much of her literary taste. In all respects, we are told, Miss Sneyd was treated as one of Mrs. Seward's family, and it was impossible to perceive that any discrimination was made by the mother between her own and her adopted child.

"It was at Buxton or at Matlock," says Mr. Edgeworth, "that André first met Honora Sneyd." Matlock Bath, about two miles from the straggling little village of Matlock in Derbyshire, was a favorite watering-place, where a pleasant freedom of social intercourse is said to have then prevailed. People coming together for the first time, and passing weeks in the same house, were content to regard each other as acquaintances and to have their enjoyments in common.

The spot itself is singularly picturesque, lying on the side of the Masson Hill, to whose summit a path was contrived through groves of fir-trees. On every hand, the eye rests upon the lofty Tors, or hills of the region; and the Lovers' Walk, by the river Derwent, was doubtless then as it is now chosen for many a happy stroll. Buxton too was celebrated for its medicinal wells, and was also in the Peak of Derbyshire. Mr. Seward had a living in the Peak, whither in his summer visits he was accompanied by his daughter, and probably by others of his household, — at all events, it was at Buxton that the two families, from Lichfield and from Clapton, were together in the summer of 1769, and it was there that the young merchant of Warnford Court became so irretrievably enamored of a lady whose charms seem by all accounts to have been sufficient to subdue less susceptible hearts than his own. A mezzotinto engraving after Romney, which was esteemed by her friends as the perfect, though unintentional resemblance of Honora Sneyd at a period "when she was surrounded by all her virgin glories, — beauty and grace, sensibility and goodness, superior intelligence and unswerving truth," — conveys an idea of charms that would justify the description of her at this period by the man who should best be entitled to pronounce a verdict. "Her memory," said her future husband, "was not copiously stored with poetry; and, though in no way deficient, her knowledge had not been much enlarged by books; but her sentiments were on all subjects so just, and were delivered with such blushing modesty, — though not without an air of conscious worth, — as to command attention from every one capable of appreciating female excellence. Her person was graceful, her features beautiful, and their expression such as to heighten the eloquence of everything she said." Blue eyes and golden hair were the inheritance of the family; but in her face there would seem to have even now been visible some hectic trait — some negative symbol of that latent disorder, which at fifteen years had threatened her life, and by which it was finally to be concluded.

Such being Honora's graces, it is no wonder that André was as heartily and as quickly impressed by them as many others were doomed to be; nor is it strange that he should speedily have awakened a corresponding sentiment in the fair one's breast. It is one of the most attractive features of his character, that — unlike many who are the life and idol of every circle but their own, and are charming everywhere but at home — André was even more prized by his nearest familiars than by the world without. The better he was known, the better he was loved; and the endearing appellation of *cher Jean*, which was constantly bestowed upon him by his family, soon found a place on the lips of his friends. A glance at his portrait will go far to explain this secret of inspiring attachment. His features, as delicate in their lines and expression as those of a woman, at once reveal a tenderness and a vivacity that could scarcely belong to a disposition not originally possessed of a very considerable degree of natural refinement. To what extent these characteristics were developed and increased by cultivation will in time appear.

It does not seem that the lovers at Buxton were long in coming to an understanding. Miss Seward, both then and afterwards, took a deep interest in the affair and looked with the fullest favor on the suitor. An opportunity was soon afforded for him to make his earliest essay at painting the likeness of a human face, and two miniatures of Miss Sneyd were the first fruits of his pencil. One of these — apparently the least perfect — he gave at the time to Miss Seward, who retained it through her life: the other was, of course, reserved by the artist for his own consolation, although the favorable reception which his addresses had received on all hands must have given him abundant reason to hope for the ultimate possession of the beautiful original. It was not until they had reflected on the youth of both parties in respect to wedlock, and the absence of present means to enable them to be provided with such a maintenance as they had each been brought up to anticipate, that the seniors looked coldly on the affair. And even then, the most that was agreed upon by Mrs. André and Mr. Sneyd, was that since an immediate marriage was out of the question, and a long engagement between two very young people, separated by a distance of a hundred miles and more, was not desirable, it was wiser that they should be kept apart as much as possible, trusting that time would either wean them from their attachment, or bring the means of gratifying it. On these terms the parting took place; but it will be seen that, as might have been expected under such circumstances, one if not both of the lovers regarded it as anything but final. It even seems, from the first of the letters presently to be given, that André accompanied Miss Seward and Miss Sneyd on their return to Lichfield; and by letters and by personal interviews, an intercourse was kept up between them for some months longer.

It was during the progress of his courtship at Buxton, that André made known to his Lichfield friends his aversion to commerce, and probably his desire for the army. The representations of Miss Seward that it was so much for his interest in every way to adhere steadily to his present employment, and above all that it was the only means by which he could procure the wealth necessary to secure his union with Miss Sneyd, prevailed upon him for a season to stick to the desk. "When an impertinent consciousness," he says, "whispers in my ear, that I am not of the right stuff for a merchant, I draw my Honora's picture from my bosom, and the sight of that dear talisman so inspirits my industry, that no toil appears oppressive." The reader may compare with some interest this confession with the sentiments, uttered at the same period, of another young occupant of a stool in a counting-house, whose career was destined to cross André's in the most interesting period of his life. "I contemn," wrote Alexander Hamilton, in 1769, "the grovelling condition of a desk, to which my fortune condemns me, and would willingly risk my life, though not my character, to exalt my station ; I mean to prepare the way for futurity."

Before André parted from "the dear Lichfieldians," to return to Clapton and his daily avocations in Throgmorton Street, a correspondence appears to have been arranged between Miss Seward and himself, the burden of which, as may well be guessed, was to be Honora. His epistles, which sometimes covered letters to Miss Sneyd, were evidently designed to pass from the hands of his fair correspondent to those of her adopted sister; while in return he should receive every intelligence of the young lady's movements and welfare, and occasionally a postscript from her own pen. There was nothing clandestine in this arrangement, little indeed as it may have accorded with the plans of the parents of the lovers. Miss Sneyd's conduct throughout, seems to have been ingenuous and discreet; while André availed himself of a fair and friendly means of obtaining that information which was naturally so desirable to one in his position. His letters were often adorned with hasty pen or pencil sketches of such objects of interest as were germain to the text, and the specimens which follow give ample proof, as Miss Seward justly observes, of his wit and vivacity. "His epistolary writings," says Mr. Sparks, "so far as specimens of them have been preserved, show a delicacy of sentiment, a playfulness of imagination, and an ease of style, which could proceed only from native refinement and a high degree of culture." "The best means, next to biography written by the person himself, of obtaining an insight into his character, is afforded," remarks Maria Edgeworth, "by his private letters." There is sufficient excuse in their own contents for here presenting those of André to Miss Seward; but the reason suggested by Miss Edgeworth affords an additional motive. It will be observed that he addresses the lady as his Julia; for no other cause that can be guessed at but that her real name was Anna. But such tricks of the pen were then counted among the delicacies of a sentimental correspondence; as is pleasantly described in *L'Amie Inconnue.*

The journey to Shrewsbury, alluded to below, was made to visit Elizabeth, Mr. Sneyd's fifth daughter, who had been brought up by and resided with her relatives, Mr. and Mrs. Henry Powys of the Abbey. The letters themselves were first printed in connection with Miss Seward's Monody upon their writer.

MR. ANDRÉ TO MISS SEWARD.

CLAPTON, Oct. 3, 1769.

From their agreeable excursion to Shrewsbury, my dearest friends are by this time returned to their beloved Lichfield. Once again have they beheld those fortunate *spires*, the constant witnesses of all their pains and pleasures. I can well conceive the emotions of joy which their first appearance, from the neighboring hills, excites after absence; they seem to welcome you home, and invite you to reiterate those hours of happiness, of which they are a species of monument. I shall have an eternal love and reverence for them. Never shall I forget the joy that danced in Honora's eyes, when she first shewed them to me from Needwood Forest, on our return with you from Buxton to Lichfield. I remember she called them *the ladies of the valley*, — their lightness and elegance deserve the title. Oh! how I loved them from that instant! My enthusiasm concerning them is carried farther even than your's and Honora's, for every object that has a pyramidical form, recalls them to my recollection, with a sensation that brings the tear of pleasure into my eyes.

How happy you must have been at Shrewsbury! only that you tell me, alas! that dear Honora was not so well as you wished during your stay there. — I always hope the best. My impatient spirit rejects every obtruding idea, which I have not fortitude to support. — Dr. Darwin's skill, and your tender care, will remove that sad pain in her side, which makes writing troublesome and injurious to her; which robs her poor *Cher Jean* of those precious pages, with which, he flatters himself, she would otherwise have indulged him.

So your happiness at Shrewsbury scorned to be indebted to public amusements? Five Virgins — united in the soft bonds of friendship! How I should have liked to have made the sixth! — But you surprise me by such an absolute exclusion of the Beaux : — I certainly thought that when five wise virgins were watching at midnight it must have been in expectation of the bridegroom's coming.

We are at this instant five virgins, writing round the same table — my three sisters, Mr. Ewer, and myself. I beg no reflections injurious to the honor of poor *Cher Jean*. My mother is gone to pay a visit, and has left us in possession of the old coach; but as for nags, we can boast of only two long-tails, and my sisters say they are sorry cattle, being no other than my friend Ewer and myself, who, to say truth, have enormous pig-tails.

My dear Boissier is come to town; he has brought a little of the soldier with him, but he is the same honest, warm, intelligent friend I always found him. He sacrifices the town diversions, since I will not partake of them.

We are jealous of your correspondents, who are so numerous. — Yet, write to the Andrés often, my dear Julia, for who are they that will value your letters quite so much as we value them? — The least scrap of a letter will be received with the greatest joy; write, therefore, tho' it were only to give us the comfort of having a piece of paper which has recently passed thro' your hands; — Honora will put in a little postscript, were it only to tell me that she is *my very sincere friend,* who will neither give me love nor comfort — very short indeed, Honora, was thy last postscript! — But I am too presumptuous; — I will not scratch out, but I *unsay* — from the little there was I received more joy than I deserve. — This *Cher Jean* is an impertinent fellow, but he will grow discreet in time;—you must consider him as a poor novice of *eighteen*, who for all the sins he may commit is sufficiently punished in the single evil of being one hundred and twenty miles from Lichfield.

My mother and sisters will go to Putney in a few days to stay some time;—we none of us like Clapton:—*I* need not care, for I am all day long in town; but it is avoiding Scylla to fall into Charybdis. You paint to me the pleasant vale of Stow in the richest autumnal coloring. In return, I must tell you that my zephyrs are wafted through cracks in the wainscot; for murmuring streams, I have dirty kennels; for bleating flocks, grunting pigs; and squalling cats for birds that incessantly warble. I have said something of this sort in my letter to Miss Spearman, and am twinged with the idea of these letters being confronted, and that I shall recall to your memory the fat Knight's love-letters to Mrs. Ford and Mrs. Page.

Julia, perhaps thou fanciest I am merry. Alas! But I do not wish to make you as doleful as myself; and besides, when I would express the tender feelings of my soul, I have no language which does them any justice; if I had, I should regret that you could not have it fresher, and that whatever one communicates by letter must go such a roundabout way, before it reaches one's correspondent: from the writer's heart through his head, arm, hand, pen, ink, paper, over many a weary hill and dale, to the eye, head, and heart of the reader. I have often regretted our not possessing a sort of faculty which should enable our sensations, remarks, &c., to arise from their source in a sort of exhalation, and fall upon our paper in words and phrases properly adapted to express them, without passing through an imagination whose operations so often fail to second those of the heart. Then what a metamorphose we should see in people's style! How eloquent those who are truly attached! how stupid they who falsely profess affection! Perhaps the former had never been able to express half their regard; while the latter, by their flowers of rhetoric, had made us believe a thousand times more than they ever felt — but this is whimsical moralizing.

My sisters' Penserosos were dispersed on their arrival in town, by the joy of seeing Louisa and their dear little Brother Billy again, our kind and excellent Uncle Girardot, and Uncle Lewis André. I was glad to see them, but they complained, not without reason, of the gloom upon my countenance. Billy wept for joy that we were returned, while poor *Cher Jean* was ready to weep for sorrow. Louisa is grown still handsomer since we left her. Our sisters Mary and Anne, knowing your partiality to beauty, are afraid that when they shall introduce her to you, she will put their noses out of joint. Billy is not old enough for me to be afraid of in the rival-way, else I should keep him aloof, for his heart is formed of those affectionate materials, so dear to the ingenuous taste of Julia and her Honora.

I sympathize in your resentment against the canonical Dons, who stumpify the heads of those good green people, beneath whose friendly shade so many of your happiest hours have glided away, — but they defy them; let them stumpify as much as they please, time will repair the mischief, — their verdant arms will again extend, and invite you to their shelter.

The evenings grow long. I hope your conversation round the fire will sometimes fall on the Andrés; it will be a great comfort to them that they are remembered. We chink our glasses to your healths at every meal. "Here's to our Lichfieldian friends," says Nanny; — "Oh-h," says Mary; — "With all my soul," say I; — "Allons," cries my mother; — and the draught seems nectar. The libation made, we begin our uncloying themes, and so beguile the gloomy evening.

Mr. and Mrs. Seward will accept my most affectionate respects. My male friend at Lichfield will join in your conversation on the Andrés. Among the numerous good qualities he is possessed of, he certainly has gratitude, and then he cannot forget those who so sincerely love and esteem him. I, in particular, shall always recall with pleasure the happy hours I have passed in his company. My friendship for him, and for your family, has diffused itself, like the precious ointment from Aaron's beard, on every thing which surrounds you, therefore I beg that you would give my amities to the whole town. Persuade Honora to forgive the length and ardor of the enclosed, and believe me truly your affectionate and faithful friend, J. ANDRÉ.

Mr. Peter Boissier, of the 11th Dragoons, and Mr. Walter Ewer, Jr., of Dyer's Court, Aldermanbury, (a son, it is said, of William Ewer, Esq., in 1778 a director of the Bank of England,) who are mentioned in the preceding letter, were valued friends of André's, and are affectionately remembered in his will.

MR. ANDRÉ TO MISS SEWARD.

LONDON, Oct. 19, 1769.

From the midst of books, papers, bills, and other implements of gain, let me lift up my drowsy head awhile to converse with dear Julia. And first, as I know she has a fervent wish to see me a quill-driver, I must tell her, that I begin, as people are wont to do, to look upon my future profession with great partiality. I no longer see it in so disadvantageous a light. Instead of figuring a merchant as a middle-aged man, with a bob-wig, a rough beard, in snuff-colored clothes, grasping a guinea in his red hand, I conceive a comely young man, with a tolerable pig-tail, wielding a pen with all the noble fierceness of the Duke of Marlborough brandishing a truncheon upon a sign-post, surrounded with types and emblems, and canopied with cornucopias that disembogue their stores upon his head; Mercuries reclined upon bales of goods; Genii playing with pens, ink, and paper; while, in perspective, his gorgeous vessels, "launched on the bosom of the silver Thames," are wafting to distant lands the produce of this commercial nation. Thus all the mercantile glories croud on my fancy, emblazoned in the most refulgent colouring of an ardent imagination. Borne on her soaring pinions I wing my flight to the time when Heaven shall have crowned my labors with success and opulence. I see sumptuous palaces rising to receive me; I see orphans and widows, and painters, and fiddlers, and poets, and builders, protected and encouraged; and when the fabric is pretty nearly finished by my shattered pericranium, I cast my eyes around, and find John André, by a small coal-fire, in a gloomy compting-house in Warnford Court, nothing so little as what he has been making himself, and, in all probability, never to be much more than he is at present. But oh! my dear Honora! — it is for thy sake only I wish for wealth. — You say she was somewhat better at the time you wrote last. I must flatter myself that she will soon be without any remains of this threatening disease.

It is seven o'clock: you and Honora, with two or three more select friends, are now probably encircling your dressing-room fireplace. What would I not give to enlarge that circle! The idea of a clean hearth, and a snug circle round it, formed by a few select friends, transports me. You seem combined together against the inclemency of the weather, the hurry, bustle, ceremony, censoriousness, and envy of the world. The purity, the warmth, the kindly influence of fire — to all for whom it is kindled — is a good emblem of the friendship of such amiable minds as Julia's and her Honora's. Since I cannot be there in reality, pray imagine me with you; admit me to your *conversationès*, — think how I wish for the blessing of joining them! and be persuaded that I take part in all your pleasures, in the dear hope, that ere very long, your blazing hearth will burn again for me. Pray keep me a place; — let the poker, tongs, or shovel, represent me. But you have Dutch tiles, which are infinitely better; so let Moses, or Aaron, or Balaam's ass be my representative.

But time calls me to Clapton. I quit you abruptly till to-morrow, when, if I do not tear the nonsense I have been writing, I may perhaps increase its quantity. Signora Cynthia is in clouded majesty. Silvered with her beams, I am about to jog to Clapton upon my own stumps; musing as I homeward plod my way — ah! need I name the subject of my contemplations?

Thursday.

I had a sweet walk home last night, and found the Claptonians, with their fair guest, a Miss Mourgue, very well. My sisters send their amities, and will write in a few days.

This morning I returned to town. It has been the finest day imaginable; a solemn mildness was diffused throughout the blue horizon; its light was clear and distinct, rather than dazzling; — the serene beams of the autumnal sun, gilded hills, variegated woods, glittering spires, ruminating herds, bounding flocks, — all combined to enchant the eyes, expand the heart, and " chase all sorrow but despair." In the midst of such a scene, no lesser sorrow can prevent our sympathy with nature. A calmness, a benevolent disposition seizes us with sweet insinuating power; the very brute creation seem sensible of these beauties; there is a species of mild chearfulness in the face of a lamb, which I have but indifferently expressed in a corner of my paper, and a demure, contented look in an ox, which, in the fear of expressing still worse, I leave unattempted.

Business calls me away. I must dispatch my letter. Yet what does it contain? — No matter. You like anything better than news; — indeed, you never told me so, but I have an intuitive knowledge upon the subject, from the sympathy which I have constantly perceived in the taste of Julia and *cher Jean.* What is it to you or me —

If here in the city we have nothing but riot,
If the Spital-field Weavers can't be kept quiet;
If the weather is fine, or the streets should be dirty,
Or if Mr. Dick Wilson died aged of thirty?

— But if I was to hearken to the versifying grumbling I feel within me, I should fill my paper, and not have room left to entreat that you would plead my cause to Honora more eloquently than the enclosed letter has the power of doing. Apropos of verses, you desire me to recollect my random description of the engaging appearance of the charming Mrs. ——. Here it is at your service:—

> Then rustling and bustling the lady comes down,
> With a flaming red face, and a broad yellow gown,
> And a hobbling out-of-breath gait, and a frown.

This little French cousin of ours, Delarise, was my sister Mary's playfellow at Paris. His sprightliness engages my sisters extremely. Doubtless they tell much of him to you in their letters.

How sorry I am to bid you adieu! Oh, let me not be forgot by the friends most dear to you at Lichfield!— *Lichfield!* Ah, of what magic letters is that little word composed! How graceful it looks when it is written! Let nobody talk to me of its original meaning, "the field of blood!" Oh, no such thing!— It is the field of joy! "The beautiful city that lifts her fair head in the valley, and says, I *am*, and there is none beside me!" Who says she is vain? Julia will not say so, nor yet Honora, and least of all their devoted   JOHN ANDRÉ.

In reference to the allusion in the last paragraph of this letter, Miss Seward very learnedly explained, that Lichfield does not signify "the field of blood," but "the field of dead bodies." The error is of little importance. Between the dates of this and the next epistle, he had visited Lichfield, and once again beheld the face of his lady-love.

MR. ANDRÉ TO MISS SEWARD.

CLAPTON, November 1, 1769.

MY ears still ring with the sounds of "Oh, Jack! Oh,

Jack! How do the dear Lichfieldians? What do they say? What are they about? What did *you* do while you were with them?" "Have patience," said I, "good people!" — and began my story, which they devoured with as much joyful avidity as Adam did Gabriel's tidings of Heaven. My mother and sisters are all very well, and delighted with their little Frenchman, who is a very agreeable lad.

Surely you applaud the fortitude with which I left you! Did I not come off with flying colors? It was a great effort; for, alas! this recreant heart did *not second* the smiling courage of the *countenance;* nor is it yet as it ought to be, from the hopes it may reasonably entertain of seeing you all again ere the winter's dreary hours are past. Julia, my dear Julia, gild them with tidings of my beloved Honora! Oh that you may be enabled to tell me that she regains her health, and her charming vivacity! Your sympathizing heart partakes all the joys and pains of your friends. Never can I forget its kind offices, which were of such moment to my peace. *Mine* is formed for friendship, and I am blessed in being able to place so *well* the purest passion of an ingenuous mind. How am I honoured in Mr. and Mrs. Seward's attachment to me! Charming were the anticipations which beguiled the long tracts of hill, and dale, and plain, that divide London from Lichfield! With what delight my eager eyes *drank* their first view of the spires! What rapture did I not feel on entering your gates! — in flying up the hall-steps! — in rushing into the dining-room! — in meeting the gladdened eyes of dear Julia and her enchanting friend! That instant convinced me of the truth of Rousseau's observation, "that there are moments worth ages." Shall not these moments return? Ah, Julia! the cold hand of absence is heavy upon the heart of your poor *Cher Jean!* — he is forced to hammer into it perpetually every consoling argument that the magic wand of Hope can conjure up; viz., that every moment of industrious absence advances his journey, you know whither. I may sometimes make excursions to Lichfield, and bask in the light of my Honora's eyes. Sustain me, Hope! nothing on my part shall be wanting which shall induce thee to *fulfill* thy blossoming promises.

The happy, social circle — Julia, Honora, Miss S——n, Miss B——n, her brother, Miss S——e, Mr. R——n, &c. — are now, perhaps, enlivening your dressing-room, the dear *blue region*, as Honora calls it, with the sensible observation, the tasteful criticism, or the elegant song; dreading the iron tongue of the nine o'clock bell, which disperses the beings whom friendship and kindred virtues had drawn together. My imagination attaches itself to all, even the *inanimate* objects which surround Honora and her Julia, that have beheld their graces and virtues expand and ripen; — my dear Honora's, from their infant bud.

The sleepy Claptonian train are gone to bed, somewhat wearied with their excursion to Enfield, whither they have this day carried their favourite little Frenchman, — so great a favourite, the parting was quite tragical. I walked hither from town, as usual, to-night. No hour of the twenty-four is so precious to me as that devoted to this solitary walk. Oh, my friend, I am far from possessing the patient frame of mind I so continually invoke. Why is Lichfield an hundred and twenty miles from me? There is no *moderation* in the distance. Fifty or sixty miles had been a great deal too much; but *then*, there would have been less opposition from *authority* to my frequent visits. I conjure you, supply the want of these blessings by frequent *letters*. I must not, will not, ask them of Honora, since the use of the pen is forbid to her declining health; I will content myself, as usual, with a postscript from her in your epistles. My sisters are charmed with the packet which arrived yesterday, and which they will answer soon.

As yet I have said nothing of our journey. We met an entertaining Irish gentleman at Dunchurch, and, being fellow-sufferers in cold and hunger, joined interests, ordered four horses, and stuffed three in a chaise. It is not to *you* I need apologize for talking in raptures of an higler, whom we met on the road. His cart had passed us, and was at a considerable distance, when, looking back, he perceived that our chaise had stopped, and that the driver seemed mending something. He ran up to him, and, with a face full of honest anxiety, pity, good-nature, and every sweet affection under heaven, asked him if we wanted anything; that he had plenty of nails, ropes, &c. in his cart. That wretch of a postilion made no other reply than, " We want nothing, master." From the same impulse, the good Irishman, Mr. Till, and myself thrust our heads instantly out of the chaise, and tried to recompense the honest creature for this surly reply by every kind and grateful acknowledgment, and by forcing upon him a little pecuniary tribute. My benevolence will be the warmer while I live, for the treasured remembrance of this higler's countenance.

I know you will interest yourself in my destiny. I have now completely subdued my aversion to the profession of a merchant, and hope in time to acquire an inclination for it. Yet God forbid I should ever love what I am to make the object of my attention!—that vile trash, which I care not for, but only as it may be the future means of procuring the blessing of my soul. Thus all my mercantile calculations go to the tune of *dear Honora.* When an impertinent consciousness whispers in my ear, that I am not of the right stuff for a merchant, I draw my Honora's picture from my bosom, and the sight of that dear talisman so inspirits my industry, that no toil appears oppressive.

The poetic task you set me is in a sad method: my head and heart are too full of other matters to be engrossed by a draggle-tail'd wench of the Heliconian puddle.

I am going to try my interest in parliament. — How you stare! — it is to procure a frank. Be so good as to give the enclosed to Honora, — *it* will speak to *her ;* — and do *you* say everything that is kind for me to every other distinguished friend of the dressing-room circle; encourage them in their obliging desire of scribbling in your letters, but do not let them take Honora's corner of the sheet.

Adieu! May you all possess that cheerfulness denied to your *Cher Jean.* I fear it hurts my mother to see my musing moods; but I can neither help nor overcome them. The near hopes of another excursion to Lichfield could alone disperse every gloomy vapor of my imagination.

Again, and yet again, Adieu! J. ANDRÉ.

CHAPTER II.

Failure of André's Courtship. — Richard Lovell Edgeworth. — Thomas Day. — Marriage and Death of Miss Sneyd.

NOTWITHSTANDING his ardor, and the presence of so powerful a friend at court as he must have had in Miss Seward, André's suit did not prosper. There is a saying, that in all love affairs there are two parties — the one who loves, and the one who is loved; and it does not seem to have been very long before Miss Sneyd came into the latter category. Separation, and consideration of the delay that must necessarily attend that acquirement of fortune upon which permission for André to renew his addresses depended, must doubtless have done much to cool her feelings, even had they originally been as warm as his own. This is at least the view taken by her friend, who at the same time commemorates the fidelity of the opposite party:

> "Now Prudence, in her cold and thrifty care,
> Frown'd on the maid, and bade the youth despair;
> For power parental sternly saw, and strove
> To tear the lily bands of plighted love;
> Nor strove in vain; — but, while the fair one's sighs
> Disperse like April-storms in sunny skies,
> The firmer lover, with unswerving truth,
> To his first passion consecrates his youth."

The lady's feelings, in short, cooled down so sufficiently, that there soon came to be no reason why she should not receive the addresses of other suitors. In 1770, Mr. Richard Lovell Edgeworth was paying a Christmas visit to Lichfield, and thus mentions the impression he received of the state of affairs between André and Miss Sneyd: it being then about eighteen months since their first meeting at Buxton, and but little over a year from the date of the letters that closed the last chapter : —

"Whilst I was upon this visit, Mr. André, afterwards Major André, who lost his life so unfortunately in America, came to Lichfield. . . . . . The first time I saw Major André at the palace, I did not perceive from his manner, or from that of the young lady, that any attachment subsisted between them. On the contrary, from the great attention which Miss Seward paid to him, and from the constant admiration which Mr. André bestowed upon her, I thought that, though there was a considerable disproportion in their ages, there might exist some courtship between them. Miss Seward, however, undeceived me. I never met Mr. André again; and from all that I then saw, or have since known, I believe that Miss Honora Sneyd was never much disappointed by the conclusion of this attachment. Mr. André appeared to me to be pleased and dazzled by the lady. She admired and estimated highly his talents; but he did not possess the reasoning mind which she required."

Mr. Edgeworth had undoubtedly what many will reckon a good opportunity of ascertaining the lady's sentiments on this subject; for Honora Sneyd eventually became his wife. Whether, however, a woman always lays bare the secrets of her youthful breast to the man whom she marries, even though he possesses "a reasoning mind," is another question. To be sure, having himself entered four times into the state of wedlock, Mr. Edgeworth had unusual means of coming to a conclusion upon this point; but it may well be doubted whether a more than common impression might not have been made on Miss Sneyd's heart by the attractions of such a person as her disappointed lover. Even while acknowledging the expediency of the course prescribed by the heads of both families, and yielding to their authority, she must have been sensible of the value of the qualities she was compelled to forego. From Mr. Edgeworth's own words it may be inferred, that at this period she had formed a high, not to say a romantic estimate of what was to be looked for in the man whom she should wed. When he left her in 1771, with a view of going abroad, he says: "In various incidental conversations, I endeavored to convince her, that young women who had not large fortunes should not disdain to marry, even though the romantic notions of finding heroes, or prodigies of men, might not be entirely gratified. Honora listened, and assented." These remarks of Mr. Edgeworth concerning Major André are entitled to considerable weight; not alone because of the well-known character for probity and discernment of the writer and of his more distinguished daughter, by whom the Memoirs were completed and edited, but also from the fact that they were given to the world while yet a sister of André was living and in England: from whom, or rather from whose circle of friends, any misstatement on this head might have met a ready correction.*

Richard Lovell Edgeworth, who ultimately became Miss Sneyd's successful wooer, is happily hit off, as he appeared in 1813, by Lord Byron. "I thought Edgeworth a fine old fellow, of a clarety, elderly, red complexion, but active, brisk, and endless. He was seventy, but did not look fifty — no, nor forty-eight even." When he first met Honora, however, he was but of twenty-five or twenty-six years, though already a man of some note. He had married on slender means, while his father yet lived; and had married unhappily. "My wife, prudent, domestic, and affectionate; but she was not of a cheerful temper. She lamented about trifles; and the lamenting of a female with whom we live does not render home delightful." He was, too, what may be called notional; and, charmed with the theories of Rousseau, must needs bring up his son after the manner of *Emile*, with bare feet and arms, and to a sturdy independence. While this connection subsisted, his visits to his friend Mr. Day brought

* The clear handwriting of Maria Edgeworth across the title-page of a presentation copy of the Memoirs, gives additional value and authenticity to the volume from which I quote.

him into constant intercourse with Miss Sneyd; "when," says he, — "for the first time in my life I saw a woman that equalled the picture of perfection which existed in my imagination. I had long suffered from the want of that cheerfulness in a wife, without which marriage could not be agreeable to a man of such a temper as mine. I had borne this evil, I believe, with patience; but my not being happy at home exposed me to the danger of being too happy elsewhere. The charms and superior character of Miss Honora Sneyd made an impression on my mind, such as I had never felt before." Other gentlemen, whom he names, intimate at the palace, were unanimous in their approbation of this lady; all but Mr. Day.

Thomas Day, the eccentric, benevolent, unpractical author of Sandford and Merton, (once the delight of all the school-boy-world,) was now residing close to Lichfield. Notwithstanding his peculiar views respecting the sex, he could not refrain from frequently tempting his fate; and what was more extraordinary, expected that with a person neither formed by nature nor cultivated by art to please, he should win some woman, wiser than the rest of her sex, though not less fair, who should feel for him the most romantic and everlasting attachment, — a paragon, who for him would forget the follies and vanities of her kind; who

> Should go like our maidens clad in grey,
> And live in a cottage on love.

His appearance was not in his favor: he seldom combed his hair, and generally set aside, as beneath the dignity of man, the graces of fashionable life. He was tall, round-shouldered, and pitted with the small-pox; — but he had £1,200 a year. Large white arms, long petticoats, and a robust frame, were, in his reckoning, indispensable qualifications to the woman he could love. And yet, as might have been expected, we very soon find him addressing Miss Sneyd, whom he had at first undervalued for her accomplishments, and who possessed in the suitable degree not one of his requirements. He had previously endeavored to supply himself with a mate precisely to his liking, by taking two orphans, (from a Foundling Hospital, I believe,) and rearing them in his own way, that he might choose one for his wife when they arrived at womanhood; but the experiment was a failure. One of his wards, he soon ascertained, would not suit him; and the other, by a somewhat slower process, came to the conclusion that he would not suit her. Anticipating the ingenious device by which, in Canning's Double Arrangement, an English baron's love of liberty and of beef is equally expressed in the title of one of the characters, he had endowed this girl with a name designed to compliment at once the river Severn and the memory of Algernon Sidney. Sabrina Sidney in time learned that the efforts of her patron to give her self-command, by unexpectedly discharging pistols close to her ear, or by dropping melted sealing-wax upon her bare shoulders, were practices little calculated to ensure her domestic happiness; and she sought repose in the arms of a less philosophical bridegroom. But early in 1771, and pending this discovery by the fair Sabrina, Mr. Day resolved to woo and win Miss Sneyd. Her friends afforded him every facility in his suit, and he was continually at her side. But, notwithstanding the friendship that grew up between them, the lady soon arrived at a conclusion adverse to his desires; and when, towards the end of the summer, he sent her by the hands of his friendly ambassador a voluminous proposal of marriage, that was probably overspread with terms and conditions, she returned him a hearty denial. She said that she would not "admit the unqualified control of a husband over all her actions; she did not feel that seclusion from society was indispensably necessary to preserve female virtue, or to secure domestic happiness. Upon terms of reasonable equality, she supposed that mutual confidence might best subsist; she said that, as Mr. Day had decidedly declared his determination to live in perfect seclusion from what is usually called the world, it was fit she should as decidedly declare she would not change her present mode of life, with which she had no reason to be dissatisfied, for any dark and untried system that could be proposed to her." This refusal sent poor Mr. Day to bed, to be bled for a fever; from which, in a space, he came forth with philosophic equanimity, to seek the hand of Miss Elizabeth Sneyd as ineffectually as he had sought her sister's.

To return to Honora; it must not be supposed that Mr. Day was blind to Mr. Edgeworth's admiration of this lady, though no one else perceived it; and as his friend was already a married man, he urged his removal from a neighborhood so dangerous to his peace of mind. In fact, when Mr. Day's fate was decided, the partially repressed passion of his envoy returned with redoubled violence, and he found it necessary to retire to the continent. But the death of his wife and his father left him, in the spring of 1773, free to pursue his inclinations; and he again came to Lichfield. Here he found Miss Sneyd, happily rid of a disorder that had threatened the destruction of her sight, and more beautiful than ever; " and though surrounded by lovers, still her own mistress." The wooing was speedy and successful, but apparently not without interruption. It is true that in 1771, he says Miss Seward declared her friend was free from any engagement or attachment incompatible with her receiving a suitor's addresses; but the little slaps, which he now and then bestows upon that lady, seem to point her out as not altogether favoring the current of his love. She had been the first, he asserts, to perceive the impression Honora had made on him, several years before; and he gives her credit for a magnanimous preference of her friend's praises to her own. But after rather ungallantly referring to her rivalry with Mrs. Darwin for the doctor's hand, he lets us perceive that at their first acquaintance Miss Seward, ignorant of his being already provided for, was not herself unwilling to make an impression upon his heart. And when he comes to the courtship of his second wife, he once or twice has occasion to notice her again. For whether because of the rapidity with which the funeral baked meats were succeeded by the marriage banquet, or because she still cherished a hope that André might yet be the happy man, she does not appear to have greatly encouraged the affair. Mr. Edgeworth, indeed, besides his intrinsic worth and a respectable position among the landed gentry, possessed advantages of fortune which André could not lay claim to; but Miss Seward was enthusiastic in her disposition, and perhaps looked upon her friend in Warnford Court as capable of founding in his mercantile pursuits a house as illustrious and as dignified as that of De la Pole, of the third Edward's reign, or of Greville, "the flower of woolstaplers," in the days of James I.; each of which sprung to nobility from successful commerce, and each of which has allied its own with the great names of literary history; with Chaucer, and with Sidney. Nor would his entrance into the army operate against this idea. In the American war, the leader who united the highest social and military rank — Lord Cornwallis — traced the first start to dignity of his house to a city merchant, and its advent to greatness to its services against domestic insurrection. And surely André — brave, wise, insinuating, indefatigable — must have been expected to achieve a very great success in whatever career his ambition and his inclinations united upon. Let only opportunity be present to such a character, and it will little matter whether he be born of cloth of gold or cloth of frieze. As Spenser has it, —

> "In brave pursuitt of honourable deed,
> There is I know not what great difference
> Between the vulgar and the noble seed;
> Which unto things of valorous pretence
> Seemes to be borne by native influence."

But if any efforts were made to preserve the lady's hand for André, they were in vain. Even on their first acquaintance, her new suitor believed himself to perceive that she was more at ease with himself than with most people; that she felt as though her character had never thitherto been fully appreciated; and he was not likely now to spare any pains to confirm this impression. His addresses were entirely successful; and on the 17th day of July, 1773, by special license, Richard Lovell Edgeworth and Honora Sneyd were married in the ladies' choir of Lichfield Cathedral, Mr. Seward performing the ceremony. "Miss Seward, notwithstanding some imaginary cause of dissatisfaction which she felt about a bridesmaid," says Edgeworth, "was, I believe, really glad to see Honora united to a man whom she had often said she thought peculiarly suited to her friend in taste and disposition." He also adds that the marriage " was with the consent of her father." Miss Seward had previously told the world that this consent was bestowed with reluctance, and published her regrets that André had not been the groom.*

Honora's subsequent life seems to have been happy. It was partly passed in Ireland, partly in England. Of an inquisitive disposition, she was pleased in bearing a share in her husband's pursuit of knowledge, and by the clearness of her judgment was of service to him in his intellectual avocations; "as her understanding had arrived at maturity before she had acquired any strong prejudices on historical subjects, she derived uncommon benefit from books." The charge of her own children and of those of her predecessor occupied much of her thoughts, and in 1778, while teaching her firstborn to read, she wrote, in conjunction with her husband, the First Part of Harry and Lucy, of which they had a few cop-

* Miss Seward says that after Mr. Edgeworth had removed Honora from "the Darwinian sphere," and Mr. Day had offered "his philosophic hand" to her sister, she sent him to France to learn a few airs and graces. He returned, however, so stilted and stiff that she was fain to confess that objectionable to her fancy as had been Thomas Day, blackguard, he was preferable to Thomas Day, gentleman.

From the similarity of name, we may suppose this gentleman was related to the parties in the great Huntingdonshire case of Day *v.* Day, (1797,) a case in which R. Sneyd, Esq., of Keel, in Staffordshire, appears as a magistrate, receiving affidavits for the plaintiff.

ies privately printed in large type for the use of their children. This was probably the earliest essay towards instilling, under the guise of amusement, a taste for science into the youthful mind. Their idea was then to have completed the work, and it was for them that Day commenced his Sandford and Merton; but Mrs. Edgeworth's sickness put a close to her literary labors. Day expanded his proposed slight tale into a delightful book, and many long years after, Maria Edgeworth included Harry and Lucy in her Early Lessons. In the meanwhile, a prey to the insidious attacks of a deep-seated consumption, Mrs. Edgeworth was sinking into the grave. Her husband, whose passion burned unabated, narrates the closing scenes with much pathos: — "The most beloved as a wife, a sister, and a friend, of any person I have ever known. Each of her own family, unanimously, almost naturally, preferred her. . . . . All her friends adored her, if treating her with uniform deference and veneration may be called adoring." It is pleasant to think that the dying pillow of such a woman was made as tranquil as man's love could compass. This appears from a letter of farewell written in her last hours to a near kinswoman: — "I have every blessing, and I am happy. The conversation of my beloved husband, when my breath will let me have it, is my greatest delight; he procures me every comfort, and, as he always said he thought he should, contrives for me every thing that can ease and assist my weakness.

'Like a kind angel whispers peace,
And smooths the bed of death.'"

It was her dying request that her husband should marry her sister Elizabeth, who, like herself, had been sought in marriage by his friend Day. This desire Mr. Edgeworth fulfilled; and she also dying, he took in fourth nuptials the sister of the late Admiral Beaufort; and here we will leave him. It was in honor of his second wife, we are told, that he gave her name to the town of Sneydborough, in North

Carolina; a province in which he possessed some landed interests. In 1780, the same year that witnessed André's death, died a second Honora Edgeworth, the only surviving daughter of Honora Sneyd. The little tale of Rivuletta, published in Early Lessons, and some drawings that are yet preserved, attest this child's resemblance in talents to her mother; — she resembled her as well in constitution, and in the source of her death.

CHAPTER III.

André joins the Army. — Visits Germany. — Condition of the Service. — He comes to America. — State of American Affairs.

EVERY historical writer, who has treated of the subject, has been under the impression that it was despair at the marriage to another of the woman whom he loved which led André to renounce his previous occupation and to enter the army. Mr. Sparks says, "From that moment André became disgusted with his pursuits, and resolved to seek relief from his bitter associations, and dissipate the memory of his sorrows in the turmoil and dangers of war." Lord Mahon, after mentioning the marriage, remarks, "André, on the other hand, to seek relief from his sorrows, joined the British army in Canada, with a Lieutenant's commission, at the outbreak of the war." The error was one into which these distinguished writers were reasonably led, but which may very properly be corrected by the "snapper-up of unconsidered trifles." It was probably through the statements of Miss Seward that the mistake originated; who asserts that André's constancy remained unshaken until he heard of Honora's wedding.

> "Though four long years a night of absence prove,
> Yet Hope's fond star shone trembling on his love;
> Till hovering Rumour chas'd the pleasing dream,
> And veil'd with raven-wing the silver beam."

The "hovering Rumour" she explains to have been "the tidings of Honora's marriage. Upon that event Mr. André quitted his profession as a merchant, and joined our army in America." Thus it would appear that the four years which elapsed between the Buxton connection of 1769 and Edgeworth's marriage in 1773, were to André, in the main, "a night of absence;" and that even a correspondence did not long subsist may be inferred from the declaration that it was to a hovering rumor that he owed the intelligence of Honora being the bride of another. Therefore the half-suppressed indignation of Mr. Edgeworth at this version of the affair, may be well understood. He complains that the author of the Monody insinuates that Major André was, in plain English, jilted by the lady; and that, " in consequence of this disappointment, he went into the army, and quitted this country." Nor must it be forgotten that during these four years Miss Sneyd had been considered by her family as entirely disengaged, and free to receive the addresses of any eligible suitor; nor that, as in Mr. Day's case, she actually had received such addresses. The fairest conclusion which we can arrive at is, that André, abashed at the discouragement his suit had encountered, and discouraged by the difficulties to be overcome ere he could be permitted to return to the siege, had given way to the original bent of his inclinations, without at all relinquishing the attachment which he no longer could have reason to expect would be presently gratified. That he should abandon the hope of ultimate success need not at all be considered.

> " None, without hope, e'er loved the brightest fair,
> Yet love will hope, where reason must despair."

His aversion to trade and wishes for a military career have already been manifested, in his letters of 1769; and it may readily be conceived that the advantages of an employment for which by nature and by education he was especially well adapted, were not without their weight in his mind. Few men, as the result proved, were more capable than he of winning a soldier's rewards; and no man of the day could have worn them with more grace;

> " Medals, rank, ribands, lace, embroidery, scarlet,
> Are things immortal to immortal man;"

and his age must have given them peculiar charms to André. The love of fame — "that last infirmity of noble minds" — was joined in him, as is shown by the whole tenor of his life, with that thirst for military glory which so long as human nature exists in its present constitution, will ever, according to Gibbon, be "the vice of the most exalted characters." So soon, therefore, as he approached his twenty-first year, we find him entering the army. The son of an American officer, who was much with him in his last days, and in whose letters André's fate always found the language of sympathy and friendship, asserts that he tore himself from the reluctant arms of the circle of devoted relatives in which he had been educated, to wear the King's livery. This information may have been obtained by Colonel Hamilton from André's own lips; but it is only confirmatory of the deduction to be drawn from his letters, that there was a strong prejudice among his friends in favor of his remaining in the compting-house. Their wishes were, however, unavailing. In January, 1772, by an account said to have been furnished by his most intimate friends, he entered the army. "His first commission," says Mr. Edgeworth, with greater particularity, "was dated March 4th, 1771." This was more than two years and four months antecedent to Miss Sneyd's marriage; but it was in the very time of those attentions of Mr. Day which all the Lichfield world, Mr. Edgeworth himself included, did not question were certain to succeed. Perhaps, therefore, Miss Seward may have confounded the two events in her memory, and attributed an effect to a wrong cause.

In the early part of 1772, André went over to Germany, and did not return to England until the close of 1773. During this period he visited most of the courts in that part of Europe. His kinsman, Mr. John André, was established in business as a musical composer and publisher at Offenbach; and the young officer's presence at her father's house was long borne in mind by a daughter, whose impression in later days was that her cousin's business in Germany was to conduct a corps of Hessians to America. This, in 1772, would have been rather premature; but it is very possible that his affairs there, away from his regiment for nearly two years, may have been in some manner connected with German subsidiaries, and under the direction of his own government.

The regiment which André had joined was the Seventh Foot, or Royal English Fusiliers: one of the oldest corps in the line, and dating its formation in the year 1685. The rank of ensign does not exist in a fusilier regiment, the grade being supplied by a second lieutenant; it was in this latter capacity that he seems to have first served. In April, 1773, the regiment had been embarked for Canada, where it performed garrison duty at Quebec for several months until it was sent to Montreal, and variously posted in Lower Canada. Before leaving England to join it, however, it is asserted that André paid a final visit of farewell to Miss Seward and to the scenes of his former happiness; which was attended by circumstances of a character so strange as to be worthy of repetition, if not of belief. During his stay, we are told, Miss Seward had made arrangements to take him to see and be introduced to her friends Cunningham and Newton, — both gentlemen of a poetical turn. On the night preceding the day appointed for her appearance, Mr. Cunningham dreamed that he was alone in a great forest. Presently he perceived a horseman approaching at great speed; but as he drew near to the spot where the dreamer imagined himself to stand, three men suddenly sprung from their concealment among the bushes, seized on the rider, and bore him away. The captive's countenance was visible; its interesting appearance, and the singularity of the incident, left an unpleasant feeling on Mr. Cunningham's mind as he awoke. But soon falling to sleep again, he was visited by a second vision even more troubling than the first. He found himself one of a vast multitude met near a great city: and while all were gazing, a man, whom he recognized as the same person that had just been captured in the forest, was brought forth and hanged upon a gibbet. These dreams were repeated the following morning to Mr. Newton; and when, a little after, Miss Seward made her appearance with André, Mr. Cunningham at once knew him to be the unhappy stranger whom he had seen stopped and hanged.

Whether this story may not belong to the class of predictions which are not heard of until the event has occurred, will not be inquired into here. A more important subject of contemplation is the condition and nature of the new life into which André had now embarked; and as the constitution of the British army was at that time so anomalous, and as much of its ill-success in the American war was directly attributable to the peculiarities of its organization, it may be as well to set a state of the case before the reader. Not long prior to hostilities, Mr. (afterwards Lord) Erskine had vigorously exposed the glaring inefficiencies of the existing system. Fifty years later Scott, *ex cathedrâ*, even more thoroughly recapitulated its abuses.

The purchasing of commissions was then at its height; and to mend matters, great men in power could always obtain a pair of colors at the War-Office for a favorite or dependant. Children in the cradle thus were enrolled in the army-lists; a school-boy might be a field-officer; and amiable young ladies are known to have drawn the pay and held the title of captains of dragoons. Of course they did no duty; but they were as fit for it as many who did. There was no military school in the kingdom; and no military knowledge was exacted of the officer who, ashamed of being suspected of possessing the first rudiments of his profession, huddled through the exercise by repeating the words of command from a sergeant, and hastened back to more congenial scenes of idleness or dissipation. These were the days when to be "a pretty fellow" was a manner of qualification for the service,— when the Amlets, and Plumes, and Brazens of the stage were fair types of a class that "swore hard, drank deep, bilked tradesmen, and plucked pigeons." The few men of social rank that had any degree of professional skill were regarded as paragons; while any talent that might exist in a subaltern was, as it is too often now, rather a curse than a blessing to its owner, unless he had money or patronage to get on with. There seems to have been no uniform system of tactics; every commandant manœuvred his regiment after his own preference, and thus, without previous concert, a brigade could not half the time execute any combined movement decently. The garb of the private was ludicrously unsuitable and absurd. More time was given to daubing the hair with tallow and flour than to the manual or drill; and the severity with which a neglected queue was punished sometimes goaded the very best corps into mutiny. In fact, the more *crack* a regiment became, the less it seems to me to have been fit for service; and there is verisimilitude, if not truth, in the story of the Hessian colonel who blew his brains out because, in reply to his boast that his dragoons dressed in a line were so equally matched that but one pigtail could be seen along the backs of all, the Duke of York pointed out the irregularity of their noses!

Such being the condition of the army, it is perhaps not too much to suppose that André, having purchased his commission, was determined to put himself on a footing so far superior to his fellows as would certainly facilitate his advancement; and that, therefore, he may have been on the continent occupied in perfecting himself in various professional branches, for which England could have afforded no facilities; since it is well known that, at a still later period in the century, Wellington was sent abroad to acquire the rudiments of an officer's education. Be this as it may, he embarked in 1774 to join his regiment, then stationed in Canada, and arrived on his journey at Philadelphia in September of that year.

It may well be asked why André should have taken this route to Canada. The travel from the Delaware to the St. Lawrence was to the full as tedious as that from England to America; and the voyage between the two countries could have as readily been performed to one river as the other. On Sunday, the 17th of the very month in which he reached Philadelphia, the ship Canadian arrived at Quebec, in sixty days from Cowes, bringing over Carleton and his family; of which Viscount Pitt, the elder son of the great Earl of Chatham, was then a member. From our knowledge of André's character, it seems unlikely that without some cause he should have missed the opportunity which taking passage in this vessel would have afforded, of coming in direct contact, through several weeks, with his commander. Or he might have sailed in other vessels to Quebec, or even to Boston, and have thus saved a long and fatiguing part of the course. Is it not probable that the selection of Philadelphia was governed by the circumstance that the meeting of the first Continental Congress was called at that place, and that there was a good deal for an intelligent eye-witness to possess himself of between Pennsylvania and Canada? His own inclination may have suggested this idea; but if it really had an existence, it was in all likelihood carried into effect by direction of Carleton himself; — a leader whom Heath, one of the chiefs of our revolutionary army, characterizes as the greatest general the British had in this country during the war, and whose retention in Canada he pronounced an especial piece of good fortune to America. This is the only manner in which André's presence in the South can be accounted for at a time when he should serve his sovereign in the North. He was a prodigiously keen observer; he doubtless noted all that he saw: and the state of things in the colonies was, beyond question, of a nature to excite the anxious attention of every considering man in authority. Domestic troubles were more than apprehended by the ministry, and the intervention of the military arm was provided for. The temper of the people and the signs of the times in America would therefore be points to which so far-sighted a person as Carleton could not be indifferent.

At this very moment, however, it is probable that our Revolution could have been turned aside by a change of British policy. The bulk of the patriotic party here were in opposition as Englishmen less than Americans. They applauded the words of Chatham and Rockingham, and regarded North as their political enemy, and the misleader of the king. They did not know that it was the king who guided his ministers, and who really is chiefly responsible for the production of measures of questionable constitutionality, and as impolitic as impracticable.*

The general tone of whig feeling in Philadelphia had from the first been cautious but firm. The public sympathy was, it is true, warmly enlisted for the Bostonians; but the public mind was not as yet filed to that hostility to England which prevailed in Massachusetts. The first Continental Congress, however, was now met; and as it was in session at Philadelphia from 5th September to 26th October, 1774, we may reasonably conclude that its doings were not disregarded by André. The secrecy in which the conduct of this body was wrapt, prevents us to-day from knowing much more than what appears on its published record; but by contemporaries, many things must have at least been surmised, which are lost to us forever. It sufficiently appears that the boasted unanimity of the assembly had no foundation in fact. At an early stage it seems to have been agreed, by

* It is curious to note how entirely North's dispositions were misunderstood. It is now known that attachment to the king rather than desire of power kept him at the head of affairs, and committed him to the most obnoxious measures. Inheriting more of the capacity than the ambition of the Lord-Keeper, he would have preferred pleasure to fame; and when he was figured in America as devising new schemes of oppression, was, perhaps, frolicking with Thurlow and Rigby, or making *bouts rimés* at the dinner-table. Of his skill in this line, an anecdote is preserved. Lord Sandwich so placed a lame Mr. Melligan that his name came to North's turn in tagging verses. The result was thus sung by the Prime Minister:—

"Oh, pity poor Mr. Melligan!
Who, walking along Pallmall,
Hurt his foot when down he fell,
And fears he won't get well again!"

way of lending weight to every conclusion, that the decision of a majority should be acquiesced in by all; and that no one should reveal anything that transpired without express permission of congress. After this arrangement had been settled upon, we are told, by a well-informed tory pamphleteer of the day, that when some strong measures were introduced and carried, the effect on the minority was like "the springing of a mine, or the bursting of a bomb" in Carpenters' Hall. So far as can be now gathered, we may infer that to this congress came several delegates who had resolved in their secret hearts upon secession from Britain, and whose aim was to produce war rather than reconciliation.* Whether or not they represented the wishes of their own constituents, they certainly did not in this fulfil the desires of the colonies generally; and it was necessary, by evasion or denial, to deceive the country at large with loyal professions, until nearly two years later, when a majority of congress was ready to unite in the resolve of independence. At the close of the war, a Boston statesman thus referred to his own services in producing the result: —

"Here, in my retreat, like another Catiline, the collar around my neck, in danger of the severest punishment, I laid down the plan of the revolt; I endeavored to persuade my timid accomplices that a most glorious revolution might

* "I had not, Sir, been in Congress a fortnight before I discovered that parties were forming, and that some members had come to that assembly with views altogether different from what America professed to have, and what, bating a designing junto, she really had. Of these men, her independency upon Great Britain, at all events, was the most favourite project. By these the pulse of the rest was felt on every favourable occasion, and often upon no occasion at all; and by these men measures were concerted to produce what we all professed to deprecate; nay, at the very time that we universally invoked the Majesty of Heaven to witness the purity of our hearts. I had reason to believe that the hearts of many of us gave our invocation the lie. . . . . I cannot entertain the most favourable opinion of a man's veracity, who intended to do it, when he swore he did not, and when he represented a people who were actually pursuing measures to prevent the necessity of doing it." — *Livingston to Laurens*, Sedg. Liv. 173.

be the result of our efforts, but I scarcely dared to hope it; and what I have seen realized appears to me like a dream. You know by what obscure intrigues, by what unfaithfulness to the mother-country, a powerful party was formed; how the minds of the people were irritated, before we could provoke the insurrection."

Had it been avowed in the Congress of 1774, that the end of some of its leaders was a democratic and independent government, it is probable that a vast majority of the American people would have repulsed them with indignation. By dissimulation, however, they maintained the control until affairs were sufficiently ripe. For indeed the issue was very clear. America was at this moment disciplining her troops with the view of resisting the enforcement of certain acts of Parliament. It was folly to suppose that this course would not end in open hostilities, unless the acts were repealed; and hostilities once begun, subjugation or independence was the inevitable result. More far-sighted than their colleagues, they perceived that it was only necessary to keep both countries moving in their present course to render a collision certain. Indeed, despite the loyal protestations that America put forth during the ensuing twelvemonth, there can be little question but that Thurlow was correct in asserting that at the end of 1774 open rebellion existed in the colonies.

Nor could anything have more entirely aided this party in congress than the course pursued in England by the leaders of the two great factions. On the one hand they were told by the most eminent men in the state, that their cause was just and their resistance laudable;—Chatham and Burke, Richmond and Granby applauded their course; Savile upheld it as "a justifiable rebellion." On the other, as though with full intent to stimulate into rage against England, every American who had not as yet drawn the sword, the halls of Parliament echoed with the denials to our countrymen of the most ordinary attributes of manhood. In the Lords, Sandwich pronounced his American fellow-subjects to be cowards, and only regretted that there was no probability of the king's troops encountering at once "two hundred thousand of such a rabble, armed with old rusty firelocks, pistols, staves, clubs, and broomsticks;" and thus exterminating rebellion at one blow. The speaker's brother might have given him a different idea of American prowess, since he had been sufficiently beaten, in the streets of Boston, by a smaller man from Roxbury, for some wild frolic. But he preferred the testimony of Sir Peter Warren as to the misconduct of the New England troops at Louisbourg in 1745; testimony which, if true, convicts them of cowardice not unlike that for which Lord George Germain, the incoming Secretary of State, had been cashiered by a court-martial. In the Commons, too, Colonel Grant, who knew the Americans well, was certain they would not fight. They possessed not a single military trait, and would never stand to meet an English bayonet. He had been in America, and disliked their language and their way of life, and thought them altogether entirely "out of humanity's reach." He forgot to add, however, that his own services among the Alleghanies had not been of a very triumphant character; and it is pleasant to believe that Cruger, an American-born, reminded him of this fact in his reply, since we find him called to order as being personal. But these boastful and injurious words had at least one good effect: they provoked the Americans. Even Washington was disturbed by such wholesale slanders, and long after, when some British troops had been badly treated at Lexington, found occasion to remind his friends in London of Lord Sandwich's language.

If such then was the sentiment in the senate, we need hardly ask how American valor was esteemed in the royal camp; but, in truth, there appears to have been such an infinite disdain of its opponents in this quarter, that, considering all things, it is almost wonderful that the king's cause was not ruined outright at the very commencement of the war As the Roman soldiery scornfully held every civilian to be a peasant, and as the Christians, improving on this, extended the word pagan to every one not of their faith, — so the English officer of that day seems to have deemed the colonist as the basest of all base *mohairs*. One gallant general thought a single regiment would be sufficient to march from Massachusetts to Georgia, and to make singing-boys of all the people. Another (the natural brother of the king) more moderately writes from Florida, that "three or four regiments would completely settle those scoundrels" in Carolina. Robertson thought it very dastardly in the Yankees to get behind a wall; and all considered it mere idiocy to look for anything like a contested field. But there were plenty of men who recollected how the very same language had been held by the king's officers before Falkirk and Preston, and what a running commentary ensued thereon.

But the most unfortunate encouragement that America received from England, was the assurance that the latter country, whether by reason of the general aversion to the war, whether because of its own comparative feebleness, would not hold out beyond a single campaign. A greater blunder was never made; and its effect was to persuade congress and the people, that an easy victory was in store for us, and to thus prevent proper preparation for a long and severe conflict. This delusion governed in great measure the action of the first and the second congress; and it is noteworthy that its chief supporters were the delegates who afterwards led the cabal against Washington. By giving forth a false estimate of the enemy's power, they very materially weakened our own; and by neglecting the means to make victory secure, they at least rendered it very doubtful. In fact, England was at that moment in admirable condition for war. The lower classes were poor, while the middle and upper were unusually rich. Commercial prosperity and the successes of the last part of the preceding war had brought into the realm an unwonted excess of the circulating coin of the world. It was estimated, that her people held more solid wealth than those of any two other states in Europe. Thus, with plenty of poor to fill up the ranks, and plenty of treasure, the country was in a good position. And as for public sentiment, there can be no doubt that the war was highly popular with the British nation until Europe joined against them, and success became hopeless. In America, at the outbreak, the circulating cash was about $3,750,000 in specie, and $26,250,000 in paper; showing a proper revenue of about $7,500,000. The population may be estimated at 2,448,000 souls, and the military capacity at from 20,000 to 30,000 men. Of course, on these estimates, a large war could not be long carried on without foreign aid; and it is therefore again a happy thing, that during the earlier years of the struggle, and before such assistance was procured, our people were persuaded that every campaign would be the last. Another fortunate circumstance was, that without pressing the people by taxes for its redemption, and in fact, without redeeming it at all, congress should have been in a position to issue millions and hundreds of millions of paper-money, wherewith to carry on the war.

Although secrecy was ordered, yet it is not likely that it was strictly preserved in regard to all the proceedings of the first congress; and in his chamber at the Indian Queen, or at the mess of the Royal Irish, or wherever he resorted, we may suppose that André picked up all the floating gossip of the day. Hardly had it met, when the whole country from Massachusetts to Pennsylvania was thrown into the utmost agitation by false tidings of the commencement of hostilities. Israel Putnam wrote to New York, that the troops and ships had began the slaughter of the people on the evening of the 2nd of September, and called for aid from every direction. This letter, sent by express, reached New York on the 5th, and was instantly transmitted to Philadelphia, where the bells were rung muffled through the day; and the people, Quakers and all, gave vent to feelings of rage and indignation. For three days the story was uncontradicted, and fifty thousand men, it was said, had prepared to march from various quarters to Boston. But there was not a jot or a tittle of truth in the tale; and Putnam had been imposed upon. The story appears to have been devised in New England by some over-anxious whig, for the purpose of taking congress by surprise at its first coming together, and plunging it into such steps of opposition as might not easily be retraced. According to the rumor of the time, proposals for a declaration of independence were even now suggested in Carpenters' Hall; but there were so many delegates who threatened to secede at once from the assembly, if such a measure was pressed, that it was withdrawn, and the association agreed on in its stead; the object of which was to distress English trade as much as possible, and thus compel a repeal of the obnoxious laws. Its effect, however, was rather to draw asunder the two countries, and to prepare a more general acceptance by America of the Declaration of Independence of 1776, than it could possibly have encountered in 1774. Thus again it was happy for this country that the secret plans of the independence party did not now prevail.

The aversion of some of the middle and southern colonies to certain measures led to the formation, in the congress of 1774, of a party that endured through all the war; and which, by unity of action and concert of purpose, generally exercised a controlling influence in the state. In January, 1775, we find a zealous tory declaring the acts of the congress to have been unwelcome to both New York and Pennsylvania; "but Adams with his crew, and the haughty Sultans of the South, juggled the whole conclave of the delegates." Before all was over, however, there was an almost open difficulty in the hall. Several leading men withdrew for several days; and it was only by compromising matters that the names of all the delegates were finally affixed to the association. These things were kept from the public as carefully as possible, and a general assertion of unanimity in all its doings put forth by congress. But something must have leaked out at the time.

On the 16th of September, the local gentry invited the fifty or sixty delegates to an entertainment at the State House, "where they were received by a very large company, composed of the clergy, such genteel strangers as happened to be in town, and a number of respectable citizens," making in the whole about five hundred persons. If André were then in the city, there is every reason to suppose that he would be of the "genteel strangers" bidden to such a scene; and the proceedings of the occasion, so far as they may be pronounced upon from the toast-master's roll, must have possessed for him an interest beyond that of a common political dinner. The King, the Queen, the Royal Family, were duly pledged; and then came the names of the party-leaders on either side of the water: Chatham, Richmond, Conway, and Burke; Hancock, Franklin, and Sawbridge. Of course, there was much said of the cause that had brought them together, and of their determination to preserve the union of the colonies and their constitutional freedom. Two toasts had interest for any military guest: "No unconstitutional standing armies," and "May British swords never be drawn in defence of tyranny"; but the general tone of the whole affair indicated clearly the public intent to adhere to demands which England would not grant, and to resist the application of laws which England was apparently resolved to enforce. The inference was easy. If neither party receded, hostilities were imminent. And on the ensuing day a practical commentary was offered in the breaking open, by a mob, of the warehouse in which the collector of the customs had just stored a cargo of smuggled sugars which he had seized, and their restoration to the importer. All this was effected in comparative openness, nor was any punishment inflicted on the offenders. It is true that, on both sides of the Atlantic, smuggling was then regarded as a dangerous rather than an immoral practice; and that in England, even ten years later, it was so hardily pursued that near Falmouth a battery was erected to cover the landing-place, the guns of which were opened on a king's ship standing in; but at the same time a much larger proportion of the magistrates and people was there ready to obey and to enforce the laws than in this country, where nearly all the merchants were engaged in illicit trade, and where the popular sentiment regarded with abhorrence any attempt from the mother-country at its restraint.

Of all these things we may be sure that André took good heed; for that he was now on a tour of observation through what was almost an enemy's country cannot be doubted, if we consider that, in addition to selecting a port so remote as Philadelphia from his ultimate destination, he left that city to visit Gage's camp at Boston, instead of repairing at once to his regiment in Canada. This expedition led him through an important section of the country, and gave him ample opportunity of ascertaining the complexion of popular feeling. There were then two public conveyances between Philadelphia and New York: a line of stages had been established in 1773, and the Flying Machine had been in operation several years longer. This last should rather have been called the Diving Machine, since it had managed to drown, among others, one of the earliest and best actresses that appeared in America, by oversetting in the ferry between New York and Staten Island; but by neither carriage was the journey between the two cities performed in less than two days. Passing through Jersey, then, he might have perceived symptoms of the prevailing strong whig feeling and turbulent spirit; and arriving at New York, may have procured some discouraging information from his brother officers stationed there. The King's Birthday in 1774 had been duly celebrated indeed by the 23rd regiment, and what other military were at New York; but by the people generally was passed over almost unnoticed. The active whigs, under the name of "Sons of Liberty," led an organized mob; and their conflicts with the soldiery were frequent and bitter. Under their auspices liberty-poles were erected, obnoxious characters hung in effigy, and instant revenge taken for the impressment of sailors by a ship-of-war. Religion and Freedom were the watchwords of the hour, and the power and license of the Liberty Boys threatened to carry everything before them. The gentry in opposition, writes Gouverneur Morris, had started the mob, for their own purposes, in Grenville's time, and now — "the heads of the mobility grow dangerous to the gentry. . . . . The mob begin to think and reason. Poor reptiles! it is with them a vernal morning: they are struggling to cast off their winter's slough; they bask in the sunshine, and ere noon they will bite, depend upon it. The gentry begin to fear this." It must, nevertheless, be confessed that, however unlawful it may have been, the action of the whigs of New York at this time, in preventing any workmen or stores being transmitted to Gage at Boston, was of real service to the American cause; and there is nothing to wonder at in the turbulence of the people, considering the encouragement they had received in such scenes ever since the period of the Stamp Act.

From New York to Boston the traveller in those days usually passed upon horseback; either going through Connecticut, or by way of Long Island to New London, and so onwards. It matters little which route André followed, so far as the temper of the people was concerned. From the moment he entered New England, he probably encountered none but ardent whigs; and as greater unanimity and more democratic habits prevailed, so was the public mind more inflamed than in New York and Pennsylvania. Through the summer and fall of 1774, the Connecticut farmers had not been sparing in their demonstrations. At Farmington the Boston Port Bill was burned by the hangman. At Windham and Norwich, a merchant from Boston named Green, suspected of loyalty and known to be in pursuit of his debts, was mobbed and driven from the town. At Bolton, the clergyman was rudely dealt with, who had proclaimed that the true reason for opposition to the introduction of the East India Company's tea was, that since the tea was sold at Amsterdam for 1*s.* and at London and Boston for 2*s.* 6*d.*, it followed that Colonel Hancock gained 1*s.* 10*d.* by every pound of tea he smuggled in from Holland, while Colonel Erving gained but 6*d.* by every pound he sold from the Company. And as this private interest, he argued, had caused the destruction of the tea in Boston harbor, he proposed that the traders with Holland there should pay the damages out of the profits from the five thousand boxes of Dutch teas they had sold within two years. In short, although there were a good many tories in Connecticut, the rule was to tar and feather all who made themselves prominent, save only in the few towns where this party happened to be the strongest. But if any luckless tory wight was caught beyond the reach of his friendly neighbors, he was forthwith seized and led from town to town, "as by law is provided in the case of strolling ideots, lunatics," &c. And so in Rhode Island:—at Providence, a public meeting requested the authorities to expel the friends of the ministry; in other places, the whigs took the law into their own hands. Through all New England, the indisposition to English sway in any form or under any circumstances, was daily more plainly to be recognized; and by the time André reached Boston, he must have perceived that an insurrection was almost inevitable.

CHAPTER IV.

Political Condition of Massachusetts in 1774. — State of Affairs at Boston.

THE province of Massachusetts Bay, and more especially the town of Boston, contained at this moment perhaps the most excited and the least loyal portion of the king's American subjects. The peculiar characteristics of this people had long led observers to believe, that the colony was impatient of any yoke; and certainly neither their traditions nor their democratical forms of government and of social life could have inspired them with any very fervent attachment to the home authority. The fall of Canada had removed the strong bond of fear, that once formed a part of the ties that united them with England; and the whig leaders already, to a greater extent than in any other part of America, looked forward to independence. Untrammelled in almost every practical sense, their commerce had long been carried on with scanty regard to the interests of Britain; and now that it was sought to enforce the old, or to bring new restrictive laws to bear on their trade, the people were thoroughly inflamed. Bold, acquisitive, hardy, and astute, they revolted at the prospect of diminished gains; fond of power, they would not endure the loss of a tittle of authority they had once possessed. This disposition was well understood by its chief men, who foresaw the inevitable result, and, like Moses on the mountain-side, looked forth to the promised land which, denied to their own feet, was yet to be trodden by their kindred. "Our fathers were a good people," wrote Otis to England; "we have been a free people; and if you will not let us remain so any longer, we will be a great people." Thus already prepared to resent the measures of government, they derived new zeal from the counsels of their spiritual guides. Great as is still the influence in secular matters of the clergy of New England, it was then enormous; and in political controversies was exercised even more powerfully than to-day, and more openly. In every ordinary action of life, it was usual to join the world's business with religious duty; and where the force of conscience failed, the effect of long continued habit controlled the conduct of men.* And the clergy of New England, naturally disturbed at the increase, under quasi-royal protection, of prelatic forms of worship, and professionally vexed at the division of their power with a growing rival, were of one voice in their arguments. Thus, while we find the churchman of New England almost universally to have been a tory, the Congregationalists, and whosoever adhered to the Calvinistic forms of wor-

---

* A conversation between James Otis and a member of the Assembly from Boston, (apparently Thomas Cushing,) "in which the satire," says Mr. Tudor, "if it bears a little hard on the character of those times, is not wholly inapplicable to most others," will better exemplify this position. Otis observed, "They talk of sending me to the next General Court." — "You will never succeed in the General Court." — "Not succeed! and why not, pray?" — "Why, Mr. Otis, you have ten times the learning, and much greater abilities than I have, but you know nothing of human nature." — "Indeed! I wish you would give me some lessons." — "Be patient, and I will do so with pleasure. In the first place, what meeting do you go to?" — "Dr. Sewall's." — "Very well, you must stand up in sermon time, you must look devout and deeply attentive. Do you have family prayers?" — "No." — "It were well if you did; what does your family consist of?" — "Why, only four or five commonly; but at this time I have one of Dr. Sewall's saints, who is a nurse of my wife." — "Ah! that is the very thing; you must talk religion with her in a serious manner; you must have family prayers at least once while she is in your house: that woman can do you more harm or good than any other person: she will spread your fame throughout the congregation. I can also tell you, by way of example, some of the steps I take: two or three weeks before an election comes on, I send to the cooper and get all my casks put in order; I say nothing about the number of hoops. I send to the mason and have some job done to the hearths or the chimneys; I have the carpenter to make some repairs in the roof or the wood-house; I often go down to the ship-yards about eleven o'clock, when they break off to take their drink, and enter into conversation with them. They all vote for me." — (*Tudor's Otis*, p. 91.)

ship as practised in that country, were as universally whigs. The former was self-confident and elate with the pride of a superior rank; the latter jealously indignant, and fearful of the establishment of an American episcopacy. This was a favorite bugbear. Among the lower classes the most dreadful apprehensions of bishops prevailed; they were esteemed as little differing from demons; and the children wept as they listened to the tale that, among other perquisites of episcopacy, every tenth-born child should be ravished from its mother's side; and were fain to pray, that death might fall upon them so soon as a bishop's foot pressed New England soil. Intelligent and educated striplings thought it their bounden duty to God to be ready to slay the first prelate that should arrive. With these sentiments, it is no wonder that the Episcopalians were closely watched, and such of their chief men as were not openly whigs, put under restraint at an early stage in the troubles; nor that hatred of the state of England was soon mingled with that of its church. No stronger evidence of the coincidence of political and religious feeling in this crisis can be found, than is presented by the address of the Provincial Congress of Massachusetts, wherein the people of New England are described as a church against which earth and hell had combined. They were moved by one religion, one cause; and the number of those who disagreed with them was too slight to militate against their proposition. And in truth, it seems but reasonable that the New England clergy should have resisted the introduction of episcopal supremacy, if such a design existed anywhere but in the hopes or the fears of the colonists. The land belonged to them and to their flocks; and it would have been utterly unjust to have subjected it to the spiritual domination of a church abhorred by the people at large. No wonder, then, that their pulpits volleyed forth the most bitter imprecations against England, and that their prayers invoked the Almighty to shatter her ships against the rocks, and to drown her armies in the depths of the ocean. "Oh Lord," prayed a fervent divine, "if our enemies will fight us, let them have fighting enough! If more soldiers are on their way hither, send them, oh Lord! to the bottom of the sea." Impelled thus by their original inclinations, stimulated by their clergy, and dexterously guided by astute leaders, the people presented a front that no royal governor could repel or confuse. It was then that what is now called a caucus system was first brought into practical use, through the skill of Samuel Adams and some other whig leaders. Before any public meeting of importance came off, the measures and men to be supported were carefully but secretly decided upon by a council of three or four chiefs. The combination of their personal adherents at the meeting was generally sufficient to decide the question, and to give the tone to its proceedings; while any opposition was effectually quashed by a lack of union or preparation among their adversaries.

The appointment of General Gage to the government of Massachusetts would, under ordinary circumstances, have been an advantage to both crown and people. His politics, so far as we know, were not harsh; — on the repeal of the Stamp Act, in 1769, his mansion at New York was brilliantly illuminated; — and he had chosen a wife in this country. In a military sense, he must have been familiar with the land; for so long before as 1755 he had led the 44th regiment under Braddock, and been wounded by the side of Washington. But the leaders of the whigs now saw in his appointment a diabolical design, amounting to more than a studied insult to the province. The Port Bill had been received at Boston on the 10th of May, 1774. Gage arrived on the 13th; and on the same day a town-meeting displayed a firm and unconciliatory temper.. On the 17th, Gage was formally proclaimed; but even at the banquet in Faneuil Hall, which formed part of the ceremonies of the day, the disposition of the people was displayed by the hisses with which they greeted his toast to his predecessor, Mr. Hutchinson. Yet, though he was thus early warned of the popular tendency, and though he never concealed the condition of things from himself or his superiors, his letters to Lord Dartmouth through the summer and fall of 1774 were calm, and often hopeful. Things were always worse than when he wrote last; but ere he wrote again, they would probably be on the mend. Thus it came that little reliance was placed on his reports; and the opposition openly declared that he had deceived ministers. " No event has turned out as he foretold, or gave reason to hope ; the next letter constantly contradicts the expectation raised by the former." But he soon saw that the civil government of the province was nearly at an end. The courts of justice were little more than a puppet-show; the judges were driven from the bench, and the juries refused to be sworn. Almost within cannon-shot of Boston, thousands of people surrounded the house of Oliver, the lieutenant-governor, and by force compelled him to sign such political papers as they chose. Danforth, Lee, and other members of the council, were similarly handled. The legislature too had, in May, almost ignored the existence of a royal governor, and, despite his proclamation of dissolution, had provided for a provincial congress. The ancient form of civil government was indeed dead, for the General Court never met more, and the power of the colony was to be divided between a royal governor and a rebel legislature till Massachusetts became an independent state. In October, 1774, twelve out of fourteen counties sent representatives to this provincial congress, at Salem; and it forthwith proceeded to act in every respect as the lawful government of the land; making provision for raising, arming, and controlling an army ; and regulating the police of the province, and its intercourse with others. One of the first questions broached was that of negro slavery ; and a letter directed to the chaplain was read, asking whether, when the masters were struggling for freedom, their slaves should not share their lot. But after debate, it was moved that " the matter now subside ;" and it subsided accordingly. Their aim seems to have been to look exclusively to the main point, and to ignore all others. Thus, in December, 1774, when the Baptist churches sought to avail themselves of the opportunity of procuring religious liberty, they were gracefully put aside by the congress. And though rumor alleged that at the same time it refused to direct the immediate taking up of arms against the king's troops until the other colonies could be involved, yet it went on accumulating guns and ammunition, and electing generals. In all that it did it had the support of the people. They who opposed its action were far more respectable in social rank than in numbers. Putnam and Willard, Saltonstall, Vassall, and Borland, Fitch, Stark, Ruggles, and Babcock, in vain sought by their character and authority to stay the tide. These were, it is true, of the first position in the colony; but the day was gone when they were to command respect and obedience. When they formed associations for mutual protection in "the free exercise of their right of liberty in eating, drinking, buying, selling, communing, and acting what, with whom, and as they pleased, consistent with God's law and the King's," they were soon broken up and driven into Boston, where Gage's troops protected them from violence. "The tories," wrote one from Boston in the summer of 1774, "lead a devil of a life; in the country the people will not grind their corn, and in town they refuse to purchase from and sell to them." An obnoxious character might look for any injury, from having his cattle taken or barns burned, up to personal indignities. Willard going to recover a debt, was mobbed and sent to the Simsbury mines; Davis was tarred and feathered; Ruggles was mobbed and driven from the county; Paine and Chandler met with little better usage; and that "ancient gentleman," as Gage calls him, "Thomas Foster, Esquire, was obliged to run into the woods and had like to have been lost." In short, the province was almost exclusively possessed by an organized party, who revenged themselves on the British Parliament in ill-treating every one that did not embrace whig principles. "There is something extremely absurd," said an American at this date, who avows his intention of eschewing politics as though they were edged tools, " in some men's eternally declaiming on freedom of thought, and the unalienable rights of Englishmen, when they will not permit an opponent to open his mouth on the subjects in dispute, without danger of being presented with a coat of tar and feathers." " The very cause for which the whigs contended," says another who himself gallantly fought for American independence, " was essentially that of freedom, and yet all the freedom it granted was, at the peril of tar and feathers, to think and act like themselves." With equal animosity the whigs of the province regarded Gage. They burned the forage coming to Boston for his troops, and sunk the boats which brought bricks for his use. Beyond the sound of his drum-beat, armed resistance was openly planned: magazines were established, exercises in arms set on foot, and weapons and ammunition of every sort, good or bad, eagerly sought after by the people. Gage's conclusion was that the object of the whig leaders was to provoke a collision and precipitate a war; and he therefore did not fail to strengthen his hands for an occasion which, it is fair to believe, he would most gladly have averted. By the time André arrived at Boston there must have been three thousand troops gathered there, besides a regiment in garrison at Castle William; and from several men-of-war in the harbor four hundred marines were drawn early in December, led by Pitcairne, a descendant of the classical panegyrist of Dundee, and equally loyal as his ancestor, though to another line. His name is celebrated in America by his connection with the first blood shed in the Revolution, which his death at Bunker Hill perhaps expiated. If we are to credit M. de Chastellux, he was in the habit of traversing the country in disguise and bringing in intelligence to Gage.

The condition of the troops was not pleasant. They were constantly insulted or tampered with by the Americans, to whom their presence was an insufferable nuisance. Desertions were privately encouraged; and before the war began, scarce an organized American military company was without its drill-master in the person of an English fugitive. Washington's men at Alexandria, and Greene's in Rhode Island, were thus taught their manual. This seduction of troops, and the allurements held out to the men to sell their equipments, added fresh fuel to the growing hatred between both parties; and frequent affrays occurred between the soldiers and the citizens. It was probably for some flagrant annoyance of this kind that Dyre, a man known as active in previous disturbances, was seized and sent in irons to England in 1774. He averred that Maddison, who seems to have questioned him pretty roughly as to the orders he might have received for the destruction of the tea from "King Hancock and the d—d Sons of Liberty," promised him, that once arrived in England, "he should be hung like a dog"; but the more temperate of the whigs seem to have thought him an untruthful fellow; and all the trouble he was put to there was to be examined by North, Dartmouth, and Sandwich, and so discharged. But sometimes the soldiers settled the matter themselves; and having fairly caught in the act a whig tempting them to sell their arms, tarred and feathered him thoroughly, and paraded him, to the air of Yankee Doodle, as "a specimen of Democracy." The example of the officers, too, was frequently anything but praiseworthy. Entertainments and dances were given on Saturday night and carried on into Sunday morning. Such things had never occurred in Boston before, and gave great offence. Nor was it unusual for a bevy of drunken officers to commit the grossest indecencies and outrages in the public streets; and violent affrays, in which they generally came off second-best, were the natural consequence. Of course, all these occurrences were perfectly adapted to inflame the people's anger, and to stimulate fresh invectives against Gage. It is true that he gave a ready ear to every complaint against his subordinates, and seldom hesitated to punish; but he was upbraided, nevertheless, as the modern Duke of Alva, as the tyrant of the town; and in the worst possible taste was told, that "the savages who chased him on the Ohio were gentle as lambs, compared with men bereaved of their liberties." The dangerous aspect of affairs soon led him to strengthen the old, and erect new works to protect the only part of his province that remained in good earnest subject to his control; and the sole communication between Boston and the main was guarded by substantial redoubts. This was a great grievance both to the Massachusetts and the Continental Congress, who saw in the fortifications a design to awe the country and enslave the town; but Gage very prudently refused to comply with a request for their reduction. "Unless themselves annoyed," he said, "the works which you call a Fortress will annoy nobody." In private, however, the Americans ridiculed these preparations. "The country lads," said Lovell, "were minded to fill the trenches with bundles of hay, and thus enter securely"; and Appleton protested that the old Louisbourg soldiers laughed at the entrenchments, and would regard them no more than a beaver-dam. Nevertheless the British occupied Boston sixteen months longer, and no attempt was ever made to put these threats into execution.

About the period of André's visit, towards the close of 1774, the army at Boston was well handled. It was brigaded under Percy, Pigot, and Jones, and a field-officer with a hundred and fifty men guarded the lines on the Neck. Their duties confined the officers to circumscribed bounds; but the beautiful appearance of the surrounding country was not lost on them. "The entrance to the harbour," wrote Captain (afterwards Lord) Harris, "and the view of the town of Boston from it, is the most charming thing I ever saw. . . . . . My tent-door, about twenty yards from a piece of water nearly a mile broad, with the country beyond most beautifully tumbled about in hills and valleys, rocks and woods, interspersed with straggling villages, with here and there a spire peeping over the trees, and the country of the most charming green that delighted eye ever gazed on. Pity these infatuated people cannot be content to enjoy such a country in peace!" But of these scenes beyond the lines the troops could have no nearer acquaintance. From the autumn of 1774, it was not safe for any ministerialist, military or civil, to be found out of Boston, where Gage remained almost in a state of siege, yet with few of its discomforts. The Americans might cut off the supplies of beef and mutton, and occasionally reduce the officers to salted diet; but the temptation of gain led them to smuggle in fresh provisions. All sorts, the officers wrote, were plenty there, and cheaper than in London, though prices had risen with the demand. "The saints" were beginning to relish the money spent in Boston; and the only regret to the spenders was the enriching of a set of people who, in their eyes, "with the most austere show of devotion, were void of all real religion and honesty, and were reckoned the most arrant cheats and hypocrites on the continent."—" In some respects," writes an officer, " our camp might as well have been pitched on Blackheath as on Boston Common; the women are very handsome, but like old mother Eve, very frail"; and in social refinements, the country was a hundred years behind England. In short, it is clear that the dislike of the provincials was amply returned by the British, chafing at the scoffs which they received, and the indignity of remaining cooped up in the presence of an antagonist whom they despised. For by many it was thought that the proceedings of congress were designed merely to intimidate the merchants in England, and that America would never be so mad as to take up arms. " Whenever it comes to blows, he that can run fastest will think himself best off," said the officers at Boston. "Any two regiments here ought to be decimated if they did not beat, in the field, the whole force of the Massachusetts Province; for though they are numerous, they are but a mere mob, without order or discipline, and very awkward at handling their arms." That it would have to come to blows was now perceived. "I see some pretty resolves from Concord," wrote Admiral Montagu, "and the proceedings from Philadelphia all seem to go on well for a Civil War." And again — "I doubt not but that I shall hear Mr. Samuel Adams is hanged or shot before many months are at an end. I hope so at least." * Nor was the language in which they were spoken of by the friends of America in England very conciliatory. "A mere army of observation," said Burke; "its only use was to shelter the magistrates of ministerial creation"; while Chatham characterized them as "an impotent general and a dishonoured army, trusting solely to the pickaxe and the spade for security against the just indignation of an injured and an insulted people." — "They are an army of impotence," he repeated, in reference to Gage's inactivity. "I do not mean to censure his inactivity; it is prudent and necessary inaction. But it is a miserable condition, where disgrace is prudence; and where it is necessary to be contemptible." Even the political rhymesters, with Lord John Townshend at their head, found occasion to celebrate the sources of ministerial embarrassment. Thus the latter addresses the pious Dartmouth: —

> "The saints, alas! have waxen strong;
> In vain your fasts and godly song
> To quell the rebel rout!
> Within his lines skulks valiant Gage,
> Like Yorick's starling in the cage
> He cries, 'I can't get out!'"

* The British seem to have believed that Samuel Adams was their most powerful and unscrupulous foe in the province. In March, 1775, one of them wrote that when Dr. Warren had pronounced, in the Old South meeting-house, an oration in commemoration of what was absurdly called a Massacre, Mr. Adams demanded that the meeting name an orator for the next anniversary of "the bloody and horrid massacre perpetrated by Preston's soldiers." Several royal officers were present to discountenance the proceedings; and one, "a very genteel, sensible officer, dressed in gold-lace regimentals, with blue lapels, moved with indignation at the insult offered the Army, since Captain Preston had been fairly tried and most honourably acquitted by a Boston Jury, advanced to Hancock and Adams, and spoke his sentiments to them in plain English; the latter told the officer he knew him, and would

Cramped up thus within the town-limits, and deprived by the countrymen of every means of erecting needful buildings for their lodging or accommodation, the British were forced to use many liberties with the public edifices of the place; and we may be sure they were little loath to convert the South Church into a riding-school. As it had been employed by the whigs for political lectures, it perhaps possessed the less sanctity in the eyes of Gage's followers; but this association of religion and horses will remind the reader of Constantine's adorning the hippodrome of his new capital with the famous and sacred serpentine pillar of brass, which had for ages commemorated, at Delphi, the glory of Marathon. Respect for the creeds of others rarely clogs the action of a power either in peace or in war.

The Americans had ample intelligence of all Gage did. Their Provincial Congress even sent in a committee to examine the surgeon's stores with the commissary in Boston, that they might, it would seem, learn what to lay in for their own army. But there was one sort of military supply that, on either side, has since the war been less loudly acknowledged than it was then eagerly sought. Before the first gun was fired at Concord or Lexington, the Massachusetts Congress had induced the Stockbridge Indians to take up the hatchet, and had regularly enrolled them in its army. The chief sachem, who went by the euphonious title of Jehoiakin Mothskin, exchanged sentiments with Mr. Hancock, and informed the Congress that if they sent for him to fight, they must expect him to fight in his own Indian way, and not in the English fashion; all the orders he wished was to know where the enemy lay. At the same period, the Americans were less successful in treating with the Six Nations, the Penobscots, Caughnawagas, &c., with whom the English had no doubt a superior influence. Their address to the

settle the matter with the General; the man of honour replied, 'You and I must settle it first.' At this the demagogue turned pale and waived the discourse." — *ii. Am. Arch. 4th ser.* 106.

Mohawks is very curious. One of the motives urged to induce the savage "to whet his hatchet" is the probable increase of popery in Canada! It is probable that most of these applications were occasioned by the wish to keep the frontiers safe, and to weaken England; but there were cases which such considerations could scarce have reached, and where the barbarian was employed simply as a warrior. "We need not be tender of calling on the savages," wrote Gage to Dartmouth, in June, 1775, "as the rebels have shown us the example by bringing as many Indians down against us here as they could collect." At a later day Washington was authorized to employ the Indians in the continental service at his discretion, and to pay them $100 for every officer, and $30 for every private that they captured; but the Massachusetts Congress was probably the first party in the war to bring them on the field. Their employment afterwards by the British was made a famous theme of reproach, by Americans as well as Englishmen, against Suffolk who had vindicated the step:—

"We've flayed the virgins, babes and wives,
With tomahawks and scalping-knives,
Which God and Nature gave us."

Without the means of connecting André directly with any incident in the occupation of Boston, a sketch of the military features of the place and time has now been given, with intent to present those points which would most probably have had a chief interest to him. Were there any reason to think that he remained with Gage so late as February, 1775, he might be suspected of a part in some such expedition as that of Brown and De Berniere, — two officers sent out in disguise by the general to make a *reconnoissance* of the country, through Suffolk and Worcester counties, where the whigs had their chief magazines; perhaps with an eye to a descent. The spies were selected apparently as having recently arrived from Canada, and therefore as less apt to be known as royal officers. They returned from a perilous and toilsome journey, well supplied with plans and sketches; and a very entertaining report of their expedition is preserved. We may imagine how André's pencil and pen would have been busied, not only with the more legitimate duty of the occasion, but with such episodes as the militia review at Buckminster's tavern, which was followed by an address from the commander, "recommending patience, coolness, and bravery, (which indeed they much needed,) particularly told them they would always conquer if they did not break, and recommended them to charge us coolly, and wait for our fire, and everything would succeed with them,—quotes Cæsar and Pompey, Brigadiers Putnam and Ward, and all such great men; put them in mind of Cape Breton, and all the battles they had gained for his majesty in the last war, and observed that the regulars must have been ruined but for them. After so learned and spirited an harangue, he dismissed the parade, and the whole company came into the house and drank till nine o'clock, and then returned to their respective homes full of pot-valor."

CHAPTER V.

Condition of Canada in 1775. — Operations on Lake Champlain and the Sorel. — Fall of Fort St. John, and Capture of André.

FROM Boston André might have passed either by land or by sea to Canada. The former route would have been the most dangerous for a known adherent of the crown; but since his arrival in America, there had probably been no necessity of his connection with the army being made public, and we may therefore conjecture, that he encountered little difficulty in getting out of the town, or on his road through the northern parts of New England. There was indeed no inconsiderable share of loyalty among the people along his path; but the whig element decidedly predominated; and perhaps the first overt act of rebellion on the continent was the capture of the fort at Portsmouth, on December 13th, 1774, by a band of three or four hundred men, acting under instructions from the Boston whigs. They rushed in by beat of drum, disregarding the four-pounders that were hurriedly and harmlessly discharged against them; and overawing the garrison of six invalids, and binding the commander, they hauled down the royal colors, and bore off (as was their chief design) all the arms and ammunition of the post. Such an event as this ought to occupy an important place in the annals of our early violations of existing laws; and taken in connection with all that had elsewhere transpired within the range of his observation since his arrival at Philadelphia, must have furnished André with matter for a very sufficient report upon the temper and designs of the Americans, if indeed such task had been assigned him. All this, however, is conjectural. We only know that he at last rejoined his regiment, the seventh, in Canada.

Sir Guy Carleton, the military and civil commander of the province of Quebec (which comprehended both Canadas) had arrived there in September, 1774. He was a man of clear and extensive judgment, great administrative faculties, large experience, and winning manners; and though turned of fifty, an active and skilful soldier. With the character of the Canadians he was well acquainted, and the extraordinary official powers that he was vested with appear to have been used so sagaciously as to procure most important advantages for England, without alienating the hearts of the people. Among our own leaders there was an opinion that it was lucky for America that the ministry should have so far gone out of their way, — as by a private arrangement with him, — to have given to Howe and Burgoyne the command of the royal arms; for the appointment, by the customs of the service, pertained to Sir Guy, and it is very certain that he would have made a better chief than either of his substitutes. He seems, too, to have been a supporter of the cabinet; yet his praises were sounded by their staunchest opponents, and the Duke of Richmond passed a most glowing eulogium upon him at this period in the House of Lords. In his present position he had the advantage of some familiarity with the patriots who were shortly to be brought against him. Montgomery and St. Clair had fought by his side when Montcalm fell, and as quartermaster of Wolfe's army he must have had some knowledge of Charles Lee and Putnam, of Starke, Schuyler, and Wooster. Such was the General under whose command André had first experience of actual war.

The people of Canada at this date, if not so warmly attached to the British government as a few years sooner they had been to that of France, were at least not generally discontented. The provisions of the Quebec act gave them little uneasiness. Unused to democratical forms of government, they did not share in the anger of the whigs in England and the more southern colonies, at a law which gave them no part in the administration of public affairs, while the free toleration of the Catholic religion was necessarily grateful to a population that was Catholic almost to a man. But our leaders in Massachusetts and elsewhere did not relish the idea of going into a war with England without striving to make allies rather than enemies of a country that lay in such dangerous contiguity to their own; and secret emissaries were already among the Canadians. In furtherance of this end, congress sent forth to them an able address, which, translated into French and distributed in manuscript, produced a good effect among that people; but it unfortunately inspired some of their principal men to examine the address to the people of England, made at the same time. This document, while it did not flatter the civil capabilities of the Canadians, inveighed with great warmth against the countenance parliament had given to their creed; which was declared to be the disseminator of impiety, persecution, and murder over all the world. These passages provoked the violent resentment of the readers, who openly cursed "the perfidious, double-faced congress," and hesitated no longer in renewing their allegiance to King George. This consequence should have been foreseen. "I beg leave," wrote over an English friend to America, in January, 1775, "to caution you against any strictures on the Roman Catholic religion, as it will be much more advantageous for you to conciliate to you the Canadians, than to exasperate or rouse the people here; let us alone to do that." The few active sympathizers that congress possessed in Canada were chiefly new-comers, whose zeal was more abundant than their discretion. On the day fixed for the Quebec act to go into force, (May 1, 1775,) the king's bust on the parade at Montreal was found to have been blackened during the night, and adorned with a rosary of potatoes and a wooden cross, to which this label was added: *Le Pape du Canada, ou le sot*

Anglois. This insult greatly exasperated the government as well as the people.

Meanwhile, matters with Gage were coming to a crisis, and Carleton left no stone unturned to put his own government in condition to render every service in its power to the crown. He seems indeed to have for a time meditated a march upon Boston, and two officers were sent out with private instructions to explore a military route. But the enterprise of the Americans, and the fortunes of war, soon gave him abundant occupation at home.

The course which an army would, it was thought, be obliged to follow in passing between Canada and the other colonies, was well known. Lake Champlain, commencing near the upper waters of the Hudson, and stretching one hundred and twenty miles to the north, pours its waters through the Sorel into the St. Lawrence, between Montreal and Quebec. This lake was commanded by the fortresses of Ticonderoga, erected near its communication with Lake George, and of Crown Point, situated farther to the north. At the head of navigation on the Sorel, Fort Chambly was erected, and twelve miles to the southward was the post of St. Johns. To garrison these places would, in time of war, demand large forces; but in peace they were of course held by slender guards. In fact, the only troops that Carleton now had in Lower Canada were the 7th and 26th regiments, numbering 717 men, all told. The 8th regiment was in Upper Canada; and all were broken up into various and scattered detachments.

As Ticonderoga was known to contain large military stores, of which we were very destitute, it was concerted to seize this post so soon as hostilities should commence. A secret emissary of the Boston Committee appears to have so managed the affair that when, on the 10th of May, three weeks after the Lexington fight, he accompanied the Americans in a night-surprise of the fortress, he was surprised to find the gates closed. A wicket, however, stood conveniently open, and, giving the Indian war-whoop, the assailants poured in "with uncommon rancour," as Ethan Allen, their chief, expressed it. The forty-four men of the 26th, who garrisoned the place, were compelled to surrender with hardly a pretence at resistance, beyond the snapping of his firelock by the sentry ; and it would seem that the only injury received by any of the victors was in consequence of a dispute between two of the leaders as to their conduct in the business, in the course of which Colonel Easton was " heartily kicked " by Colonel Arnold.

The Americans on this occasion were not numerous, but they were active. Crown Point, Skenesborough, and St. Johns were visited without delay, the public stores seized or destroyed, and a few more soldiers taken prisoners. But the secret of the expedition had leaked out before the blow was struck, and large reinforcements were actually on their way to Ticonderoga when it was captured. There is even reason to suppose that André was of the party. It consisted of one hundred and twenty men, with six pieces of cannon ; and was but twenty miles from St. Johns when that place fell. To these appear to have been joined forty more from Chambly. On the 19th May they fell upon Allen, who was then at St. Johns. He retreated with trifling loss, and the British resumed possession of the post.

So long as he retained the command of the Sorel, Carleton knew that a serious invasion of Canada was unlikely. He therefore at once set about strengthening his hands in this quarter. Over five hundred regulars were soon gathered for the defence of Chambly and St. Johns, drawn chiefly from the 7th and 26th regiments, with a few from the naval and artillery services; and a number of Canadian levies, and all the ship-carpenters from Quebec, were joined with them. The summer was passed in building vessels wherewith to regain the control of Lake Champlain, and in fortifying St. Johns. This post was situated on a level space near the riverside, and, so long as it could hold out, was thought to be a perfect safeguard against any attempt on Chambly. The latter fort was therefore but weakly garrisoned, and appears to have been regarded by the English as a place of deposit for the bulk of their stores, and one to which they might safely resort should the other work become untenable. The provisions for St. Johns were even kept there, to be issued forth from time to time as wanted. By the end of August, two vessels were nearly ready to receive their masts, and two strong square forts erected. These were about a hundred yards apart, connected towards the water by a small breastwork. A ditch, fed from the river, and strong pickets, or chevaux-de-frise, encompassed them about; and they were well supplied with artillery. The hesitancy of congress to set on foot an invasion of a neighboring province, gave the English unusual facilities for carrying on their toil uninterruptedly. That body had indeed approved of the private enterprise which wrested Ticonderoga from the king's hands; but it was not until June that it took steps to provide for a continental army and to appoint its generals. On the 27th, a few days later, Major-General Schuyler was directed to repair to Ticonderoga and, if expedient, to invade Canada; but it was not before the 30th that Articles of War for the government of its soldiery were actually adopted. A number of Americans were already assembled at Ticonderoga when Schuyler arrived there on the 18th July, and many more came in during the summer; so that towards its close upwards of 2000 men were expected to move to the Sorel. But, as may be easily believed, this force was stronger in numbers than effectiveness. Drawn from different colonies, unaccustomed to serve together, impatient of discipline, their ranks were filled with jealousies and disputes.* The most

* "About ten o'clock last night I arrived at the landing-place, the north end of Lake George, a post occupied by a captain and one hundred men. A sentinel, on being informed I was in the boat, quitted his post to go and awake the guard, consisting of three men, in which he had no success. I walked up, and came to another, a sergeant's guard. Here the sentinel challenged, but suffered me to come up to him, the whole guard, like the

OPERATIONS ON LAKE CHAMPLAIN AND THE SOREL. 77

undaunted courage cannot long supply the lack of subordination in a soldier; and this defect seems to have been one great cause of Schuyler's trouble. He alleges that even from a partisan so valiant and important as Ethan Allen, he was obliged to exact a solemn promise of proper demeanor before he reluctantly gave him permission to attend the army. Nor was desertion unknown: "We held a court-martial at every other stage," wrote a New York officer, "and gave several of the unruly ones Moses's Law, *i. e.* thirty-nine."

Apprehensive that the enemy's vessels would be ready for service before the full force with which he designed entering Canada could be brought up, Schuyler appeared before St. Johns, with upwards of 1000 men, on the 6th of September. A landing was made within two miles of the place, and after some brisk skirmishing the troops halted for the night. But no Canadians repaired to their aid, as had been hoped for, which, with other prudential considerations, induced the American leaders to return on the 7th to the Isle-aux-Noix, not far distant. On the night of the 10th a detachment of 800 men, under Montgomery, again landed near the fort; but the noise which a part made in marching through the tangled woods occasioned a panic among the rest, from which there was no recovering them; and it was necessary, on the next day, to lead them back, after a very trifling skirmish. On the 17th, however, they were once more embarked, and, Schuyler's illness preventing his accompanying them, the subsequent conduct of the siege devolved upon Montgomery. It is difficult to estimate the strength of his forces, by reason of the numbers who were constantly sent back to Crown Point on the sick-list; but it was probably

---

first, in the soundest sleep. With a penknife only I could have cut off both guards, and then have set fire to the block-house, destroyed the stores, and starved the people here. . . . But I hope to get the better of this inattention. The officers and men are all good-looking people, and decent in their deportment, and I really believe will make good soldiers as soon as I can get the better of this *nonchalance* of theirs. Bravery, I believe, they are far from wanting." — *Schuyler to Washington,* July 18, 1775.

not far from 2000 men. A party was stationed between Chambly and St. Johns to interrupt the communication; and though it was routed by an expedition from the fort, subsequent reinforcements arrived to the Americans, and on the 18th the British were in turn compelled to fly. The investment continued, but bad weather and the feebleness of the beleaguering army retarded its progress not a little. The fort was held by Major Preston, of the 26th, with upwards of 500 men; among whom was a large part of the 7th, with André as their quartermaster. Major Stopford of the 7th, with nearly 100 of that regiment, commanded at Chambly. In Montgomery's opinion it was necessary to erect certain works to insure the reduction of St. Johns; but he had to do, as he soon acknowledged, with "troops who carried the spirit of freedom into the field, and thought for themselves." His ideas were not approved of by his inferiors, and he was compelled to lay the plan aside. This is but an instance of the crude organization of our army at this early day. Wooster, the third in rank in that region, held command of his Connecticut men as a colonial and not a continental regiment, explaining that they were allies of the other Americans, but soldiers of Connecticut; and Schuyler says that it was with no little difficulty that any useful service was at length obtained from them. With others of his officers, Montgomery's relations were extremely embarrassing. Many of them reported directly to their respective colonial authorities, and of course commented freely on all that occurred. The ill effects of such a system are evident; but there was then no help for it. A New Hampshire officer informs the government that he alone has the execution of any successful measure; the failures are due to Allen and others. Another officer, a captain, kept up a correspondence with Governor Trumbull of Connecticut, in which, professing his own piety, he feels called upon to complain of the profanity of head-quarters; Montgomery, besides, is no general, though he may indeed possess courage. On the other hand, courage was the very quality which Montgomery seems to have found lacking in some of his followers. He reports to Schuyler the cowardly conduct of an officer of the same name as this critical writer, and adds: "Were I furnished with power for that purpose, he should not live an hour after his trial, if the court condemn him." This spirit of insubordination, which induced Montgomery's army to prefer mutiny to the sacrifice to his positive commands of their own opinion as to the best way of besieging St. Johns, must be duly considered by every one who follows our military history at this period. It prevailed widely; and the purest patriotism, and the irksome use of flattery and persuasion, were too often needed to enable a general to retain his commission or to effect anything with his troops. Montgomery was wearied of his place, and anxious to get rid of it; for matters soon came to such a pass that he was obliged to inform his chief subordinates (or, rather, insubordinates), that unless they would obey his orders he should at once abandon the leadership and leave them to their own devices. At the same period Schuyler, disgusted with the disorders that he could not subdue, was resolved no longer "to coax, to wheedle, and even to lie, to carry on the service," and made up his mind to retire; while Washington, for similar causes, declared that no earthly consideration should have wooed him to accept the chief command, had he foreseen what was before him. Yet there were many good soldiers in our ranks, and discipline only was required to render them all such. Meanwhile the siege went on slowly. Both parties suffered from want of sufficient necessaries of war. The garrison fought often knee-deep in mire, and their opponents, in addition to the injudicious nature of their works, labored under a deficiency of ammunition. At this juncture, an enterprise, suggested by some Canadians whom Major James Livingston had prevailed on to espouse the American cause, was crowned with success, and gave an unexpected turn to affairs. With 300 of them, and in coöperation with a detachment from Montgomery's army, he attacked Fort

Chambly. On the 18th of October, Major Stopford of the 7th, with nearly 100 of his men, surrendered this post, in which, as in a place of security, were lodged not only the stores for St. Johns, but the women and children of the troops that defended it, and to which the beleaguered garrison already meditated a retreat. It may be noted that Livingston, whose conduct on this occasion so greatly promoted the event that reduced André to captivity, was the same officer who, a few years later, was indirectly the cause of his final and fatal arrest. "The capture of Chamblée occasioned many others," wrote Sir Henry Clinton, long after. Lamb also, the artillery officer at West Point on this last occasion, now pointed the guns against the walls within which André fought. The colors of the 7th were among the spoils taken at Chambly. They were sent to Philadelphia; and their keeping, after presentation to congress, being probably confided to the President, they were, wrote John Adams to his wife, "hung up in Mrs. Hancock's chamber with great splendor and elegance."* These were the first standards captured in this war.

The garrison of St. Johns was now put on half allowance, and the siege was more vigorously conducted. Montgomery's men seem at length to have permitted his views to be carried out; and on the 29th October, a battery was erected, under the fire of the fort, on an eminence to the north which entirely commanded it. On the next day ten guns and mortars were

* The 7th lost its colors again before the war was ended. One of these, taken at Yorktown, is preserved, as the gift of Washington, at Alexandria, Va. It is of heavy twilled silk, seventy-two inches long by sixty-four wide, and presents the red and white crosses on a blue field. In the centre, in silk embroidery, is the crown above a rose surrounded by a garter with the legend, *Honi soit qui mal y pense*. The royal warrant of July 1, 1751, prescribes for the 7th: — "In the centre of their colours the Rose within the Garter, and the Crown over it: the White Horse in the corners of the second Colour." This colour now also bears by royal warrant the words: — Martinique, Talavera, Albuhera, Badajoz, Salamanca, Vittoria, Pyrenees, Orthes, Peninsula, Toulouse; — memorials of victories that may well obliterate the scenes of America.

mounted, and preparations made for a general cannonade and assault. Tidings of affairs had however been conveyed to Carleton, who marched with a strong force of irregulars to relieve the place. His design was to attack the American intrenchments, while Preston at the same time should make a sally from within. But on the 30th October, Sir Guy's party was intercepted and defeated, and he was compelled to retreat to Montreal. On the evening of November 1st, the new battery and the old four-gun work having kept up an incessant fire through the day, which was briskly returned from the forty-eight pieces of the fort, Montgomery sent a flag to Preston with one of the prisoners taken at Carleton's defeat, and a request that, since relief was now hopeless, the post should be surrendered. To this Preston replied, promising to offer proposals if relief should not appear within four days. These terms were peremptorily declined. Another prisoner of superior rank was sent to Preston, with a declaration from Montgomery, that the only means to insure the honors of war for the garrison and the safety of the officers' baggage, was to surrender at once. The Englishman yielded, and on the 2nd, articles of capitulation were signed. The troops were allowed all the honors of war. "This was due," said Montgomery, "to their fortitude and perseverance." The officers were to retain their side-arms; their firearms were to be kept in pledge; the effects of the garrison were not to be withheld unless a prisoner should escape, in which case his property was to be given as plunder to the Americans; and the prisoners were to pass into Connecticut, or such place of detention as congress might provide. A quartermaster from each corps was also to go on parole to Montreal to settle its business and bring up its baggage. For the 7th, this duty fell upon André; seven of its officers had been taken at Chambly, and thirteen more were now captives with most of its privates. About sixty men only remained at liberty. These had been retained by Carleton, and shared in the defence of Quebec. At 9 A. M., on the 3rd November,

1775, the Americans entered St. Johns; and the English, to the number of six hundred, marching out and grounding their arms on a plain to the westward, became prisoners of war. They were immediately embarked for Ticonderoga.

The principal losses to either side during this siege seem to have been by desertions. Of our people, but nine were killed, and four or five wounded. " You know we take good care of ourselves," wrote Montgomery. Nor could the British casualties have been very numerous, since the defence was conducted with hardly an attempt at a sortie; though such measures might have been very advantageous to the besieged. But for the capture of Chambly, and the final adoption of our general's plan of investment, the fort would not have fallen at all, either by assault or starvation; for assault was only practicable from that quarter whence our men had at first shrunk, with an impression that they were to be betrayed and trepanned under the guns of the place. Besides, at the time of surrender, very many of our troops were importunate to go home. Their enlistments were nearly out, and they were utterly unaccustomed to the severities of military life, or to prolonged absence from their families. Few indeed of the hundreds of sick that were sent to Ticonderoga ever returned to camp. " The greater part of them are so averse to going back, that they pretend sickness and skulk about; and some, even officers, go away without leave; nor can I get the better of them," wrote Schuyler to congress. Had the siege endured much longer, probably half of our army would have retired. As it was, Howe, at Boston, had little idea that all was not going on well on the Sorel, till the Americans furnished him with a newspaper account of our victories. On the 14th November, Washington published the grateful intelligence to the army beleaguering Howe: and the countersign for the day was " Montgomery"; the parole, " St. Johns." A thousand copies of the account of the capture were printed by congress for distribution in England.

CHAPTER VI.

André's Captivity. — Detained in Pennsylvania. — Treatment of Prisoners. — André's Relations with the Americans. — His Letters to Mr. Cope. — Exchange and Promotion. — Sir Charles Grey. — Sir Henry Clinton and the Operations on the Hudson.

THE stipulation that their effects should not be withheld from the garrison of St. Johns does not seem to have been observed. It but was too customary on both sides, at this time, to disregard the rights of the vanquished and defenceless. The British, being better disciplined, did their spiriting rather more gently than our troops. The American baggage, protected by the capitulation of Fort Washington in November, 1776, was only partially plundered; while about the same period Washington, by flogging and cashiering, was striving to make the Nyms and Bardolphs of our ranks refrain from stealing large mirrors, women's raiment, and the like, from private houses, to prevent their falling into the enemy's hands. It was with difficulty that André got away with the baggage of the 7th from Montreal, whither our army had marched. On the 13th November, 1775, Montgomery writes to Schuyler : —

"I wish some method could be fallen upon of engaging *gentlemen* to serve; a point of honour and more knowledge of the world, to be found in that class of men, would greatly reform discipline, and render the troops much more tractable. The officers of the 1st regiment of Yorkers, and Artillery Company, were very near a mutiny the other day, because I would not stop the clothing of the garrison of St. Johns. I would not have sullied my own reputation, nor disgraced the Continental arms, by such a breach of capitulation, for the universe; there was no driving it into their noddles, that the clothing was really the property of the soldier, that he had paid for it, and that every regiment, in this country especially, saved a year's clothing, to have decent clothes to wear on particular occasions."

But there were, first or last, other and less scrupulous hands to be met; which, as they did not hesitate to spoil the goods of congress, were probably not idle among those of a captive enemy, protected only by a guard of honor. "I have been taken prisoner by the Americans," wrote André to a friend at home, "and stript of every thing, except the picture of Honora, which I concealed in my mouth. Preserving that, I yet think myself fortunate." * At Ticonderoga the officers of the 7th and 26th applied to the Americans for blankets and shoes for their men, who were almost barefooted; but there were none to spare. Schuyler, however, who had received the hospitalities of the 26th when travelling in Ireland, advanced means to the officers of both regiments to supply these necessities. They were then sent, under a guard of a hundred men, for Connecticut; where the Committee of Safety had provided for their distribution, and for the assignment of the privates as laborers. This was a practice with our government through the contest, as it was afterwards of Napoleon's; but it was warmly resented by the English. Gage, especially, complained that the pris-

---

* *Extract from Miss Seward's Will:* — "The mezzotinto engraving from a picture of Romney, which is thus inscribed on a tablet at top, *Such was Honora Sneyd*, I bequeath to her brother Edward Sneyd, Esq., if he survives me; if not, I bequeath it to his amiable daughter, Miss Emma Sneyd, entreating her to value and preserve it as the perfect though accidental resemblance of her aunt, and my ever dear friend, *when she was surrounded by all her virgin glories — beauty and grace, sensibility and goodness, superior intelligence, and unswerving truth.* To my before-mentioned friend, Mrs. Mary Powys, in consideration of the true and unextinguishable love which she bore to the original, I bequeath the miniature picture of the said Honora Sneyd, drawn at Buxton in the year 1776, by her gallant, faithful and unfortunate lover, Major André, in his 18th year. That was his first attempt to delineate the human face, consequently it is an unfavorable and most imperfect resemblance of a most distinguished beauty."

oners of war should be made to work "like negro slaves to gain their daily subsistence, or reduced to the wretched alternative, to perish by famine or take up arms against their king and country." Up to Montgomery's arrival at the Sorel, indeed, there were no prisoners of war to speak of subject to the control of Congress; and no systematic preparations for their disposition had been made. It was now, however, ordered that the officers taken at St. Johns should continue their course to Connecticut, while the privates should be brought to Pennsylvania, where there were greater conveniences for subsisting so many men. But it was to guard against such a separation that the officers had obtained Schuyler's promise that they should not be parted from their soldiers. On the one hand, it was important that they should see that their followers were not abused; on the other, that attempts to seduce them into the American service should be thwarted. Accordingly, when the instructions of Congress reached the officer who was leading the prisoners to Connecticut by way of the Hudson River, he could only obey them so far as to bring on with him to Pennsylvania all of the 7th that were taken at St. Johns, officers as well as privates. As he came down the Hudson, however, André was encountered by Knox, — afterwards one of the Board that pronounced on his fate, and now on his road to the north to select cannon for the siege of Boston, from the spoils on Champlain. Chance compelled the two young men to pass the night in the same cottage, and even in the same bed. There were many points of resemblance between them. Their ages were alike; they had each renounced the pursuits of trade for the profession of arms; each had made a study of his new occupation; and neither was devoid of literary tastes and habits. Much of the night was consumed in pleasing conversation on topics that were rarely, perhaps, broached in such circumstances; and the intelligence and refinement displayed by André in the discussion of subjects that were equally interesting to Knox, left an impression on the mind of the latter that was never obliterated. The respective condition of the bedfellows was not mutually communicated till the ensuing morning as they were about to part; and when Knox a few years later was called on to join in the condemnation to death of the companion whose society was so pleasant to him on this occasion, the memory of their intercourse gave additional bitterness to his painful duty. Joshua Smith also asserts that he dined at this time with André, at the house of Colonel Hay of Haverstraw; though the features of the young officer were faded from his remembrance when he was called to guide him from our lines in 1780.

Congress having ordered that its prisoners of war should be kept in the interior of Pennsylvania, André and his companions were now carried to Lancaster. The officers were paroled to keep within six miles of their appointed residence, to approach no seaport, and to hold no correspondence on American affairs. The sale of bills on England, otherwise unlawful, was legalized to them; and the men were ordered to be fed as the continental privates, but to be paid and clad by their own government. The new and unsettled state of affairs made the condition of prisoners doubly painful. They had no money, and could not get any. They were compelled to lodge at taverns, for no private house would receive them; and their expenses could not be met by a proffered loan of two paper dollars a week from Congress. It was decided to separate them from their men, and they in vain protested against this measure. Their complaint to Congress was that, while the officer was thus parted from his soldiers, they were enlisted by the Americans; and again, that the privates at Lancaster had received neither their clothes nor their pay, and that it was unjust in the extreme to thus deprive their leaders of the means of satisfying them. The local Committee of Safety, at the head of which was Edward Shippen (a lady of whose family was at a later day the friend of André and the wife of Arnold), could not maintain order among the men but by a military guard. In January, 1776, they represent this to Congress. They also strongly paint the distress of their prisoners. The women and children are in a state of starvation. The men are half frozen by want of sufficient covering " against the rigor and inclemency of the season." This committee seems to have given what assistance it could to the captives, and, at the same time, to have declined separating officers and men. Accordingly, Congress handed over the disposition of the business to the State Committee, with instructions to imprison such officers as would not give a parole; and in March, 1776, orders for their removal from their men at Lancaster and Reading were issued. Their money had not yet arrived, and they were compelled to leave their lodging-bills unsettled. The Lancaster Committee reported this to Congress, saying that the tavern-keepers, with whom the continental authorities had lodged the officers, had finally refused to accommodate them longer, and that some of the inhabitants, out of courtesy, had therefore been induced to afford them rooms, with candles, fuel, and breakfasts; their own servants were in attendance, and a mess-dinner for them all was established. Among the bills thus rendered, we find Michael Bartgis's claim for £7 6s., for a chamber, fire, and lights, supplied to Lieutenants Despard and André of the 7th.

There is no great cause to suppose that these prisoners were either well treated or patient. An American officer of reputation, himself just released from long confinement at New York, remarks upon the ungenerous slights put upon the captives at Reading, by that class of whigs whose valor was chiefly displayed in insulting those whom better men had made defenceless; and if their affronts were resented, the officer stood a good chance of being soundly cudgelled, and clapped into gaol. More than one who had surrendered to Montgomery attempted to abscond.*

* After alleging instances of our ill-treatment of prisoners, an English account continues: " When the garrison at St. Johns capitulated, because

The prisoners alleged, and with truth perhaps, that the fear of persecution deterred many of the inhabitants from showing them kindness. In André's case this apprehension certainly did not prevail. From some of the people of Lancaster he received kind words and kind deeds; and relations of friendship were established that still exist in the memory of their descendants. The local authorities were less pleased with the behavior of the 26th than with that of the 7th; and there could have been no one in either regiment better qualified than himself to win the favor of his new neighbors. His disposition may be described, if it cannot be accurately delineated. In him were most judiciously combined the love of action and the love of pleasure: the moving powers of every spirit that rises from the common level, and which, when properly directed and controlled, are well represented as the parents respectively of the useful and the agreeable in man. "The character that unites and harmonizes both," says Gibbon, "would seem to constitute the most perfect idea of human nature." When business was concerned, André was zealous, active, and sagacious: and his leisure hours were given to elegant and refining relaxations. A taste for painting, poetry, music, and dramatic representations, comprehends as well a knowledge of the outward face of nature as of the thoughts and passions that stir mankind; and correctness of eye, ear, and hand; of judgment, fancy, and observation; is fostered and strengthened by the arts upon which

they had no provisions and no place to retire to, the rebels were so much afraid of them, even when unarmed, that Schuyler addressed the officers, telling them he was in their power, and depended on their honour. It would have been no wonder if such people had been well treated; yet so scandalously ill were they afterwards used, that some of the young officers resolved rather to run the hazard of perishing in the woods in attempting to escape to Canada, than continue to submit to it."—*Royal Penn. Gaz.* May 15, 1778. This story has probably thus much truth in it. Schuyler may have so addressed 600 men whom he sent off under a guard of 100. That they were ill-treated afterwards was no fault of his, though he promised to hang an absconding prisoner if he could catch him. And after capturing them while yet fully armed, the Americans would hardly have feared unarmed men.

it feeds. In his present strait, not Goldsmith's flute was more useful to its master beside "the murmuring Loire" than the brush and pencil to André's familiar hand. Whether as a mere amusement, or as a means of ingratiating himself with the people of Lancaster, he set about teaching some of their children to draw. The late Dr. Benjamin Smith Barton, of scientific reputation, was thus initiated into the art of sketching, and became no mean draughtsman. His family still preserves specimens of André's skill, some of which are of singular merit. His style was easy and free, and his favorite designs studies of the human figure, or from the antique. In certain circles he thus became a welcome guest, and was wont to share in their parties of pleasure. Among the inhabitants who were distinguished by their courtesy to the captives was Mr. Caleb Cope, a Quaker gentleman of loyal proclivities. His son had a strong natural taste for painting, and soon became a favorite pupil of André's: so much so, that he constantly pressed the father to place the lad in his charge and suffer him to be brought up to that art. On one occasion he urged that he was anxious to go back to England, but could not do so without a reasonable excuse for quitting the army; that he had now an offer to purchase his commission; and that with this boy to look after, a fair pretext for returning home would be afforded. But the father was inflexible, and in March, 1776, the master and pupil were separated, and the former sent to Carlisle. A correspondence was however kept up between Mr. Cope and himself.

ANDRÉ TO CALEB COPE.

SIR:— You wou'd have heard from me ere this Time had I not wish'd to be able to give you some encouragement to send my young Friend John to Carlisle. My desire was to find a Lodging where I cou'd have him with me, and some quiet honest family of Friends or others where he might have boarded, as it wou'd not have been so proper for him to live with a Mess of officers. I have been able to find neither and am myself still in a Tavern. The people here are no more willing to harbour us, than those of Lancaster were at our first coming there. If, however, you can resolve to let him come here, I believe Mr. Despard and I can make him up a bed in a Lodging we have in view, where there will be room enough. He will be the greatest part of the day with us, employ'd in the few things I am able to instruct him in. In the meanwhile I may get better acquainted with the Town, and provide for his board. With regard to Expence this is to be attended with none to you. A little assiduity and friendship is all I ask in my young friend in return for my good will to be of service to him in a way of improving the Talents Nature hath given him. I shall give all my attention to his morals, and, as I believe him well dispos'd, I trust he will acquire no bad habits here. Mr. Despard joins with me in compliments to yourself, Mrs. Cope, and Family. I am, Sir, your most humble servant, JOHN ANDRÉ.

Carlisle, April the 3d, 1776.

André and Despard obtained lodgings with a Mrs. Ramsey, in the stone house that now stands at the corner of Locust Alley and South Hanover Street, in Carlisle; and for them and eight other officers a mess was established. Each had his servant from the regiment, dressed in the hunting-shirts and trousers that then were so commonly worn, particularly by our troops. The ardent whigs of the place feared lest their discourse should corrupt the weak-minded within their allotted bounds and were anxious to imprison them, but could find no pretext. At last André and his comrade were detected in conversation with two tories. The latter were sent to gaol; and letters in the French language being found on their persons, André and Despard were forbidden for the future to leave the town. As no one could be found competent to translate the letters, their contents were never known. The two officers had provided themselves with very handsome fowling-pieces and a brace of beautiful pointer dogs. The guns they forthwith broke to pieces, says tradition, affirming "that no —— rebel should ever burn powder in them,"— an exclamation that savors of Despard's style.* On another occasion a person named Thompson, who had once been an apprentice to Mr. Ramsey, and was now a militia captain, marched his company from the northern part of the county to Carlisle, and drawing it up by night before the house, swore loudly that André and Despard should forthwith be put to death. The entreaties of Mrs. Ramsey at length prevailed on this hero to depart, shouting to her lodgers as he went that they were to thank his old mistress for their lives. On the 5th of August, the rumor spread through Lancaster that Captain Clark's company, of Cumberland County, on its way through Carlisle to that town, had wantonly attacked the royal officers there, and, firing through the windows, had wounded André. As Clark's arrival was looked for that night, the Lancaster Committee appear to have feared a massacre would ensue of the privates in their gaol, similar to that perpetrated in the same place, and by people from the same region, a number of years previously, upon the Christian Indians who had fled from the wrath of the Paxton Boys. They ordered the gaol to be well supplied with water before sunset, and provided for calling out the local militia, if needs were; and the prisoners were assured that they should be protected, if possible. These, however, were not inclined to imitate their predecessors and die singing hymns and praying. They armed themselves with stout cord-sticks, and

* This was an Irish officer, who, in 1781, very bravely supported Nelson in Nicaragua, and was executed for treason in 1803. He was one of the very few English officers that brought back from America democratical ideas. A democratical soldier was indeed an anomaly in the service of that day. "Three distinguished heroes of this class," wrote Scott to his son, "have arisen in my time: Lord Edward Fitzgerald, Colonel Despard, and Captain Thistlewood; and, with the contempt and abhorrence of all men, they died the death of infamy and guilt." Even in America, Mr. Cope had warned Despard that his recklessness and disregard would certainly bring him to some bad end.

resolved to die hard. On Clark's approach, the alarm vanished: he denied the story altogether, and put its propagator in the guard-house. The man then had only to say that, at Carlisle, he had seen two persons firing their pieces down the street, and that he had heard, from the house where the officers' servants dwelt, that André was wounded. There was probably no truth in this last assertion; but there was much ill-will against the officers from the following cause:— Early in 1776, Foster, with some English and a number of savages, had encountered a body of Americans at the Cedars, on Lake Champlain, who surrendered to the number of 500. Foster alleged that his Indians, infuriated at the loss of their sachem, were for murdering the prisoners, and were only content to spare them on condition of marking each man's ear with a knife, and threatening to slay outright all who should ever return with this distinction. He then paroled them, to go home and be exchanged for a like number of the English taken at St. Johns. The American government would not fulfil this convention; and the clipped men, arriving at their own abode, were often full of hatred to those for whom they were to have been exchanged. This event occasioned great embarrassments in effecting exchanges during the war; for the enemy always insisted on the men of the Cedars being accounted for. But while some of the officers surrendered their paroles and were sent to prison,— "a dreadful place, that will be prejudicial to their health," says the whig committee,—and others, disregarding it, fled through the wilderness to their friends, André is described as quietly confining himself to his chamber and passing his days in reading, with his feet resting on the wainscot of the window and his dogs lying by his side. This was the wisest course; for any infringement of the strict letter of their parole was now visited on the officers with imprisonment; and new restrictions were imposed. They were sent to gaol if they went out except in uniform; they were not permitted to leave their chambers after nightfall; some were deprived, as they complained to congress, of their servants; others subjected to threats and insults. These matters are set down in the records of the times. Disagreeable as they are to repeat, there can be no reason for their omission here, save one: if there were any cause to question their truth, they would gladly be stricken out.

— Pudet hæc opprobria nobis
Et dici potuisse, et non potuisse refelli.

ANDRÉ TO CALEB COPE.

DEAR SIR: — I am much oblig'd to you for your kind Letter and to your son for his drawings. He is greatly improv'd since I left Lancaster, and I do not doubt but if he continues his application he will make a very great progress. I cannot regret that you did not send your son hither: We have been submitted to alarms and jealousys which wou'd have render'd his stay here very disagreeable to him and I wou'd not willingly see any person suffer on our account; with regard to your apprehensions in consequence of the escape of the Lebanon gentlemen, they were groundless, as we have been on parole ever since our arrival at this place which I can assure you they were not. I shou'd more than once have written to you had opportunitys presented themselves, but the post and we seem to have fallen out, for we can never by that channel either receive or forward a line on the most indifferent subjects. Mr. Despard is very well and desires to be remembered to yourself and family. I beg you wou'd give my most friendly compliments to your Family and particularly to your son my disciple, to whom I hope the future posture of affairs will give me an opportunity of pointing out the way to proficiency in his favourite study, which may tend so much to his pleasure and advantage. Let him go on copying whatever good models he can meet with and never suffer himself to neglect the proportion and never to think of finishing his work, or imitating the fine flowing lines of his copy, till every limb, feature, house, tree, or whatever he is drawing, is in its proper place. With a little practise, this will be so natural to him, that his Eye will at first sight guide his pencil in every part of the work. I wish I may soon see you in our way to join our own friends with which I hope by Exchange we may be at length reunited. I am, Dear Sir, &c.

Carlisle the 3rd Septr. 1776.

THE SAME TO THE SAME.

Your Letter by Mr. Barrington is just come to hand. I am sorry you shou'd imagine my being absent from Lancaster, or our troubles could make me forget my friends. Of the several Letters you mention having written to me only one of late has reach'd Carlisle, viz. that by Mr. Slough. To one I received from you a week or two after leaving Lancaster I return'd an Answer. I own the difficulties of our Correspondence has disgusted me from attempting to write. I once more commend myself to your good family and am sincerely Yrs. &c.
J. A.

I hope your son's indisposition will be of no consequence.*

THE SAME TO THE SAME.

Dear Sir : — I have just time to acquaint you that I receiv'd your Letter by Mrs. Calender with my young Friend's drawings, which persuade me he is much improv'd, and that he has not been idle. He must take particular care in forming the features in faces, and in copying hands exactly. He should now and then copy things from the life and then compare the proportions with what prints he may have, or what rules he may have remember'd. With respect to his shading

---

* This letter was probably written early in September. On the 24th August the Council at Philadelphia ordered that Mr. Barrington should be sent on parole from Lancaster gaol to Cumberland County.

with Indian Ink, the anatomical figure is tolerably well done, but he wou'd find his work smoother and softer, were he to lay the shades on more gradually, not blackening the darkest at once, but by washing them over repeatedly, and never until the paper is quite dry. The figure is very well drawn.

Captn. Campbell who is the bearer of this letter will probably when at Lancaster be able to judge what likelyhood there is of an Exchange of Prisoners which we are told is to take place immediately. If this shou'd be without foundation, I shou'd be very glad to see your son here. Of this you may speak with Captn. Campbell, and if you shou'd determine upon it, let me know it a few days before hand when I shall take care to settle matters for his reception. I am, &c.

Carlisle the 11*th Oct.* 1776.

My best compliments to your family and particularly to John. Mr. Despard begs to be remember'd to you.

THE SAME TO THE SAME.

DEAR SIR:—I cannot miss the opportunity I have of writing to you by Mr. Slough to take leave of yourself and Family and transmit to you my sincere wishes for your welfare. We are on our road (as we believe, to be exchang'd) and however happy this prospect may make me, It doth not render me less warm in the fate of those persons in this Country for whom I had conceiv'd a regard. I trust on your side you will do me the Justice to remember me with some good will, and that you will be persuaded I shall be happy if an Occasion shall offer of my giving your son some farther hints in the Art for which he has so happy a turn. Desire him if you please to commit my name and my friendship to his Memory, and assure him, from me, that if he only brings diligence to her assistance, Nature has open'd him a path to fortune and reputation, and that he may hope in a few years to enjoy the fruits of his labour. Perhaps the face of affairs may so far change that he may once more be within

my reach, when it will be a very great pleasure to me to give him what assistance I can. My best compliments as well as Mr. Despard's to Mrs. Cope and the rest of your family. I am truly, &c.
Reading the 2nd Decr. 1776.*

Towards the close of this year most of the prisoners made by either side in Canada were exchanged, and André thus obtained his freedom by their means, through whom he had lost it. The skeleton of the 7th was transferred from that province to New York; recruits and new clothing were sent out from England; and in the end of December the regiment, including the men lately discharged from Pennsylvania, marched into town with tolerably full ranks. André did not, however, long remain in it: on the 18th January, 1777, he received a captaincy in the 26th, which had been so augmented that each company consisted of 64 men, exclusive of commissioned officers.

Sir William Howe, who now commanded in chief, had appeared on Long Island (where, indeed, it was supposed Amherst had advised his wintering in 1775–6, and thence commanding the neighboring colonies) in the preceding summer, and had given Washington's army a severe defeat.† The skill with which our general availed himself of his adversary's carelessness, however, wrested the fruits of victory from the English; and 9000 men were safely borne away, whose retreat might have been prevented by the least exercise of

---

* These letters were communicated to me by Caleb Cope, Esq., of Philadelphia, grandson of the gentleman to whom they were addressed. The memory of their writer was tenderly cherished by the young man they so constantly allude to, who in after-years could never refer to André's story without deep emotion. The correspondence did not cease here; letters came to Mr. Cope up to the time when André was about to proceed to meet Arnold at West Point; but unfortunately they appear to have been lost or destroyed.

† " We have had what some call a battle, but if it deserves that name, it was the pleasantest I ever heard of, as we had not received more than a dozen shot from the enemy, when they ran away with the utmost precipitation." — *Lushington's Harris;* i: 74.

VICTORIES OF TRENTON AND PRINCETON.

forethought. New York was occupied; Fort Washington taken with its 2000 Americans; and Washington compelled to retreat through Jersey into Pennsylvania, with Cornwallis thundering at his heels and pressing the pursuit with hot urgency. Had Howe (as he might easily have done) passed a force from Staten Island to Brunswick, where much of our ammunition, light artillery, &c., had been sent on in advance, it could have destroyed them all, and in every human probability have intercepted the retreat and crushed our army between itself and Cornwallis. This was the opinion, not only among our men, but in the royal lines; and Clinton had vainly urged that the Rhode Island expedition should have been "landed at Amboy, to have coöperated with Lord Cornwallis, or embarked on board Lord Howe's fleet, landed in Delaware, and taken possession of Philadelphia." *

Our affairs now began to look very desperate. We had been driven out of Canada. Washington, though invested by Congress with a dictatorship, saw his forces fluctuating between 2000 to 3000 men, disorganized, and one might have feared, almost ripe for dissolution. Numbers in the seat of war were daily resuming fealty to the crown, and the contagion spread even into the higher ranks of the army.† Congress had adjourned to Baltimore. The paper-money had depreciated. Lee, on whom many relied as on a second Charles of Sweden, was led away captive by Harcourt's dragoons while yet the pen was wet which had testified to Gates his contempt for his chieftain: — "entre nous, a certain great man is most damnably deficient." At this crisis, his strength swollen by militia to 5000 men, Washington aimed a deadly blow at the chain of posts unwisely established and carelessly maintained across Jersey. Rahl was cut to pieces; Cornwallis out-generalled; and the victories of Trenton and Princeton, which in a European campaign might scarce figure as more than brilliant affairs, were as the

* Paine's American Crisis, No. I. — Sir H. Clinton's MS.
† Warren; i. 353.

breath of life to the fainting cause of American Independence.

Howe might vainly console himself with the reflection that the neglect of his subordinates had invited surprise, and that an exasperated population withheld intelligence from their Hessian plunderers. These contingencies he should have provided against. The fault was his own, and it was Washington's care to gloriously profit by it.*

On his arrival at New York, André had prepared and presented to Howe a memoir upon the existing war. In it he doubtless set forth the conclusions taught him by a year's active service in Canada, with the astute and energetic Carleton; by his temporary intercourse as a prisoner with the generous Schuyler and Montgomery, and their followers in the north; by his long confinement among the rural population of Pennsylvania; and by the impressions he had received, and the comparisons he was able to make of the relative positions of affairs in 1774, when Congress first met, and in 1777, when

---

* "There were who thought (and who were not silent) that a chain across Jersey might be dangerous. General Howe wrote to General Clinton thus, a few days before the misfortune, — 'I have been prevailed upon to run a chain across Jersey; the links are rather too far asunder.' . . . . General Grant [was] principally to blame; he should have visited his posts, given his orders, and seen they had been obeyed. . . . I am clear it would have been better if Sir W. Howe had not taken a chain across Jersey; but General Grant is answerable for everything else. . . . . The two very judicious and officerlike movements of Lord Cornwallis against Tippoo, in 1791 and 1792, proves what he himself thinks of his conduct in 1776. He had driven Washington over the Assumption, and the Delaware was impassable; the Assumption no where but at its bridge, that at Trenton. His Lordship held that at Allen's town; he held the string too. His Lordship, thinking that Washington would wait for him till the next day, deceived by his fires, &c. into this belief, neglects to patrole to Allen's town — over which Washington's whole army, and the last hope of America, escaped. I am sure no Hessian Corporal would have been so imposed upon. . . . 'Tis a wonder Washington did not march to Brunswick. . . . . Unless we could refrain from plundering, we had no business to take up winter-quarters in a district we wished to preserve loyal. The Hessians introduced it. Truth obliges me to assert, and I have proofs in the addresses and the letter, that Lord Percy and I effectually stopped it in Rhode Island. I could produce a very curious proof." — *Clinton's MSS.*

he rejoined the army. Since he came to America he had kept up a journal in which both pen and pencil were tasked to record his adventures and wanderings among Americans, Canadians, and savages. Everything of interest that he saw — bird, beast, or flower — was preserved by his brush in its native hue, and the volume exhibited not only views and plans of the regions he had traversed, but of the manners and apparel of their inhabitants. Even through captivity, he had saved this precious memorial from the hands of his captors; and it may well be believed to have been of material service to him now. His memoir was well received; — Sir William was delighted with its ability and intelligence. He at once took the writer into favor; and it was perhaps in consequence that, on the 18th of January, 1777, he got his company in the 26th. But a staff appointment was his legitimate sphere, and there was for the time none such vacant. He therefore remained on line duty. His regiment was fortunately not one of those that Tryon led in April, 1777, to Danbury; otherwise he might have met Benedict Arnold face to face, and shared in the questionable glories of what Clinton honestly confesses to have been "a second Lexington."* In the beginning of the summer he was named aide-de-camp to Major-General Grey.

Charles Grey was the fourth son of Sir Henry Grey of Howick, to whom he eventually succeeded — his next brother being killed in a duel by Lord Pomfret. He came of a knightly Northumbrian family, and of an ancient line. "The Hows of Grai," says Sir Philip Sidney, "is well known inferior to no Hows in England, in greater Continuance of Honour, and for number of great Howses sprung from it to be matched by none, but by the noble Hows of Nevel." At nineteen he was aide to Prince Ferdinand, and wounded at Minden. At the peace of 1763, when he retired on half-pay, he was colonel and aide to the king. In our war, he had the local rank of Major-General, and was distinguished for

* Clinton MS.

his dashing enterprise; and afterwards served with such credit in other quarters, that he was, in 1801, raised to the peerage as Baron Grey de Howick, and subsequently advanced to a viscountcy. So great was the opinion of his merit that, when the mutiny of the Nore threw all England into fear and confusion, his political opponent, Sheridan, advised Dundas "to cut the buoys on the river, send Sir Charles Grey down to the coast, and set a price on Parker's head." By these means only, he said, could the country be saved; and he threatened to impeach ministers that very night, if they were not resorted to. Grey brought home with him a high estimate of Washington, though he thought him constitutionally nervous.*

Personal friendship had now led Sir Charles to Howe's camp. The other generals were all provided with aides. He brought none with him when he arrived at New York on the 3d of June, and willingly listened to his general's recommendation of "a young man of great abilities, whom for some time he had wished to provide for." André was appointed his aide-de-camp, and thenceforth could have been but little with his regiment, though his rank in it was still retained. He doubtless accompanied Grey in the movement

* General Grey was father of the celebrated Reform Peer, whose name was once in every mouth, and whom Cobbett so injured by the publication of the *Grey List*, which showed that, when prime minister, he had saddled his kindred on the nation, to the rate of £170,000 per annum. It was also said that, so far from imitating "the fair platonist," Lady Jane, his way of life might have been classed by her tutor, old Roger Ascham, with that which the young nobility of the day brought home from Venice. An anecdote of Gen. Grey, whether true or false, was told among the tories in the war. An officer going home with despatches was thus instructed by him: "You will first go to Lord G. Germain; he will ask you such and such questions; you will answer them *so and so*. You will then be sent to Lord North, who will ask you these questions; you will thus answer them. You will then be sent to the King, who will also ask you, &c.; you are also to give him these answers. You will then be examined by the Queen. She is a sensible woman. You must answer with caution; but of all things be careful that you say nothing that will condemn the conduct of Gen. Howe."
—*Davis's Burr*; ii. 32.

of force that Howe made into Jersey on the 14th of June, but the column to which he was attached did not come into action. This was at a juncture when our army, inferior in strength, had nothing to hope from being forced into a general engagement; which, for that very reason, was desired by the enemy. We were encamped in a very defensible, but by no means impregnable ground.* It was the British policy to seduce us from these lines; and by a simulated retreat, they partially succeeded. "This feint of Sir William Howe," confesses Clinton, "was well imagined and well executed, but Washington began to grow wary." The Americans fell back with slight damage to their posts in the hills, securing the passes which Cornwallis had sought to occupy; and there was nothing left for the foe but to return to the place whence he came, to boldly essay the hostile camp, or to leave our people in their security, and, by intercepting their supplies, or even crossing the Delaware, finally force Washington to march out. This last seemed to many of the English the most feasible manœuvre. "I had planned this very move in 1779," wrote Clinton, some years later, "under promise of early reinforcements, and had taken every previous step to it; but reinforcements not arriving till September, I was obliged to relinquish it." † On this occasion, however, Howe thought it wisest to go quietly back towards New York; whence he soon sailed with the bulk of the troops. Clinton was left to hold the city with what remained; "making in all 7000; great proportion of which were raw provincials." ‡

From Sir Henry's own manuscript notes, it may be as well to insert here some further narrative of the doings of the royal arms on the Hudson. It will be recollected that, while he was "forbid to do anything offensive that could endanger

---

* "In this position Washington had the Rariton in front so as [to be] strongly posted, but not entirely secure: for his communication might have drawn him from it." — *Clinton MS.*

† Clinton MS. ‡ Ibid.

New York," it was impossible for Clinton to remain indifferent to the fate of Burgoyne. In his own words: —

"When Sir H. Clinton had received a reinforcement of 1700 recruits from Europe, and had determined on a move up the Hudson, he wrote to Sir W. Howe his intention and his motives for doing it; though he considered an attempt on the forts as rather desperate, he thought the times required such exertions. He feared he should not succeed, but flattered himself he had nothing to apprehend but failure without any fatal consequences to New York. Sir W. Howe in answer told him that if his object was not of the greatest consequence, and almost certain of success, and in a short time, he was ordered to return, and send to Sir W. Howe the troops he had moved with, as Washington reinforced by Putnam had been enabled to attack him on the 9th, and that if he was not joined by the troops I had moved with, or till he was, he could not open the Delaware. I mention this fact and Sir W. Howe's reasons for withdrawing the force I had moved with: had I received this letter of Sir W. Howe's before I had moved, it must have stopt me; but receiving it afterwards, by a miracle succeeded in taking the forts. I should have felt myself satisfied in proceeding had I any hopes of success. I had dispatched G. Vaughan with 1700 men to feel for Burgoyne; coöperate with him; nay, join him if necessary. Vaughan had advanced near 100 miles and had 40 more to go to Albany, and 60 more to join Burgoyne. He wrote me word the 19th he could hear nothing certain of Burgoyne, but had apprehensions. Alas! Burgoyne had surrendered the 17th. Had I moved 6 days sooner I should have found McDougal there, and consequently must have failed; besides I could not risk a move of that sort unless Burgoyne had expressed a wish that I should; and I did not receive his answer accepting my offer till the 29th. Had I made the attempt on the east side, and even beaten Putnam, I had still the Hudson to pass, and I had no boats, nor no vessel to protect my landing: thus, therefore, I must have failed. Had I delayed my attack after I had passed the Thunderberg 6 hours, Putnam would have passed that river and gained the forts, for though Sir James Wallace prevented his doing it from Peekskiln, he might have done so by a detour, and I must have been foiled. I tried the Impossible: a tolerable good arrangement, good luck, and great exertion of Officers and Men succeeded. From the information I received just as I was landing at Howe's point, and which I dare not communicate to anybody, I had little hopes of doing more than covering Burgoyne's retreat to Ticonderoga, which I had no doubt of his attempting the 12th; for as to his supposing I could take the forts and penetrate to Albany, and keep up the communication afterwards, he could not expect it." *

This interesting statement refers to Clinton's movement against the American works at Verplanck's and Stony Points — one of the most creditable performances of the war. These works commanded the navigation of the Hudson and impeded the transmission of aid to Burgoyne. "Lord Rawdon, then aide-de-camp to Sir H. Clinton, had been sent to reconnoitre Verplanck's Point; but he could not get near enough to ascertain the practicability of a landing." † Despite this, the English set forth by water with 3000 men, and easily made good their landing at Verplanck's, on the eastern side of the river. Alarmed lest their plan should be to push on directly to Burgoyne, Putnam hurried to secure the passes above, while Clinton adroitly circumvented him by throwing 2100 of his little army to the western bank, and hastening to attack our forts Montgomery and Clinton. A dangerous and difficult mountain — the Donderberg — had to be surmounted ere his troops could come to the assault; and, destitute of artillery, there was nothing left for them but to storm. It was late in the day when they drew near, "by a detour of seven miles, having also a long defile to pass under a steep cliff, at the end of which was Fort Montgomery, con-

* Clinton MS. † Ibid.

sisting of eight redoubts joined by an intrenchment." That post was inferior in strength to Fort Clinton, from which it was separated by a passable stream; and both were assailed as the day was closing. "Had not both these forts been attacked at the same instant, neither would have been carried without great loss," observes Sir Henry, who himself directed the more dangerous onset against Fort Clinton. "This attack was delayed till that of the left was judged to have become serious, and till it was dark, that the troops might be less exposed in moving up to it." The enterprise was successful. The forts were carried with a rush; and an immense quantity of military stores were captured or destroyed. Nevertheless there was a prodigious risk in the whole affair; and the English leader candidly owns how much his safety was due to the enterprise of "Sir James Wallace, who, by stopping the rebel boats in Peekskiln, prevented Putnam from passing to the forts."*

But however detrimental these successes were to our cause, they were more than atoned for by the fall of Burgoyne. That Clinton's object was the relief of that general is pretty certain; and to that extent his expedition was a failure.

"Sir H. Clinton, thinking G. Burgoyne might want some coöperation (though he had not called for it in any of his letters), offered in his of the 12th September to make an attempt on the forts as soon as the expected reinforcements should arrive from Europe. Gen. Burgoyne fought the battle of Saratoga on the 19th, and on the 21st tells Gen. Clinton that an attempt or even a menace of an attempt would be of *use*. Sir H. Clinton received this letter the 29th of September, and moved the 2nd of October. On the 27th Sept., G. Gates [Burgoyne?] had received information that his gallies, gunboats, &c., on Lake George had been surprised and destroyed by Gen. Lincoln, and he had consequently lost his communication with Canada. 'Tis pity he had not

* Clinton MS.

instantly fallen back to recover them; but thinking, 'tis presumed, he was under orders to Albany, he requests to know of me whether I can meet him there or supply him afterwards, and says he will stay to the 12th October for my answer." *

But the results of the second Saratoga battle, on the 7th October, rather modified the British plans.

"On the very day of this action, by giving the enemy jealousy for the East side, Sir H. Clinton landed on the West, gained the mountain of Thunderberg, and by a tolerably well combined move, and the wonderful exertion of the troops under his command, took all the forts by assault." †

This accomplished, the partial attempt to succor Burgoyne and to bring him supplies was proceeded in, and Vaughan was embarked for that purpose — "after the chain was broken, the chevaux-de-frieze removed, and provision for 5000 men for 6 months prepared. . . . . General Vaughan had orders to proceed immediately as high as his pilots could carry him to feel for Burgoyne, coöperate with him, and join him if required."

But on the 13th October, Burgoyne was compelled to open negotiations for surrender; and neither Clinton nor Vaughan accomplished more for his relief than the destruction at Esopus. Disappointed in their chief hope, the British presently returned to New York: — that such was mainly the motive of the expedition sufficiently appears by the important private memorandums of Sir Henry himself, as above printed.

* Clinton MS. † Ibid.

CHAPTER VII.

The British embark for Philadelphia. — Brandywine, the Paoli, and Germantown. — André's Humanity. — Occupation and Fortification of Philadelphia. — Character of the City in 1777.

PRECIOUS time was spent in fruitless attempts to bring Washington to battle on equal ground in Jersey, ere Howe resolved to circumvent our army by means of the fleet, and to approach Philadelphia from another quarter. This scheme, disapproved by some of his immediate subordinates, was carefully concealed from the rest of the troops, who, on the 23d of June, 1777, were embarked at Amboy, in perfect ignorance of their destination.* The *media scientia* of the schoolmen — the calculation of possible consequences of events that did not happen — can alone determine the effect of another plan of the campaign. Had a powerful force marched northwardly to act in connection with Burgoyne, the surrender at Saratoga might have been prevented, the royal army increased in strength, and time still left to operate against Philadelphia ere the season closed. A few ships of war threatening the New England coast or cannonading Boston, might have drawn to another quarter the militia that thronged to the aid of Gates. Nor did all his labor eventually much better Howe's situation. At Brunswick he was but sixty miles from Philadelphia; at Elk, he was sev-

---

* "I owe it to truth to say there was not, I believe, a man in the army, except Lord Cornwallis and General Grant, who did not reprobate the move to the southward, and see the necessity of a coöperation with General Burgoyne. . . . General Clinton told Lord G. Germain, April 27th, — and Sir W. Howe repeatedly, after his return to America — his humble opinion that Philadelphia had better close than open the campaign, as it required an army to defend it." — *Clinton MS.*

enty; and if our army's position was less strong at Brandywine, its spirit was better and its force increased.

When he appeared in the Chesapeake, his brother the Admiral with line and plummet and in seaman's garb leading the boat that guided the fleet's course, it was questioned at Philadelphia whether Sir William aimed at Baltimore, or a yet higher point. All doubts vanished on the 25th of August, when he landed. The debarcation was finished on the 27th; and on the 28th, he marched seven miles and fixed head-quarters at the head of Elk, posting the troops two miles off. On the 3rd of September, he led part of his army to Aickin's tavern; the light infantry and yägers skirmishing with the American advanced parties for a mile and a half, and losing a dozen men in killed and wounded. Knyphausen had been detached across Elk Ferry to Cecil Court-house to collect stores, and now rejoined at Aickin's; and on the 6th, Grant's division also came up. Hence, by easy stages, with Galloway in his coach following in the rear, Howe passed on through a fertile and friendly country; while on Sunday, the 24th of August, our army had marched through Philadelphia to meet him. Cheerful but half naked, their hats adorned with green boughs, and drum and fife sounding merrily, they came down Front and up Chestnut streets, and so over the Schuylkill. On the 11th of September, the citizens hearkened to the roar of the artillery; and gathering by groups, according to their political inclinations, in the squares or public places, speculated in hope or in fear upon the results of the day.

It was an unfortunate day for America, but less so than might have been. With 13000 men, and in the best position the region afforded, Washington waited the attack. He could do no better. By a larger and better force, and by manœuvres as well conceived as executed, he was surprised and driven from the ground. At four A. M., Howe and Cornwallis marched from Kennett's Square with their left column, led by Grey, Mathew, and Agnew, and crossing the Brandywine above and undiscovered, fell on our right flank and rear, while Knyphausen forded the stream in front. This column had advanced seven miles from Kennett's Square, and coming on the field about ten A. M., began a heavy cannonade. When it was seen that Howe had arrived, it passed the ford, storming the breastworks we had thrown up. As Moncrieff rushed on with the leading files, he saw an American howitzer charged with grape, and pointed to sweep away, in a moment more, himself and all about him. The matross stood in the act of applying the burning match ere he followed his retreating comrades. "I will put you to death if you fire!" shouted Moncrieff; and the man, startled from his self-possession, dropped the match and fled. Grey's brigade, consisting of the 15th, 17th, 44th, and two battalions of the 42d, was the reserve of Cornwallis's column, and was not engaged. Its character was so high, that it was preserved intact as a recourse in case Knyphausen failed; in which event Cornwallis might have had his hands full. And but for the false intelligence of Sullivan's videttes, who were drinking at a tavern when they should have been scouring the roads, Washington would probably have turned the tables on the German, by himself crossing the Brandywine and crushing the opposite force before the other column came to its aid. Nightfall found our army, its artillery destroyed, in a retreat that might have easily been made a route. Had the pursuit been pressed it must have perished. The fatigues of the day induced Howe to remain that night on the battle-field. Since daybreak, to four P. M., when the onset began, one part of his men had marched seventeen, the other seven miles. Of the former, Grey's brigade of from 2000 to 3000 choice troops were on the spot, ready to go into action; two battalions of the guards and four of grenadiers had been astray in a wood and little engaged; nor had the 16th dragoons been employed. The greater part of Knyphausen's column had borne no active part, for the retreat began almost as soon as it moved forward. It was very fortunate thus for America, that the darkness, which came on just as the whole British army was brought into possession of our position, persuaded Howe to discontinue the pursuit; for he had at command a force which, if not perfectly fresh, was abundantly so in comparison with the fugitives, many of whom had marched as much through the day as Knyphausen, and all would have had as long a journey as their pursuers ere they should be overtaken. An immediate pursuit would have gone far to demoralize and break up our troops, and prevented many from rejoining their regiments who were with them the next day.*

Knyphausen's command moved on the 12th towards Chester; and on the 16th, the sick and wounded being sent to Wilmington, the army advanced to Goshen, where the yägers and light infantry dispersed some parties of our men. On the 18th, starting before dawn, it struck the Lancaster road, and coming two miles towards Philadelphia, turned into that of Swedes Ford. Here an opportunity rose to give Grey's division that active service it had missed on the 11th. Washington was advised on the 18th that the English thought him crushed, and were leisurely bringing on their main army; having advanced into the country only the picked light troops. On the 19th, Wayne wrote that he was closely watching them, resolved to attack the instant they moved. He had approached within half a mile of their left flank at reveille-beat that morning, but found them perfectly supine. "There never was nor never will be a finer opportunity of giving the enemy a fatal blow, than at present, — for God's sake, push on as fast as possible." During the day he kept on guard; and, persuaded that his position and force were unknown to the enemy, was confident of success in the move-

---

* " They lost an all important night, and this was, perhaps, their greatest fault during a war in which they committed so many errors."—*Laf. Autob.*
" 'Tis pity Sir W. Howe could not have begun his march at nightfall instead of eight o'clock in the morning."—*Clinton MSS.* Napier's words, however, give the best comment: " Had Cæsar halted because his soldiers were fatigued, Pharsalia would have been but a common battle."

ments that were to "complete Mr. Howe's business." He was encamped in the woods near the Paoli Tavern, on the Lancaster road (which André had travelled before) about three miles in the rear of Howe's left. He had 1500 men and four guns; and Smallwood with 1150 Maryland militia, and Gist with 700 men, were to join him the next day to harass Howe as he passed the Schuylkill. Of course, it was important to break up this design; and before one A. M., of the 21st, Grey marched against him, through forests and a narrow defile, with the 42nd and 44th, and the 2d light infantry. The nature of the service was dangerous. Wayne's corps was known through the war for its stubborn and desperate conduct in fight; and his whole own life was characterized by a "constitutional attachment to the arbitrament of the sword." Surprise and speed were necessary to success, for Smallwood lay but a mile off. To insure it, the Englishman enforced a measure that he had learned in Germany, and by which he got in America the sobriquet of *No-flint Grey.* He made his men uncharge their pieces, and knock out the flints. Not a shot could be fired; they were to rely entirely on the bayonet. Wayne himself always upheld his own faith in the marvellous virtues of cold steel; but though he was apprised of Grey's movement, and took, as he thought, every proper precaution, he had little opportunity on this occasion to practise resistance. At four A. M. his pickets were forced, and the light of his fires guided the enemy to his camp. The Americans, unable to form, and struggling irregularly or not at all, were instantly bayonetted. Our accounts put the killed and wounded at 150; the English version says 300 and upwards; two guns and seventy or eighty prisoners were taken, and while Wayne's men were in hasty flight, and Smallwood in march for their relief, the English with but twelve casualties returned in triumph with eight wagon-loads of arms, baggage, and stores. The army then moved towards Valley Forge, and destroyed what supplies were there that they could not remove. Thus we lost 7,000 barrels of flour for one item. Having now cleverly got between Washington and the Schuylkill, Howe passed that stream unopposed below the Forge and descended towards Philadelphia, destroying powder-mills, and taking a few prisoners and cannon on the route. On the 25th, he moved in two columns to Germantown; and on the 26th, says a royal eye-witness, at eleven A. M., Cornwallis, with 3000 men, and accompanied by Harcourt, Erskine, and a cavalcade of distinguished officers, as well as Galloway, Story, the Allens, and other leading tories, entered the town among the loudest acclamations of the loyal population who had "too long suffered the yoke of arbitrary power." Other citizens have described the scenes of that day: the grenadiers, steadfast and composed, splendidly equipped, with their music sounding the long unheard strains of God save the King, as they caught at the children's hands in passing, with friendly greeting; the bearded Hessians, terrible in brass-fronted helmets, keeping step to wild strains that to the popular ear spoke of plunder and pillage in every note; the closed houses; and the throngs of citizens, clad in their best array, that lined the streets which they had patrolled by night since the 23rd, in suspicion that the retiring Americans were disposed to fire the town. A deputation besought Howe not to give it up to plunder. On the 25th, he sent a letter to Thomas Willing, assuring the people that they should not be disturbed if they remained tranquil. Meantime the main army rested at Germantown, while strong detachments moved against the American posts that still commanded the Delaware and prevented the arrival of the fleet.

The loss of Philadelphia was grievous to the Americans, and almost unlooked for;* and Washington determined, by a

* "Sept. 19, 1777. This morning about 1 o'clock an express arrived to Congress giving an account of the British Army having got to the Swedes Ford on the other side of Schuylkill, which so much alarmed the gentlemen of the Congress, the military officers, and other friends to the general cause of American Freedom, that they *decamped* with the utmost precipitation and in the greatest confusion; insomuch that one of the delegates,

surprise and coup-de-main, to give Howe such a blow, ere his transports could come up, as to overturn the plan. Germantown, where he now lay, was a long, narrow village of sombre moss-grown houses, solidly built of a dark stone, and each surrounded with its own enclosure, that extended for two miles along the road leading southwardly to Philadelphia. The British were encamped at right angles across the town; Grey's brigade being on the line that stretched from the left to the Schuylkill. The people of the neighborhood were not open tories, but they were averse to the war; and Howe appears to have had a warning of what was stirring. He afterwards denied that he was surprised; but it is not probable that he anticipated anything like so heavy an attack as he received from our whole army at dawn on the 4th October. Sullivan and Wayne led the advance, and encountered first the post where, with the 40th, was encamped the 2nd light infantry that had given us so much trouble at the Paoli. These stood their ground for nearly an hour, till their ammunition began to fail. Our men now took ample revenge. Driving all before them in their rage, they plied the bayonet furiously; and it was not until many were thus slain, that they listened to their officers and gave quarter. The attack was vigorously pressed, with a promise of being successful; but a dense fog caused everything to fall into confusion. About 120 men of the 40th threw themselves into a large stone house, from which they kept up a heavy fire; the drum beating a parley to summon a surrender was mistaken for a retreat; a panic seized our bewildered troops; and while one band believed itself in the full tide of victory, another would be hastily retreating thinking all was lost. Turning his front to the village, Grey led his brigade to close quarters with our people there, and repulsed them. They gave way about

by name Fulsom, was obliged in a very *Fulsom* manner to ride off without a saddle. Thus we have seen the men, from whom we have received, and from whom we still expected protection, leave us to fall into the hands of (by their accounts) a barbarous, cruel and unrelenting enemy." — *Morton MS.*

the same time in other quarters; and the retreat becoming general, the pursuit was maintained by the enemy's cavalry as far as the Blue Bell Tavern, full eight miles. It cannot be denied that in this action the regulars on both sides behaved with great spirit; and that the American retreat, occurring as it did, was the sudden result of one of those circumstances that no precaution can guard against with new troops. But though the discipline of both armies, according to Grey, was bad, that of ours was the worst. " You have conquered General Howe," said a foreign officer of rank to Washington, " but his troops have beaten yours." On the first and tremendous sound of the firing, Cornwallis's grenadiers took the alarm Starting from Philadelphia at a full trot, they ran the whole way to Germantown, and came breathless to the field just as all was over. The Highlanders, too, came on at speed, keeping pace with the cavalry. In fact, the detonations were so furious and incessant and from so many quarters, and the thickness of the fog so overwhelming, that while the combat lasted, it was impossible to tell in what force or with what success the Americans came on. At 11 A. M., the prodigious clatter of battle suddenly hushed, and the retreat was conducted in comparative stillness.

The casualties on either side were severe. Chief among the enemy was General Agnew, whose brigade had supported Grey's. He is said to have been slain by an inhabitant who, lying in ambush, aimed at a decoration on Agnew's breast, and shot him down. Nor was our loss slight; and the next day the enemy were busily employed in burying our dead. " Don't bury them with their faces up, and thus cast dirt in their faces," said a kindly-hearted British soldier; " for they also are mothers' sons." It is said by a distinguished American officer, who afterwards carefully examined the field, that our retreat was providential, and the best thing that could have happened for us; since the force in opposition, and the thoroughly defensible position of the village (by reason of its numerous stone houses with enclosures, each of which could be made a stronghold by broken parties of the enemy), would have brought about our annihilation with returning light. Clinton on the contrary suggests, in relation to the unhappy delay which was made before Chew's House, that the 40th occupied, and which was attacked, as the British owned at the time, with a " singular intrepidity ": — " Had Washington left a corps to observe this house, and proceeded, there is no saying what might have been the consequence." *

During the contest, a Lieutenant Whitman, of Reading, was struck down by the enemy, and left for dead. He managed to crawl from the scene to a house in Washington Lane, where he was sheltered and cared for. Soon after the action, on discovering that an American officer was thus concealed within their lines, the British put both Whitman and his host under arrest. In this emergency the wounded man, having had probably some knowledge of André during his confinement at Lancaster or Carlisle, contrived to procure an interview with him; which terminated in André's obtaining a withdrawal of the arrest, and permission for Whitman to remain unmolested in Germantown until he was in a condition to return to his home. Such circumstances as these present the best evidences of the nature of that disposition which so entirely endeared its possessor to all whom he encountered.

A Philadelphian who, preserving friendly relations with the English, writes nevertheless very impartially, thus describes the posture of affairs on the day after the battle, and the language then held in the royal quarters: —

"*Oct. 5th.* This morning I went to Germantown to see the destruction and collect, if possible, a true account of the action. From the accounts of the officers, it appears that the Americans surprised the Picquet Guards of the English, which consisted of the 2nd Battalion Grenadiers, some infantry, and the 40th regiment: altogether about 500. The English sustained the fire of the Americans for near an hour

* Clinton MS.

(their numbers unknown) when they were obliged to retreat, the ammunition of the Grenadiers and Infantry being expended. The 40th regiment retreated to Chew's House, being about 120 men, and supported the fire of the Americans on all sides. The Americans came on with an unusual firmness, came up to the doors of the house, which were so strongly barricaded they could not enter. One of the Americans went up to a window on the side of the house to set fire to it, and just as he was putting a torch to the window he received a bayonet through his mouth which put an end to his existence. The Americans finding the fire very severe retreated from the house: a small party of the Americans, which had gone in near the middle of Germantown, and had sustained the fire in the street for some time, perceived the British coming up in such numbers that they retreated. General Grey with 5000 men pursued them to the Swedes Ford. His men being very much fatigued and very hungry and the Americans running so fast, that the General gave over the chase, and returned to his old encampment. The greatest slaughter of the Americans was at, and near to Chew's Place: most of the killed and wounded that lay there were taken off before I got there; but three lay in the field, opposite to Chew's Place. The Americans were down as far as Mrs. Maganet's tavern. Several of their balls reached near to Head Quarters. From all which accounts I apprehend, with what I have heard, that the loss of the Americans is the most considerable. After I had seen the situation at Chew's House, which was exceedingly damaged by the balls on the outside, I went to Head Quarters, where I saw Major Balfour, one of General Howes aide-de-camps, who is very much enraged with the people around Germantown for not giving them intelligence of the advancing of Washington's army; and that he should not be surprised if General Howe was to order the country for 12 miles round Germantown to be destroyed, as the people would not run any risque to give them intelligence when they were fighting to preserve the liberties and properties of the peaceable inhabitants. On our setting off we see His Excellency the General attended by Lord Cornwallis and Lord Chewton: the General not answering my expectations." *

At this time the grenadier and the light infantry company of each regiment was separated from its companions, and marshalled respectively in battalions; which explains the apparent weakness of some of the English corps, thus deprived of a large part of their nominal strength. On the 19th October, the army moved at daylight for Philadelphia; McLane, and a few American light-horse disguised as British, following close on their heels to the heart of the city, picking up a few royal officers and just missing the adjutant-general and Howe himself.† The General's quarters were at the house of our General Cadwalader, who was with Washington. His men, in fine condition and anxious to be led against the Americans, were encamped from below Kensington on the Delaware nearly to the Schuylkill. The cause named in despatches for this move was to obtain a more convenient position for the reduction of our river-forts; but in camp it was attributed to the lines at Germantown being too large for ready defence. The experience of the 4th was not lost.

* Morton MS.

† Allan McLane was one of the best men in our service. In the emergency of the war, he consumed all the table and household linen of his family in clothing his troopers, and throughout was as active in our cause as he was intelligent and brave. On one occasion he entered Philadelphia disguised as a countryman; and having transacted his business, was returning to camp, when he was overhauled by an English picket. The commanding officer questioned him narrowly; but the supposed peasant was adroit in his replies, and ready to agree that Washington would not adventure an attack. The Englishman gave him meat and drink, and dismissed him after he was thoroughly warmed at the watch-fire. McLane hurried to his own station, led out his troopers and some infantry, and presently brought away captive the whole party of the outpost that had so hospitably entertained him. Had he failed in the onset, or been taken, his fate would certainly have been the gallows. This authentic anecdote shows that a patriotic soldier will shrink from no means of helping the state at the peril of his own life.

Howe's plan was now to fortify this city, so that it could be held by a small garrison, while he took the field. The troops that entered with Cornwallis had been quartered at the State House, the Bettering (or Poor) House, &c., and had at once set to fortifying the river front against our ships and galleys. The disposition made of the main army placed the Hessian grenadiers on Noble and Callowhill, between 5th and 7th streets; the British grenadiers, 4th, 40th, and 55th, &c., on the north side of Callowhill, from 7th to 14th streets; eight other regiments were on the high grounds of Bush Hill, from 14th Street in about a line with Vine to the upper Schuylkill Ferry, near which was a Hessian post; while the yägers were on a hill at 22d Street and Pennsylvania Avenue. Infantry corps were at 8th, near Green streets and by 13th, on the Ridge Road. The 16th dragoons and three foot regiments were by a pond between Vine and Race, and 8th and 12th streets; and a body of yägers at the Point House on the Delaware. When winter came on, the men were quartered in the public buildings and in private houses, and in the old British barracks in the Northern Liberties. The artillery were on Chestnut, from 3d to 6th streets, and their park in the State-House Yard, now Independence Square. On the north side of the town, ten redoubts, connected by strong palisades, were erected, from the mouth of Conoquonoke Creek, on the Delaware near Willow Street, to the Upper or Callowhill Street Ferry. They were thus situated: — near the junction of Green and Oak streets, where the road then forked for Kensington and Frankford; a little west of Noble and 2nd streets; between 5th and 6th, and Noble and Buttonwood streets; on 8th street, between Noble and Buttonwood; on 10th, between Buttonwood and Pleasant; on Buttonwood, between 13th and Broad; on 15th, between Hamilton Street and Pennsylvania Avenue; at 18th Street and Pennsylvania Avenue; at 21st and Callowhill streets; and on the Schuylkill bank near the Upper Ferry. These works were begun on the 1st of October. The country before them towards the Schuylkill was hilly, but towards the Delaware level and comparatively open, though dotted with woods and cut up by the stout rail-fences of farms. The latter were soon seized for fuel by the English, and orchard and grove went down for the palisades and abatis of the works; the lines of which were still evident in 1780, as well as the ruined houses and defaced fields.they had occasioned. The work at the right, or Delaware end, was a large, square battery, with a handsome saw-shaped parapet, each redan of which held three men.* On the 23d of October, a body of English brought up the floating bridge from the lower (Gray's), and established it at the Middle Ferry, where it was guarded by the camp of the 71st, and a fascine redoubt at Chestnut Street. It was thought by some, however, that the Upper Ferry, as nearer to the camp and possessing advantages of ground, was its proper place.

It is difficult to recognize to-day the Philadelphia of 1777, though it was then the largest and, in many senses, the metropolitan city of America. Its extent was from Christian Street on the south to Callowhill on the north, and its greatest width east and west was to 9th Street, between Arch and Walnut. Its legitimate population, when all were at home who were now with our army, may have possibly approached 30,000. The exact returns of the city and liberties, made to Howe, in October, 1777, show 4,941 males under eighteen; 4,482 over eighteen and under sixty; and 12,344 females of all ages; a total of 21,767. The only streets parallel with the river, that were closely built up, were 3d, Water, and Front;—groves and gardens, hills and ponds, were interspersed through the greater portion of the place. Above 6th or 7th streets was generally open country, and the low meadows of Moyamensing and Passyunk abounded in game. The Delaware shore was open in places where there were not wharves; and the better classes resided in its vicinity, in

---

* The streets are named as they now exist, without regard to the open lands when the works were thrown up.

Water, and Market, and below Dock in Chestnut and Walnut streets; after the war their mansions became the resorts of trade. Such as it was, Jefferson declares Philadelphia to have been handsomer than London, far handsomer than Paris. Social rank too was strongly marked. The gentry consisted as well of the original Quaker families — rich, respectable, but by religion averse to the gayeties of the world — as of another class, chiefly of the English church, who often were or had been connected with the proprietary government, and who gave its tone to the fashionable society of the day. Many of these had travelled abroad, and their houses were decorated with valuable prints, or copies of great masters. Lord Carlisle describes the good style of living among the chief people in 1778; and the pleasures of the table being almost the only carnal vanity that it was lawful for a Quaker to indulge in, we need not wonder that even then the city was famous for its choice Madeira and French wines, and its West India turtle. John Adams went into ecstasies over the fare that was set before him. Chastellux says the formal dinner-hour was five or six P. M., and goes into the details of the repast as minutely as Adams: the roast meat and warm side-dishes, the sweet pastry and confectionary; and, the cloth being removed, the fruit and nuts, the toast-drinking, and the coffee that warned the guests to rise. The ladies he found singularly well-informed and attractive, and praises the skill with which the harpsichord was touched, and the pretty timidity of the songstress. They dressed, he says, with elegance. Another Frenchman paints them as tall and well-formed; their features regular, and complexions fair but often without color; their carriage less graceful than noble. The hair was often dressed without powder, and brought up high over the top of the head. It was the belles of this place and time whom Mrs. Adams characterized as "a constellation of beauties." "With what ease," says another lady, "have I seen a Chew, a Penn, an Oswald, an Allen, and a thousand others, entertain a large circle of both sexes; the conversation, without the aid of cards, never flagging nor seeming in the least strained or stupid." The leaders of this circle were decidedly loyal; they rather ignored Mrs. Washington when she passed through the town in 1775–6, and were in the height of their glory during Howe's occupation; of all which the whigs took ample revenge, by shutting them out from the assemblies, after the British had gone away. Nevertheless it may be remarked, that probably in no other American city is there so large a proportion of the better society composed of the same families whose members constituted it a century ago as in Philadelphia.* The dress of the gentry was generally a little in arrear of the English fashions. Powdered heads with clubs and queues; silver or gold-laced coats of broadcloth, of almost every hue save red (which color, on any but a soldier's back, bespoke, at this time, "a creole, a Carolinian, or a dancing-master"); knee-breeches and stockings, low shoes and large buckles, made up their attire. Gold watches were rare; silver were used, even by men of rank. Every one of a certain class was at least known by appearance; a strange gentleman was instantly observed. Many of these large-acred men were moderate in their political views, favoring neither extreme, but content to abide the result. Some, indeed, embarked their all on either venture. Cadwalader and Dickinson followed Washington; Galloway, Allen, Clifton, sided with the crown; but the most adopted the resolution of Ross, who, says Graydon, stuck to his ease and Madeira, and declared for neutrality; let who would be king, he well knew that he should be subject. The large private houses were few, but their appearance was stately and imposing. That in High, near 6th Street, occupied as Sir

---

* Burnaby, who travelled through America in 1760, particularly notices the beauty and elegance of the women of this city, and the love of pleasure and the cultivated tone that distinguished its society. In 1778, the reader will be amused to hear that among the young ladies of Philadelphia there were no books so charming as Juliet Grenville, Caroline Melmuth, and the History of Mr. Joseph Andrews.

William Howe's quarters, was subsequently Washington's abode.

The distinction, so strictly drawn before the war, between the gentleman and the tradesman, had not yet worn out; and people still dressed and lived according to their station. The workman was apparelled with leather breeches, checked shirt, coarse flannel jacket, and neat's hide shoes. Porridge was the morning and evening meal. Domestic servants were usually negro slaves, or German and Irish redemptioners, who were bought and sold for a term of years. The generality of houses were plainly furnished with rush-bottomed chairs, pewter platters, wooden trenchers, delft-ware, and the like. Silver tankards and China punch-bowls were evidences of prosperity, as were the small mirrors in wooden frames, and the mahogany tea-boards that are still to be sometimes met with in the lumber-rooms of old-time houses. Glass tumblers were rarely seen; a dipper for the punch-bowl, or a gourd or cup for the water-pail, supplied those who did not have recourse to the vessel itself. About a dozen churches were to be found in the town; but the Americans had removed all the bells ere Howe's arrival, lest they should be melted by the enemy. Chastellux draws a striking picture of the contrast between the silent watchfulness of the Quaker service and the music and chanting of the next place of worship he entered, which appears to have been one of the Church of England. The streets were but in part paved and lighted; and bridges in several places were thrown across Dock Creek, which flowed up into the very heart of the town. As for the inclinations of the majority of the people that Howe found there, it seems clear that they were loyal, though indisposed perhaps to take an active part. A proposition to blacken the front of every tory's house, that was in vogue among the ultra whigs on the return of the city to the American sway, was quietly put aside lest, it would seem, it should proclaim their strength. Just so the Romans forbade a distinguishing livery to their slaves;

quantum periculum immineret si servi nostri numerare nos cœpissent. Dr. Franklin says that the Quakers, then a numerous and wealthy people in Pennsylvania, had given to the Revolution "every opposition their art, abilities and influence could suggest"; and it is probable that the ill-usage which many of the sect received from the whigs during the war would have led to armed resistance, were such a step consistent with their pacific principles. As it was, their sympathies were largely with the British; nor were there wanting others who, unrestrained by conscientious scruples, were apparently ready to serve the crown. Nor, however we may condemn their actions who whether passively or actively resisted American Independence, should we universally impugn their motives. The lot of the tories of the Revolution was cast in the same land with the whigs; their education was under the same political and social influence; many of them were of character unblemished by aught but the final heresy, and of families honorably identified through generations with the history of the country and with its private benefactions; some gave their lives, others princely estates, to witness the sincerity of their belief. To the one side as to the other we may look for and find equally conduct susceptible of the imputation of pure or of impure instigation. That the tories erred, was and is the conviction of our side of the house. The very act by which they thought to establish their fidelity sealed their guilt. But the standard of success, by which they are so often judged, is a poor test of truth. Weighed in this scale, another turn to affairs would have made them heroes and justified the old Jacobite paradox:—

> Treason doth never prosper — what's the reason?
> Why, when it prospers, 'tis no longer treason.

CHAPTER VIII.

Affairs at Philadelphia. — Disorders and Discontents. — Fall of Red Bank. — André follows Grey with Howe to Whitemarsh. — Character of Sir William Howe.

IN the spring of 1777 a clever Philadelphia writer had divided the people into five classes. The Rank Tories came first. The Moderate Tories were such as preferred the English connection of 1763, valued worldly prosperity, hated New England, and loved the Rank Tories. The Timid Whigs distrusted American power, the cost of the war, and the continental paper-money; but were not disinclined to Independence, if it could be got. Avarice was supposed to be their mainspring. The Furious Whigs, says the writer, injure the cause of Liberty as much by their violence as the Timid Whigs by their fears. They think the destruction of Howe's army less important than the detection and punishment of the most insignificant tory; that the common forms of justice should be suspended towards a tory criminal; and that a man who only speaks against our common defence should be tomahawked, scalped, and roasted alive. They are likewise all cowards, who skulk under the cover of an office, or a sickly family, when they are called on to oppose the foe in the field. Woe to the community that is governed by this class of men. Lastly, he enumerates the Staunch Whigs — temperate, firm, and true; friends to their country, but holding life and goods as less than American Independence. The three orders first named now prevailed in Philadelphia; and it is not too much to say that a majority of them owed to this circumstance their conversion to opposite sentiments. The conduct of the royal army was far from satisfactory.

The Quakers, habitually benevolent yet tenacious of the rights of property, were shocked at once by its looseness of morals and its severity of discipline. Their effects had been already diminished by American exactions, yet they were reported to have made a free gift of £6,000 to the British on their arrival, and to have subsequently been called on for £20,000 more. Their first grievance was the pillaging to which the citizens were subjected, and to which many of the army became so accustomed during the war, that its reduction on the peace was the means, according to Scott, of inundating Great Britain with ruffians of every description; so that in Edinburgh alone six or seven disbanded soldiers would be under sentence of death at the same time. While yet at Germantown, the 33rd, though a pattern regiment in the field, was distinguished for its light fingers; but the Hessians were the boldest operators. Their pay, which was to come from their own sovereign, was not provided regularly, and their discipline consequently was bad enough to give Howe trouble in correcting it. With the English privates they did not get on pleasantly; arrogant, full of the idea of immediate allotments of land, and of living in free quarters with unlimited license to plunder, they incensed the inhabitants to such a degree, that many a farmer who hesitated to slay his fellow-countrymen, thought as little when he had the opportunity to shoot a Hessian as a hawk. Their officers could not understand why war should not be waged here as they had seen it in Europe. "No American town," they said, "has been laid under contribution; and what is there to destroy? Wooden houses deserted of their inhabitants, pigs, and poultry!" In the general confusion that prevailed between the arrival of the army and its final going into quarters, no doubt unusual license prevailed; and the newspapers of the day are filled with notices of robberies, several of them upon British officers. Seventeen watchmen were hitherto sufficient to protect the city; but when the army and fleet swelled the population to the neighborhood of 50,000, a hundred and

DISORDERS AND DISCONTENTS.

twenty were scarce thought enough. A stringent proclamation of the General's as to these practices was issued on the 7th November; but it proved a dead letter against the disorders that in one or another form had irritated some of the best people. The neighboring farms were freely spoiled by the soldiery. On the 28th September one of Harcourt's dragoons had four hundred lashes for such an offence, and another was hanged; and their commander gave the utmost offence to the distressed proprietors by his peremptory refusal to listen to their intercessions to spare the backs and the lives of his troopers who had robbed the king's liegemen. About the same time a foraging party brought in a great number of cattle from the neighborhood of Darby, to the discontent of their owners. On the 19th October a hundred Hessians went foraging, or rather robbing, among the farms where now stands the Naval Asylum. Their officer permitted them to take all the vegetables they could find. A person interested thus describes the scene:—

"Being afraid they would take our cabbage, I applied for a guard for the house and garden, which was immediately granted, and by that means prevented our cabbage from being plundered. After they had taken all John King's cabbage they marched off. [I] brought our cabbage home. It was surprizing to see with what rapidity they run to and with what voraciousness they seized upon John King's cabbage and potatoes, who remained a silent spectator to their infamous depredations."

The Hessians repeated their visit the next day, taking everything in the way of hay, vegetables, &c., that they could lay hands upon, until a squad of Harcourt's dragoons arrived and interfered, and made them go back. But for weeks the thing was continued; the officers sanctioned the plunder of vegetables, &c., till the people were thoroughly provoked. They were even compelled at last to remove and conceal their fences lest the British should take them for fuel; and the fields were thus left open and unprotected.

Nor was it till the 9th January, 1778, when the patrol was ordered to stop and examine every one found in the streets without a lantern between tattoo (8.30 p. m.) and reveille, that a real check was given to the nocturnal housebreaker.*

A succession of skirmishes had ensued along the lines ever since the British arrived. On the 27th September, a cannonade was kept up from 9 to 10 a. m. between four guns in their shore-batteries and our little fleet of a frigate of 34, and a ship of 18 guns, four row-galleys, and a schooner, till the frigate grounded and struck, and the others retired. The schooner as she came down lost her foremast and was abandoned. At 3 p. m., about 100 of our men attacked about 30 British on the ground now occupied by the Naval Asylum, (probably of Harcourt's dragoons who were posted there,) and killed or wounded three of their officers and two men. On the 4th October, after shots had been exchanged for an hour without effect, three American columns, with two field-pieces, appeared on the opposite side of the Schuylkill, at the Middle Ferry, and opened a general fire on 30 dismounted dragoons who guarded it. Reinforcements arriving to the latter, our men retreated leaving their guns by the water-side, but soon returned and bore them away. Only one man (an American) was wounded in this affair, which was witnessed by many of the citizens. On the 6th, 300 wounded British were brought from Germantown and lodged in the Seceders'

---

* As the necessity of the case had so long failed to produce such an order, we may suppose some personal motive now prevailed. Perhaps the affair last preceding its appearance may have had an effect. The following notice is from the Pennsylvania Ledger, Jan. 7, 1778. It would be curious if the initials referred to André: — "*Three Guineas Reward.* Was stolen out of a house in Walnut Street, Sunday evening last, the following articles, viz. A claret coloured ratteen suit of clothes, lined with blue satin, with spangled gold buttons; a pair of white cassimer breeches; some shirts marked J. A. with several other things: also a ladies black silk hat and cloak. Whoever will secure the thief and effects shall receive the above reward; and for the effects without the thief Two Guineas upon their delivery to the Printer."

and the Pine Street Presbyterian churches, and the old theatre; and the worst injured in the City Hospital. The wounded Americans, who were already neglected, were placed in the Presbyterian church and in two new houses in 4th Street. On the 12th, our patrols were ranging through all the vicinity, and seizing obnoxious tories. On the night of the 6th, 300 militia had entered Chester and captured the loyal sheriff of Sussex County, for whose arrest the Delaware government had offered $300 reward; and at 4 A. M., on the 15th, a party cut the rope of the Middle Ferry and exchanged platoon fires with the light dragoons. On the evening of the 16th, the troops left at Wilmington, who it was supposed would have attacked Red Bank, where our flag was hoisted that very morning, arrived at Philadelphia, leaving their sick and wounded at Gray's Ferry. A number of Hessians followed on the 20th.

Howe had written to Clinton that he was not strong enough to open the Delaware, and ordered reinforcements to be sent to him. On the 21st October, Donop with 2500 Hessians marched against Red Bank, crossing the Delaware in flat-bottomed boats sent up by night from the fleet, and passing from Cooper's Ferry to Haddonfield, where a quantity of stores were captured. This post and that on Mud Island, each about five miles below Philadelphia, together with the chevaux-de-frise they protected, controlled the navigation of the Delaware. Till it was free Howe's position was a simple cul-de-sac: parted from his supplies, and scarcity already exhibited, he rested within a triangle of which the Delaware and Schuylkill were the sides and his works the base. If the attack meditated in the American camp was thus made dangerous, so also was his own removal: for our army in at least equal numbers lay before him, and so long as the fleet could be shut out there was a prospect of reducing him by starvation, or by a ruinous and imperfect retreat across Jersey. The importance of clearing the way was therefore well understood by "the great count," as he was called in Philadelphia, when, for the especial distinction of himself and his men, Donop applied out of turn for this command. For the Americans he had indeed a most sovereign contempt; but it is possible that other circumstances may have governed his conduct. There were feuds in the army; and his countrymen had been freely spoken of. The Americans with great reason regarded them with utter abhorrence. The English Opposition, unmindful of the treaty stipulations that sent them, perhaps against their inclinations, to this country, lavished continual contumely on their heads. To the sea-stock of old hock wine their chief had laid in ere sailing, ministers were invoked to add the irresistible temptation of plenty of sour-krout for "the dear-bought cut-throats"; and in the coach that De Heister insisted on carrying with him over the ocean, it was almost wished that he might lie coffined beneath the waves like Pharaoh in his chariot. Their services were ridiculed, and an English nobleman sang, in relation to officers of the Brunswick corps, —

> "We shall not with much sorrow read
> How Sclatzen, Knotzen, Blatzchun bleed
> ——— Unless we break a tooth."

Howe was opposed politically to ministers, and it is probable these and other diatribes reached head-quarters; and though André, by long residence in Germany, was prepared to live in friendly relations with Donop, all of the army were not. De Heister had already gone home in a rage; and it is not likely his subordinates were less sensitive. A sufficient rampart, too high and steep to be carried without ladders and surrounded by an abatis and ditch, constituted the fort; it was defended by 300 valiant men. On the morning of the 22nd October, Donop halted just beyond its cannon-shot, and a drum followed by an officer brought a summons to surrender. "The King of England," were the words, "orders his rebellious subjects to lay down their arms; and they are warned that if they stand the battle they shall receive no quarter." The garrison replied that they were content neither to give quarter nor to take it. At 4 P. M., the enemy's guns opened on the place, and the Hessians rushed to the storm. The first outwork was carried; and, with shouts of triumph and waving of hats, — as thinking the day their own, — they advanced against the abatis. But Donop seems to have now entertained no such thought of victory. Though he saw success was almost impossible, he resolved to proceed; and giving his watch and purse to a bastard son of Lord Bute's, who was with his party, he plunged into the thickest of the fight. It was said at the time in Philadelphia that he considered his orders to be peremptory, and indeed they were so esteemed there; but Howe in his despatch of the 25th simply observes that they were "to proceed to the attack"; while in his Narrative he affirms them to have been discretionary, according to the chances of succeeding. It is probable that Donop's haughty spirit could not brook the shame, after all that had passed, of returning alive and unsuccessful. But the rampart was unattainable without ladders or pioneers. A front and a flank fire mowed down the assailants. The drummer that had approached the fort in the morning beat the charge at their head: he was a marked man, and fell on the first fire; and with him the officer who brought the summons. The leaders smote vainly with their swords on the abatis, and the men strove to tear it down; they fell by scores in the attempt. Donop himself, distinguished by his courage and by his handsome person, on which was displayed the order he bore, was struck in the hip, swooned, and was left for dead. A few of his men sheltered themselves beneath the parapet; the rest fled. When all was over, a feeble voice was heard among the heaps of slain, saying, " Whoever you are, draw me hence." He was extricated, and our men demanded of him if he was still determined to give no quarter. " I am in your hands," he replied; " you may revenge yourselves." Ascertaining that it was Mauduit, a French officer, who had taken him up — " Je suis content," he cried; " je meurs entre les mains de l'honneur même."

Every care was given him, for Washington was anxious that he should be saved; but he died in three days. He was intimate with St. Germain, the French minister of war; and his last hours were bestowed on a letter recommending Mauduit to his favor. "It is finishing a noble career early," he calmly said when the end approached; "but I die the victim of my ambition and of my sovereign's avarice." In England, Townshend satirically suggested that proper care and twenty pounds sterling would have provided ladders, and saved to the Treasury the cost of 600 slain Hessians at forty pounds a man.

> "Sir William's Conquests raise a smile.
> Lo, Red-Bank yields, and eke Mud Isle,
> Which Hessians storm'd — pell-mell!
> The ditch was wet — they had no bladders,
> The wall was high — they had no ladders,
> So Donop fought and fell!"

But it was not until a month later that the works, so skilfully planned by the unfortunate Coudray, were beaten down by the royal batteries to an extent which compelled their evacuation, and left Lord Howe master of the stream. Meantime small parties of our people kept up a constant disturbance along the lines, approaching within half a mile of the Kensington outposts. A royal detachment, crossing the Schuylkill on the 22nd, broke up the floating bridge at Gray's, and brought it up to the Middle Ferry. On the 26th the picket on the farther side was attacked for fifteen minutes by our people till a regiment had crossed the bridge for its relief; but soon after the floods came out and carried the structure away. These little affairs kept the enemy perpetually in motion. They were busied also with building two floating batteries on the Schuylkill, which, though when launched were too leaky for use, were presently put in better trim and sent down against Red Bank. Three or four brigs and sloops with provisions seem to have slipped up from the fleet on the 11th November; but over 300 sail still lingered below, by whose absence 12,000 men had already been detained in idleness for seven precious weeks. Excessive rains and the cutting of the dykes retarded the English works. In relieving guard, their men marched sometimes breast-deep in water. The American works were however now ceasing to be tenable; that on Mud Island was abandoned on the 16th; and on the 18th, Cornwallis, with Grey and 2500 men, crossed the Schuylkill at the Middle Ferry to attack Red Bank. On the way to Chester André saw a few more of the horrors of war. At the Blue Bell Tavern the American picket retreated within doors and from the windows shot down a couple of grenadiers. Their comrades burst in and, ere their officers could prevent, bayoneted five of our men. The rest were taken. Plunder prevailed on the road, and the houses of whigs were consumed. By 11 A. M. the British were crossing the Delaware at Chester, and, with the troops just come from New York, were so rapidly pushed against Red Bank, that it was impossible to relieve it. The place was evacuated on the 20th. Of the vessels that had been sheltered by its guns some were fired and, at four A. M. on the 21st, came drifting up the river on the flood-tide to within two miles of the city; but carried back by the ebb, exploded harmlessly after flaming for five hours. In the thick fog that prevailed, the gondolas passed by, despite the heavy firing of the English frigate Delaware. It was thus known that Red Bank had fallen; and as the design of a forward movement hinged on that event, the loyal believed that Cornwallis was now to pass up to Burlington and thence get into Washington's rear. On the morning of November 24th the fleet began to come in and business to revive. Cornwallis brought 400 cattle from Jersey on the ensuing day; and on the next, while sixty-three sail were in sight between the town and Gloucester Point, Lord Howe came on shore and the citizens made up their minds that Sir William would not pursue Washington that winter. They learned their mistake, however, on the following day; for so ill were

Howe's secrets kept that it was the town-talk that the main army would march on the 2nd December. Detachments were sent over Schuylkill; suspected spies were seized; and various country-houses, some the property of tories, were fired because the American pickets had found them a convenient ambush whence to shoot down the enemy. Most of the buildings along the lines were by this time destroyed; and it was even expected that Germantown would soon be burned.

Leaving a few regiments to guard the city, the British army marched forth by the Germantown road at eight P. M., December 4th, the van led by Cornwallis and the rest by Knyphausen. Howe's object was to find a weak place in the fortified camp at Whitemarsh, or to tempt our army, now strongly reinforced, into a battle for the recovery of Philadelphia; but the public impression was that he had gone out to fight Washington wherever he found him. The camp fires were lighted at Chestnut Hill, which, soon after, a body of Americans under Irvine attempted to occupy. They were discomfited, however, by Abercromby with the light brigade, and the general made prisoner. Here the English remained till the 7th; when, reluctant to essay Washington's right, they moved at one A. M. towards his left, and took post on Edgehill. A sharp skirmish was created by Morgan, whose rifles disputed the ground as long as they could, while to the left Grey encountered and easily put to flight a considerable party, chiefly of militia. Grey's night-march led him to their outposts. He formed with the Queen's Rangers on his left, the light infantry of the guards on his right, and his brigade in the centre. The Hessians and Anspach Chasseurs, with the field-pieces, were in the van. The Americans were outflanked on either side, and outrun by the guards, who turned their flight across the fire of the centre and left. This affair appears to have occurred in Cheltenham township, Montgomery county.

On the 8th, Howe abandoned all hope of finding a vulnerable place in our lines, and Washington restraining his personal desire to go forth and give them the meeting they sought, the British turned their faces homewards. At four P. M., Grey and Cornwallis, whose troops were the last to move, retired. At that precise time Simcoe was watching the entrance of a squad of our dragoons into a trap he had cunningly baited, when André galloped up with peremptory orders to withdraw. The others were already on the march; and at nine P. M., to the confusion and amazement of Philadelphia, the British ingloriously reëntered the lines.* As they came down the Old York Road, they burned, for some reason, the Rising Sun Buildings; but, except 700 cattle and the spoils of every farm-house that lay in a Hessian's path, there was nothing at all to show for all this effort and parade. Ere sailing for England, Cornwallis foraged the country beyond Schuylkill towards Chester; routing Potter as he went, and finding a success very grievous to all who had anything to lose, and who fruitlessly claimed redress from head-quarters. Another large force went to Darby on the 22nd; and stripping it of 1000 tons of forage returned on the 28th with a parcel of prisoners; of whom two officers and thirty men had been cunningly beguiled into ambuscade by a couple of the 17th dragoons. At seven P. M. on Christmas Eve, the city was enlivened by a brisk but unsupported cannonade with twelve-pounders on the lines between 3rd and 4th streets; and this was its last taste of battle in the year 1777. The troops, on the 30th and 31st December, went into good winter-quarters. With the exception of a transport, that was swept from her moorings by the ice to be stranded and

---

* This failure is attributed to the conduct of Lydia Darrach, a midwife of Philadelphia. The royal adjutant-general was billeted in the same house; and when he sent for some chief officers to give them their instructions and the general plan of action, he particularly ordered that all else in the house should go to bed. By aid of a friendly keyhole his precautions were frustrated; and the woman herself, without being suspected, bore the important details to our people, who were consequently enabled to anticipate every move of the enemy.

plundered on the Jersey shore, nothing more occurred of sufficient note to excite attention.

The severities of the winter of 1777-8 were keenly felt by the poor of Philadelphia; and even the better classes, no longer able to procure fresh provisions by means of the river, which was obstructed by ice on the 30th of December, found additional aggravation in the spirit that permitted the Americans to hold their position at Valley Forge, and thence to restrain supplies from the country by severities which at this day seem hardly just. "The laws of war," said Marshal Conway, "sanction the infliction of death on those who furnish food to an enemy only when such aids are needful to existence; not where they are rather matters of luxury." The army commissariat was always capable of being replenished by the fleet, and there was no longer hope or attempt to reduce Howe by starvation; but the inhabitants were on another footing. They remembered, in their hunger, how the officers who entered on the 26th of September, with all their civility to the people, professed the most bitter determination to pursue our army to the last extremity; but their amazement is also recorded at the self-confidence of the English and their contempt of the Americans, whom they stigmatized as " a cowardly and insignificant set of people." There were not wanting, even in Congress, men who had heard Cope's officers at Preston hold the same terms of the Scots, declaring they would never remain to face the British bayonet: yet who had seen these very boasters fly pusillanimously before the Highlanders without striking a blow. The impulse that at first led to the formation of Loyal Associations and Provincial Corps had not been fostered. The Quakers even were at one time expected by their antagonists to appear in arms. "Thee and thou, in Philadelphia," wrote an American officer (Oct. 6th, 1777), " now find a religion will not serve that doth not turn weathercock-like. They begin to say to each other — ' Will thee take a gun, — hope thee will appear in the field;'"— but when flour was at three guineas the hundred, and other things in proportion, they rather thought of obtaining assistance through Dr. Fothergill, from their friends in England, to be repaid at the end of the troubles, than of fulfilling the predictions of their enemies. Nor was a British army longer to be esteemed invincible by rebels. Burgoyne's was a case in point. On the 3rd of October, imperfect rumors of the first battle at Stillwater flew from lip to lip. Gates was beaten. A letter was in town, with a postscript in Irish which told how a partial engagement on the 18th of September had been unfavorable to Burgoyne; but that returning on the 19th to bury his dead, a general action ensued in which he was entirely successful, and was in full march on Albany. A man who had been in Albany on the 19th was at once arrested; but he of course knew nothing of Sir John's advance. His fall was known to Washington on the 18th of October; but Howe's army scouted at the story, while the citizens believed it. The Frenchman who brought in Donop's wounded officers was questioned on the possibility of such an event. "I know the fact is so," he answered, "you must explain it as you can." Foremost in capacity among the local loyalists was Galloway. Sir William employed him in municipal affairs, but in other respects gave him the cold shoulder. Galloway was not insensible of the supineness of the campaign, nor, as he believed, of the cause. His friends shared in his discontent, and he has recorded its origin. At Philadelphia, he says, Howe found 4482 fencible inhabitants, of whom about 1,000 were Quakers and perhaps fifty secret foes. An eleventh of the whole population had fled. A militia of 3500 men should have been forthwith organized; that, with the shipping and 1000 regulars, could have held the lines against anything but Washington's main army, which Howe might thus be at liberty to attack at Valley Forge. He should have invited the loyal men of the Chesapeake and Delaware peninsula to rise, and supplied them with arms and ammunition, and a few regulars. In three days he would have had

2000 tories in the field, who would soon increase to 6000 or 8000. A covering post at Wilmington would put Washington between it and the loyalists, should he march against them; while the army at Philadelphia would be but one day's distance by water, or two by land. He cited the fact that even with the insufficient means that were taken to raise men, over 1100 of the Philadelphians joined the British; but particularly was he sensitive of the refusal to permit him to raise a regiment. A warrant for a single troop was vouchsafed him; in two months it was full and efficient. The General put aside his services in the recruiting line, and gave the warrant to "an unpopular country tavern-keeper, for whom he [Howe] thought his servants in the kitchen the most proper company." Fifty gentlemen from Monmouth, New Jersey, brought their services to Sir William, "but the General was inaccessible; they could not, after several days attendance, procure an audience." Such are the charges Galloway brought forward; and it is no wonder he found ready listeners.

Sir William and Lord Howe were the sons of the second Viscount Howe, and were in an illegitimate way kinsmen to the King. The late King William spoke of Lord Howe as "indeed a sort of connexion of the family." When that coarse, vulgar, vicious little profligate, George Louis, the first of the Hanoverian line, came over to reign in England, he brought among his German mistresses a Madame Kielmansegge, whose mother had filled a questionable position near his own father. Once in England, she was of course placed on the pension and the peerage rolls; and in 1721, while his wife languished out her life in a dungeon, George created her Countess of Leinster and of Darlington, and Baroness Brentford. By the usual means of her office, though her appearance was far from pleasing, she accumulated wealth. Walpole paints the fright into which his childhood was thrown by an interview with this "fat woman of Brentford." "The fierce, black eyes, large and rolling beneath two lofty arched eyebrows; two acres of cheeks spread with crimson, an ocean of neck, that overflowed and was not distinguished from the lower parts of her body, and no part restrained by stays, — no wonder that a child dreaded such an ogress." The child that she bore to the king was, in 1719, married to Lord Howe; and though she was never publicly acknowledged as George's daughter, her own child was always treated by Princess Amelia, daughter of George II., as of the blood-royal. There were whispers also of a relationship of the same nature as with the Howes, between George III. and Lord North; their resemblance was so great, according to Wraxall, as to be pointed out by George's father to Lord Guilford. — The ill feeling between North and Howe, so natural to the royal line, would not belie this tale.

John Adams asserts that the Howes were poor, brave men, who had wasted their estates in election contests and had now nothing to sell but their votes and their swords. Sir William represented Nottingham in the Commons; and the expenses of carrying that town in 1768 were said by Lord Chesterfield to have been full £30,000 to the winner, and not less to the losing candidate. Letters from London in 1775 aver that both Howe and Clinton went with reluctance to America; but they were told they must do this or starve. In Parliament he was in the chair of Committee of the Whole House, on the 20th of March, 1775, when the Commons considered American affairs. From nine P. M. to one A. M. it was one scene of confusion and altercation, during which a member called on him to publish in the Colonies, that whenever evidence in their favor was produced, the prime minister " was either fast asleep, and did not hear it; or, if awake, was talking so loud as even to prevent others from hearing it." As next in command to Gage, he led the assault at Bunker Hill, where his " disposition was exceeding soldier-like; in my opinion, it was perfect," said Burgoyne. Others however discovered in this action his habitual neglect to press fortune to the utmost, when Clinton was vainly urging the pursuit of the Americans crowded on a narrow causeway. It would seem that ministers were then perplexed to find a suitable chief commander. With little show of probability, Prince Ferdinand was spoken of on either side; but this nomination would never have suited Germain (who was soon to represent America in the cabinet), for it would have brought him into direct contact with the man by whose means he had been himself cashiered for misconduct at Minden. The veteran Amherst was also mentioned; and a contemporary historian alleges the post was even tendered to the aged Oglethorpe, who, in 1745, had been refused any command whatsoever. The ancient Jacobite however sturdily refused the appointment, unless he were permitted to comply with American demands; and this the ministry would not think of. Accordingly, Dartmouth informed Howe on the 2nd of August, 1775, of his prospective position, and bade him transmit a full statement of everything that he would need to insure success. Yet the nature of his politics at this time may, perhaps, be fairly deduced from an address of his constituency to the throne that was in his absence presented by his brother, the Viscount. The constitutionality of the steps against America was questioned, their expediency denied, and especially was regretted the presence, in such a service, of their representative — "a descendant of that noble family which in every walk of glory has equalled the Roman name." Howe himself averred that he accepted the command by desire of his friends in opposition; and it is not to be denied that, if his conduct in this country was detrimental to the triumph of the British arms, it was at least often stamped with sterling traits. At Bunker Hill, where he was struck by a spent ball, he would have preserved the wounded Warren. He captured Fort Washington in a manner to indicate that he prized the lives of his men. He might have made a more dashing attack, but not a surer or safer. To his prisoners he was not so considerate; and the treatment that he suffered them to receive would alone pollute his fame. Ethan Allen, not backward himself to inflict scourging or exile where a disputed land-title was concerned, lifts up his voice against Sir William's commissary of prisoners, a native of Allen's own region; and declared that "legions of infernal devils, with all their tremendous horrors, were impatiently ready to receive Howe and him, with all their detestable accomplices, into the most exquisite agonies of the hottest regions of hell-fire." As for his provost-marshal, Major Cunningham, "a burly, ill-natured Irishman, of sixty years," humanity shrinks from the recital of his cruelties, and almost regrets that it cannot find reason to believe that the justice of the nation he so long disgraced did not provide him a halter. Few worse men have dangled from a gibbet. There is satisfaction in the reflection that, when the British evacuated New York in 1783, the insolence of office led him to quarrel with the man who had a little prematurely hoisted the American flag; and that he was soundly belabored with a broomstick by an indignant virago. His quarters in Philadelphia were plundered by robbers of his own ranks; foremost among whom was a hag named Marshall, well-known on the battle-field as the "bag and hatchet woman,"— a title that sufficiently indicates her horrid trade. Cunningham's prison was in Walnut Street below 6th, and the neighboring Potter's Field (now Washington Square) received his victims. It was at the time told of this human beast, that when charity supplied a vessel of broth to his starving captives, he would divert himself by kicking it over, and seeing the prisoners fall sprawling on the earth, striving to lap up the food with their tongues. As for the hulks in which our people were shut up at New York, we need not go behind the confession of Sir William Napier — "The annals of civilized nations furnish nothing more inhuman towards the captives of war than the prison-ships of England." The fact seems to be that Howe prized his own comfort too highly to disturb himself much about his duties. Charles Lee, who long had him in the highest love and reverence, describes him as being "naturally good-humored, complaisant, but illiterate and indolent to the last degree, unless as an executive soldier, in which capacity he is all fire and activity, brave and cool as Julius Cæsar." Yet his enemies also asserted that since 1776 he had never met Washington but in force really superior; and nineteen occasions were cited in which he might have overturned the Americans. At Long Island his men were hardly restrained for three days from attacking our lines. He lingered in camp, when he should have passed to New Rochelle and hemmed up his foe in New York. At Brandywine, by the most judicious manœuvres, he enclosed Washington between his two columns and impassable waters. He indolently suffered the defeated party to remain undisturbed all night within eight miles of the field, and, by five days' inactivity, lost all the fruits of victory. At Germantown, it was Musgrave who saved the day; and even then there was no general pursuit. Nothing was extenuated, and not a little set down in malice. The people were discontented with his private life. He appropriated to himself Mrs. Pemberton's coach and horses; he was fond of his bottle; he kept a mistress;—even the more discreet among his own officers were abashed at his luxurious habits, and his inaccessibility to affairs of importance. Across the ocean, Burns caught up the story of his slothful ease.

> "Poor Tammy Gage within a cage
> Was kept at Boston ha', man,
> Till Willie Howe took o'er the knowe
> For Philadelphia, man.
> Wi' sword and gun he thought a sin
> Guid Christian blood to draw, man:
> But at New-York, wi' knife and fork,
> Sir-loin he hacked sma', man."

The Admiral and himself, bitterly remarks a contemporary, had alike the sullen family gloom; but while Lord Howe was devoted to business, his brother hated and avoided it. "Their uniform character through life has been, and is to this day, haughty, morose, hard-hearted, and inflexible." This aversion to public affairs, and the consequent pecuniary disorders that ensued in their management, may perhaps give another color to the allegation that Sir William was privately interested in various transactions by which riches were got at the expense of government. He was said to be a secret partner with Coffin, a large military shopkeeper who attended the army. Certainly the expenditures of his campaigns were beyond all reasonable bounds. In every profitable branch of the service, wrote Wedderburne at the time, the peculation was as enormous as indecent. Both the troops and the treasury were robbed: "the hospitals are pest-houses and the provisions served out are poison. Those that are to be bought are sold at the highest prices of a monopoly." No wonder the most loyal Englishman winced at this wanton and fruitless waste of taxation, and apostrophized his country, insulted by Americans, —

" Who force thee from thy native right
Because thy heroes will not fight;
— Perfidious men, who millions gain
By each protracted, slow campaign!"

The French officers in Washington's camp were amazed at Howe's inactivity. "After Brandywine," said Du Portail, " he might have exterminated our army"; and his sluggishness while they were at Valley Forge was an ineffable blunder. "Had he moved against them in force, they could not have held their encampment," says Marshall. An opinion was (no doubt falsely) at this time attributed to La Fayette, that as any general but Howe would have beaten Washington, so any other than Washington would have beaten Howe; and ministers trembled lest Gates should march from Saratoga and, joining the main army, subdue Philadelphia and its garrison. But Sir William was already anxious to retire. There was ill blood between Germain and himself; and not even the king could persuade the Colonial Secretary to treat his General with proper confidence. In July, 1778, he returned to London, " richer in money than laurels," says Walpole. "The only bays he possessed," said another, "were those that drew his coach." His reception by the cabinet was not encouraging; and he endeavored to cast the blame of his want of success at its door. In this he but partially succeeded. A parliamentary investigation took such a turn that it was dropped on motion of his friends. He was not reëmployed in the war; and the nation, and even his own constituents of Nottingham, seem to have been content to have done with him.

> "General Howe is a gallant commander —
> ——— There are others as gallant as he"

was the general conclusion. In 1799 he succeeded to his brother's Irish titles; and died childless in 1814. In person he was tall and portly, full six feet in height, and, to Philadelphia eyes, of stately and dignified manners. His enforced withdrawal from the field of professional service was in some measure compensated by the social and political influence which secured him in a lucrative and honorable office under the crown.

CHAPTER IX.

The British Army in Philadelphia. — Features of the Occupation. — Sir William Erskine. — Abercrombie. — Simcoe. — Lord Cathcart. — Tarleton. — André's Social Relations in the City. — Verses composed by him. — Amateur Theatricals. — Misconduct of the Royal Arms. — The Mischianza. — André's Account of it. — Howe removed from the Command.

The year 1778 found the British at Philadelphia in snug quarters, unembarrassed by the cares of the field and, except for occasional detachments, free from other military duties than the necessary details of garrison life. The trifling affairs that occurred during the remainder of the season, served rather as a zest to the pleasures which engaged them, than as a serious occupation. Our army lay the while — from the 19th December to the 18th June — at Valley Forge, on the west side of the Schuylkill. The camp was placed on the rugged hill-side of a deep valley, through which flows a creek. On the east and south it was fortified with a ditch six feet wide and three feet deep, and a mound four feet high that might easily be overthrown (said Anbury, an English officer who visited the spot,) by six-pounders. On the left was the Schuylkill, over which a bridge was built by the Americans to keep up their communications. On every arch was carved a general's name ; that in the centre bore Washington's, and the date of its erection. The rear was protected by a precipice and thick woods. From December to May, continues our authority, Howe could have readily carried these lines ; at any time in the spring he could have besieged them. The sufferings of the men were intolerable ; they deserted by tens and by fifties ; and they often appeared in Philadelphia almost naked, without shoes, a tattered blanket strapped to their waists — but with their arms. These they were always allowed by the English to sell. It is incredible that, however bad his intelligence from the country-people might be, Howe could not have found guides among these to lead him to our camp. It is known that there were not provisions in store to enable Washington to hold out. He must have abandoned his lines or starved; and he had not sufficient means to remove his equipage. Sickness prevailed; eleven hospitals were kept up at one time. None but the Virginia troops were provided with anything like enough clothing; and, to crown all, Congress was busier with schemes to supplant and remove Washington, than to listen to the grievances of his followers and supply their just demands.* It was for us a fortunate though a most unwarlike turn that occupied such soldiers as Abercrombie, Tarleton, Musgrave, Simcoe, and De Lancy with the ordering of a ball-room or the silken trappings of the stage, rather than the harsh realities of the field. In other scenes they proved themselves gallant and dangerous antagonists.

The general demeanor of the officers billeted at Philadelphia in private houses is described as very agreeable. Candles, fire, and a chamber were provided by the householder. The guest would return of an evening, take his candle, and after a little fireside-chat retire to his apartment. One unfortunate wight indeed, who had been wounded in the

---

* General Knox and Captain Sargent, both of the artillery, were delegated by their comrades to represent their necessities. The committee having heard them, one of its members took occasion to remark that much had been very well said about the famine and the nakedness of the soldiers; yet he had not for a long time seen a fatter man than one of the gentlemen who had spoken, nor one better dressed than the other. Knox, who was of corpulent habit, was mute — probably with indignation; but his subordinate rejoined that this circumstance was due to the respect his companions bore not only to themselves, but to Congress. The General's rank prescribed his appointment; but, beyond that, the corps could not hesitate to select as their representatives the only man among them with an ounce of superfluous flesh on his body, and the only other who possessed a complete suit of clothes.

neck at Germantown and who was saddled on one of the best families in the town, used to keep the neighborhood of 2nd Street and Taylor's Alley aware of his existence by the frantic volleys of oaths that he would pour out when, as he sat by the open window, every turn of his head to watch what went on below would throw him into new pains; but such cases were exceptional. Several of them too had mistresses; and this, though offensive to morality, was neither disguised nor kept in the dark. Lieutenant-Colonel Birch of the dragoons — a man of high fashion at the time — was of these; and Major Crewe, whose jealousy of Tarleton was one of the *esclandres* of the day. "I saw," said a distinguished citizen, "a grand review of 18,000 British troops, on the commons that extended from Bush Hill to Southwark. They had just received their new clothing, and made a fine appearance. A very lovely English girl, the mistress of Major Williams of the artillery, drove slowly down the line in her open carriage with handsome English horses and servants. Her dress was cut and trimmed after the fashion of the regiment's; the facings were the same, and the plumes. The woman was singularly beautiful."

No sooner were they settled in their winter-quarters, than the English set on foot scenes of gayety that were long remembered, and often with regret, by the younger part of the local gentry. Weekly balls, each conducted by three officers of repute, were given in the public rooms at Smith's City Tavern, in 2nd Street. Convivial associations were formed, to dine at the Bunch of Grapes or the Indian Queen. Mains of cocks were fought at a pit that was opened in Moore's Alley. As spring came on, cricket-matches were discussed. The advertisements in the newspapers give many curious hints of the levity of manners and morals that was fast springing up in the lately staid and demure city. Thefts were not infrequent; wet-nurses were in constant demand; comely white bondwomen were escaping from servitude. To-day Lord Rawdon's spaniel is lost near Schuylkill, and is to be brought back to Mrs. Sword's in Lodge Alley; to-morrow an exhibition of glowing pictures, or a sale of books rather more free than had usually found market there; or perchance a lecture on electricity at the college. The presence of so many young officers, not a few of them distinguished by rank or by fortune, lent new life to every occasion of amusement. The Marquis of Lindsay, who in this year became Duke of Ancaster, was the nephew of André's old colonel, Lord Robert Bertie; and Stopford, his major in Canada, was also here, a ball-manager. Lord William Murray, Lieutenant-Colonel (afterwards Earl) Harcourt, Sir Henry Calder, Sir Thomas Wilson, and many other men of rank were with the troops. Here too was Sir William Erskine, who a year or so later resigned his quartermaster-generalcy, not for ill health it is said, but because the General gave no heed to his recommendation for an ensigncy. Erskine remained long in the service, and many stories are told of him. He protected the English rear at the retreat from Dunkirk, and in the midst of the confusion, with charming frankness and in the broadest Scotch, shouted to his comrade in this war, Dundas, as he passed, — "Davie, ye donnert idiot, where's a' your peevioys (pivots) the day?" — Sir David being one of those tedious tacticians who could not take one step forward without going a dozen about. Erskine was not an able officer, as Wellington afterwards found out in the Peninsula. There, too, was the Hessian captain Frederick Münchausen, aide to Howe, whose name was so ominously significant of incorrect despatches; and Abercrombie, apparently the same who later served and died so gallantly in Egypt, and whose mortification when the British arms were finally grounded at Yorktown — hiding his face and gnashing his sword-hilt as he turned away — is so picturesquely related by one of Rochambeau's staff. Of those, however, who seem to have been of André's more immediate circle were Simcoe, the famous partisan officer; Captain Battwell; Sir John Wrottesley; Captain De Lancy, afterwards his successor in the adjutant-generalcy; Major Stanley (father of the late Earl of Derby); and Major Lord Cathcart. This last was of an ancient Scotch family long distinguished in arms, who rose to command in chief before Copenhagen in 1807; he was created an English Viscount and Earl, and died so lately as 1843.*

Another young officer at Philadelphia, whose part in the

* Cathcart married in America (April 10, 1779) the daughter of Andrew Eliot, once collector at Philadelphia and uncle of the first Lord Minto, better known as author of the beautiful pastoral of Amyntas — "My sheep I neglected, I broke my sheep-hook," — than by his title. Mr. A. Eliot was one of the commissioners to procure André's release. A MS. letter of the time thus pleasantly describes the nuptials: "We live, it is true, for a little while, when Beauty strikes the strings at General Pattison's concerts: but this is only on the first day of a week that sickens before it is concluded. . . . An't you tired of moralizing? I'll tell you news: Lord Cathcart — "Poh, I heard it before!"

"However, you just heard that he was married to Miss Eliot, but the story here is that he took himself in merely to pass the time away in winter-quarters; and because Miss E. was a lively, pretty girl, he made violent love to her, wrote letters, &c. &c. Miss E. listened and believed — 'For who could think such tender looks were meant but to deceive?' Whether his Lordship flew off afterwards, I know not: but Mr. E. laid the letters and the whole affair before Sir Henry. Sir H. advised Cathcart to marry: Cathcart wished to be excused till the end of the war: and the General informed him that after having gone so far, he must marry Miss E., or quit his family. A fine girl, a good fortune, to a Scotch Lord with a moderate one, were not to be despised. You know the Peers of Scotland, having no legislative privileges, are not of that consequence that the Lords of England or even those of Ireland are. And so his Lordship married Miss Eliot, and they will soon sail for England, it is said." — Lady Cathcart appears to have had a place at court, and Peter Pindar celebrates her at Weymouth, in connection with the king's insensate manners: —

> "Cæsar spies Lady Cathcart with a book;
> He flies to know what 'tis — he longs to look.
> 'What's in your hand, my lady? let me know.' —
> ' A book, an't please your majesty.' — ' Oho!
> Book's a good thing — good thing — I like a book
> Very good thing, my lady — let me look —
> War of America! my lady, hæ?
> Bad thing, my lady! fling, fling *that* away.' "

A sister of Cathcart's married Sir Thomas Graham, afterwards Lord Lynedoch, a distinguished cavalry officer; another was Duchess of Athol, and a third Countess of Mansfield.

war was not unnoted, was Banastre Tarleton. Born at Liverpool, the son of an eminent merchant, he forsook, like André, the compting-room for the army, and when the contest began obtained a cornetcy of dragoons. Sir W. Erskine was his first patron; afterwards Clinton and Cornwallis prized and promoted him. Well but heavily made, with large muscular legs, a good soldier's face, dark complexion, small, piercing, black eyes, about five feet eight inches in height, and a capital horseman, he was the very model of a partisan leader. At this time he was but about twenty-one, and though Howe did not employ cavalry much, was always vigorous and active; "when not riding races with Major Gwynne on the commons, making love to the ladies." In England he had been guilty of some excesses; and a whimsical speech from the box of a theatre about one of his own kindred was quoted as an evidence of his "flow of spirits and unrestrained tongue." At the Mischianza his equipage bespoke the man. His device was a light dragoon; his motto, *Swift, vigilant, and bold*, — and his squire's name was Heart. On his return he was elected to Parliament by his native place, and was one of the most distinguished among the whig circles; now jesting at Fox's swollen legs, now taking the odds from Sheridan that Pitt will not be First Lord of the Treasury on the 18th of May, 1795. Despite his distinguished services he was coldly received by George III., who less regarded how his soldiers fought than how they voted.* An ill-advised boast, in the presence of a lady of influence, that he had not only slain more men in America, but had more nearly approached the feats of Proculus in Gaul than any other soldier in the royal army, so incensed his hearer that she determined he should lose his seat at the next election, — and she carried her point. Tarleton's repu-

---

* Tarleton, it is said, has been honored with a private conference, in which his Majesty took no other notice of his services than just to say — "Well, Colonel Tarleton, you have been in a great many actions, had a great many escapes." — *MS. London, Feb.* 6, 1782.

tation for cool but reckless daring attended him in England. When a mob threatened Devonshire House, he quietly threw up a window and said, — " My good fellows, if you grow riotous, I shall really be obliged to *talk* to you." They immediately dispersed. In 1798 he married a daughter of the Duke of Ancaster, and in 1817 was a major-general, but not on active service. He always maintained, till the event falsified his judgment, that Wellington would fail in Portugal. On the coronation of George IV. he was made a Baronet and K. B. His fortunes do not seem to have been continually prosperous; — on the 5th of September, 1798, he writes from Sussex: "I have thought proper to proceed to Lord R. Spencer's friendly mansion, for two purposes: to read, and to subsist for nothing — being very, very poor." The portrait by Sir Joshua Reynolds represents him in a martial attitude on the battle-field. His own figure is finely drawn; but the horses are outrageously in defiance of nature, and fully warranted the contemporaneous criticism that was bestowed upon the production: —

> "Lo! Tarleton dragging on his boot so tight!
>   His horses feel a godlike rage,
>   And long with Yankees to engage —
> I think I hear them snorting for the fight.
>
> " Behold with fire each eyeball glowing!
>   I wish, indeed, their manes so flowing
> Were more like hair — the brutes had been as good
>   If, flaming with such classic force,
>   They had resembled less that horse
> Call'd Trojan — and by Greeks compos'd of wood."

Tarleton's ravages in America have made his name a household word in many regions; but an exception may be cited to his general reputation in Jefferson's testimony to the care he gave to the house of Monticello when it was in his power.

It was natural that the presence of such a gay and brilliant throng should create an impression on Philadelphia society that long remained uneffaced, and which in after-years induced many, particularly of the softer sex, to look back with real regret to the pleasant days, the festive nights that prevailed during the British occupation. One of these in recording her own sentiments probably uttered the thoughts of many more:

> "Oh halcyon days, forever dear,
> When all was frolic, all was gay:
> When Winter did like Spring appear,
> And January fair as May!
> When laughing Sol went gaily down,
> Still brighter in the morn to rise:
> And gently glancing on the town
> O'er British ensigns moved his eyes.
> When all confessed the gallant youth
> Had learned in camps the art to please;
> Respectful, witty, friends to truth,
> Uniting valour, grace, and ease!"

But of all the band, no one seems to have created such a pleasing impression or to have been so long admiringly remembered as André. His name in our own days lingered on the lips of every aged woman whose youth had seen her a belle in the royal lines; and though the reminiscences of a bygone generation are not implicitly to be relied on, there is reason to believe that in this instance they are in the main correct. He is described as of five feet nine inches in height, and of a singularly handsome person,—well-made, slender, graceful, and very active; a dark complexion, with a serious and somewhat tender expression; his manners easy and insinuating. He was an assured favorite with some of the best people in the city, and despite their indignation at Grey's behavior at the Paoli. This André warmly upheld, as in entire conformity with the usages of war; and they who disagreed with these assertions still cherished the aide-de-camp, who vindicated the deeds he had shared in, as "a most charming man." If the serious business of life was a part of his lot, there was yet ample scope for the exercise of those elegant arts in which he excelled. His infirmities, if any there were, sprang, like Charles Townshend's, from a noble cause — that lust of fame which is "the instinct of all great souls"; and his comely person, his winning speech, his graceful manners, procured him universal acceptance.

> "Whate'er he did 't was done with so much ease,
> In him alone 't was natural to please:
> His motions all accompanied with grace;
> And paradise was opened in his face."

Warm friendships sprung up between many of the officers and the towns-people; and among those in which André was concerned, was that with the family of Edward Shippen, which was destined to bear such an important part in his career. In rank, character, and fortune Mr. Shippen was among the first men of his time. That he was, to say the least, lukewarm in the war has often been charged. Certainly he was constantly fined for neglect of militia duty, in seasons when every zealous whig might have been looked for in arms; but after all was over, he was worthily dignified by the highest professional offices in the state, and at the hands of men who had been the most conspicuous supporters of the Revolution.* With Miss Redman, André was also intimate; the buttons playfully severed from their coats by Stanley and himself, and presented to her as parting-keepsakes when they left Philadelphia, are yet preserved, as also are a number of silhouettes of himself and various of his friends, cut by him for this lady. For her, too, he wrote, on the 2nd January, 1778, these pretty *vers de société*, to a German air that he had perhaps composed or picked up in his wanderings:—

> Return, enraptur'd hours,
> When Delia's heart was mine;
> When she with wreaths of flowers
> My temples would entwine.
>
> When jealousy nor care
> Corroded in my breast —

---

* Fines of £6 and of £13 are affixed to his name on various occasions in the returns of Capt. Paschal's company, 2nd battalion. See Accts. Lieuts. and Sub-Lieuts. Philadelphia City: 1777-1783.

> But visions light as air
> Presided o'er my rest.
>
> Now, nightly round my bed
> No airy visions play;
> No flow'rets crown my head
> Each vernal holiday.
>
> For far from these sad plains
> My lovely Delia flies;
> And rack'd with jealous pains
> Her wretched lover dies.

Some may find allusion in these lines to the writer's affair with Miss Sneyd. There is no evidence that his heart was bound by new ties while in this country; and his freedom from the grosser passions of his fellows was especially observed. It was likewise noticed, as an instance of his courtesy, that neither while a prisoner at Lancaster, or in power as Grey's aide, did he ever join in the contemptuous language so often applied to the Americans. He did not speak even of those in arms as rebels; *colonists* was the gentler phrase by which he referred to them.

During all the war, the favorite amusement of the British army was amateur theatricals. Wherever it found itself in quarters, at once a dramatic corps sprung up. In 1775-6, when beleaguered in Boston, Burgoyne and his fellows fitted up a playhouse (in an abandoned meeting-house, it is said); the roof of which, according to an English writer, was destroyed by American shells, and the wardrobe and curtain much injured. Here the officers gave Tamerlane, The Busybody, and the like. It opened with Zara, to which Sir John wrote an apposite prologue; and the bills were sent to Washington and to Hancock. It might well have closed with another of Burgoyne's bantlings — The Blockade of Boston; the performance of which was disagreeably interrupted by practical skirmishings on the outposts. In 1779-80 the captives of Saratoga, detained at Charlottesville, erected a theatre for themselves. At Philadelphia, the royal officers were more fortunate in finding one standing to their hand. On the south side of South Street (to be out of the bounds of the city, the regulations of which were opposed to the stage), near 4th, was a large, ugly, ill-conditioned wooden building, the third public playhouse that had been opened in or about Philadelphia. It was built in 1760, and was long disused. The scenes of war outshone the mimic pageantries of the sock and buskin; and one at least of the old company, Francis Mentges, a dancer, was now an officer of some repute in our army. The house was not a good one. The great square wooden columns, that supported the upper tier and the roof, interrupted the view from the boxes; the stage was lighted by plain lamps without glasses; everything betokened ill-taste and dilapidation. But any theatre was better than none; and it was without hesitation decided to make the most of this shabby barn. The stage-box on the east side was probably that occupied by Howe; it was afterwards appropriated to Washington, who himself was partial to the drama, and during his Presidency made a point of attending the representations of The Poor Soldier. Above the entrance was the Rabelaisian motto — *Totus mundus agit histrionem;* which the tyros translated, "We act Mondays, Wednesdays, and Fridays." The military amateurs were slow to verify this rendering in the frequency of their performances. Having resolved on their plan, André and Oliver De Lancy — "a lusty, fat, ruddy-looking young fellow between 20 and 30 years of age," went to work to prepare the needful scenery and decorations. André's readiness with the brush has already been declared. On this occasion he produced effects that might have stood beside the scenic labors of Hogarth, De Loutherbourg, or Stansfield himself. His foliage was uncommonly spirited and graceful. The two amateurs made several very useful and attractive additions to the old stock scenery; one of which, from André's brush, demands, says Durang, a particular record.

"It was a landscape presenting a distant champagne country, and a winding rivulet extending from the front of the picture to the extreme distance. In the foreground and centre a gentle cascade (the water exquisitely executed) was overshadowed by a group of majestic forest-trees. The perspective was excellently preserved; the foliage, verdure, and general colouring was artistically toned and glazed. . . . It was a drop-scene, and hung about the middle of the third entrance, as called in stage-directions. The name of André was inscribed in large black letters on the back of it, thus placed no doubt by his own hand on its completion; — sometimes a custom with scenic artists." *

On the 24th December, 1777, matters were sufficiently advanced for the undertakers to determine on the piece they should first appear in, and to advertise for an accountant or sub-treasurer, a swift and clear writer for the distribution of parts, and for practised scene-shifters and carpenters. The play first resolved on was perhaps The Wonder, or A Woman keeps a Secret. It was advertised for as " wanted immediately for the use of the theatre, to borrow or buy," on the 3rd January; but if there was any one point on which the Presbyterian and Quaker agreed, it was in aversion to theatres, and the piece was not soon forthcoming. Accordingly, on the 14th January, for the benefit of the widows and orphans of the army, were given the comedies of No One's

* Few persons of taste who have ever seen this drop will hesitate to confirm its praises. The " Old South," as the theatre came to be known, sank from the hour when playhouses might lawfully exist within the city limits. It became at last the resort of the most depraved of both sexes, and the witness of their infamies. In 1821, it was burned down; and despite every effort to save the scenery, particularly the drop painted by André, its contents were consumed. Some part of the walls yet stand. For years previously throngs of the vulgar had crowded the house every Fourth of July, to witness a piece well suited to their tastes and understandings, and founded on his fate.

There is still preserved at Philadelphia a figure of a British grenadier, cut out of half-inch board, six feet high, with rounded edges, and painted to the life, which tradition says was made by André. If so, it was probably a stage decoration. It got into American hands. and was used in practical joke to heartily frighten some of our officers.

Enemy but his Own, and The Deuce is in Him. The characters were represented by officers of the army and navy; the doors opened at 6 P. M., and the play began at 7; the tickets were a dollar for box or pit, and half a dollar for the gallery. No money was to be taken at the door, nor were more tickets sold than the house would hold. I have had the fortune to stumble upon a collection of specimens of all these theatrical bills, tickets, notices, &c., with an indorsement of the number struck off of each, that had been preserved by James Humphreys, the printer, together with all the handbills of proclamations and the like issued during the Occupation. From these may be deduced some idea of what the house held. Of notices of performance, 1000 copies would be printed; and 660 box-tickets. And so popular did the entertainment soon become, that the doors were opened ere sunset, and they who wished places kept for them had to send their servants to the house at 4 P. M.

The first performance was eminently successful. Despite the legislative prohibition of public theatricals, amateur representations were in great vogue with the more refined and cultivated classes in various parts of America. In staid Connecticut, the late venerable Bishop Griswold at the early age of seven shone as a page in Fair Rosamond in 1773, and in 1781, was great as Zanga in The Revenge. In Pennsylvania, particularly among the churchmen and moderate dissenters, a like taste prevailed; and though the playhouse could only be reached on foot, by miry and unlighted paths (for there were no hackney-coaches in those days, and very few private coaches), the ladies did not shrink to trip thither and back home after nightfall. The house was opened for the season and the play introduced by the following prologue, which there is much reason for attributing to André, both in com position and delivery: —

PROLOGUE.

Once more, ambitious of theatric glory,
Howe's strolling company appears before ye.

O'er hills and dales and bogs, thro' wind and weather
And many hair-breadth 'scape, we've scrambled hither.
For we, true vagrants of the Thespian race,
Whilst summer lasts ne'er know a settled place.
Anxious to prove the merit of our band,
A chosen squadron wanders thro' the land.
How beats each Yankie bosom at our drum —
—'Hark, Jonathan! zaunds, here's the strollers come!'
Spruced up with top-knots and their Sunday dress,
With eager looks the maidens round us press.
—'Jemima, see — an't this a charming sight —
Look, Tabitha — Oh Lord! I wish 'twas night!'
Wing'd with variety our moments fly,
Each minute tinctur'd with a different dye.
Balls we have plenty, and *al Fresco* too,
Such as Soho or King-street never knew.
Did you but see sometimes how we're arrayed,
You'd fancy we design'd a masquerade.
'T would tire your patience was I to relate here
Our routs, drums, hurricanes, and Fêtes Champêtres.
Let Ranelagh still boast her ample dome;
While heaven's our canopy, the earth's our room.
Still let Vauxhall her marshall'd lamps display,
And gild her shades with artificial day:
In lofty terms old vaunting Sadler's Wells
Of her tight-rope and ladder-dancing tells,
But Cunningham in both by far excels.

Now winter * —— Hark! and I must not say No —
'But soft, a word or two before I go.'
Benevolence first urged us to engage,
And boldly venture on a public stage:
To guard the helpless orphan's tender years,
To wipe away the afflicted parent's tears,
To sooth the sorrows of the widow'd breast,
To lull the friendless bosom's cares to rest;
This our design — and sure in such a cause
E'en Error's self might challenge some applause.
With candor then our imperfections scan,
And where the Actor fails, absolve the Man.

* Stage-bell rings.

The success of the first night was really beyond expectation, and a notice was issued begging gentlemen not to bribe the door-keepers : " The Foreign Gentleman who slipped a Guinea and a half into the hands of the boxkeeper, and forced his way into the house, is requested to send to the office of the theatre in Front-street, that it may be returned." Such advertisements do not occur nowadays. The performances during the rest of the season were as follows: On the 26th January, The Minor, and The Deuce is in Him; on the 9th February, The Minor, and Duke and No Duke; on the 16th, Constant Couple, and Duke and No Duke. The illness of a chief actor and other causes prevented any more plays till March 2nd, when The Constant Couple and The Mock Doctor were given; on the 9th, The Inconstant and The Mock Doctor, with a display of fireworks; on the 16th, The Inconstant, and Lethe; on the 25th, The First Part of King Henry IV., and The Mock Doctor; on the 30th, The First Part, &c., and Lethe. Then one of the *actresses* fell sick; Passion Week came on; and nothing was played before The Wonder and The Mock Doctor, on the 24th April. The Liar and A Trip to Scotland were played on the 1st May; a copy of Douglas was advertised for on the 2nd; on the 6th were represented The Liar, and Duke and No Duke; and on the 19th, Dr. Home's play of Douglas, and the Citizen. This was the last performance. When the curtain fell, the officers resorted to a sort of club-room that was established in the large apartments of the City Tavern, where their weekly balls were held; and here Charles Lee was introduced in March, 1778, after witnessing the evening's play. The bills give no distribution of parts, and we cannot tell what characters came to André's share; but we may well believe that in Douglas he appeared as the young hero whose feigned conditions so much resembled his own.

> "Obscure and friendless, be the army sought,
> Resolved to hunt for fame, and with his sword
> To gain distinction which his birth denied.
> In this attempt, unknown he might have perish'd
> And gain'd with all his valor but oblivion.
> Now graced by thee, his virtue serves no more,
> Beneath despair. The soldier now of hope,
> He stands conspicuous; fame and great renown
> Are brought within the compass of his sword."

And in another passage of the same play, we find language that indeed expresses what seems to have been the key-note of André's character. "Living or dead, let me but be renown'd," appears truly to have been the unaltered wish of his soul.

Without going into too many particulars, there is abundant testimony that gambling, races, plays, and gallantries occupied more of the attention of the royal officers, during this winter, than was at all consistent with the good of the service.

The military feats about Philadelphia, in the earlier part of 1778, were neither numerous or important. Howe aimed at little more than keeping a passage clear for the country-people, within certain bounds, to come in with marketing. The incident known as the Battle of the Kegs was celebrated by Hopkinson in a very amusing song that, wedded to the air of Maggy Lauder, was long the favorite of the American military vocalists; but it hardly seems to have been noticed at Philadelphia, until the whig version came in. The local newspapers say that, in January, 1778, a barrel floating down the Delaware being taken up by some boys exploded in their hands, and killed or maimed one of them. A few days after, some of the transports fired a few guns at several other kegs that appeared on the tide; but no particular notice of the occurrence was taken. These torpedoes were sent down in the hope that they would damage the shipping. The Queen's Rangers and other troops were constantly employed in patrols and forages, but, beyond bringing in Americans whom they caught stopping and stripping the market-people, there was little to be done. Howe, too, set on foot several loyal corps of the vicinity that proved very useful. Hovenden, with his Philadelphia Light Dragoons and some of Thomas's Bucks County Volunteers, made a foray on the 14th of February, and brought in a number of prisoners. On the next day 400 Americans came within 600 yards of one of the pickets, "and after making a terrible howling," and exchanging fires, retired leaving three dead. On the 18th,

Hovenden and Thomas passed up to Jenk's fulling-mill in Bucks, and thence to Newtown, surprising the Americans posted there to intercept market-people, and bringing in thirty-four prisoners as well as two coach-loads of things from Galloway's country-seat. This was doubtless a prime object of the move; and it is thus we can account for the loss of invaluable papers (particularly Franklin's) respecting our history, that were left in Galloway's hands. On the 23rd, Hovenden went thirty miles up the Skippack Road, and returned on the 24th, with 130 fine cattle and some prisoners. He reported the Americans as excessively severe on market-people, and that Lacey had burned the mills about the city to the infinite misery of the town-folk; to whose poor, salted beef was now publicly distributed. Some of the Americans had great reputation as market-stoppers; these, when caught, were decorated with their spoils — eggs, women's shoes, and the like — and so paraded through the streets to gaol; or were publicly whipped in the market-place, and drummed out of town.* Simcoe very much applauds the skill with which a loyalist, pretending to be an American commissary, turned a fat drove of Washington's cattle into British beef. Such little stratagems, however, were usually crowned by our people with a halter. In these patrollings the two antagonists occasionally came in contact.

* "On Saturday last, a rebel light horseman, loaded with several wallets across his shoulders, and a large basket on his arm, full of market-truck, of which he had robbed the country people coming to market, was brought in, having been taken a few miles from the lines at the very time he was plundering. The drollery of his appearance afforded no little amusement to the populace."—*Penn. Ledger*, Apr. 22, 1778. Galloway says that it was usual to give 200 lashes to the market-people caught coming to town; or to send them in to Howe, with G. H. branded on their flesh with a hot iron; and the local journals of March, 1778, tell of several persons, taken on their way to buy provisions, being court-martialled at Wilmington and sentenced, some to be hung, others to be flogged. They got off with being tied to the gallows and thus receiving 250 to 500 lashes from "wired cats that cut large pieces from them at every stroke." Some enlisted with the Americans to avoid punishment, and then deserted. So, at least, says the Ledger, No. 153.

On the 20th of March a large party of American horse were encountered beyond Schuylkill by the mounted yägers, and defeated with loss. On another occasion, during the occupation, Generals Cadwalader and Reed with one follower riding and reconnoitring through the country, had stopped at the house of a Quaker to whom they were known. Passing on, and being caught in a rain, they had turned the blue cartouche cloaks they wore so that the red lining was exposed to the shower, and were hastily galloping back to camp when, as they repassed the Quaker's house, he came rushing out to them. "Gentlemen, gentlemen!" he cried, mistaking their scarlet for British uniform, "if you will only turn back you will certainly catch General Reed and General Cadwalader, who have just gone down that road!" His confusion at discovering his blunder may be guessed; and it afterwards came near to hang him when Reed was in power. For piloting Abercrombie on the 1st of May, when Lacey's post at the Crooked Billet was broken up, John Roberts actually was hung, after whig supremacy was established at Philadelphia.

The opening of the campaign of 1778 found the British councils at London in great perplexity. Howe's recall was a settled thing; but it was as yet unknown whether the Americans would listen to the new commissioners sent to them, or ally themselves with France. Lord Amherst, a great authority with the king, advised that in the latter contingency the royal armies should be withdrawn from the continent to the West Indies; and in any event, that a retreat from Philadelphia to New York should at once be made. Meanwhile, Sir William was looking about for an opening to cover his retirement with an active lustre; stimulated, perhaps, thereto by the friendly satire of his subordinates, one of whom (afterwards General Meadows, then the lieutenant-colonel of the 55th, Howe's own regiment) bluntly reproached his commander's slothful devotion to pleasure, and asked him if he did not think it was now time to get out of his bed and to get on his horse. On the 1st of April, the army was ordered to be ready, with three days' provision and at a moment's warning, for an enterprise on the 5th. But no large movement was made. A detachment of 1400, indeed, by a night-march relieved Billingsport, where our people were besieging some refugees; and, on the 24th and the 26th, parties (one led by De Lancy) went forth successfully against bodies of Americans. Transports were now fast coming in with forage from New York, and troops and stores from Cork; on the 7th of May, Clinton was at Billingsport; and on the 8th he arrived at Philadelphia. On the 10th, an expedition sent on the 7th to Bordentown to burn the American frigates and stores there returned, having succeeded perfectly. On the night of April 30th, Abercrombie led a party of light troops, with which were some of James's and Hovenden's loyalists, against Lacey near the Crooked Billet. By the British account, Lacey resisted at first, but was forced to fly, and was pursued four miles. His loss was 80 to 100 killed, and fifty taken; besides ten wagons of baggage and stores. His huts, and what equipage could not be brought off were burned.

No longer relying on militia, in whatever strength, to fulfil the ends required of a stout outlying force between himself and the enemy, Washington on the 18th of May ordered La Fayette, with five guns and 2500 of the flower of the army, to pass over the Valley Forge bridge, and take post in his front. The Marquis accordingly placed himself at Barren Hill, on this side of the Schuylkill, and about midway between the two armies. But the Quaker with whom he quartered himself is said to have promptly communicated the circumstance to Howe. The news reached Philadelphia that La Fayette's "tattered retinue had abandoned their mudholes" and were advancing towards Germantown. An attack was instantly concerted. There were plenty of men in Howe's ranks who knew every inch of the ground; some of the loyalist troopers were residents of the place itself, and were the best of guides. So inevitable appeared success that Sir William, ere setting forth, invited ladies to meet La Fayette at supper on his return; while Lord Howe, who went along as a volunteer, prepared a frigate for the immediate transmission to England of the expected captive. In a war like this, where public opinion was so powerful, the effect of such an event would have been prodigious. It is pleasing to reflect, not only that the design failed, but that its failure was due to an officer who held American soldiership in the extreme of contempt, and whose whole American history, whether before or during the war, is a tissue of arrogance and shortcomings.

"I was present at this move," says Sir Henry Clinton; "it was made before I took the command. As Sir W. Howe was there, I gave no opinion about the plan or execution."* To an unprofessional man, there seems to be room for but one opinion about either. The plan was admirable; the execution imperfect. With 5,000 men, Grant marched on the evening of the 19th by the Delaware Road to a sufficient distance; when, turning to the left by Whitemarsh, he was at sunrise a mile in La Fayette's rear, and between him and the Valley Forge bridge. At a later hour, Grey (and of course André) brought up 2,000 men by a more direct road on the south side of the Schuylkill, and established himself at a ford two or three miles in front of La Fayette's right flank. A force was also stationed at Chestnut Hill. Thus the Americans were so environed, that in no direction could they march without encountering an enemy, unless they could repass the river; and there was but one ford (Matson's) now available for this purpose, which was even nearer to Grant's position than their own.

Howe had, by a wonder, ordered matters so cleverly that not the least whisper of his intentions reached our people beforehand. It was on a play-night that the expedition set forth, and most of the officers were witnessing Douglas when

* Clinton MS.

the troops were getting under arms or actually in motion.
But so large a force could not leave town without the knowledge of Washington's faithful intelligencers; and by the time they reached their positions, the fact was known in our camp. Grant's advance was, at sunrise, halted at a spot where the road forked; one course leading to Barren Hill, another to Matson's Ford. For an hour and a half his column stood at ease; the men unfatigued, but chagrined and angry, the General in doubt what line to pursue. He was vainly urged to take possession of Matson's Ford; but thinking, probably, that his situation would enable him either to attack La Fayette by the one road, whether he moved on it or remained at Barren Hill, or to intercept him by the other if he tried for the ford, he remained idle. Nevertheless, the British advance was now no secret. Simcoe, who led Grant's column at the prescribed pace of two miles an hour, had just after dawn encountered a patrol that retired before him; two officers, who had made an early start from Barren Hill to Jersey, hastened back with tidings of the enemy's approach; and an American on the road, seeing them on their way, had hastened across the country to give warning. From Valley Forge also alarm-gun after alarm-gun now pealed forth. The post was withdrawn from this side of the bridge; preparations for its destruction were made; and it was even alleged that Washington almost looked forward to retreating, with all he could carry, towards the Susquehannah.

La Fayette proved himself adequate to the occasion. In a moment, as it were, his dangers were revealed, and the one possible means of extrication resorted to. Dispositions were made in the church-yard as though to receive Grey; his artillery, by a well-directed fire, encouraged the idea that he purposed to engage. His real aim was of course flight, and by the ford; but to attain it, he must pass within a short distance of Grant, who was nearer to it than himself. By feigned movements as though for an attack, and an occasional display of the heads of columns, he for a time persuaded the Englishman that an action was imminent. Meantime his troops, as fast as they could come up, were hurrying across the ford, till at last the artillery only and a body of Oneida savages remained on this side the stream. These were also now brought over, and on the high grounds beyond our men were secure. Grant at last came up, and ordered the advance to move on; but too late. They saw but a party of our troops dotting the surface of the water, like the floats of a seine. The prey had escaped. Grant was hopelessly in their rear; and when Grey's column closed in, there was nothing between the British lines. The only skirmishing even that seems to have occurred was between a body of light-horse and the Oneidas. Neither had ever encountered a like foe; and when the cavalry unexpectedly rode among the savages, the whooping and scampering of the one, and the flashing swords and curveting steeds of the other party, excited such a common terror that both fled with the utmost precipitation. Irritated and empty-handed Howe marched back to town, with no one but his own officers to blame for his ill-success.* On the 24th of May, he surrendered the command to Clinton, and arrived in England on the 2nd of July. One of the last acts of his authority was to ordain a lottery, on the 15th of May, directed by substantial citizens, to raise £1,000 for the poor of the city.

Whatever may have been his shortcomings to ministers, it is certain that Howe was beloved by his troops. He was ever careful of them in battle, and in quarters his own indulgences were shared by them. Dissipation, gambling, relaxation of discipline, may have indeed tainted the army; but they knew their leader to be personally brave, and capable in the field; and by his very errors their own comfort was

* " It will no doubt have struck whoever reads this, that La Fayette escaped exactly by the same means the garrison of Fort Lee had done: with this difference, that Lord Cornwallis had not been informed of the situation of Newbridge, and Sir William Erskine repeatedly entreated General Grant to march directly to Matson's Ford. Had he done so, not a man of La Fayette's corps would have escaped." — *Clinton MS.*

THE MISCHIANZA.

increased. It was therefore resolved, by a number of those most conspicuous in the pursuit of pleasure and attachment to the General, to commemorate their esteem for him by an entertainment not less novel than splendid. This was the famous Mischianza of the 18th of May, 1778; the various nature of which is expressed by its name, while its conception is evidently taken from Lord Derby's fête champêtre at The Oaks, June 9th, 1774, on occasion of Lord Stanley's marriage to the Duke of Hamilton's daughter. Burgoyne was the conductor of this elegant affair, with its masques, fireworks, dancing, &c.; and for it he wrote his play,—The Maid of the Oaks. The regatta, or aquatic procession, in the Mischianza was suggested by a like pageant on the Thames, June 23rd, 1775. Each of these festivities—the first of the kind in England—had been much talked of and admired at the time.

Both in the plan and execution of this affair, André's near alliance with head-quarters led him to be much concerned. His brush as well as his taste was engaged in the decorations, nor was his pen idle. A mock tournament—perhaps the first in America—was a part of the play; and for this he selected as esquire his brother William Lewis André, now a lieutenant in the 7th. The appointed scene was at the country-seat of Mr. Wharton: then a fine stately mansion, surrounded with large trees and its grounds extending uninterruptedly to the Delaware; now pent about with factory buildings and houses, and occupied as a public school.* Here

---

* The proprietor of this estate is described as a man of no little social importance. He was usually styled *Duke* by reason of his manners. When Sir William Draper was at Philadelphia, Mr. Wharton, in visiting him, entered hat in hand. Sir William condescendingly bade him be covered: he would dispense with those marks of respect, he said, which he knew it was ungrateful to Friends to render. The visitor, however, coolly replied that he had uncovered for his own comfort, the day being warm, and that whenever he found it convenient he should certainly resume his hat. He was utterly outgeneralled though during the occupation by a private soldier. The man had laid aside his musket to trespass on Mr. Wharton's grounds. The owner, possessing himself of it, by threats of carrying it to the guard-house

Sir Henry Calder was lodged, whose name is subscribed to the invitations. It was not a bad season for one branch of the festivity; remarkably fine green turtle, just arrived from New Providence, and choice Claret and Madeira wines, were then in market and doubtless contributed to the cold collation that crowned the whole. Much of the decorations, as the Sienna marble, &c., was on canvas, in the manner of stage-scenery. The supper-room was built however for the occasion, and at every toast given in it, a flourish of music was answered with three cheers. The mirrors, lustres, &c., which adorned the scene were borrowed, says Watson, from the town-folk, and all were returned uninjured, with the ornaments that had been added still appended. Nothing in short more disastrous than the loss of a silver watch, for which a guinea reward, " and no questions asked," was offered, seems to have occurred. The young ladies of Philadelphia present numbered about fifty; the remainder being married women. The intended wife of Captain Montresor was the leader of one rank, while the second was headed by the future bride of another officer.* The queen of the Mischianza, however, is said to have been a lady who, in describing it afterwards, represented André as "the charm of the company." His

---

compelled the man to humiliate himself thoroughly by way of penance; but no sooner was his piece returned, than he fell on the Quaker, and by menaces of wounds and death made him pass under the Caudine Forks in the most comprehensive sense of the term.

* One of David Franks' daughters was married to Captain (afterwards General) Oliver De Lancy; and another to Colonel (afterwards General Sir Henry) Johnston of the 28th, who was surprised by Wayne at Stony Point, and whom Cornwallis in Ireland thus describes, July 15, 1799: "Johnston, although a wrong-headed blockhead, is adored for his defence at New Ross, and considered as the Saracen of the South." His wife was celebrated in America for her undaunted wit, that, generally exercised on the Americans, sometimes found a British subject. It was she who corrected Sir H. Clinton when he called on a ball-room band for "Britons strike home!"—"Britons go home, you mean," she cried.—And see Littell's Graydon, 469.

Fac-similes of André's drawings of costumes, &c., and of a Mischianza ticket, are in *Smith and Watson;* 1847.

designs for the costumes of the ladies of the Burning Mountain, and the Blended Rose, are still preserved. The latter was a Polonaise, or flowing robe of white silk, with a spangled pink sash, and spangled shoes and stockings; a veil spangled and trimmed with silver lace, and a towering head-dress of pearls and jewels. The former had their white Polonaises bound with black, and sashes of the same. The wharves and house-tops towards the water were thronged with spectators as the boats, filled with these gayly dressed nymphs and not less brightly clad gallants, passed from the northern part of the city to the scene of pleasure. But André himself has given a full account of the whole proceeding.

ANDRÉ TO A FRIEND.

PHILADELPHIA, May 23, 1778.

For the first time in my life I write to you with unwillingness. The ship that carries home Sir William Howe will convey this letter to you, and not even the pleasure of conversing with my friend can secure me from the general dejection I see around me, or remove the share I must take in the universal regret and disappointment which his approaching departure hath spread throughout the whole army. We see him taken from us at a time when we most stand in need of so skilful and popular a commander; when the experience of three years, and the knowledge he hath acquired of the country and people, have added to the confidence we always placed in his conduct and abilities. You know he was always a favourite with the military; but the affection and attachment which all ranks of officers in this army bear him, can only be known by those who have at this time seen them in their effects. I do not believe there is upon record an instance of a Commander-in-Chief having so universally endeared himself to those under his command; or of one who received such signal and flattering proofs of their love. That our sentiments might be the more universally and unequivocally known, it was resolved amongst us, that we should give him as splendid an entertainment as the shortness of the time, and our present situation, would allow us. For the expences, the whole army would have most chearfully contributed; but it was requisite to draw the line somewhere, and twenty-two field-officers joined in a subscription adequate to the plan they meant to adopt. I know your curiosity will be raised on this occasion; I shall therefore give you as particular an account of our *Mischianza* as I have been able to collect. From the name you will perceive that it was made up of a variety of entertainments. Four of the gentlemen subscribers were appointed managers — Sir John Wrottesley, Col. O'Hara, Major Gardiner, and Montresor, the chief engineer. On the tickets of admission, which they gave out for Monday the 18th, was engraved, in a shield, a view of the sea, with the setting sun, and on a wreath, the words *Luceo discedens, aucto splendore resurgam.* At top was the General's crest, with *vive! vale!* All round the shield ran a vignette, and various military trophies filled up the ground.

A grand regatta began the entertainment. It consisted of three divisions. In the first was the Ferret galley, having on board several General-Officers, and a number of Ladies. In the centre, was the Hussar galley with Sir William and Lord Howe, Sir Henry Clinton, the Officers of their suite, and some Ladies. The Cornwallis galley brought up the rear, having on board General Knyphausen and his suite, three British Generals, and a party of Ladies. On each quarter of these gallies, and forming their division, were five flat boats, lined with green cloth, and filled with Ladies and Gentlemen. In front of the whole were three flat boats, with a band of music in each. Six barges rowed about each flank, to keep off the swarm of boats that covered the river from side to side. The gallies were dressed out in a variety of colours and streamers, and in each flat boat was displayed the flag of its own division. In the stream opposite the centre of the city, the Fanny armed ship, magnificently decorated, was placed at anchor, and at some distance ahead lay his Majesty's ship Roebuck, with the Admiral's flag hoisted at the foretop-mast-head. The transport ships, extending in a line the whole length of the town, appeared with colours flying, and crowded with spectators, as were also the openings of the several wharfs on shore, exhibiting the most picturesque and enlivening scene the eye could desire. The rendezvous was at Knight's Wharf, at the northern extremity of the city. By half after four, the whole company were embarked, and the signal being made by the Vigilant's manning ship, the three divisions rowed slowly down, preserving their proper intervals, and keeping time to the music that led the fleet. Arrived between the Fanny and the Market Wharf, a signal was made from one of the boats ahead, and the whole lay upon their oars, while the music played *God save the King*, and three cheers given from the vessels were returned from the multitude on shore. By this time, the flood-tide became too rapid for the gallies to advance; they were therefore quitted, and the company disposed of in the different barges. This alteration broke in upon the order of procession, but was necessary to give sufficient time for displaying the entertainments that were prepared on shore.

The landing-place was at the Old Fort, a little to the southward of the town, fronting the building prepared for the reception of the company about four hundred yards from the water by a gentle ascent. As soon as the General's barge was seen to push for the shore, a salute of seventeen guns was fired from the Roebuck, and, after some interval, by the same number from the Vigilant. The company, as they disembarked, arranged themselves into a line of procession, and advanced through an avenue formed by two files of grenadiers, and a line of light-horse supporting each file. This avenue led to a square lawn of two hundred and fifty yards on each side, lined with troops, and properly prepared for the exhibition of a tilt and tournament, according to the customs and ordinances of ancient chivalry. We proceeded through the centre of the square. The music, consisting of all the bands of the army, moved in front. The Managers, with favours of white and blue ribbands in their breasts, followed next in order. The General, Admiral, and the rest of the company, succeeded promiscuously.

In front appeared the building, bounding the view through a vista formed by two triumphal arches, erected at proper intervals in a line with the landing-place. Two pavilions, with rows of benches rising one above the other, and serving as the wings of the first triumphal arch, received the Ladies; while the Gentlemen ranged themselves in convenient order on each side. On the front seat of each pavilion were placed seven of the principal young Ladies of the country, dressed in Turkish habits, and wearing in their turbans the favours with which they meant to reward the several Knights who were to contend in their honour. These arrangements were scarce made when the sound of trumpets was heard at a distance; and a band of Knights, dressed in ancient habits of white and red silk, and mounted on grey horses richly caparisoned in trappings of the same colours, entered the lists, attended by their Esquires on foot, in suitable apparel, in the following order:

Four trumpeters, properly habited, their trumpets decorated with small pendent banners. A herald in his robes of ceremony; on his tunic was the device of his band, two roses intertwined, with the Motto, *We droop when separated.*

Lord Cathcart, superbly mounted on a managed horse, appeared as chief of these Knights; two young black slaves, with sashes and drawers of blue and white silk, wearing large silver clasps round their necks and arms, their breasts and shoulders bare, held his stirrups. On his right hand walked Capt. Hazard, and on his left Capt. Brownlow, his two Esquires, the one bearing his lance, the other his shield.

His device was Cupid riding on a Lion; the Motto, *Sur-*

mounted by Love. His Lordship appeared in honour of Miss Auchmuty.

Then came in order the Knights of his band, each attended by his Squire bearing his lance and shield.

1st. Knight, Hon. Capt. Cathcart, in honour of Miss N. White. — Squire, Capt. Peters. — Device, a heart and sword; Motto, *Love and Honour.*

2nd. Knight, Lieut. Bygrove, in honour of Miss Craig. — Squire, Lieut. Nichols. — Device, Cupid tracing a Circle; Motto, *Without End.*

3rd. Knight, Capt. André, in honour of Miss P. Chew. — Squire, Lieut. André. — Device, two Game-cocks fighting; Motto, *No Rival.*

4th. Knight, Capt. Horneck, in honour of Miss N. Redman. — Squire, Lieut. Talbot. — Device, a burning Heart; Motto, *Absence cannot extinguish.*

5th. Knight, Capt. Matthews, in honour of Miss Bond. — Squire, Lieut. Hamilton. — Device, a winged Heart; Motto, *Each Fair by Turn.*

6th. Knight, Lieut. Sloper, in honour of Miss M. Shippen. — Squire, Lieut. Brown. — Device, a Heart and Sword; Motto, *Honour and the Fair.*

After they had made the circuit of the square, and saluted the Ladies as they passed before the pavilions, they ranged themselves in a line with that in which were the Ladies of their Device; and their Herald (Mr. Beaumont), advancing into the centre of the square, after a flourish of trumpets, proclaimed the following challenge:

" The Knights of the Blended Rose, by me their Herald,
" proclaim and assert that the Ladies of the Blended Rose
" excel in wit, beauty, and every accomplishment, those of the
" *whole World;* and, should any Knight or Knights be so
" hardy as to dispute or deny it, they are ready to enter the
" lists with them, and maintain their assertions by deeds of
" arms, according to the laws of ancient chivalry."

At the third repetition of the challenge the sound of

trumpets was heard from the opposite side of the square; and another Herald, with four Trumpeters, dressed in black and orange, galloped into the lists. He was met by the Herald of the Blended Rose, and after a short parley they both advanced in front of the pavilions, when the Black Herald (Lieut. Moore) ordered his trumpets to sound, and then proclaimed defiance to the challenge in the following words:

"The Knights of the Burning Mountain present them-"selves here, not to contest by words, but to disprove by "deeds, the vain-glorious assertions of the Knights of the "Blended Rose, and enter these lists to maintain, that the "Ladies of the Burning Mountain are not excelled in beauty, "virtue, or accomplishments, by any in the universe."

He then returned to the part of the barrier through which he had entered, and shortly after the Black Knights, attended by their Squires, rode into the lists in the following order:

Four Trumpeters preceding the Herald, on whose tunic was represented a mountain, sending forth flames. — Motto, *I burn for ever.*

Captain Watson, of the guards, as Chief, dressed in a magnificent suit of black and orange silk, and mounted on a black managed horse, with trappings of the same colour with his own dress, appeared in honour of Miss Franks. He was attended in the same manner with Lord Cathcart. Capt. Scot bore his lance, and Lieut. Lyttelton his shield. The Device, a Heart, with a Wreath of Flowers; Motto, *Love and Glory.*

1st. Knight, Lieut. Underwood, in honour of Miss S. Shippen. — Squire, Ensign Haverkam. — Device, a Pelican feeding her young; Motto, *For those I love.*

2nd. Knight, Lieut. Winyard, in honour of Miss P. Shippen. — Squire, Capt. Boscawen. — Device, a Bay-leaf; Motto, *Unchangeable.*

3rd. Knight, Lieut. Deleval, in honour of Miss B. Bond.— Squire, Capt. Thorne. — Device, a Heart, aimed at by several arrows, and struck by one ; Motto, *One only pierces me.*

4th. Knight, Monsieur Montluissant, (Lieut. of the Hessian Chasseurs,) in honour of Miss B. Redman. — Squire, Capt. Campbell. — Device, a Sunflower turning towards the Sun ; Motto, *Je vise à vous.*

5th. Knight, Lieut. Hobbart, in honour of Miss S. Chew. — Squire, Lieut. Briscoe. — Device, Cupid piercing a Coat of Mail with his Arrow ; Motto, *Proof to all but Love.*

6th. Knight, Brigade-Major Tarlton, in honour of Miss W Smith. — Squire, Capt. Heart. — Device, a Light Dragoon ; Motto, *Swift, vigilant, and bold.*

After they had rode round the lists, and made their obeisance to the Ladies, they drew up fronting the White Knights ; and the Chief of these having thrown down his gauntlet, the Chief of the Black Knights directed his Esquire to take it up. The Knights then received their lances from their Esquires, fixed their shields on their left arms, and making a general salute to each other, by a very graceful movement of their lances, turned round to take their career, and, encountering in full gallop, shivered their spears. In the second and third encounter they discharged their pistols. In the fourth they fought with their swords. At length the two Chiefs, spurring forward into the centre, engaged furiously in single combat, till the Marshal of the Field (Major Gwyne) rushed in between the Chiefs, and declared that the Fair Damsels of the Blended Rose and Burning Mountain were perfectly satisfied with the proofs of love, and the signal feats of valour, given by their respective Knights ; and commanded them, as they prized the future favours of their Mistresses, that they would instantly desist from further combat. Obedience being paid by the Chiefs to this order, they joined their respective bands. The White Knights and their attendants filed off to the left, the Black Knights to the right ; and, after passing each other at the lower side of the quadrangle, moved up alternately, till they approached the pavilion of the Ladies, when they gave a general salute.

A passage being now opened between the two pavilions, the Knights, preceded by their Squires and the bands of music, rode through the first triumphal arch, and arranged themselves to the right and left. This arch was erected in honour of Lord Howe. It presented two fronts, in the Tuscan order; the pediment was adorned with various naval trophies, and at the top was the figure of Neptune, with a trident in his right hand. In a nich, on each side, stood a Sailor, with a drawn cutlass. Three Plumes of Feathers were placed on the summit of each wing, and in the entablature was this inscription: *Laus illi debetur, et a me gratia major.* The interval between the two arches was an avenue three hundred feet long, and thirty-four broad. It was lined on each side with a file of troops; and the colours of all the army, planted at proper distances, had a beautiful effect in diversifying the scene. Between these colours the Knights and Squires took their stations. The Bands continued to play several pieces of martial music. The Company moved forward in procession, with the Ladies in the Turkish habits in front; as these passed, they were saluted by their Knights, who then dismounted and joined them; and in this order we were all conducted into a garden that fronted the house, through the second triumphal arch, dedicated to the General. This arch was also built in the Tuscan order. On the interior part of the pediment was painted a Plume of Feathers, and various military trophies. At top stood the figure of Fame, and in the entablature this device, — *I, bone, quo virtus tua te vocet; I pede fausto.* On the right-hand pillar was placed a bomb-shell, and on the left a flaming heart. The front next the house was adorned with preparations for a fire-work. From the garden we ascended a flight of steps, covered with carpets, which led into a spacious hall; the panels, painted in imitation of Sienna marble, enclosing festoons of white marble: the surbase, and all below, was black.

In this hall, and in the adjoining apartments, were prepared tea, lemonade, and other cooling liquors, to which the company seated themselves; during which time the Knights came in, and on the knee received their favours from their respective Ladies. One of these rooms was afterwards appropriated for the use of the Pharaoh table: as you entered it, you saw, on a pannel over the chimney, a Cornucopia, exuberantly filled with flowers of the richest colours; over the door, as you went out, another presented itself, shrunk, reversed, and emptied.

From these apartments we were conducted up to a ball-room, decorated in a light, elegant stile of painting. The ground was a pale blue, pannelled with a small gold bead, and in the interior filled with dropping festoons of flowers in their natural colours. Below the surbase the ground was of rose-pink, with drapery festooned in blue. These decorations were heightened by eighty-five mirrours, decked with rose-pink silk ribbands, and artificial flowers; and in the intermediate spaces were thirty-four branches with wax-lights, ornamented in a similar manner.

On the same floor were four drawing-rooms, with sideboards of refreshments, decorated and lighted in the same stile and taste as the ball-room. The ball was opened by the Knights and their Ladies; and the dances continued till ten o'clock, when the windows were thrown open, and a magnificent bouquet of rockets began the fireworks. These were planned by Capt. Montresor, the Chief Engineer, and consisted of twenty different exhibitions, displayed under his direction with the happiest success, and in the highest stile of beauty. Towards the conclusion, the interior part of the triumphal arch was illuminated amidst an uninterrupted flight of rockets and bursting of baloons. The military trophies on each side assumed a variety of transparent colours. The shell and flaming heart on the wings sent forth Chinese fountains, succeeded by fireworks. Fame appeared at top, spangled with stars, and from her trumpet blowing the following device in letters of light, *Tes Lauriers sont immortels.* — A *sauteur* of Rockets, bursting from the pediment, concluded the *feu d'artifice.*

At twelve, supper was announced, and large folding doors, hitherto artfully concealed, being suddenly thrown open, discovered a magnificent saloon of two hundred and ten feet by forty, and twenty-two in height, with three alcoves on each side, which served for side-boards. The ceiling was the segment of a circle, and the sides were painted of a light straw-colour, with vine-leaves and festoon-flowers, some in a bright, some in a darkish green. Fifty-six large pier-glasses, ornamented with green silk artificial flowers and ribbands; a hundred branches with three lights in each, trimmed in the same manner as the mirrours; eighteen lustres, each with twenty-four lights, suspended from the ceiling, and ornamented as the branches; three hundred wax-tapers, disposed along the supper tables; four hundred and thirty covers; twelve hundred dishes; twenty-four black slaves, in oriental dresses, with silver collars and bracelets, ranged in two lines and bending to the ground as the General and Admiral approached the saloon: all these, forming together the most brilliant assemblage of gay objects, and appearing at once as we entered by an easy ascent, exhibited a *coup d'oeil* beyond description magnificent.

Towards the end of supper, the Herald of the Blended Rose, in his habit of ceremony, attended by his trumpeters, entered the saloon, and proclaimed the King's health, the Queen and Royal Family, the Army and Navy, with their respective Commanders, the Knights and their Ladies, the Ladies in general; each of these toasts was followed by a flourish of music. After supper we returned to the ball-room, and continued to dance till four o'clock.

Such, my dear friend, is the description, though a very faint one, of the most splendid entertainment, I believe, ever given by an army to their General. But what must be most grateful to Sir W. Howe is the spirit and motives from which it was given. He goes from this place to-morrow; but, as I understand he means to stay a day or two with his brother on board the Eagle at Billingsport, I shall not seal this letter till I see him depart from Philadelphia.

Sunday, 24th. I am just returned from conducting our beloved General to the water-side, and have seen him receive a more flattering testimony of the love and attachment of his army, than all the pomp and splendor of the *Mischianza* could convey to him. I have seen the most gallant of our officers, and those whom I least suspected of giving such instances of their affection, shed tears while they bid him farewel. The gallant and affectionate General of the Hessians, Knyphausen, was so moved, that he could not finish a compliment he began to pay him in his own name, and that of his Officers who attended him. Sir Henry Clinton attended him to the wharf, where Lord Howe received him into his barge, and they are both gone down to Billingsport. On my return, I saw nothing but dejected countenances.

Adieu, &c.*

I have no hesitation in attributing to André two forms of a poetical address, designed to be spoken on the occasion in honor of Howe, but which Sir William, however gratified, wisely forbade. The first seems intended for recitation by a celestial guest.

> Down from the starry threshold of Jove's court
> A messenger I come, to grace your sport;
> And at your feet th' immortal wreath I lay,
> From chiefs of old renown, who bid me say,
> Like you, they once aspir'd to please the fair,
> With all the sportive images of war.

---

* This letter is printed from the Gentleman's Magazine, Aug. 1778, collated with the version of The Lady's Magazine, 1793. It may have been addressed to Mr. Ewer; but more probably to Miss Seward, to whose literary connection both with André and The Lady's Magazine I am inclined to attribute the insertion of various scraps of military intelligence from America, some of which bear marks of sources of information not always open.

Round Arthur's board, when chivalry was young,
In justs and tilts their manly nerves they strung:
Scorning to waste the intervals of peace
In sordid riot, or inglorious ease.
Martial and bold their exercises were;
Though Gothic, grand; though festive, yet severe:
Design'd to fire the breast to deeds of worth
And call th' impatient soul of glory forth.
Thus train'd to virtue, when the trumpet's sound,
And red cross streaming, led to holy ground;
Or violated rights, and Freedom's call,
Bade them chastise the perfidy of Gaul;
Each lover, mindful of his plighted vow
A hero rose, inflam'd with patriot glow.
The cause of beauty his peculiar care;
His motto still — " The brave deserve the fair."

Air, in Artaxerxes.

" The soldier, tir'd of war's alarms,
  Exults to feast on beauty's charms,
    And drops the spear and shield:
But if the brazen trumpet sound
He burns with conquest to be crown'd,
    And dares again the field."

Oh! be th' example copied in each heart;
Let modern Britons act the ancient part;
And you, great Sir, these parting rites receive
Which, bath'd in tears, your hardy veterans give;
Veterans approv'd, who never knew to yield
When Howe and Glory led them to the field.
To other scenes your country's sacred cause
Now calls you hence, the champion of her laws.
Your Veterans, to your brave successor true,
By honouring him, will seek to honour you.

And ye, bright nymphs, who grace this hallow'd ground,
In all the blooming pride of beauty crown'd,
Still strive to sooth the hero's generous toils,
With what he deems his best reward, your smiles.

The other, a little less flattering in tone, is accompanied by stage-directions. It contains also a provident compliment to the rising sun.

ADDRESS

INTENDED TO HAVE BEEN SPOKEN AT THE MISCHIANZA, BY A HERALD HOLDING IN HIS HAND A LAUREL-WREATH WITH THE FOLLOWING INSCRIPTION:

Mars, conquest-plum'd, the Cyprian Queen disarms;
And Victors, vanquish'd, yield to Beauty's Charms.

After hanging the Wreath on the Front of the Pavilion, he was to have proceeded thus:

Here then the laurel, here the palm we yield,
And all the trophies of the tilted field;
Here Whites and Blacks,* with blended homage, pay
To each Device the honours of the day.
Hard were the task, and impious to decide
Where all are fairest, which the fairer side.
Enough for us, if by such sports we strove
To grace this feast of military love;
And, joining in the wish of every heart,
Honour'd the friend and leader ere we part.

When great in arms our brave forefathers rose,
And loos'd the British Lion on his foes;
When the fall'n Gauls, then perjur'd too and base,
The faithless fathers of a faithless race,
First to attack, tho' still the first to yield,
Shrunk from their rage on Poictiers laurel'd field;
Oft, while grim War suspended his alarms,
The gallant bands, with mimic deeds of arms,
Thus to some favourite chief the feast decreed,
And deck'd the tilting Knight, th' encountering steed:
In manly sports that serv'd but to inspire
Contempt of death, and feed the martial fire,
The lists beheld them celebrate *his* name
Who led their steps to victory and fame.
Thro' every rank the martial ardor ran;
All fear'd the chieftain, but all lov'd the man:
And, fired with the soul of this bright day,
Pay'd to a *Salisbury* what to *Howe* we pay.
Shame to the envious slave that dares bemoan
Their sons degenerate, or their spirit flown;—
Let maddening Faction drive this guilty land,
With her worst foes to form th' unnatural band:
In yon, brave crowd, old British courage glows
Unconquer'd, growing as the danger grows.

* The Knights so distinguished.

> With hearts as bold as e'er their fathers bore
> Their country they'll avenge, her fame restore.
> Rouz'd to the charge, methinks I hear them cry,
> Revenge and glory sparkling from each eye, —
> "Chain'd to our arms while Howe the battle led,
> "Still round these files her wings shall Conquest spread.
> "Lov'd tho' he goes, the spirit still remains
> "That with him bore us o'er these trembling plains.
> "On Hudson's banks * the sure presage we read
> "Of other triumphs to our arms decreed:
> "Nor fear but equal honours shall repay
> "Each hardy deed where Clinton leads the way!"

It need not be thought however, that honors such as Rome might have rendered to a conqueror were now paid without criticism to a general who had made no conquests. McLane took the occasion to beat up the lines so thoroughly that he was pursued to the Wissahiccon Hills; but the promoters of the gala kept their fair guests tranquil. Others whose *forte* was the pen rather than the sword, were not so soon silenced. Galloway was never weary of the theme.

— "We had seen the same General, with a vanity and presumption unparalleled in history, after this indolence, after all these wretched blunders, accept from a few of his officers a triumph more magnificent than would have become the conqueror of America, without the consent of his sovereign or approbation of his country, and that at a time when the news of war with France had just arrived, and in the very city, the capital of North America, the late seat of Congress, which in a few days was to be delivered up to that Congress." †

---

* "The North-river expedition from New York, last autumn."

† — Galloway's Reply, &c. See also Towne's Confession (written by Dr. Witherspoon), Philadelphia, 1783; and Strictures on the Philadelphia Mischianza, or Triumph upon leaving America unconquered (London printed, Philadelphia reprinted, 1783): that I am inclined to attribute to Galloway. This tract ascribes the *fête* to Sir William's flatterers, "promoted by his favour, or possibly enriched by his connivance." — "He bounced off with his bombs and burning hearts set upon the pillars of his triumphal arch, which, at the proper time of the show, burst out in a shower of squibs and crackers and other fireworks, to the delectable

Colonel Johnston, who married Miss Franks, had his quarters in the house of Edward Penington, a leading Friend, at the corner of Crown and Race streets. It was thus the headquarters of the 28th, and was also the resort of a number of grave elderly officers who, like the better class of tories, had a high opinion of Washington. When the Mischianza was in every one's mouth, a young person of the family asked of an old major of artillery what was the distinction between the Knights of the Mountain and the Rose. — " Why, child," quoth he, " the Knights of the Burning Mountain are tom-fools, and the Knights of the Blended Rose are damned fools — I know of no other difference between them." Then, placing a hand on either knee, he added in a tone of unsuppressed mortification — " What will Washington think of all this!"

amazement of Miss Craig, Miss Chew, Miss Redman, and all the other Misses, dressed out as the fair damsels of the Blended Rose and of the Burning Mountain for this farce at Knight-errantry."

CHAPTER X.

Evacuation of Philadelphia. — Battle of Monmouth. — D'Estaing's Arrival. — André accompanies Grey against New Bedford. — His Satirical Verses on the Investment of Newport. — Aide to Clinton. — Character of this General. — André's Verses upon an American Duel.

THE instructions under which Clinton was to take command had involved an early and vigorous campaign, and preparations at Philadelphia were made accordingly. On the 23d of May, however, the orders of March 21st were received, which, in consideration of the hostile intervention of France, looked to a retreat to New York and large detachments thence to the West Indies.* A council of war was held, and the evacuation of Philadelphia provided for. The immense military stores, together with 3000 of the civil population who feared to meet the wrath of the incoming Americans, were to be sent in the fleet; the troops, with their provision-trains, &c., for lack of room on board, were to march by land. All were busied with preparations for removal. Knyphausen bade farewell to the pleasant quarters in 2nd Street, where he should no more spread butter on his bread with his thumb. André's lodgings were at the house of Dr. Franklin, a full description of which, with all its furniture down to the pictures of the king and queen and of the Earl of Bute, "in the room for our friends," is given by Mrs. Franklin to her husband, in 1765. His daughter,

* "The first orders Sir H. Clinton had were to bring Washington to action, to detach an expedition against seaports, &c., when the promised reinforcements should arrive (12000 recruits) to complete his army. On the interference of the [French?] near 12000, instead of sent, were taken from Sir H. C. He was ordered to embark the army and proceed to New York, where the commissioners were to open communication, and then to detach to W. Indies, &c." — *Clinton MS.*

Mrs. Bache, had abandoned the place on Howe's approach. On her return she complained of some spoliations though not so great as she had expected "from the hands of such a rapacious crew." "A Captain André also took with him the picture of you, which hung in the dining-room." One might almost fancy André rummaging the bales of dead letters that, while Franklin was at the head of the American post-office, were piled away in the garrets of this house.*

Before passing from Philadelphia, mention may be made of another ghost story, about as well authenticated as such stories usually are, in which André and his fate were again prefigured. The Springettsbury Manor-house, in the present neighborhood of 20th and Spring-garden Streets, was then a favorite resort for rural entertainments. Though long disused by the Penns, its proprietors, the house and grounds were kept up, and officers were accustomed to provide dinner-parties there. Two ladies of the family of my informant, who had known André, were on their way hither, to dine with Washington and some other American officers, where André and his comrades had often feasted before. As they passed through the groves of cedars and catalpas that surrounded the mansion, they perceived simultaneously a corpse dangling from a limb, clad as a British officer, which presently, as they drew nearer, swung around as though by a natural torsion of the rope. The face then was visible, calm, and stiff, as in death; but they immediately recognized it as Captain André's. On approaching the spot the illusion vanished. At dinner they did not conceal their adventure, but related it with a faith that provoked the polite

* In some severe strictures on his character published after his death, it was positively alleged that André took away with him from the Library Company of Philadelpcia a copy of the *Encyclopédie*, which had been presented by Dr. Franklin. Franklin's benefactions to this institution were not numerous, and it is easy to discover that no such work was among them, and that there is no earthly cause to believe that André was guilty of any peccadillo of the nature imputed to him. Certainly it does not appear that any one acquainted with the affairs of the Library ever entertained such a thought.

ridicule of Washington to the extent at last of hearty laughter at their credulity: a circumstance especially remarked by one of them, who never previously had seen him laugh. Many years later, when he was President, this lady again dined with Washington at Philadelphia; and took occasion, she says, to remind him of his mirth. He was much disturbed, she said, and bade her never to refer the subject to him more; that it was a matter he would not recur to, since it had already greatly troubled and perplexed him. The narrator of this tale, it may be added, was a lady of distinguished mental endowments, well versed even in Hebrew and Greek studies; while her comrade was daughter and sister of two of the first medical men of their day. It was hardly through ignorance therefore that they could have fallen into their delusion.

Meanwhile André in the flesh was busily employed. "Sir Henry Clinton made no secret of his intention of quitting Philadelphia;"* but at Valley Forge it was not for some time known whither his course would be directed. The commissioners, arriving on the 6th of June, 1778, found him almost ready to move. A great number of baggage-wagons were gathered at Cooper's Point, on the Jersey shore of the Delaware; and most of the artillery and stores, with several regiments, were passed over that river and secured by temporary works. On the night of June 17th, the lines were manned as usual, and the troops led out of quarters and bivouacked on the ground beyond the built-up parts of the town. This was to guard against the plunder or incendiarism of a retreating army, and to avert from Philadelphia the calamity which there is too much reason to suppose was unauthorisedly inflicted in 1776, by some of our troops, as they evacuated New York. At three A. M., on the 19th, the army marched across the commons and crossed at Gloucester Point, three miles below the centre of the city. By ten A. M. the rear-guard came over, and the march for New York began. Lord

* Clinton MS.

Howe supervised the water-carriage, and was the last man to embark. The chief of the fleet had already dropped down to Reedy Island; and a few of the most important of the loyalists, who had lingered to the last moment in the places that were to know them no more, now dejectedly sailed after it. "When we left Philadelphia," wrote one of these, "the night of the 17th of June, the finest night I ever saw, was obscured by the most melancholy reflections I ever felt." They were two days and two nights to Reedy Island, and thirteen days to the Capes. The weather was hot and calm; and visiting about was kept up among the ships. "How melancholy was the idea that the fleet might be compared to a town peopled by our friends! Alas, it was a town founded by misfortune, and inhabitants connected by similarity of misery." The bulk of the tories, however, went with the army:—"and took their baggage with them, which was a great incumbrance during the march."*

Many of the soldiers, especially of those who had married in town, hid themselves in cellars and such places and remained behind, and the deserters ere Clinton reached New York were estimated at 1000; but perhaps the last man to quit Philadelphia was Lord Cosmo Gordon. He slept at his quarters all night and so late the next day, that the family out of kindness at length awakened him, the news of "his friends the rebels" being in town. It was as much as he could do to slip to the waterside and find a skiff to carry himself and his servant over. Two hours after the rearguard was gone, the American dragoons galloped through the streets.

Nothing could have been more cleverly managed than the evacuation. So silently was it conducted, that many of the inhabitants knew of it only when they went about in the morning, and found not a British regiment remaining. "They did not go away; they vanished." But the real difficulties of the retreat were only begun. Clinton did not

* Clinton MS.

calculate to forage on his journey, and the quantities of stores and baggage that the transports could not receive or his troops could not dispense with, formed a line of march twelve miles long. He anticipated an attack, and as he sat on a rock and reviewed the prolonged train, he was half-inclined to destroy all his incumbrances on the spot. But this, he thought, would be made too great a handle for triumph to his enemies; so he manfully resolved to confide the issue to the swords of his followers and his own skill. His retreat, necessarily slow, was perfectly deliberate and nothing resembling flight. The first day's march was but five miles; and though it would seem as clear that his object must have been an uninterrupted passage as that ours was to fall on his cumbered and attenuated line, the Englishman, by our best American judgment, rather invited a general action. He does not himself discountenance this idea. "Perhaps Washington was not quite mistaken," says he. "Perhaps Sir Henry Clinton was as desirous of bringing it to one decisive stroke, as Washington seemed desirous of avoiding it."* He likewise kept his own counsel, and not until June 24th was it known, even to his officers, what was his purposed route or destination.

During May and June our army at Valley Forge had been constantly exercising and preparing for combat on a moment's warning. On the 22nd of June it crossed at Coryell's Ferry to the same side of the Delaware with Clinton. It was stripped of all ineffective and heavy baggage, and put into trim fighting condition, and the arms were carefully cleaned and inspected. On the 24th, two day's provision was cooked; and on the 27th, the troops were ordered to be provisioned till the 29th, inclusive, and to be kept compact and ready to move at the shortest notice. Other precautions were taken: — "The drums to beat on the march. When the rear is to come up, a common march; to quicken the march, a grenadier's march. These signals to begin in the rear under the direction of the brigadier of the day, and are

* Clinton MS.

to be repeated by the orderly drum of every battalion from rear to front. An orderly drum to be kept ready braced with each battalion for this purpose. When the whole line is to halt for refreshment, the first part of the General will beat, and this to be repeated by every orderly drum down to the rear."*

These signals were very necessary; but it was impossible that in a few hours a whole army should be taught to regulate its conduct by the rattle of a bit of sheepskin, and it was a just complaint on the 28th that our regiments had no distinguishing uniforms or standards, and were deficient in instruments proper to sound a retreat, a halt, a march or a charge.

Though the advice of his council was against a general action, Washington was now prompted by his own inclinations and the circumstances of the case to steps that rendered an engagement almost unavoidable. On the 27th June, with our advance under La Fayette at but five miles distance, Clinton foresaw the coming conflict. Encamped in a strong position he passed a quiet night, and by five o'clock of the next morning Knyphausen was on his march with all the baggage and a large part of the troops, including the Pennsylvania and Maryland Loyalists, and most of the Hessians. That the march should have been so dangerously cumbered was, it would appear, entirely due to Clinton's military pride. He himself confesses the error of thus overloading the legitimate operations of his men:— "Sir H. Clinton was certainly to blame for permitting it. The reason was explained above. He lost not a cart, however." †

The position of our people was well weighed by the royal general. Morgan hung over his right and Dickinson over his left; while the advance of our main army was at Englishtown, less in the rear than on the left of his abode on the the night of the 27th, with the remainder of our people not far behind. Years of reflection served only to confirm Clin-

* MS. Am. O. B. June 27, 1778. † Clinton MS.

ton in his original opinion that the real aim of the Americans was against his baggage. — " Washington, so little desirous does he seem to have been of risking a general action, had passed the South river and put three or four of its marshy boggy branches between his army and that of the British." *

It is not proposed here to give a detailed account of the battle of Monmouth. Its story has been often and well told, and the circumstances that lend it a peculiar interest as liberally canvassed. In common justice, however, to the reputation of the turbulent and irregular Lee, whose prestige was on this day so fatally damaged, I must acknowledge that his conduct before the enemy seems to me to have been unworthy of the censure it received.

The flower of the king's soldiery, it will be recollected, rested with their general on the place of their encampment till the day was well advanced, and Knyphausen fairly under way. In such a well-chosen situation, with various natural defences or impediments intervening between himself and our men, it was entirely impossible, Sir Henry thought, for the Americans to gain any advantage while he held the position: for it was difficult for them to traverse at all the bad ground to reach him; and the ranks would necessarily fall into such disorder in the passage as to easily be cut down as fast as they appeared. Not far away were the Middletown Hills, where he would certainly be secure; and it was evident, therefore, he must be attacked now or never. His own idea was that we aimed at his baggage; and accordingly he perhaps resolved to give us such a handling here as would prevent any large bodies being thrown forward on his flanks. It is difficult to get at the precise numbers of either army. Sir Henry loosely estimated his opponents at near 20,000. Washington's own force certainly amounted to 10,684 effective rank and file, exclusive of Maxwell's brigade and perhaps of Morgan's regiment of 600 men, and Cadwalader's

* Clinton MS.

400 continentals and 100 volunteers. If these, and Dickenson's 1000 Jersey militia, who hung on the enemy's line, are to be added, it would swell the total directed against him to 13,000 or 14,000 men. The British were less, says Marshall, than 10,000; and if we allow for the desertions, &c. that he claims, we may put them at about 9,600. A large part of these were started with the baggage under Knyphausen at daybreak: with Cornwallis and the balance, at least 5000 or 6000 of the elite of the army, Clinton himself remained until 8 A. M.

Of the battle fought on Sunday, June 28th, 1778, I shall have but little to say. The circumstances of the case appear to be as follows. Between the two opposing armies stretched some very dangerous ground. Lee's advance, embarrassed by this and by the powerful front presented by the retiring enemy, quickly fell back, pursued in their own turn. Lee vindicates this policy in the declaration that the more extensively he was followed, the better for our cause it would have been: for as our main army came up, it would find a comparatively fruitful victory in every English regiment that had put the morasses referred to between itself and the remainder of Clinton's troops. The interruption of this plan by Washington, and the resumption of the attack ere yet the enemy were fairly launched from their stronghold, he seems to have considered capital errors; and it is certainly plain that our whole force through the whole day effected nothing much beyond what Lee might have done, nor succeeded in driving Clinton a rood's distance from the place he held when the fray begun. Sir Henry's own story, too, is in perfect concurrence with Lee's:—

"Sir Henry Clinton had been ordered to embark the army at Philadelphia, and proceed to New York. For various reasons he ventured to disobey the King's commands, and by that disobedience saved both army and navy. The principle of the British army was retreat at this period. Washington's avant guarde passes to marshy boggy branches at single bridges and attacks the British rearguard; probably with no other intent than to amuse while another corps attempted the baggage. The British rearguard forces Lee back over all these branches beyond the Lake. Lee is met by Washington arriving in column from Englishtown. Here of course the business would have finished; but the ungovernable impetuosity of the light troops had drawn them over the morass, and till they returned it became necessary to mask the 4th ravine to prevent the enemy from passing it and cutting [off] the above corps; and the 1st Guards and 33rd regiment, under Col. Meadows and Webster, maintained the ground exposed to a crossfire, and with severe loss, till the light troops had retired over the bog in safety. . . . The great Frederick, on hearing Sir Henry Clinton's account of this action and Lee's defence at his trial, said that when two opposite gentlemen agree in describing the ground and events of the day, they must both be right." *

The heat was in the last degree oppressive. Men fell dead in the ranks without a wound; and the panting Hessians swore that in such an atmosphere they would fight no longer. Night at last brought relief. At 10 P. M. Clinton arrayed his weary bands, and led them to where Knyphausen was halted, three miles away in the Nut Swamp. The moon setting on that night at 10.55 P. M., barely sufficed to light his path. Our army, we are told, was unaware of the march; but it is probable that it had little desire of renewing a contest in which, it is pretty clear, it had as yet gained no solid advantage. For whether the end was to kill or capture Clinton's troops, or to get possession of his baggage, we were successful in neither. The battle was at most a drawn one; and the only interruption the baggage received was when a small party would run across the road between the carts, without being permitted to attempt anything. There was no attack on it, and it had no losses at all.

The merits, however, of the battle of Monmouth were

* Clinton MS.

loudly disputed and variously canvassed. There were not wanting military men in either army to condemn in pointed terms the character of Washington's strategy; while Lee's conduct soon raised a hornet's nest about that general's ears. What were the words Washington used to him when they met on the battle-field are unknown to me, but they were undoubtedly very strong in phrase as well as tone. La Fayette was a party to the conversation. He avers that the excitement of the scene drove the precise language from his memory. This personal altercation probably brought to a head the ill-blood between the two generals; and but for Lee's intemperate tongue after all was over, we might never have heard anything of his misconduct upon the field. It is certain that on the 30th June, he was appointed major-general for the ensuing day by Washington, and that no exception in his disfavor was made in the earlier orders from head-quarters. The Orderly Books of June 29th say:—

"The Commander in Chief congratulates the Army upon the victory obtained over his Britannic Majesty's troops yesterday, and thanks most sincerely the gallant officers and men who distinguished themselves upon the occasion, and such others who by their good order and coolness gave the happiest presage of what might have been expected had they come to action. General Dickenson and the Militia of his State are also thanked for their noble spirit in opposing the enemy on their march from Philadelphia, and for the aid they have given by harassing and impeding their march so as to allow the continental troops to come up with them. . . . A party consisting of 200 men to parade immediately to bury the slain of both parties; General Woodford's brigade to cover the party. The officers of the American Army are to be buried with the military honours due to men who nobly fought and died in the cause of liberty and their country. . . . The several detachments except those under Col. Morgan are to join their respective brigades immediately."

On the other hand, Clinton's course was freely and variously criticized. On the motion for thanks to him and Cornwallis, Mr. Coke in the Commons declared that the whole march from Philadelphia to New York "was universally allowed to be the finest thing performed during the present war:" while the Earl of Shelburne characterized it as the "shameful retreat from Philadelphia, when the General escaped with his whole army, rather by chance and the misconduct of the enemy, than by the natural ability of the force under his command." With sounder cause, military critics have questioned the wisdom of the British course. Why, when a safe retreat was the manifest object, should Sir Henry have avoided the shorter route by the Raritan, and taken the longer road to Sandy Hook? This question Sir Henry himself has answered, by a reference to the position of his adversaries:— "Gates in front beyond the Raritan: Washington in the rear and left behind the Milestone Creek, with the Fords of Raritan on his left to join or be joined by Gates." * Why did he pause for two days at Monmouth, when Washington was closing on his skirts, and his paramount object should have been to get a communication with the fleet? "No military man," quoth Clinton scornfully, "can ask this question." † And to Stedman's recapitulation of the dangerous straits to which his army would have been reduced had Washington turned either of the British flanks, Sir Henry tranquilly replies: "When the author knows the country a little better, and possible military movements in it a little better, this question may be answered." ‡ From the various circumstances of the case, and particularly from the royal commander's evident selection of the position he fought in, and his remaining on it till the encounter actually occurred, it may be presumed that he had, or thought he had good cause to expect at least so much success as he experienced. "Tell General Phillips," said he to Major Clarke, "*that on that day I fought upon velvet:* he will fully understand me." For my own part, though I have preferred

---

* Clinton MS. † Ibid. ‡ Ibid.

to give the story in the original language of its actors, I am unable to conjecture the reasons wherefrom Clinton derived such sanguine anticipations of victory in every contingency. That he should have expected to secure the preservation of his baggage by just such a check as he gave our people is plausible enough; but that his troops should have preserved their equanimity under the very probable event that Stedman suggests, is not to my comprehension so plain. Probably the matter would appear in a different light to a professional eye.

Once among the Middletown Hills, the English were out of danger from the Americans. The march to Sandy Hook was easy; the baggage was transported, by aid of the fleet, over a bridge of boats; and after delaying a little in hope of encountering our army, the rest of the enemy's force followed to Staten Island.

On July 5th, the very day that Clinton passed from the main land to Staten Island, D'Estaing's fleet appeared on the Virginia coast. But for an unusually long voyage it might have found Howe's vessels yet in the Delaware; and well-informed writers reckon that an earlier arrival at Sandy Hook would have prevented Sir Henry's crossing. He himself was of different opinion. "If all the enemies' combined fleet had been laying at Sandy Hook, Sir H. Clinton, commanding with gallies and gun-boats the inner channel, could always have got to Salem [Staten] Island either from South Amboy or Mount Pleasant." * On the 11th D'Estaing with twelve ships of the line, six frigates, and 4000 troops, anchored without the Hook, designing an attack on the British squadron in the harbor. Howe's armament was considerably inferior, consisting of but six ships of the line, four of fifty guns, and some smaller craft; and his vessels were very insufficiently manned. But he had control over the crews of a vast number of transports: 2000 naval volunteers pressed forward to engage in the expected action, of whom at least

* Clinton MS.

1000 were accepted; and the anger and indignation that pervaded all ranks amply supplied any deficiencies of his muster-rolls. Mates and masters of merchantmen sought places at the guns among the common sailors; and it is highly probable that had D'Estaing got over the bar and into the harbor, he never would have got out again in command of his own ships. But there was not water, he thought, for his larger vessels; and in the moment when, by favorable conjuncture of wind and tide, the whole British population were agog in anticipation of attack, he put up his helm and by preconcerted arrangement with Washington bore away for Rhode Island. Scarcely was he out of sight, however, when sail after sail of Byron's command came dropping in, shattered and weather-beaten; all of which must have fallen into his hands but for his withdrawal. With these, though still inferior to the French, Howe sailed to find them.

Meantime Sullivan, Greene, and Lafayette, with 10,000 men, were assembled against Pigot, well entrenched with 6000 at Newport. On D'Estaing's arrival success seemed certain; and the militia of Massachusetts, led by Hancock in person, pleased themselves with the idea of at last getting rid of so abhorred and dangerous a neighbor. But dissensions sprung up between the French and American leaders, in which the former were chiefly to blame. Howe's fleet appeared; D'Estaing stood out with the weathergage to fight him; a storm sprung up, and the French only reappeared at Newport to notify their intention of proceeding forthwith to refit at Boston. The remonstrances and the anger of our generals were equally vain. D'Estaing went away, and the siege was abandoned. Clinton, who had sailed with 4000 men to relieve Pigot, no sooner knew the French fleet to be gone, than he endeavored either to intercept Sullivan's retreat, or to find means to fall upon Providence. Grey's division was with him; and when he found it impossible to carry out his original ideas he dispatched this officer against New Bedford, — one of the chief among the minor seaports that lined the New England coast, — and wrought infinite mischief to British commerce. On the 5th September, at five P. M., Grey anchored in Clark's Cove, and at six, debarking with very slight loss, he ravaged the Acushnet River for six miles. The fort was dismantled and burned, its guns demolished, and its magazine blown up; upwards of seventy sail of privateers and their prizes consumed; and numbers of buildings containing very great quantities of stores reduced to ashes. From Buzzard's Bay he passed through the baffling tides of Quick's Hole (which can never be forgotten by any one who has ever sailed over them), to Martha's Vineyard; where he levied a contribution of 300 oxen, 10,000 sheep, all the arms of the militia, and £1000 in paper-money, being the sum of the public funds on hand. Taking or destroying what vessels he found there, Grey returned from the island to New York. His esteem for his aide, however, and his desire to leave him, at his own approaching withdrawal from America, on the best possible footing at head-quarters, probably induced the general to send by his hands in the first instance a very brief account of his doings to Clinton. "I write in haste," he says, "and not a little tired; therefore must beg leave to refer you for the late plan of operations and particulars to Captain André." The value of such language, repeated from the commander-in-chief to the minister at London, and reiterated in the official gazettes, can readily be appreciated by all military men.* It was probably in the unemployed hours of his voyage to New York that André found leisure to commemorate the first fruits of the French Alliance in these lines: —

YANKEE DOODLE'S EXPEDITION TO RHODE ISLAND.

From Lewis Monsieur Gerard came
To Congress in this town, Sir;

---

* This Bedford foray, and not the Paoli affair, is alluded to by Germain to the Royal Commissioners, 4th November, 1778, as the wise and ably executed expedition under Grey. — *Reed's Reed,* i. 436.

They bow'd to him, and he to them,
  And then they all sat down, Sir.
    Chorus: Yankee Doodle, &c.

Begar, said Monsieur, one grand *coup*
  You shall *bientôt* behold, Sir.
This was believed as Gospel true,
  And Jonathan *felt bold*, Sir.

So Yankee Doodle did forget
  The sound of British drum, Sir;
How oft it made him quake and sweat
  In spite of Yankee rum, Sir.

He took his wallet on his back,
  His rifle on his shoulder,
And *veow'd* Rhode-Island to attack
  Before he was much older.

In dread array their tatter'd crew
  Advanc'd with colours spread, Sir;
Their fifes played Yankee Doodle doo,
  King Hancock at their head, Sir.

What numbers bravely cross'd the seas
  I cannot well determine;
A swarm of Rebels and of fleas
  And every other vermin.

Their mighty hearts might shrink, they tho't;
  For all flesh only grass is;
A plenteous store they therefore brought
  Of whisky and molasses.

They swore they'd make bold Pigot squeak,
  So did their *good* Ally, Sir,
And take him prisoner in a week;
  But that was all my eye, Sir.

As Jonathan so much desir'd
  To shine in martial story,
D'Estaing with *politesse* retir'd
  To leave him all the glory.

He left him what was better yet;
  At least it was more use, Sir:

He left him for a quick retreat
A very good excuse, Sir.

To stay, unless he rul'd the sea,
He thought would not be right, Sir;
And continental troops, said he,
On islands should not fight, Sir.

Another cause with these combin'd
To throw him in the dumps, Sir:
For Clinton's name alarm'd his mind
And made him stir his stumps, Sir.
Sing Yankee Doodle Doodle doo, &c.*

While D'Estaing, under cover of formidable works on George's Island where he had mounted 100 heavy guns, was repairing his fleet, Congress and Washington were striving to allay the heats into which our generals were thrown by his withdrawal from Newport. Though they succeeded in stilling the angry tongues of superior officers, the passions of the populace were still inflamed; and in a riot that sprung up in Boston, some of the Frenchmen were very severely handled. When Howe returned to New York from a fruitless cruise before Boston, and found reinforcements that gave him the superiority, a serious move was under consideration.

"After Lord Howe had been joined by the greater part of Byron's squadron, Sir H. Clinton offered himself with 6000 troops to accompany Lord H. to Boston Bay, to attempt a landing on Point Alderton; to endeavor from thence to attack or destroy the batteries on the islands covering D'Estaing's fleet; or, by seizing Boston, deprive that fleet of

---

* This piece is reprinted, with useful notes, in Moore's Ballads of the Revolution. The first verses refer to the terms in which the American papers related Gerard's reception by Congress; and in this connection, the lines were originally pretended to have been written at Philadelphia. They are printed here from the text given by Rivington's tract, 1780; which, though it does not name the author, contains two other pieces by André, and one by his friend and literary coadjutor, Dr. Odell. Internal evidence also points to André as the writer.

its necessary supplies, and force it to quit its position. Lord H. seemed at first to relish the proposal, but afterwards declined it, for reasons I am persuaded the best, tho' he never communicated them to me. From what I have heard since, I really believe we could have succeeded. D'Estaing had only eleven, and Lord Howe twenty-one sail of the line."*

The fact is, that the Admiral had made up his mind to go home as soon as the fleet was stronger than D'Estaing's. On the 26th of September, "Black Dick," as he was called, left the coast, with the regret of all who had served under him. His successor, the inefficient Gambier, held command to the following March, when he was removed, wrote a loyalist, "to the universal joy of all ranks and conditions. I believe no person was ever more detested by navy, army, and citizen, than this penurious old reptile." In later years he brought shame on the service at the Basque Roads, and became in Hood's satire the great Gambogee of the Hum-Fum Society.

André's next active service was when Clinton pushed heavy foraging detachments up the North River, and destroyed the privateers of Egg Harbor. Lest his aim might be the Highlands, troops were so posted by Washington as to interrupt and discover such a movement. Of these was Baylor's regiment of dragoons which, on the 28th of September, was quartered at Taapan or Herringtown, a small hamlet on the Hackensack River. Against these Grey so skilfully led a night-attack, that the Americans had no opportunity of saving themselves, but by dispersion and flight. In affairs of this nature, it is not the custom of war to lose time in receiving and disarming prisoners, and sending them to the rear; nevertheless, "the whole of the fourth troop," says Marshall, "were spared by one of Grey's captains, whose humanity was superior to his obedience to orders." We may well suppose that this captain was the general's aide. Among the Americans who fell was Major Clough,

* Clinton MS.

who had aided with these troopers in disturbing the lines of Philadelphia, on the night of the Mischianza. This stroke, however, on a smaller scale but in the very style of the Paoli, was greatly censured in our camp, and denounced as little else than a massacre.* A reinforcement of 3500 men from England had reached Clinton on the 25th of August, but their arrival had been so delayed by a détour to the channel island of Jersey, that they were too late to be of much use in this campaign.†

At this period, André again changed his regiment. The 26th was ordered home; but such was the reluctance to part with so valuable an officer, that his superiors went to the trouble of an arrangement by which he might still remain with Clinton. The 44th, in which his brother was a captain, was ordered to Canada. A captain of the 54th, which was to continue in America, wishing to sell, it was settled that he should take, instead of his own, the younger André's company in the 44th, which he forthwith sold to Sir Thomas Wallace; to whom the purchase-money was advanced by Sir James Wallace of the navy (apparently no relation) to the amount of £1500 or £2000. John André had the vacated captaincy in the 54th, and his brother took that in the 26th, choosing to go to England rather than Canada. Grey also leaving this country, André, with the provincial rank of major, was appointed an aide to Sir Henry Clinton. Considering the relations that existed between this general and his predecessor, it at least was no slight compliment to an officer's merits that both should be so ready to oblige him.

Sir Henry Clinton was the son of Admiral George Clinton, once governor of New York, who was second son of the

---

* I am inclined to think André celebrated these and other feats of the light infantry in appropriate verse; but compositions that savor of his style cannot be introduced here without evidence of authorship. See The British Light Infantry; A Medley for the Light Infantry; The Sacrifice, etc.; printed in *The Loyalist Poetry of the Revoludio*n.

† "Two months of most important operations lost by this Don Quixotic move to Jersey." — *Clinton MS.*

ninth Earl of Lincoln. The Clintons came from Geoffrey de Clinton, the builder of Kenilworth, who, though a *novus homo* in 1129, was the father of princely lines. In the old days, when baronies were held by tenure and not by writ, it may be supposed that the Clintons were not a house of the first magnitude, since they do not appear among the twenty-five great guardians of Magna Charta, in the beginning of the thirteenth century: not an unlucky circumstance for them in the end, as not a male descendant of the "Iron Barons" is a peer to-day. In person, Sir Henry was short and stout, with a full face and prominent nose: his manners reserved, and though polite, not popular with the world at large. He had long been accustomed to arms in the best practical schools of Europe; and Prince Ferdinand bore very honorable testimony to his capacity. At Bunker Hill, without waiting for orders, he flew to lead the reinforcements for Howe which were wavering in uncertainty whither to march; and was of essential service. These officers, who " never differed in one jot of military sentiment" at this period, became afterwards rivals and foes. He was regarded by many, however, as more conspicuous for honesty, zeal, and courage, than for military genius. It was complained that he never knew when to strike. In our army, a plan for his seizure was canvassed and abandoned on the ground that his measure was exactly ascertained, and any change in the command would be for the worse. "I should be very sorry," wrote Livingston at the time of Cornwallis's fall, "to have Clinton recalled through any national resentment against him, because, as fertile as that country is in the production of blockheads, I think they cannot easily send us a greater blunderbuss, unless peradventure it should please his majesty himself to do us the honour of a visit." He was accused, and not without appearance of reason, of an habitual indecision, that in a man vested with a great public trust often approaches imbecility. An instance of this trait occurred when he suffered the American and French armies to pass from his own vicinity to that of Cornwallis. It was evident that they must attack either the one British commander or the other; and success in either undertaking was ruin to the cause of the crown. An abler officer would perhaps have anticipated an assault on New York by finding a lucky chance to strike at the enemy himself; but when it was once plain that the allies were definitely gone to Virginia, it was folly not to send instant and abundant relief to the Chesapeake; and it was worse than folly for a commander-in-chief to consider personal punctilio or private jealousies, when great state interests are concerned. He seems to have had a landed estate too in America; but all the information I have on this subject consists in his notice of the measures for confiscation of whig estates in Carolina, established by Cornwallis in 1780.

"I know no great use in this act of severity; it was not even reported to me till it had been represented to and approved by the minister; it produced retaliation, and I was the sufferer, though a British subject and born a subject. My estate was confiscated and sold, and I can get redress nowhere."*

To me, Sir Henry appears as a good man, and, in many respects, as an excellent officer, but deficient in the genius necessary for the first post. In private he was amiable and humane; the correspondent of Gibbon and the confidential friend of Sheffield. He died governor of Gibraltar, December 13th, 1795. The spirit of faction that permeated through both army and navy in this war, renders it sometimes difficult to get at the real state of certain cases; and his retirement from America was respectably believed to have been less of a resignation than a removal. He thus notices such a surmise:—

"As this author chuses to insinuate that Sir Henry Clinton had been superceded in the command by Sir Guy Carleton, Sir H. C. takes leave to repeat what the King was

* Clinton MS.

pleased to say to him at the first audience he was *called* to after his return from America. — 'I always wished to see 'you, Sir Henry, in the command of my armies in America : 'but the Duke of Newcastle was so exceedingly pressing for 'your return that I was obliged at last to acquiesce.' — Sir H. Clinton had asked three times every year to have leave to resign the command, but his majesty would never before consent." *

Both armies going into winter-quarters, little more occurred in this year of an active nature for André to bear part in. The French fleet was in the West Indies, where Byron was vainly endeavoring to inveigle it to action ; and the loyalists in New York were in constant hope of D'Estaing's destruction, and a consequent withdrawal of his court from the quarrel. " D'Estaing's blockade by Byron at Martinique — one of the most fortunate events of the war — must revive the spirits of the most drooping Tory in Philadelphia. The game is in our own hands, and we may expect to hear next of the taking of D'Estaing. A treaty between England and France follows of course ; and we must then shed tears of pity for poor America, laid in ruins to gratify the fatal ambition of a few artful men." †

But the usual luck of " the hardy Byron " of the poet — more appropriately known as Foul-weather Jack by his sailors — did not desert him. D'Estaing was not taken; and all the tears tory eyes could command were in the end wanted for their own misfortunes. Of as little real importance, (considering that one of its heroes afterwards sat in judgment on the author's life,) was the following squib, published by André in Rivington's Gazette. It is a perfectly fair paraphrase, so far as details are concerned, of the pompous account of a duel between Lieutenant-governor Gadsden of Carolina, and Major-general Howe of our army, provoked by the former's published letter reflecting injuriously upon his opponent's military conduct. As Gadsden

* Clinton MS.   † Loyalist MS. New York, 1778.

was not in Howe's line of service, and would neither retract nor apologize for his language, a challenge passed; and in the consequent duel Howe's ball grazed his antagonist's ear after which an honorable reconciliation was effected by the seconds, Col. Bernard Elliott and Gen. Charles Cotesworth Pinckney. The initials in the verses are in strict accordance with those used in the American newspapers; but the latter would fix the date of the encounter on Sept. 5th. The introductory lines are of course a mere blind: —

ON THE AFFAIR BETWEEN THE REBEL GENERALS HOWE AND GADDESDEN.

CHARLESTOWN, S. C., Sept. 1st, 1778.

We are favored with the following authentic account of the affair of honour, which happened on the 13th of August, 1778. Eleven o'clock was the hour appointed for Generals H. and G. to meet; accordingly, about ten minutes before eleven — but hold, it is too good a story to be told in simple prose.

  It was on Mr. Percy's land,
   At Squire Rugeley's corner,
  Great H. and G. met, sword in hand,
   Upon a point of honour.
    Chorus: Yankee Doodle, doodle doo, &c.

  G. went before, with Colonel E.,
   Together in a carriage;
  On horseback followed H. and P.
   As if to steal a marriage.

  On chosen ground they now alight,
   For battle duly harnessed;
  A shady place, and out of sight:
   It shew'd they were in earnest.

  They met, and in the usual way
   With hat in hand saluted;
  Which was, no doubt, to shew how they
   Like gentlemen disputed.

  And then they both together made
   This honest declaration, —

That they came there, by honour led,
    And not by inclination.

That if they fought, 'twas not because
    Of rancour, spite, or passion:
But only to obey the laws
    Of custom and the fashion.

The pistols, then, before their eyes
    Were fairly primed and loaded;
H. wished, and so did G. likewise,
    The custom were exploded.

But, as they now had gone so far
    In such a bloody business,
For action straight they both prepare
    With mutual forgiveness.

But lest their courage should exceed
    The bounds of moderation,
Between the seconds 'twas agreed
    To fix them each a station.

The distance, stepp'd by Colonel P.,
    Was only eight short paces;
"Now, gentlemen," says Colonel E.,
    "Be sure to keep your places."

Quoth H. to G., — "Sir, please to fire;"
    Quoth G., — "No, pray begin, Sir:"
And truly, we must needs admire
    The temper they were in, Sir.

"We'll fire both at once," said H.;
    And so they both presented;
No answer was returned by G.,
    But silence, Sir, consented.

They paused awhile, these gallant foes,
    By turns, politely grinning;
'Till, after many *cons* and *pros*,
    H. made a brisk beginning.

H. missed his mark, but not his aim;
    The shot was well directed.
It saved them both from hurt and shame;
    What more could be expected?

Then G., to shew he meant no harm,
  But hated jars and jangles,
His pistol fired across his arm:
  From H., almost at angles.

H. now was called upon by G.
  To fire **another shot, Sir;**
He smiled and, " after that," quoth he,
  " No, truly I cannot, Sir."

Such honour did they both display
  They highly were commended;
And thus, in short, this gallant fray
  Without mischance was ended.

No fresh dispute, we may suppose,
  Will e'er by them be started;
And now the chiefs, no longer foes,
  Shook hands, and so they parted.
    Chorus: Yankee Doodle, doodle doo, &c.

Through all the war, the British loved to ridicule our people with the burden of this song. Yankee Doodle was with them the most withering sarcasm. Sometimes they met a retort in kind hardly so grateful. Percy's drums beat this air when he set out for Lexington; and Gates's musicians repeated it when the arms were grounded at Saratoga. The idea was not new. When Cumberland crossed the Spey against Charles Edward, it was thought a wise thing to insult the Scots with the air —

  " Will you play me fair play,
    Bonnie laddie, Highland laddie?"

CHAPTER XI.

New York in 1778. — André's Political Essay. — His Favor with Clinton. — Receives the Surrender of Fort La Fayette. — Letter to Mrs. Arnold. — Commencement of Arnold's Intrigue. — Appointed Deputy Adjutant-General. — Siege of Charleston. — Letter to Savannah. — Accused of entering Charleston as a Spy.

The city of New York, for the rest of the war the British head-quarters, was far in 1778-9 from its present metropolitan condition. Though about a mile in length, by half a mile in width, it was inferior in population and in importance to Philadelphia. Its narrow, clean, and well-paved streets were lined with neatly-built houses of wood or brick, and these for convenience of the harbor being chiefly clustered along the East River, were thus subjected to difficulties in the supply of fresh water. The ruin caused by the conflagration of 1776 yet subsisted, and in The Burnt District the blackened skeletons of 500 dwellings stretched along Broadway, from Whitehall Slip up to Rector Street. To this devastation was added that of the fire which broke out at one A. M. on the 10th of August, 1778, and consumed 300 houses. The best people then lived in Wall or Pearl streets; and to arrive at the present abodes of fashion, one must have ridden through several miles of country. Ponds, hills, and open fields extended where now is nothing but leagues of stone walls and solid pavements; and the mutilated statues of Chatham and King George bore public witness to the civic discord that had brought them from their high estate. But no dilapidation deprived the English soldier for the first time entering the port, of "the most beautiful scene that could be imagined." On the one hand were spread the fertile shores of Long Island, abounding in game, studded with country-seats and thriving villages, and the garden-spot of the coast; on the other, wide forests rose above the rough irregularities of Staten Island, in strong and luxuriant contrast to the nakedness of that on which the city stood, whence almost every tree had been removed. Powerful works defended all parts of the town. The old fortifications at The Battery, enlarged to receive ninety-four heavy guns, were strengthened with stone with merlons of cedar joists and filled in with earth; they commanded alike the entrances of the North and East rivers. Along the course too of either stream a series of breastworks were raised, connecting with each other in the strong ground towards Kingsbridge by well-ordered and powerful lines that followed the heights and extended across the island. In this upper part of the works, the first British post to be met after crossing from the main-land over Harlaem River to York Island, was Fort Charles: a strong redoubt overhanging and commanding Kingsbridge. Next, as we approach New York city, were the works that rising one above the other bristled with their guns the steeps of Laurel Hill. The road to the town led through a pass on the right, where again was lofty ground, on which stood Fort Knyphausen, once Fort Washington, and so narrow was the path between the two ascents that the British closed it with a gate. Continuing on by where is now the Central Park, the ground remained singularly strong; at McGowan's Pass, it was believed that a few companies properly handled could keep an army at bay. The chief difficulty with these extensive works, however, was the great force necessary to defend them. Sufficiently manned, they were perhaps impregnable; but to do this compelled the detention of thousands of troops from prolonged enterprise in the field.

The English had other posts without the limits of the island. At Sandy Hook were some heavy gun and mortar batteries. On the main-land above Morrisania was the small work called Number Four, usually garrisoned by a captain's guard and hardly capable of being preserved in a serious investment of the place. A regiment held the post where Paulus Hook stretches out from the Jersey shore into the North River. Formidable works were erected at Brooklyn Heights on that part of Long Island opposite to the city. The New Fort here would accommodate 1000 or 1500 men. Brooklyn itself was then a small, scattered village, with a capital tavern famous for its fish-dinners, which the royal officers were accustomed to consume to an extent that soon made a rich man of the landlord. These fish-loving gentry relate in melancholy wise the deprivation that fell upon the town by reason of the war. They tell that New York had long been dependent on the eastern coasts for its lobsters till a well-boat was shattered in Hell-Gate, and the escaping prey populated the neighboring depths. Here they flourished in cold and in boiling water until the tremendous cannonading of the Long Island battle disturbed their retreats; they passed away, and their accustomed haunts knew them no more. It was through this same whirlpool of Hell-Gate that Sir James Wallace, pursued by a French fleet into the eastern end of Long Island Sound, steered the Experiment in 1777. The passage was daring and perilous; but he brought her safely through. On Staten Island too Clinton had strong posts with 1000 or 1500 men; and here André, with other young officers, was in the habit of visiting Simcoe's quarters, where the landlord's pretty daughter bloomed in rustic seclusion and tempted many a gallant across the waters and the hills.

If the population of New York was lessened by the migration of its whigs, it was abundantly recruited by the incoming troops and tories. It was well understood that Ministers were for manifold reasons resolved to hold out longer here than in any other place; and though many of the loyalists, "once lords of thousands," now languished in comparative destitution at London, there were throngs at New York to supply their absence. Nor was involuntary increase wanting.

"Our little half-demolished town here seems crowded to

the full, and almost every day produces fresh inhabitants. Two or three days ago five or six wagon-loads of women and children were sent in from Albany, in imitation of the prudent policy of Philadelphia. It was impossible to see them without pain, driving about the streets in the forlorn attitudes which people fatigued with travelling and riding in wagons naturally fall into, making fruitless searches for their husbands and fathers." *

Dicing, drinking, fine dressing, and amateur theatricals, made New York as gay to the English as Philadelphia. Their stage was raised at the John Street Theatre, with Beaumont the surgeon-general as manager, and Major Williams of the artillery for principal tragedian. Colonel French was the low-comedy man, and André, Stanley, De Lancy, &c., had various parts. Female characters, where an officer had not in his train a woman competent to the performance, were assigned to the youngest ensigns; and Macbeth, Richard III., and the Beaux Stratagem, were ventured upon. The bottle was not neglected: hard drinking prevailed, and it was a point of social honor to press the glass upon guests; and during morning visits the punch-bowl was freely circulated and healths drank by the ladies. Clinton's quarters were at No. 1, Broadway; but he also maintained a country-seat in Dr. Beekman's house at the corner of 52nd Street and First Avenue, where he lived more at ease; and every day might be seen with his staff taking his constitutional gallop up Broadway to what was then The Fields. The loyalists, however, who found refuge here, were comforted neither with the military government of the city, nor the social eclipse into which they were thrown by "the Lords, and Sir Georges, and dear Colonels," of its garrison. The fashion of a fine gentleman's wearing two watches, which was ridiculous at Philadelphia, was esteemed highly polite in New York. The custom introduced by Admiral Digby of closing the windows for a half-past four o'clock dinner-party,

* Loyal MS.

and dining by candle-light, was as novel to the American stranger as the religious exactitude with which, through rain or snow, the New Year's calls were paid. At Philadelphia, after the evacuation, the loyal young people seem to have formed a sort of coterie of their own, that made it easy for their scrupulous parents to keep away "the lively French and the gallant Continentals"; but in New York, with half-a-dozen admirers to every handsome girl, such care was hopeless. "You cannot imagine what a superfluity of danglers there is here; so that a lady has only to look over a list of a dozen or two when she is going to walk, or to dance, or to sleigh." The tory manuscript from which I quote gives animated sketches of the city belles of this day.

"Of those I mentioned to you before, Miss T—— is said to be the greatest beauty: tall, genteel, graceful in her motions, with fine, light hair, dark speaking eyes, a complexion superior to the boasted one of Miss K——. She seldom fails to captivate those who see her; but to me she wants the greatest of female charms: she wants sensibility of features. Her sister less celebrated is more pleasing: neither so tall, so fair, nor so regularly featured, I would sooner, were I to offer my hand to a lady's *person*, make choice of Miss Betsy T—— than her sister, who I ought to have called Mrs. B——.

"Miss L——, the sentimental Miss L——, is tall and delicate, features not regular, eyes not lively. There is a modest dignity in her appearance that no one could offend — it is the dignity of true unaffected innocence and simplicity.

"Mrs. F——'s person resembles N—— P——'s: of course good, but she is not that beauty I expected to have found. Her complexion is pale, her hair the colour of Juliet's. She appears delicate and languishing, and she has the misfortune of having a fine face ruined by a very bad mouth, wide and unexpressive. . . . I cannot pretend to do justice to the Miss M——s: — Mild, delicate, thoughtful, there is an air of pensive languor and unaffected modesty over the whole appearance of Miss Beulah that would awe impudence itself into respect and sympathy. Neither tall, fair nor genteel, she pleases the more for being the more uncommon; and with a pair of eyes that cannot strictly be called handsome, but which say everything that the owner pleases — a forehead open and ingenuous — cheeks that bloom continually with the softest tints of the rose, and a mouth formed by the hands of the graces — joined to an abundance of dark flowing hair — confirms more conquests than the fluttering blaze of Mrs. B—— or the tall dignity of Mrs. F—— are ever able to produce. But Susan — the sweet, sprightly, amiable Susan — how shall I describe thee! How shall I paint that flow of cheerfulness, that elegance, natural elegance, of expression; that wit, that sense, that sensibility, that modesty, that good-nature, and that winning air of artless youth; every one of which thou possessest to such a superior degree! Still more difficult is it to describe a person, on which beauty and gracefulness have been lavished, but which I believe never raised in thee a vain idea! Eyes large, full, black, and the most expressive I ever beheld: fine dark hair: a faultless nose — but it is in vain to particularize every beauty where all is beauty.

" — Two months ago one of the plainest little mortals, all awkwardness and simplicity, without a thread of superfluity in her dress, eloped with a captain in the army. She was just come to town, and her parents, apprehensive that a girl of sixteen could not be safely trusted alone in a place so full of allurements, guarded her with the most peevish caution. Before they heard where she was they concluded she was locked up, murdered, anything sooner than in the company of an officer. After much difficulty and negotiation a marriage was effected, and Mrs. C—— now makes her *entrée* at public places in all the elegance of fashion. And behold the parents, whose name is P——, are now 'under dealings' for consenting to the marriage of their daughter. 'What would you have done in such a case?' I asked a plain-coated Friend.

'Done'—replied the benevolent Christian—'I would have cast her off to the contempt and beggary she deserved!' 'But could you forget she was your child?'—'Yes, I would tear the remembrance of her from my bosom!'

"— We have lately had one admitted into that mysterious order: a Miss P——. Yet she would not be affronted with the *a:* it was Miss P—— celebrated for her beauty, wit, and accomplishments; indeed so immensely sensible, that he was thought a bold officer who ventured on her. It was the Hon. Capt. Smith, eldest son of Lord Strangford of Ireland. All the observations made upon her since are that her eyes are brighter than ever. A pretty Miss G—— of the age of fourteen, finding marriages so very fashionable and thinking them very clever, eloped with a Hessian officer for want of a better. Father and mother as usual inconsolable and inexorable: 'Parents have flinty hearts, you know, and children must be wretched.'"

Under the influences that then prevailed in New York it was fashionable to be loyal; and in such social assemblies as pretended to a tone of literary cultivation we can easily conceive that André would not fail to put forth what power of intellectual entertainment he possessed. Indeed, his pen was probably rarely idle; and though it is not practicable to trace with certainty his political essays, I have no doubt that he was a constant contributor to the pages of Rivington's Gazette. Fortunately we are able to identify at least one of these papers, from which a fair idea of his manner may be inferred. At the mansion of Mr. Deane he is related to have won the praises of both sexes by an extempore upon Love and Fashion, which he delivered on the evening of January 6th, 1779; nor was a Political Dream, that he also read aloud on the same occasion, less applauded. It was printed in Rivington's newspaper shortly afterwards; and it will be seen that the author was anything but sparing in his censure of those Americans who were signalized by severity against the tories. Chief-justice McKean, who presided at the conviction of Carlisle and Roberts, two Philadelphia loyalists; Livingston of New Jersey, the implacable foe of toryism, and the supporters of our cause generally, were handled with little compunction; and the concluding paragraph seems even directed against his own former patron and late commander, Sir William Howe.

A DREAM.

"I was lately in company where the Metempsychosis became the subject of conversation, and was ably explained by a gentleman of erudition, who traced it from the Brachmans in the East, to Pythagoras in the west, and very learnedly demonstrated the probability and justice of this ancient system. How it was possible to deny that when mankind degraded themselves from the character of rational beings, it became proper that they should assume the figure of those beasts to whose properties they were already assimilated. On the other, how pleasing was it to trace the soul through its several stages, and to behold it rewarded or punished according to its deserts in a new state of existence. Many fanciful observations immediately occurred to the company. Besides several pair of turtle-doves, some cock sparrows, and one or two butterflies whom we found among our acquaintances, we were led to take a survey of superior characters. We entertained ourselves with viewing the soul of Louis XIV. transmigrated into a half-starved jackass, loaded with heavy panniers, and perpetually goaded by a meagre Frenchman, who, from the most humble of his slaves, was become the master and tormentor of this absolute and universal monarch. Alexander the Great, for whose ambitious views this whole orb had been too confined, was changed into a little sorry horse, and doomed to spend his life in the diurnal drudgery of turning a mill to which he was constantly fixed with blinds over his eyes. Charles of Sweden made his appearance in the figure of a Russian bear, whilst his wiser competitor was placed at the head of a warlike and industrious monarchy of bees. The poetical soul of Sappho continued to warble in the character of the "Love-lorn Nightingale," and that of our countryman Pope (into which those of Homer, Horace, Juvenal, and Lucretius had been before blended and transfused) was again revived and admired in the melodious Swan of Twickenham.

"Full of the ideas which this singular conversation had suggested, I retired to my chamber, and had not long pressed the downy pillow before the following vision appeared to my imagination: —

"I fancied myself in a spacious apartment, which I soon discovered to be the hall wherein the infernal judges administered justice to the souls which had animated the bodies of men in the superior regions. To my great surprise, instead of those grim personages which I had been taught to expect, I found the judges (who were then sitting) to be of a mild, gentle, and complacent appearance, unlike many dispensers of justice in the vital air, who add terror to severity, and by their very aspect not only awe the guilty, but discourage the innocent. At one end of the table, after a short interval, appeared a numerous crowd of various shades, ushered in and conducted by Mercury, whose business it was to take charge of the criminals and see the sentences executed. As dreams are of an unaccountable nature, it will not (I presume) be thought strange that I should behold upon this occasion the shades of many men who, for aught I know, may be still living and acting a conspicuous part upon the worldly theatre. But let this be as it will, I shall go on to relate simply what appeared to me, without troubling myself whether it may meet with credit from others.

"The first person called upon was the famous Chief-justice McKean, who I found had been animated by the same spirit which formerly possessed the memorable Jeffries. I could not but observe a flash of indignation in the eyes of the judges upon the approach of this culprit. His more than savage cruelty, his horrid disregard to the many oaths of allegiance he had taken, and the vile sacrifice he had made of justice to the interests of rebellion, were openly rehearsed. Notwithstanding his uncommon impudence, for once he seemed abashed, and did not pretend to deny the charge. He was condemned to assume the shape of a blood-hound, and the souls of Roberts and Carlisle were ordered to scourge him through the infernal regions.

"Next appeared the polite and travelled Mr. Deane, who from a trickling, hypocritical, New England attorney, was metamorphosed into a French marquis, with all the external frippery that so eminently distinguishes the most trifling characters of that trifling nation. The judges deliberated for a time whether they should form their sentence from the badness of his heart, or the vanity of his manners; but in consideration of the many mortifications he had lately experienced, they at length determined upon the latter, and the most excellent ambassador to his most Christian majesty skipped off, with very little change, in the character of 'The monkey who had seen the world.'

"The celebrated Gen. Lee, whose ingratitude to his parent country was regarded with the utmost detestation, assumed (by direction of the court) the figure of an adder: a reptile that is big with venom, and ready to wound the hand that protects, or the bosom that cherishes it, but whose poison frequently turns to its own destruction.

"The black soul of Livingston, which was 'fit for treason, sacrilege and spoil,' and polluted with every species of murder and iniquity, was condemned to howl in the body of a wolf; and I beheld, with surprise, that he retained the same gaunt, hollow, and ferocious appearance, and that his tongue still continued to be red with gore. Just at this time, Mercury touched me with his wand, and thereby bestowed an insight into futurity, when I saw this very wolf hung up at the door of his fold, by a shepherd whose innocent flock had been from time to time thinned by the murdering jaws of this savage animal.

"The President of the Congress, Mr. Jay, next appeared

before the tribunal, and his trial was conducted with all the solemnity due to so distinguished a character. I heard, with emotions of astonishment and concern, that in various human forms he had been remarkable for a mixture of the lowest cunning and most unfeeling barbarity; that having, in his last shape, received from nature such abilities as might have rendered him useful in his profession, and even serviceable to the public, he had, by a semblance of virtue, acquired the confidence of his fellow-citizens, which he afterwards abused to all the horrid purposes of the most wanton rebellion, and that being indefatigable in the pursuits of ambition and avarice, by all the ways of intrigue, perfidy, and dissimulation, he had acquired the station of a chief justice, and, in imitation of the infamous Dudley, had framed and enforced statutes that destroyed every species of private security and repose. In fine, that by his whole conduct he had exemplified his own maxim that princes were not the worst and most dreadful of tyrants,* and had given a fresh demonstration that power could never be well used when lodged in mean and improper hands.

"The court immediately thought fit to order that this criminal should transmigrate into the most insidious and most hateful of animals, a snake; but to prevent his being able any longer to deceive, and thereby destroy, a large set of rattles was affixed to his tail, that it might warn mankind to shun so poisonous a being.

"The whole Continental Army now passed in review before me. They were forced to put on the shape of the timid hare, whose disposition they already possessed. With ears erect, they seemed watching the first approach of danger, and ready to fly even at the approach of it. But what was very singular, a brass collar was affixed to the neck of one of their leaders, on which I saw distinctly the following lines: —

'They win the fight, that win the race.'

* See a pamphlet called (I think) The Nature and Extent of Parliamentary Power considered.

Alluding to the maxim he had always pursued, of making a good and timely retreat.

"This timorous crew having hastily retired, I beheld a great and magnanimous commander of antiquity, transformed into a game-cock, who at once began to crow and strut about as if he was meditating a combat, but upon the appearance of a few cropple crowned hens, he dismissed his purpose, and I could see him at some distance from the hall, brushing his wing, and rustling his feathers at every Dame Partlet in the company. The oddity of this transformation, and of the circumstances attending it, excited in me such a disposition to laugh, that I immediately awakened, and was forced reluctantly to resign the character of *A Dreamer.*"

André's conspicuous merit and amiable character had soon made him the most important person of Clinton's staff, and won the admiration of all who had business with the General. He would promptly inform them whether or not he could engage in their affairs. If he declined, his reasons were always polite and satisfactory; if he consented, the applicant was sure of an answer from Sir Henry within twenty-four hours. Clinton's confidence was evidenced, in the spring of 1779, by his appointment of André, with Colonel West Hyde of the Guards, as commissioners to negotiate with the Americans an exchange of prisoners. They met Colonels William Davies and Robert H. Harrison on our behalf at Amboy, on the 12th May, and remained till the 23rd in a fruitless effort to agree upon terms. The Americans objected in the first place that Clinton's delegation of powers for a general permanent cartel were insufficient. Hyde and André thought they perceived a design to procure the introduction of terms in their commission that might confess the Independence of America, and stood on their guard. A present exchange was then considered; but here again difficulties arose as to giving up officers and men together. The Americans knew the difference between the value of their own soldiery, whose enlistments were running out, and those of the enemy, who would at least serve out the war; and no terms were proposed by either side that the other would accept. The business thus ended, Clinton determined to open the campaign of 1779 with a blow at the posts on Verplanck's and Stony Points, which commanded King's Ferry and the opening passes to the highlands. Every step taken at New York was promptly communicated to Washington by his efficient spies in that city; and he had good cause to think the heavy forces now moving were not to be confined in their operations to the mere reduction of these works, but were ultimately designed to take ground that would interrupt his communications and divide his army. "Washington had his cattle from the Eastern provinces," said Clinton in regard to the campaign of 1777, "and his corn from the Western. Could we have taken a position on either of these communications we might have risked an action or retired."* If he now aimed at West Point, however, he was fated to be thwarted by the active providence of his enemies.

On the 31st May, Clinton debarked a little below Haverstraw, on the west bank of the Hudson, and approached Stony Point. As he drew near, Collier with the Vulture and other light war-ships came also in sight, and the unfinished works were with hardly a show of opposition abandoned by the Americans. Guns were at once haled up by the British, and a fire opened upon Fort La Fayette on Verplanck's, against which Vaughan had led a column on the eastern shore. During the night, the Vulture and a galley anchored above the fort, and so cut off a retreat by water. On the following day, unable to return a fire equal to what they received, the little garrison beat a *chamade*. The batteries were stilled, and André was dispatched to receive the surrender.

"On the Glacis of Fort Fayette, *June* 1st, 1779.

"His Excellency Sir Henry Clinton and Commodore Sir George Collier grant to the garrison of Fort La Fayette

* Clinton MS.

terms of safety to the persons and property (contained in the fort) of the garrison, they surrendering themselves prisoners of war. The officers shall be permitted to wear their side-arms. JOHN ANDRÉ, Aid-de-Camp." *

The possession of these posts was of no little importance to either army, and Clinton remained on the scene long enough to put them in condition for a stout defence. Then he left garrisons, and descended the river. On the night of July 15th, Stony Point was retaken by Wayne. Discipline, it is said, was so relaxed in the king's army, that officers entrusted the password to a countryman who supplied them with fruit. Having thus a guide, and all the dogs in the country round being killed on the day previous, lest their barking should betray his movements, Wayne silently advanced. The outer sentries were approached and gagged, and after a sharp but short resistance, the fort was stormed and over 500 prisoners taken. These, and the glory of an affair which was justly considered one of the most gallant things in the war, were all the advantages gained by the stroke. Circumstances prevented the reduction of Fort La Fayette. Stony Point was abandoned; and the British put a stronger garrison in it than ever.

During the remainder of the campaign Clinton led no other expedition in person. The fortification of New York was carried on vigorously, and André's labors were chiefly those of the pen. To his former acquaintance Miss Shippen, now the wife of General Arnold, he wrote as follows: —

---

* This transaction was ridiculed by an American writer (perhaps Gov. Livingston) in the New Jersey Gazette, 29th Dec. 1779. "Sir William Howe could not have invested this insignificant place with more unmeaning formality. No display of ostentatious arrangements was overlooked on this occasion; and Mr. André, your aid, as if in compliance with the taste of his General, signed a capitulation, in all the pomp of a vain-glorious solemnity on the very edge of the glacis, which he had gained under cover of a flag. What, Sir Henry, could you intend by this farce? What excuse will a person of Mr. André's reputed sense find for this parade?"

" Head-Quarters, New York, the 16th *Aug.* 1779.

"Madame. — Major Giles is so good as to take charge of this letter, which is meant to solicit your remembrance, and to assure you that my respect for you, and the fair circle in which I had the honour of becoming acquainted with you, remains unimpaired by distance or political broils. It would make me very happy to become useful to you here. You know the Mesquianza made me a complete milliner. Should you not have received supplies for your fullest equipment from that department, I shall be glad to enter into the whole detail of cap-wire, needles, gauze, &c., and, to the best of my abilities, render you in these trifles services from which I hope you would infer a zeal to be further employed. I beg you would present my best respects to your sisters, to the Miss Chews, and to Mrs. Shippen and Mrs. Chew. I have the honour to be, with the greatest regard, Madam, your most obedient and most humble servant,

"John André."

In March or April of this year General Arnold, commanding at Philadelphia, had, under the feigned name of Gustavus, began a secret correspondence with Clinton; who committed the matter to the hands of André. The latter wrote over the signature of John Anderson; and was replied to as "Mr. John Anderson, Merchant, to the care of James Osborn, to be left at the Reverend Mr. Odell's, New York." Though at the outset the English had no clue to their correspondent's identity, the character and value of his informations soon led them to suspect it; and it is supposed by some that this letter to Mrs. Arnold was written with the view of making clear to her husband the character of its author, and to invite a return of confidence. This may possibly have been the case; but all my investigations show that the lady had not any suspicion of the dealings between the parties, or was ever intrusted by either side with the least knowledge of what was going on. Equally false, in my judgment, is the charge that she tempted her husband to treason. Her purity and elevation of character have not less weight in the contradiction of this aspersion, than the testimony of all chiefly concerned in the discovery and punishment of the crime.

This correspondence must have engrossed much of André's time. His letters are said to have been "numerous and significant"; though there is no reason to believe that, so far as Mrs. Arnold was concerned, its limit ever exceeded the one just printed. To or from Arnold he at this period had probably nothing of a precise nature either to suggest or require. The earliest communication is said to have generally recommended to the American's imitation the example of Monk, and urged his intervention to procure peace on a substantial basis for his unhappy country. The distresses of America, the power of England, the superiority of a British to a French and Spanish alliance were strongly drawn; and instead of the old colonial subserviency, it was insinuated that the continental affairs of the united provinces should be committed to a purely national council resembling the British parliament, which should be so connected with the throne that, indissolubly bound together in the chains of equality, of commerce, and of mutual interest, the two lands should peacefully govern all the world.*

Besides the labor and anxiety of this intrigue, André had a private uneasiness to employ his mind. In July, D'Estaing had captured Granada, an island in which much of the family estate was invested. The terms offered to Macartney were so severe, so repugnant to the laws of nations and the principles of justice, that the governor and inhabitants preferred submitting at discretion. On taking possession, D'Estaing showed little lenity. The people were plundered and abused to an extent that persuaded the Count Dillon — the most distinguished soldier of the French command — to intervene at the head of his regiment for their protection.

* See Appendix No. I.

This course, in such direct contrast to that of De Bouillé in like circumstances, threatened André and those nearest and dearest to him with early poverty. His General, however, though tenderly attached to him, and doubtless entirely sympathizing with his private griefs, seems not to have left him their undisputed prey. In the summer heats he resorted on occasions to the cooler shores of Long Island. Quogue was one of his haunts; where he would taste the sea breezes, and gather for his table every delicacy that the island could produce. He is remembered as a jovial liver, who pushed the bottle freely; while André with his bright, fresh face and symmetrical figure, and wearing his hair unusually long, is described by an islander in whose house he passed three nights, as presenting "the finest model of manly beauty he had ever seen." About this period, too, circumstances brought about a considerable amelioration of his professional condition. It would appear that without the knowledge or approbation of the Commander-in-chief, the Minister had established certain points of provincial rank very unsatisfactorily to the regular corps. In bringing about this step, Innes, Drummond, and the adjutant-general Lord Rawdon—all prime favorites of Sir Henry's—were said to be concerned. His indignation was great, and the offenders were made to feel it. Rawdon was detached from head-quarters to the South, and his duties naturally devolved on that one of the deputies of the office who enjoyed the most confidential relations with Clinton. This was no other than André. We are told that Major Stephen Kemble, the brother-in-law of General Gage, who had long filled the deputy's post, had written to some one or other in excessively severe terms of the conduct of Sir Henry. By some mischance these documents were made known at head-quarters. The writer of course resigned his office, and went to his regiment (the 60th) in the West Indies, where he earned promotion and distinction. The vacant deputy adjutant-generalcy was forthwith bestowed upon André; and thenceforward all the business at head-quarters of the department passed through his hands. It was thus about the beginning of the fall of 1779, that he commenced the virtual discharge of the adjutant-generalcy, in which he continued till his death. When Clinton had dismissed Lord Rawdon, the vacant charge was pressed on Rawdon's personal friend, Lieut.-Col. Charles Stuart, of the 26th, whom delicacy forced to refuse; wherefore, as chief deputy, André went on with all its duties until he was promoted to the station itself, as well as its responsibilities. In October, his friend Simcoe was captured, returning from a daring enterprise to the Raritan, in which by a forced march, without halt or refreshment, of over eighty miles, his cavalry burned a number of large flat-bottomed boats, built for an expedition against New York. Simcoe was treated with much severity, which was, by the efforts of his comrade André, and his courteous and particular opponent Harry Lee, at last so modified that he was exchanged. André, setting aside for the time a bold but well conceived plan for his rescue, wrote proposing he might be sent to New York on parole, as by similar indulgence Colonel Baylor had been permitted to go to Virginia. Simcoe forwarded this application from the state of New Jersey, in whose power he was, to Washington, and rather complains that as it had been neglected by Governor Livingston, so it was unanswered by the General; but in a day or two after he was sent to New York. Arriving at Staten Island, December 31st, he found Clinton gone, and the chance of accompanying him lost. A letter from André was put into his hands — "If this meets you a free man, prepare your regiment for embarkation, and hasten to New York yourself." On the 26th, Clinton had sailed for Charleston.

The war-ships and transports of this expedition were commanded by Mariot Arbuthnot, Vice-Admiral of the Blue, an old sailor, an amiable man, and a bad tactician. It is evident that Sir Henry and himself could not pull together where the king's service was concerned. He was the nephew of "Arbuthnot the polite," the friend of Pope, Swift, and

Gay, the famous physician of Queen Anne, the elegant author of John Bull; — was born in 1711, and died in 1794. His flag-ship was damaged by a storm on the voyage; — instead of signalling the squadron to pursue its appointed course, he led the whole convoy after himself, to the great detriment of the public good. "The good old Admiral lost his bobstay in a gale of wind — bore away — obliged the fleet to follow. It got into the gulf-stream, and bad weather did the rest."* As a consequence it was not until January 31st, 1780, that a part of the armament reached Savannah, whither such of the vessels as were not lost followed. A captured transport brought into Charleston, on the 23rd, the first sure tidings of the expedition.

Notwithstanding the peculiar importance of the city — in a manner the gate of the South — Washington was always, it is said, of opinion that evacuation was preferable to an uncertain defence. He would rather lose a town than an army. The possession of Charleston had hitherto secured to the Americans the control of the state; but since Clinton's repulse from its approaches in 1776, care had not been taken to make it, as its value deserved, absolutely impregnable. Nevertheless its works were strong. Lying between the intersection of the Cooper and Ashley rivers, it could only be invested by land upon one of its three sides, where a chain of redoubts and batteries, mounting over eighty guns and mortars, and stretching from stream to stream, was itself further protected by a double abatis, a deep water canal flowing from Ashley to Cooper, and other fortifications. The Ashley shore was lined with batteries with fifty guns; on that of the Cooper, thirty-three were mounted; and across its mouth was a boom composed of eight sunken vessels, with chains, cables, and spars lashed between their lower masts. Five armed ships with 124 guns, and some galleys, were arrayed behind this *cheval-de-frise*. The fortifications on the island in the harbor were also strong and in good condition;

* Clinton MS.

and it was not thought probable that a hostile fleet could come up to the town.

Having, by aid of the loyalists, obtained horses (all that he sailed with being lost at sea), Clinton on the 11th of February landed about thirty miles south of Charleston, and easily and deliberately approached the city. He waited reinforcements, and thus gave Lincoln time to increase his defences. "Every delay proved of use," says Sir Henry; "it induced Lincoln to collect his whole force at Charleston, and put the fate of both Carolinas on that of the town."* On the 29th of March, the British passed Ashley River, ten miles above the city, under the guidance of Captain Elphinstone of the navy; and on April 1st broke ground before our lines. The fleet meanwhile had forced its way up, shutting out relief from the sea; and on the 14th, the only communication that had still been kept open was closed by the enterprise of Tarleton.†

The city was defended, as nearly as can be computed, by about 2600 regulars and upwards of 3000 local or other militia, among whom was perhaps Andrew Jackson, the future soldier and ruler of the Union. There were besides about 1000 armed sailors; so that the whole defensive force was called 7000. The enemy's strength was probably but little greater. "They had 7000,"—says Clinton,—"we not more than 5000."‡ But he does not appear to include herein the 2500 men that reinforced him from New York.

About this time André wrote as follows, apparently to the adjutant of the garrison at Savannah:—

"HEAD-QUARTERS BEFORE CHARLESTON, the 13th *April*, 1780.

"SIR: I shall be much obliged to you to find out for me

---

* Clinton MS.

† "Captain Elphinstone had infinite merit from the hour of our starting from Savannah to our reduction of Charleston; at the siege of which he commanded a detachment of the royal navy. . . . This does infinite credit to Col. Tarleton. His officer-like decision gained the advantage — the only chance we had of passing the Cooper."— *Clinton MS.*

‡ Clinton MS.

whether such a person as is herein described has ever been prisoner in your hands, and what has become of him; as I am requested by some of my relations to make this inquiry. I have received your several letters, and shall inform the General of the resignation you make of your pretensions to purchase Major Van Braam's commission, and also of the succession proposed of Ens. Fatio and Mr. Clarke to Captain Carden. By a letter received from Col. Steil I find Mr. De Crousac recommended to succeed in a vacant Lieutenancy. I fear this young gentleman has been wronged, from his never having been heard of. He may however I hope be redressed by filling the vacancy of Lieut. Maltey, resigned.

"I must beg you to observe that the Fortnight States are to be signed by the commanding officer of the troops, and not by the Deputy Adjutant General: which I request you to be kind enough to rectify in the future ones to be transmitted. I have the honour to be, Sir, your most obedient and most humble servant, JOHN ANDRÉ, Dy. A. Gen.

"Be so good, Sir, as to omit no opportunity of sending convalescents here. A vessel may possibly be sent round to receive them — but Gen. Prevost will I dare say in the mean time dispatch what he can."

On the 6th May the third parallel was finished, and the British thus enabled to sap the waters of the canal, which was then made a cover for their Yägers to gall with close rifle-shots the defenders of the lines; while balls, bombs, carcasses and fireballs were showered on the town. The fire-brigade was in constant service; and wherever the enemy saw by the smoke that they had kindled a house, there they would drop a bomb. As provisions began to run short with the besieged, a shell filled with rice and molasses was thrown in delicate raillery into their ranks; and in the same spirit was returned charged with sulphur and hog's lard for the benefit of the Scots regiments. Desertions were not numerous, though there were sufficient facilities for stealing through

THE FALL OF CHARLESTON.

the investments to enable Du Portail to be conveyed into the town after the last parallel was begun. Late as it was, this officer advised an immediate evacuation; but the wishes of the citizens and the hopes of relief prevailed on Lincoln to hold out. On the 10th April he had refused to yield; on the 8th May he was again summoned to surrender a post that was rapidly ceasing to be tenable. As he would not accept the proposed terms, the siege was continued until the 11th, when he notified Clinton of his willingness to receive them. Though it was now, by their own opinion, optional with the English to storm the town or insist on its surrender at discretion, a milder counsel prevailed. As might be expected, the capitulation was disadvantageous to the garrison. Their necessities and the laws of war entitled Clinton to prescribe hard conditions; but the most bitter pill to swallow must have been the manner of surrender. Lincoln had demanded to march out with the honors of war — drums beating, colors flying, and shouldered arms. It was answered that when the arms were grounded his colors should not be uncased, nor should his drums beat a British or German march.* The garrison, consisting of every adult who had borne arms in the defence of the town, became prisoners of war; and on the 12th May Clinton took possession.

The fall of Charleston was a dreadful blow to America, and its results were of the highest importance. That it did not yield till the last moment is undoubtedly true, unless we receive Napoleon's axiom that no fortification should succumb without at least one assault; but it ought not to have been defended at all, unless successfully. The wishes and the gallantry of the citizens and the failure of expected succor, apologize for Lincoln's fatal error of judgment. On the other hand, this event must always be esteemed a great credit to Clinton. The siege was well-conceived, and ex-

---

* This severity was exactly retorted at Yorktown, when Cornwallis's troops were compelled to march out with colors cased and drums beating neither a French or American march.

ecuted in the best vein of military judgment. With a force numerically not exceeding that of his foe, and with but trifling loss to himself, he compelled nearly 7000 men strongly fortified to lay down their arms.*

After the fall of the city, we are told that there was an opinion current in our army that André had been present in its lines during the siege as a spy; and in 1822 it was declared that two gentlemen of repute still surviving at Charleston, affirmed at least the existence of the report in 1780. One of these had been an officer of Clinton's; the other, a resident of the place through and after the siege. Another witness goes further. Edward Shrewsberry, a suspected tory, but of good condition, was ill at his house in East Bay. His brother, a whig, leaving the lines to visit him, found repeatedly there a young man clad in homespun, to whom he was introduced as a Virginian belonging to the troops then in the city; and as such he considered the stranger. After the capitulation, meeting the same person at the same place, he was again presented to him as Major André; and taxing his brother with the identity of the two characters, they were confessed to have been one and the same man. To another visitor, his son records that the stranger in homespun had been represented " as a back countryman, who had brought down cattle for the garrison to the opposite side of the river," — an assertion that passed unsuspected and unchallenged until months after, when André had been hanged and the visitor who related the story was returned from confinement at St. Augustine's, when the whig Shrewsberry informed him that the cattle-driver he had seen with his brother was no other than Major André in disguise. These declarations, coming from distinct and respectable sources, seem to bear the marks of truth; and that the circumstance, if it really occurred, was not singular, appears from the case of Col. Hamilton Ballen-

* The Return of prisoners to the army at the surrender, May 12th, 1780, is signed by André, as Deputy Adjutant-General. Those made by the Fleet, including seamen, &c., do not figure therein. — *Rememb.* x. 76.

dine, who, in the very beginning of the siege, fell into an American picket that he mistook for Clinton's. When challenged, he gave his name in reply; and being told that was not sufficient, he produced from his pocket draughts of the American works that he had made or obtained. He was informed of his error as to the party of the captors, and sent to Lincoln, by whose orders he was instantly hanged. It is but just to add that, if this story of André's having been a spy at Charleston received credence in respectable quarters, it was afterwards questioned by gentlemen of equal character in our service.

CHAPTER XII.

Clinton returns to New York. — Proposed Attack on Rochambeau. — Plans for a Loyal Uprising. — Anecdotes of André. — The Cow-Chase.

DURING Clinton's absence, the unusual severity of the winter had frozen the waters about New York so firmly that the whole train of our army might safely have passed over. Lest such an attempt should be made, the loyal inhabitants petitioned to be embodied; and an additional force of nearly 6000 men was thus arrayed for the defence of the city, of whom about 1000 were armed and uniformed at their own cost — "many of the most respectable citizens serving in the ranks of each company." There was apparent need for this display when the Hudson to Paulus Hook presented a causeway of ice of but 2000 yards from shore to shore; but unfortunately the miserable state of our army prevented any advantage from the opportunity being taken. The spirits of the loyalists, however, were wonderfully cheered by these musterings; many deserters and others came in from Jersey, where Chief-justice Smith advised Knyphausen now to raise the royal standard, in the idea that militia and continentals would hasten to join it, and the state be subdued before Clinton's return and without his aid. This plan was tried on June 7th, but nothing came of it; the English returned after some plundering and skirmishing with a loss of 500 killed, wounded, and missing, and closely observed by Washington's army, now reduced to but 3000 or 4000 men.

Leaving 4000 men with Cornwallis, and Carolina and Georgia to all appearance entirely reduced, Sir Henry hurried back to New York; justly apprehending a design of the French armament now on the coast to make with Washington a conjoined attack on his lines. In fact his convoy had already been in the power of the French as it passed the Chesapeake, and had only escaped by De Ternay's mistaking the large troop-ships for firstrates. On the 12th July, Rochambeau's men were in Newport harbor.

Clinton's first design, to fall at once on Washington or West Point, was thwarted by the inopportune and prolonged absence of Knyphausen. "This premature move in Jersey, at a time when Sir H. Clinton least expected it, prevented a combined move against Washington that might have been decisive:"—and Washington himself wrote that their combination would make the British "equal to almost anything they may think proper to attempt."* The next thought was to carry the French position at Newport by a *coup-de-main*. Arbuthnot was solicited ere yet their arrival was known to have transports in readiness for 6000 men. On the 18th July, news of their position was conveyed to him by Clinton, and means of embarkation pressingly called for. These, however, were so long in coming that not till the 27th was the army embarked on the Sound, and conveyed to Huntingdon Bay; where it awaited the return of a vessel despatched by Sir Henry to the Admiral blockading the French at Newport. Meantime Rochambeau had so strengthened his works with heavy guns and mortars, and furnaces for heating balls, that a joint attack of army and fleet was deemed out of the question, and the moment for a *coup-de-main* long gone by. Sorely disappointed and with not a little grumbling the troops on the 31st returned to Whitestone.† They burned for an

---

* Clinton MS. Marshall, iv. c. 5.

† Stedm. ii. 246.—" Mr. Stedman seems totally ignorant of the object of this move. It had been proposed that 6000 men under Sir H. Clinton should have been landed in Escort Passage to meet the French on their embarkation [debarkation?]: but as the Admiral was not informed of their arrival till ten days after, and that they had been reinforced and had had time to fortify, it would not have been quite so prudent for the army alone to attempt:—and if the Admiral had seen the propriety of taking an active part with the Navy, he would have accepted the proposal of Sir H. C. This is all that need be said, and perhaps Mr. Stedman affords us the best reason

equal encounter with the French; and officers applied to the adjutant-general as an especial favor for such employment. "The General assures you," he replied to Simcoe, "that the Rangers shall be pitted against a French regiment the first time he can procure a meeting." These regiments were the Bourbonnais, Soissonnais, Santonge, and Deux Ponts; and Lauzun's Legion.

Among other objects that now commanded André's attention was a correspondence with the chief tories of that loyal region lying between the Chesapeake and Delaware bays; which was intended to terminate in the successful uprising of several thousand men in arms for the king, under the protection of a strong British detachment. There were great hopes of this measure when matters should be ripe, for the district was populous and unquestionably abundant in loyalists; but it was nipped by unforeseen events.

Various anecdotes are preserved that show with what gentleness of spirit André bore his honors. When Lamb, one of the Convention troops of Saratoga, escaped from his officers and from the Americans — "honorable desertions," Burgoyne called them, since instead of being allowed to go to England as the capitulation provided, Congress retained them prisoners for exchange — and with a party of his comrades was sheltered by the country people till he got to New York, he was received at Head-quarters by André, who taking him into the parlor, closely questioned him of his route, his risks, the numbers of the Americans, their treatment of prisoners, &c.; and finally rewarded himself and his comrades in Sir Henry's name, and proffered them either a free passage home or service in any regiment they chose. Of his lenity to prisoners also we have a trivial but doubtless authentic anecdote from a Mr. Drewy.

for not attempting anything." — *Clinton MS.* "It was reported some time after that the French were in such consternation at being blocked up by a superior fleet, that had we proceeded, at our arrival they would have run the ships aground and thrown their guns overboard." — *MS. Journal, Lt. Mathew, Coldstream Guards.*

"A foraging party from New York made an inroad into our settlement near that city. The neighbours soon assembled to oppose them; and though not above fifteen years old, I turned out with my friends. In company was another boy, in age and size nearly my own speed. We had counted on a fine chase; but the British were not to be driven so easily as we had expected. Standing their ground, they not only put us to flight, but captured several of our party; myself and the other boy among them. They presently set off with us for New York: and all the way as we were going, my heart ached to think how distressed my poor mother and sisters would be when night came and I did not return. Soon as they brought me in sight of the prison, I was struck with horror. The gloomy walls and frightful guards at the doors and wretched crowds at the iron windows, together with the thoughts of being locked up there in dark dungeons with disease and death, so overcame me that I bursted into tears. Instantly a richly dressed officer stepped up, and taking me by the hand, with a look of great tenderness said,—'My dear boy, what makes you cry?' I told him I could not help it, when I compared my present sad prospect with the happy one I enjoyed in the morning with my mother and sisters at home. 'Well, well, my dear child,' said he, 'don't cry, don't cry any more.' Then turning to the jailer ordered him to stop till he should come back. I was struck with the wonderful difference between *this* man and the rest around me. He appeared to me like a brother; they like brutes. I asked the jailor who he was. 'Why, that's Major André,' said he angrily, 'the adjutant-general of the army; and you may thank your stars that he saw you; for I suppose that he has gone to the general to beg you off, as he has done many of your —— rebel countrymen.' In a short time he returned, and with great joy in his countenance called out—'Well, my boys, I've good news for you! The General has given you to me, to dispose of as I choose; and now you are at liberty. So run home to your fond parents, and be good boys: mind what they tell you; say your prayers; love one another; and God Almighty will bless you.'"

The month of July, 1780, furnished André with an occasion for the best known of his verses, which seem to have been written as much to gratify his own keen perception of the ludicrous as to retaliate in kind the satirical assaults that were made by the other side upon himself and his friends. On the 20th, our army was stationed in the upper part of Bergen county, New Jersey; and St. Clair having the light infantry during La Fayette's visit to Rochambeau, Wayne of course commanded the Pennsylvania line. With its two brigades, some guns of Proctor's artillery, and Moylan's dragoons, amounting in all, perhaps, to less than 2000 men, he started from camp on an expedition that would have long ago been forgotten but for the comic strain in which a foeman commemorated its results.* The object was to harry Bergen

* The composition of the Cow-Chase may have been suggested by the fact that André had boarded with John Thompson, the woodcutting agent at New York. He also probably visited the scene of action with Clinton. The piece was written at Head-quarters, No. 1, Broadway, and was given for publication to Rivington, whose Gazette was a thorn in the side of the whigs of the neighborhood. Among his friends he was a merry, jovial, companionable person enough; but to his enemies he was a perfect pest. The Rev. Dr. Witherspoon, in his pretended recantation of Towne, says:— "However, take it which way you will, there never was a lie published in Philadelphia that could bear the least comparison with those published by James Rivington in New York. This, in my opinion, is to be imputed to the superiority not of the printer, but of the prompter or prompters. I reckon Mr. Tryon to have excelled in that branch, and probably he had many coadjutors. What do you think of 40,000 Russians, and 20,000 Moors, which Moors too were said by Mr. Rivington to be dreadful among the women? as also of the boats building at the forks of Monongahela to carry the Congress down the river to New Orleans? These were swingers."— He made great fun too of Governor Livingston, who had imprudently taken the pen against him. "If Rivington is taken, I must have one of his ears; Gov. Clinton is entitled to the other; and General Washington, if he pleases, may take his head," writes Livingston in 1780; and if the Cow-Chase was felt nowhere else, it hit hard here. Fifty years after, Livingston's descendant and biographer comments on "the scurrilous and abusive Cow-Chase, which no one can read without lessening his sympathy for the

Neck and to break up a blockhouse at Bull's Ferry by Fort Lee, where seventy refugees under Cuyler were posted to protect the British woodcutters; and to disperse any forces that might be found in the vicinity. But Cuyler defended himself most spiritedly, though his wooden walls were pierced with fifty-two cannon balls in one face only; and when Wayne retired, hung on his skirts, seizing stragglers, and rescuing some of the spoil. His loss was twenty-one killed and wounded; Wayne's being sixty-four. To the survivors of "the brave Seventy" the king conveyed his especial approval of their valor and fidelity.

It is hardly needful to observe that this poem — which, says Mr. Sparks, with much that is crude and coarse, contains several stanzas of genuine humor and satire — is modelled on Chevy Chase. The manuscript copy as well as the original editions have several notes, that are distinguished here from my own by being put in brackets. In retort to the names bestowed on the airs in vogue at American festivities, a writer in Rivington's paper suggested that the managers of the Phil-

unfortunate André," apropos of Stirling who had intermarried with the family. The poem was written and printed at intervals; the first canto appearing on the 16th August, the second on the 30th, and the third on the 23rd Sept. 1780. Dunlap reports that Rivington said he received the last canto from the author on the day before he set out to meet Arnold; it was published on the very day of his capture; which must have contributed to the great vogue it has always obtained. I have printed the version in this volume from André's original autograph MS., collated with these editions. Cow-Chase, in Three Cantos, Published on Occasion of the Rebel General Wayne's Attack of the Refugees' Block-House on Hudson's River, On Friday the 21st of July, 1780. New York: Rivington, 1780, 8vo. pp. 69: — and The Cow-Chase, an Heroick Poem, in Three Cantos. Written at New York, 1780, by the late Major André, with Explanatory Notes by the Editor.

"The man who fights and runs away,
"May live to fight another day,"
Said Butler in his deathless lay.
"But he who is in battle slain
"Can never rise to fight again;"
As wisely thought good General Wayne.

London; Fielding, 1781. 4to. pp. 32. It is also printed by Dunlap, with his tragedy of André, (Lond. 1799,) and in Moore's Bal. Rev.

adelphia Assembly Balls should thenceforth add to the tunes of Burgoyne's Surrender, Clinton's Retreat, and the like, the new dancing-measure of A Trip to the Block-House, or The Woodcutter's Triumph.

THE COW-CHASE.

CANTO I.

ELIZABETH-TOWN, August 1, 1780.

To drive the kine one summer's morn
　The Tanner took his way;*
The calf shall rue, that is unborn,
　The jumbling of that day.

And Wayne descending steers shall know,
　And tauntingly deride;
And call to mind, in every low,
　The tanning of *his* hide.

Let Bergen cows still ruminate,
　Unconscious in the stall
What mighty means were used to get—
　And lose them after all.

For many heroes bold and brave
　From New Bridge and Tapaan;†

---

* [General Wayne's *legal* occupation.] By the way, this order may explain the last scenes of the cattle taken:—"One of the drafts acquainted with the management of hides and tallow from each wing to be sent to the Commissary of Hides at the Magazine."—*MS. Am. Orderly-book*, Aug. 11, 1780.

† [Village in New Jersey] on Wayne's line of march.

And those that drink Passaick's wave,*
And those that eat soupaan; †

And sons of distant Delaware,
And still remoter Shannon;
And Major Lee with horses rare,
And Proctor with his cannon.‡

All wondrous proud in arms they came;
What hero would refuse
To tread the rugged path to fame
Who had a pair of shoes? §

At six, the host with sweating buff
Arrived at Freedom's Pole: ‖
When Wayne, who thought he'd time enough,
Thus speechified the whole.

"Oh ye, whom Glory doth unite,
Who Freedom's cause espouse;
— Whether the wing that's doomed to fight,
Or that to drive the cows —

---

* [A river in New Jersey.]

† [Hasty Pudding, made of the meal of Indian Corn.] The corpulent Van Bummels, dwellers on the pleasant Bronx, says the learned Diedrich Knickerbocker, "were the first inventors of suppawn or mush and milk."

‡ The numbers of Irish in the Pennsylvania line often caused it to be called, in the war, the line of Ireland. Lee, of the dragoons, — Light-horse Harry as he was styled, — was distinguished by the superior equipage of his corps, and its dashing achievements. He says that Wayne's brigade though good fighters were over-fond of pleasure, and moved with larger trains than any equal corps in the service.

§ "They are of a thin, long-legged make, most of them without shoes and stockings, and without coats, and sometimes they throw away their arms when they are close pursued." — *MS. Mathew's Journ.*

‖ [Freedom's — *i. e.* Liberty Pole, — a long tree stuck in the ground.] Its place was between Orangetown and Tinack. — *MS. Am. O. B.* Aug. 22, 1780.

"Ere yet you tempt your further way,
   Or into action come;
Hear, soldiers, what I have to say;
   And take a pint of rum.

"Intemp'rate valour then will string
   Each nervous arm the better:
So all the land shall IO sing,
   And read the General's letter.*

"Know, that some paltry Refugees
   Whom I've a mind to fight,
Are playing h—l among the trees
   That grow on yonder height.

"Their fort and block-houses we'll level,
   And deal a horrid slaughter:
We'll drive the scoundrels to the devil,
   And ravish wife and daughter.

"I, under cover of th' attack,
   Whilst you are all at blows,
From English-Neighbourhood and Tinack †
   Will drive away the cows.

"For well you know the latter is
   The serious operation:

---

* This letter is probably the same printed in Almon's Remembrancer, x. 290, and credited to the Pennsylvania Packet, Aug. 1, 1780. It is from Washington to the President of Congress, July 26, 1780, and after narrating the story of the expedition, the failure of the attack on the block-house by reason of the cannon being "too light to penetrate the logs of which it was constructed," and the "intemperate valor" of our men that occasioned so great loss to themselves, he concludes: "I have been thus particular, lest the account of this affair should have reached Philadelphia much exaggerated, as is commonly the case upon such occasions."

† [Villages in New Jersey.]

And fighting with the Refugees
  Is only — demonstration."

His daring words, from all the crowd
  Such great applause did gain,
That every man declar'd aloud
  For serious work — with Wayne.

Then from the cask of rum once more
  They took a heady gill;
When, one and all, they loudly swore
  They'd fight upon the hill.

But here — the muse hath not a strain
  Befitting such great deeds:
Huzza, they cried. Huzza for Wayne!
  And shouting ——

CANTO II.

Near his meridian pomp, the sun
  Had journey'd from th' horizon;
When fierce the dusty tribe mov'd on
  Of heroes drunk as poison.

The sounds confus'd of boasting oaths
  Reecho'd through the wood:
Some vow'd to sleep in dead men's cloaths,
  And some — to swim in blood.

At Irvine's nod 'twas fine to see
  The left prepared to fight;
The while the drovers, Wayne and Lee,
  Drew off upon the right.

Which Irvine 'twas, Fame don't relate;
   Nor can the Muse assist her:
Whether 'twas he that cocks a hat,
   Or he that gives a glister.

For greatly one was signalized
   That fought at Chestnut Hill;
And Canada immortalized
   The vender of the pill.

Yet the attendance upon Proctor
   They both might have to boast of;
For there was business for the doctor
   And hats to be dispos'd of.*

Let none uncandidly infer
   That Stirling wanted spunk;
The self-made Peer had sure been there,
   But that the Peer—was drunk.

But turn we to the Hudson's banks,
   Where stood the modest train
With purpose firm, tho' slender ranks,
   Nor car'd a pin for Wayne.

For them the unrelenting hand
   Of rebel fury drove,
And tore from every genial band
   Of Friendship and of Love.

And some within a dungeon's gloom,
   By mock tribunals laid,

---

* [One of the Irvines was a hatter, the other a physician] Dr. William Irvine, after two years' captivity in Canada, now commanded the 2nd Pennsylvania regiment. Brigadier James Irvine of the militia was, it will be recollected, taken at Chestnut Hill, Dec. 1777.

THE COW-CHASE.

Had waited long a cruel doom
   Impending o'er their head.

Here one bewails a brother's fate;
   There one a sire demands;
Cut off, alas! before their date
   By ignominious hands.

And silver'd grandsires here appear'd
   In deep distress serene;
Of reverend manners, that declar'd
   The better days they'd seen.

O curs'd rebellion! these are thine;
   Thine are these tales of woe!
Shall at thy dire insatiate shrine
   Blood never cease to flow?

And now the foe began to lead
   His forces to th' attack;
Balls whistling unto balls succeed,
   And make the blockhouse crack.

No shot could pass, if you will take
   The Gen'ral's word for true;
But 'tis a d——ble mistake,
   For every shot went thro'.*

The firmer as the rebels press'd
   The loyal heroes stand.
Virtue had nerv'd each honest breast,
   And industry each hand.

---

* Wayne attributed his failure to the lightness of his pieces, which he thought made no impression on the walls of the house. In this he was probably mistaken. *Spark's Wash.* vii. 117. *Rem.* x. 261.

"In valour's phrenzy * Hamilton
"Rode like a soldier big,
"And Secretary Harrison
"With pen stuck in his wig.

"But lest their chieftain Washington
"Should mourn them in the mumps,†
"The fate of Withrington to shun
"They fought *behind* the stumps." ‡

But ah, Thadæus Posset, why
Should thy poor soul elope?
And why should Titus Hooper die,
Ah die — without a rope?

Apostate Murphy, thou to whom
Fair Shela ne'er was cruel,
In death shalt hear her mourn thy doom,
— "Auch, would you die, my jewel?" — §

Thee, Nathan Pumpkin, I lament,
Of melancholy fate:

* [*Vide* Lee's Trial.] — "When General Washington asked me if I would remain in front and retain the command, or he should take it, and I had answered that I undoubtedly would, and that he should see that I myself should be one of the last to leave the field: Colonel Hamilton flourishing his sword immediately exclaimed — that's right, my dear General, and I will stay, and we will all die here on this spot... — I could not but be surprized at his expression, but observing him much flustered and in a sort of *phrenzy of valour*, I calmly requested him," &c. Lee's Defence in Trial (ed. 1778), p. 60. — Harrison also mentioned in this verse had met André at Amboy: where this personal peculiarity may have been noticed.

† [A disorder prevalent in the rebel lines.]

‡ [The merit of these lines, which is doubtless very great, can only be felt by true connoisseurs conversant in ancient song.]

For Witherington needs must I wayle
As one in doleful dumps;
For when his legges were smitten off
He fought upon his stumpes. — *Chevy Chase.*

§ See the Irish song in Smollett's *Rehearsal.*

THE COW-CHASE.

The grey goose, stolen as he went,
In his heart's blood was wet.*

Now as the fight was further fought,
And balls began to thicken,
The fray assum'd, the Gen'rals thought,
The colour of a licking.

Yet undismay'd the chiefs command,
And, to redeem the day,
Cry, SOLDIERS, CHARGE! — they hear, they stand,
They turn — and run away.

CANTO III.

Not all delights the bloody spear,
Or horrid din of battle:
There are, I'm sure, who'd like to hear
A word about the cattle.

The Chief, whom we beheld of late
Near Schralenberg haranguing,
At Yan Van Poop's † unconscious sate
Of Irvine's hearty banging.

Whilst valiant Lee, with courage wild,
Most bravely did oppose
The tears of woman and of child
Who begg'd he'd leave the cows.

* Against Sir Hugh Mountgomery
So right the shaft he sett,
The grey goose-wing that was thereon
In his hearts blood was wett.— *Chevy Chase.*

The queer American names in the text are not an unfair hit at the Zerubbabel Fisks and Habakkuk Nutters and Determined Cocks, whose patronymics are immortalized by Irving.

† [Who kept a dramshop.]

But Wayne, of sympathizing heart,
  Required a relief
Not all the blessings could impart
  Of battle or of beef:

For now a prey to female charms,
  His soul took more delight in
A lovely Hamadryad's * arms,
  Than cow-driving or fighting.

A Nymph, the Refugees had drove
  Far from her native tree,
Just happen'd to be on the move
  When up came Wayne and Lee.

She in mad Anthony's fierce eye
  The Hero saw pourtray'd;
And, all in tears, she took him by
  The bridle of his jade.†

" Hear" — said the Nymph — "Oh great Commander,
  " No human lamentations;
" The trees you see them cutting yonder
  " Are all my near relations.

" And I, forlorn, implore thine aid
  " To free the sacred grove:
" So shall thy powers be repaid
  " With an Immortal's love!"

Now some, to prove she was a Goddess,
  Said this enchanting fair

---

* [A deity of the woods.]
† [A New-England name for a horse, mare, or gelding.]

Had late retired from the *Bodies*,*
    In all the pomp of war.

That drums and merry fifes had play'd
    To honor her retreat:
And Cunningham himself convey'd
    The lady thro' the street.†

Great Wayne, by soft compassion sway'd,
    To no enquiry stoops;
But takes the fair afflicted maid
    Right into Yan Van Poop's.

So Roman Anthony, they say,
    Disgrac'd th' imperial banner,
And for a gypsy lost the day;
    Like Anthony the tanner.

The Hamadryad had but half
    Receiv'd redress from Wayne,
When drums and colours, cow and calf,
    Came down the road amain.

All in a cloud of dust were seen
    The sheep, the horse, the goat;
The gentle heifer, ass obscene,
    The yearling and the shoat.

And pack-horses with fowls came by,
    Befeather'd on each side,

---

* [A cant appellation given among the soldiery to the corps that has the honour to guard his Majesty's person.]

† That is, the lady had been drummed out of the lines as a common drunkard or thief. Cunningham was the Provost-Marshal. "There are a number of women here of bad character, who are continually running to New York, and back again. If they were men, I would flog them without mercy." — A. Burr, commanding on American lines in Westchester county, to Gen. McDougall: Whiteplains, Jan. 21, 1779.

Like Pegasus, the horse that I
    And other poets ride.

Sublime upon his stirrups rose
    The mighty Lee behind,
And drove the terror-smitten cows
    Like chaff before the wind.

But sudden, see the woods above
    Pour down another corps
All helter-skelter in a drove,
    Like that I sung before.

Irvine and terror in the van
    Came flying all abroad;
And cannon, colours, horse, and man,
    Ran tumbling to the road.

Still as he fled, 'twas Irvine's cry,
    And his example too:
"Run on, my merry men all — for why?
    The shot will not go through?"

— Five Refugees, 'tis true, were found
    Stiff on the blockhouse floor:
But then, 'tis thought the shot went round,
    And in at the back door. —

As when two kennels in the street,
    Swell'd with a recent rain,
In gushing streams together meet
    And seek the neighboring drain:

So meet these dung-born tribes in one,
    As swift in their career;
And so to New Bridge they ran on —
    But all the cows got clear.

Poor Parson Caldwell, all in wonder,
  Saw the returning train:
And mourn'd to Wayne the lack of plunder
  For them to steal again.*

For 'twas his right to seize the spoil, and
  To share with each commander,
As he had done on Staten-Island
  With frost-bit Alexander.†

In his dismay the frantick priest
  Began to grow prophetic:
You'd swore, to see his lab'ring breast,
  He'd taken an emetick.

"I view a future day," said he,
  "Brighter than this day dark is:
And you shall see what you shall see —
  Ha! ha! one pretty Marquis.‡

"And he shall come to Paulus Hook,
  And great atchievements think on:

---

* Rev. James Caldwell of New Jersey, an active whig and deputy quarter-master general, whose wife was barbarously shot by a newly enlisted soldier of Knyphausen's command in the preceding summer, on no other provocation, as was alleged, than that she vituperated him from her window as he passed. In connection with this case, Bishop Griswold, of the diocese including Vermont, writes at Bennington in 1818: "With what detestation is frequent mention made of the British soldier's killing a woman in New Jersey. But how rarely, if ever, do we hear of the barbarity of Col. F——, who, in the battle of Bennington, deliberately aimed at, shot through the breast, and instantly killed the wife of a British officer?" Mr. Caldwell was himself killed by an American soldier, Nov. 24, 1781. In proof of his patriotic zeal, local tradition relates that when Knyphausen came to Springfield, he collected the hymn-books of his church for wadding to the American muskets. "Put a little *Watts* into them," he said to our soldiers.

† [Calling himself, because he was ordered not to do it, Earl of Stirling, though no sterling Earl.] He led a foray into Staten Island, Jan. 1780, in which 500 of his men were frost-bitten.

‡ [Lafayette.]

And make a bow, and take a look,
Like Satan over Lincoln.

" And all the land around shall glory
To see the Frenchmen caper,
And pretty Susan tell the story
In the next Chatham paper." *

This solemn prophecy of course
Gave all much consolation ;
Except to Wayne, who lost his horse
Upon the great occasion.

---

* Miss Susannah Livingston (born 1748), the governor's daughter, was suspected of political authorship. Perhaps " an intercepted epistle to Tabitha from New York," dated Aug. 27, 1780, may be attributed to her:

" Sir Harry, it seems, was more sullen than ever ;
And André complained of much bile on the liver."

And again:

" Alas, my sweet sister, I cannot but fear
That something not good is to happen us here.
The knight he is either involved in deep gloom,
When no one but André dare enter his room," &c.

Though her father had no mercy for " the British scoundrels," his house of Liberty Hall was protected in the invasion of June, 1780, by Lt. Col. Gordon; who on account of his sister, the dowager Duchess of Gordon and her husband Gen. Morris, was always very civil to the ladies of Lord Stirling's connection. On this occasion he promised safety to the young ladies, " so amiable in appearance as to make it scarcely possible to suppose they are daughters of such an archfiend as the cruel and seditious proprietor of the mansion "; and in token of the same was presented with a rose from Miss Susan's hand. During the day a guard was kept at the house; nevertheless from behind it (and by a servant, it was charged), he himself was shot through the thigh. The whole business figured in the newspapers. This was the same Gordon that slept so soundly at Philadelphia. He got into trouble in this expedition; was tried; and afterwards insisted on fighting and killing Lt. Col. Thomas of the 1st Guards, who had testified against him. Miss Livingston married John Cleves Symmes, the father-in-law of President Harrison.

Since this note was written, I have seen a statement printed in Rivington's paper, July 22nd, 1780, denying that any musket was fired from Livingston's house, and alleging that the rose was bestowed not upon Gordon, but on Colonel Wurmb of the Hessians.

His horse that carried all his prog,
    His military speeches,
His corn-stalk whisky for his grog,
    Blue stockings, and brown breeches.

And now I've closed my epic strain,
    I tremble as I shew it;
Lest this same warrio-drover Wayne
    Should ever catch the poet!*

* It has been said that Wayne was brigadier of the day when André was taken. This was not so. Huntington had that post (MS. Am. O. B.); nor was Wayne of the board that pronounced on his fate. A biographer however tells us that he was delivered to Wayne's keeping at Tappaan.

Though the introduction of breeches into burlesque heroicals is sanctioned by the usage of poets from King Stephen's days down to those of Tam O'Shanter, it is possible that André here had a particular pair as a model:—

> "His breeches were of rugged woollen,
> And had been at the siege of Bullen;
> To old King Harry so well known,
> Some writers held they were his own.
> Tho' they were lined with many a piece
> Of ammunition bread and cheese,
> And fat blackpuddings, proper food
> For warriors that delight in blood." &c.
> —*Hud. Pt.* i. *c.* i. v. 309.

Under André's signature to a MS. of The Cow-Chase are endorsed, says Mr. Frank Moore, these lines:—

> "When the epic strain was sung
> The poet by the neck was hung,
> And to his cost he finds too late,
> The dung-born tribe decides his fate."

CHAPTER XIII.

Progress of Arnold's Treason. — Condition of American Affairs in 1780. — Plans for Surrendering West Point. — Letters between André and Arnold. — An Interview Concerted. — André's Last Hours in New York.

THE secret correspondence with Arnold, begun in 1779, had at an early stage been intrusted by Clinton to André's exclusive management. The information received was valuable, and often highly important; nor was it long questionable from what quarter it came. In an elaborately disguised hand Arnold wrote over the signature of Gustavus, — a pseudonym perhaps suggested by the romantic story of Gustavus Vasa, in whose love of military glory, undaunted boldness, and successful revolt against the unwonted lords of his native land, he might persuade himself his own character found a counterpart. On the other part, the fictitious name of Anderson was but a transparent play upon André's own. The accuracy and nature of the intelligence soon gave Clinton concern to know with certainty its author; and once satisfied in his mind that this was no other than Arnold, he took his cue from circumstances, and delayed the final consummation until a period when the loss of a correspondent so valuable would be compensated by weightier gains than the individual defection of an officer of rank. Thus he continued to receive the most momentous revelations of our affairs; and it may possibly have been that through these means a knowledge was acquired of the condition of Carolina that led to the fall of Charleston. It is certain that his slow approaches after landing were as well calculated to bring reinforcements to the city as to himself; and it is not likely that Arnold could have borne any very great love to Lincoln, who had been raised over his head from the militia directly to a continental major-generalcy, and at a juncture when the neglect of his own claims by Congress amounted to little less than a positive insult. If we may believe Marbois, tidings of the expected aid from France were undoubtedly communicated to Sir Henry, with the additional news that no plans of combined operations were to be settled by Washington and Rochambeau until its arrival. This information, concealed at the time by Congress from even its own army, was thus made known to the enemy; and if Arnold could not in advance tell him the precise force to arrive or its intended plan of action, he at least might advise him of Washington's ruse, and that La Fayette's and Rochambeau's invasion of Canada was but a false light hung out to beguile the foe. On August 3rd, 1780, he was appointed to the command of West Point and its dependencies; and it was forthwith concerted that his treason should be fully developed with the greatest possible advantage to the British.*

The moment was truly a favorable one. The English were weary of the continued strife, and really anxious for peace with America on almost any terms that might not involve Independency. The mess-rooms no more, as in Howe's days, echoed the toast of "A glorious war and a long one!" The royal officers now pledged "A speedy accommodation of our present unnatural disputes!" On the other hand, America too was tired of the war. A cloud of witnesses of the best authority testify to the probability of a majority of our people being desirous of accomodating the quarrel, and of reuniting with England on conditions of strict union, if not of mediated dependence. The public chest was empty. The miserable bubble by which it had hitherto been recruited was

---

* It is curious that so long before as 1776, Colonel Zedwitz of our army entered into negotiations with the enemy almost identical with those now conducted by Arnold. The delivery of the forts on the North River was the ultimate design of either traitor. Zedwitz was guilty; but he was acquitted because the court did not think his offence merited death!

on the verge of explosion, and the continental paper money, always really worthless though long sustained by the force of laws and bayonets, was now rapidly approximating its ultimate value. The ranks were supplied with children, whose service for nine months was bought for $1500 apiece. Hundreds even of the staff officers, said Greene in May, 1780, were ruined by the public charges they had been forced to incur, while every obstacle was opposed to a settlement of their accounts lest their demands on government should become fixed. "However important our cause, or valuable the blessings of liberty," he continues to Washington, "it is utterly impossible to divest ourselves of our private feelings, while we are contending for them." — "It is obvious that the bulk of the people are weary of the war," said Reed in August. "There never has been a stage of the war," said Washington, "in which the dissatisfaction has been so general and so alarming." The army ill-paid, ill-fed, ill-clad, avenged its sufferings and its wrongs by such means as lay in its hands. Martial law was published to procure its supplies in states that had not a hostile ensign within their borders. Regiment after regiment rose in mutiny; nor could the rope or the scourge check the devastation and desertion that marked the army's course. At this very period, despite the repeated sentences of courts-martial, and the general orders for the officer of the day on his individual authority to flog any straggler within the limit of fifty lashes, we find in Washington's own words the most unwelcome evidences of the necessities of his followers and their consequent marauds along the banks of the Hudson.* Not until the end

---

* Without regard to the question of the soldier's right to quit a service where he is defrauded of his pay and detained beyond the term of his enlistment, it may simply be remarked that at no time were the lash and the cord more active than in 1779 and in 1780. The many-thonged and knotted cat which cut to the blood at every stroke, and the gauntlet, where a double file of soldiers anointed the culprit's naked body with blows from one end of their lane to the other, were in constant requisition. Flogging went beyond a hundred lashes; and sometimes the criminal was again and

of August was the pay due in the preceding March forthcoming. In September Hamilton found the army a demoralized, undisciplined mob: disliking the nation for its neglect, dreaded by the nation for its oppressions. The description of an East Indian government, wielding with one hand a truncheon while the other was stretched forth to plunder, seemed in the fears of many about to be realized in our own land. Our chiefs with mortification and regret confessed the day impending when, unless the war was carried on by foreign troops and foreign treasure, America must come to terms. "Send us troops, ships, and money," wrote Rochambeau to Vergennes; "but do not depend upon these people nor upon their means." Yet it was known that the aid of France and Spain was merely sporadic; that their finances forbade the hope of permanent subsidies. In 1774 neither fear nor flattery, we are told, could swell the taxes of France beyond $90,000,000, to be levied from 24,000,000 of people, and there was now reason to fear that, without some great stroke on our part, she would soon abandon us as a profitless ally, and make her own peace with Britain.

Congress too, rent by faction and intrigue, no longer commanded the entire confidence of the whigs. Its relations with the states were not satisfactory, and with the army were decidedly bad. Jealousy on the one hand, aversion and distrust on the other, daily widened the unacknowledged breach. In August it threatened such an exercise of its power as drew the warning from Washington that if the deed were perpetrated, he questioned much "if there was an officer in

again remanded, that his torn and inflamed back might be more bitterly rent. As for the death penalty, it was necessary in 1779 when our army was in danger of dissolution by desertions, to authorize its immediate infliction upon any one caught in the act. Harry Lee not only hanged the first man that he detected in this offence, but sent his lopped and bloody head to Washington. The spectacle had a happy effect on the men; but our officers dreaded the result of its being made known to the public. Its repetition was forbidden, and Washington ordered a party at once to bury the mutilated corpse ere it should fall into the hands of the enemy. — *Thacher*, 223; *Lee on Jefferson* (*ed.* 1839), 150; *MS. Am. O. B.*

the whole line that would hold a commission beyond the end of the campaign, if he did till then. Such an act, even in the most despotic governments, would be attended with loud complaints." The party hostile to the Chief, deep-rooted in New England and pervading Jersey, Pennsylvania, and Virginia, which from the beginning of the war to its end dreaded lest the tyranny of a Commodus should lurk behind the wise virtues of a Pertinax, though foiled in a former effort to displace him, still retained power to hamper his movements and embarrass his designs. It was very evident that his removal would be the signal for the army's dissolution, and the inevitable subjection of the infant state; but it was yet feasible to limit his powers, deny his requirements, and in a hundred ways exhibit a distrust of his capacity or integrity that would have caused many soldiers to throw up the command.

Much of all this was known to the British. Their intelligencers appear to have existed in the most unsuspected and dangerous quarters; and at this very epoch public officers were betraying trust and unreservedly revealing our affairs in New York. Such was Heron, of the Connecticut legislature, who left West Point with a flag on the 30th of August, and was probably the bearer of Arnold's letter of that date to André. He dined with Arnold, parted with him on that day, and brought to the English leaders the most important oral information of matters in the Highlands and of the country and army generally. "Mr. Heron is confident the whole rebellion must fall to the ground soon from the internal weakness of the country, and the still greater weakness of the party that have hitherto fomented the troubles, who lose ground every day, and divide from each other. *All subdivisions are for peace with Great Britain on the old foundations.*"

The reduction of West Point had long been the hope of the enemy; but to accomplish it without loss of life would indeed have been a triumph for Clinton and a most brilliant conclusion to the campaign. Mr. Sparks has clearly mapped out the advantages he must have contemplated in this contingency. In the first place, the mere acquisition of a fortress so important, with all its dependencies, garrison, stores, magazines, vessels, etc., was an achievement of no secondary magnitude. The supplies gathered here by the Americans were very great, and once lost could not have been readily, if at all, restored. The works were esteemed our tower of salvation; an American Gibraltar, impregnable to an army 20,000 strong. Even though yet unfinished, they had cost three years' labor of the army and $3,000,000; and were thought an unfailing and secure resort in the last emergency. But the ulterior consequences of its possession were of even greater importance. It would enable Sir Henry to have checked all trade between New England and the central and southern states. It was, in Washington's eyes, the bolt that locked this communication. The eastern states, chiefly dependent for their corn-stuffs on their sisters in the union, were commercial rather than agricultural communities; and the power that at once commanded the seaboard and the Hudson might easily bring upon them all the horrors of famine. From Canada to Long Island Sound a virtual barrier would have shut out New England from its supplies, as the wall of Antonine barred the free and rugged Caledonians from the Roman colonies and the south of Britain. A modern writer, ridiculing the idea that the possession of West Point would have been really serviceable to Clinton, diverts himself with a picture of the hardy New England yeomanry turning out for a week to reduce the hostile garrisons and returning to their farms in triumph; but it may well be questioned whether, with the river at its command, such a post as West Point could have been so subdued in a week, or a month, or in twenty years. But even these advantages were of less moment than those more immediate. The French under D'Estaing had already bickered with the Americans. It was hoped that similar ill-blood might arise in Rochambeau's camp, and be fanned into a flame. It was shrewdly and correctly suspected by Clinton that the allies meditated a combined attack on New York. To execute this movement with West Point strongly garrisoned by the British would be impossible; and nothing was more likely than that the French should have all their jealousies aroused by the defection of one of the most distinguished American generals, and the surrender of the most important American citadel, on the very ground of repugnance to the alliance. Ignorant of the extent of the plot, it would be difficult for them to repose in confidence with an American army by their side, and a British before them and in their rear. Nations get experience by such examples as that of Count Julian on the field of Xeres; and the failure of the campaign was the immediate contingent result of Arnold's success; the dissolution of the alliance and the ruin of the American cause not a remote one.

It was supposed that Washington's plan of attack was to advance himself upon the lines at Kingsbridge and perhaps menace Staten Island; while the French, landing on Long Island, should threaten New York from that quarter. To meet and counteract this scheme, Clinton intended to receive the surrender of West Point in the very moment when Washington should have fairly resolved on his designs, gathered all his necessary stores into West Point, and set his troops in motion. Under pretence of an expedition to the Chesapeake, which the Americans believed was on foot, the English ships, with transports of a peculiar draught of water properly manned, were kept at a convenient place for immediate use; and the men destined for the service held ready for embarcation at any moment. Of these was the corps commanded by Simcoe, from whom Clinton did not conceal his real designs, and who was accordingly busied in procuring information.

"My idea of putting into execution this concerted plan with General Arnold with most efficacy, was to have deferred it till Mr. Washington, coöperating with the French, moved upon this place to invest it, and that the Rebel Magazines should have been collected and formed in their several Depots, particularly that at West Point. General Arnold surrendering himself, the Forts and Garrisons, at this instant, would have given every advantage which could have been desired: Mr. Washington must have instantly retired from King's bridge, and the French troops upon Long Island would have been consequently left unsupported, and probably would have fallen into our hands. The consequent advantage of so great an event I need not explain."*

On the 31st of August Clinton formally asked the king's approbation of André as Adjutant-General,—"whose faithful discharge of the duties of that office for nearly a twelvemonth have made me consider him as worthy of the appointment." † There had already been some delay in changing his provincial to a regular majority: and ministers perhaps thought there was more of favoritism than merit at the bottom of all. To remove such inference, Dalrymple, Mathew, and Pattison, who went over with this despatch, probably bore oral information from Clinton of what André was concerned in. The details were not yet to be safely trusted on paper to the fortunes of the sea. Robertson refers to these generals, on the 1st of September, as able to tell everything to the minister that he is silent about, and on the 21st more plainly intimates that government must know what great things the General and Admiral were meditating:—"So I will only say in general that since the year 1777 I have not seen so fair a prospect for the return of the revolted provinces to their duty." In London, Mathew and the others on their arrival gave out that it was all over with the Americans; that news would presently be received of an irreparable blow that would ruin them forever. Their silence after tidings of André's death came in induces the belief that they had been trusted with and referred to Arnold's meditated treason.

* MS. Clinton's Desp. 11 Oct. 1780. State Paper Office; Received Nov 13.
† MS. Clinton's Desp. 31 Aug. 1780. S. P. O.; Rec. 14 Oct.

How far soever the secret may have been confided in the British camp, it was inviolably kept in the American; and while Clinton was waiting the motions of the allies to strike his blow, news of the total defeat of Gates at Camden induced him to suspend further steps till it appeared what Washington's course would be. The reports of his spies and the force still reserved, convinced him that New York remained the object; and Arnold soon confirmed this conclusion. For various reasons, however, the plan already concerted of moving upon West Point was abandoned, and other steps resorted to. It would seem that, despite Sir Henry's language lately quoted, there was yet much to be arranged. The time for approach and surrender might indeed be settled in the mysterious and covert phrase of the correspondence between Anderson and Gustavus; but the manner of attack, which was of course to turn on that of defence, and the price of the performance, could not be so easily hit upon. From what we can gather, it may be inferred Arnold's terms were greater than Clinton thought reasonable; and this very circumstance may have induced the former to insist on an agreement beforehand with an authorized agent. On the other hand, Sir Henry was desirous (inconsistent with the previously concerted arrangement as it may seem) to verify Arnold's identity, and to settle beyond peradventure the hour and means of his appearance before West Point. He therefore agreed to the proposal that André should be sent to meet him. Meanwhile the correspondence had been kept up; the following is the letter that was perhaps sent in by Heron:—

ARNOLD TO ANDRÉ.

"*August* 30*th*, 1780.—Sir: On the 24th instant I received a note from you without date, in answer to mine of the 7th of July, also a letter from your house of the 24th July, in answer to mine of the 15th, with a note from Mr. B——, of the 30th July; with an extract of a letter from Mr. J. Osborn of the 24th. I have paid particular attention to the contents of the several letters; had they arrived earlier, you should have had my answer sooner. A variety of circumstances has prevented my writing you before. I expect to do it very fully in a few days, and to procure you an interview with Mr. M——e, when you will be able to settle your commercial plan, I hope, agreeable to all parties. Mr. M——e assures me that he is still of opinion that his first proposal is by no means unreasonable, and makes no doubt, when he has had a conference with you, that you will close with it. He expects, when you meet, that you will be fully authorized from your House; that the risks and profits of the copartnership may be fully and clearly understood.

"A speculation might at this time be easily made to some advantage with *ready money;* but there is not the quantity of goods *at market* which your partner seems to suppose, and the number of speculators below, I think, will be against your making an immediate purchase. I apprehend goods will be in greater plenty, and much cheaper, in the course of the season; both dry and wet are much wanted and in demand at this juncture; some quantities are expected in this part of the country soon. Mr. M——e flatters himself, that in the course of ten days he will have the pleasure of seeing you; he requests me to advise you, that he has ordered a draft on you in favor of our mutual friend S——y for £300, which you will charge on account of the *tobacco.* I am, in behalf of Mr. M——e & Co., Sir, your obedient humble servant, GUSTAVUS.

" Mr. John Anderson, Merchant,

" To the care of James Osborne, to be left at the Reverend Mr. Odell's, New York."

Translated from its commercial phraseology into plain English, this letter teaches us that on the 7th July Arnold had declared the probability of his obtaining the command of West Point, and the inspection he had just made of its defences; and had written again on the 15th, when the projections connected with the arrival of the French may have been mentioned. The terms on which he was to surrender were also doubtless named. To these André had replied in two notes; and, if we may suppose that B. stood for Beverly Robinson and J. Osborn for Sir H. Clinton, communications from these were likewise apparently conveyed. It may be easily gathered also that the present strength of the garrison both in militia and continentals was indicated; and that the feasibility of a *coup-de-main,* and the danger of the troops at Verplanck's retarding such an undertaking, were suggested. It will be observed that Gustavus writes as agent for Mr. M———e : elide the dash, and we have Mr. Me ; in other words, himself. The reader will recollect Arnold's old motto — *Sibi totique:* it was indeed for himself that he now acted.

In this letter, the demand for an interview with a confidential agent of Clinton's — a man of Arnold's " own mensuration " — with André in fact — was repeated : and Clinton agreed that the meeting should take place. Several fruitless efforts — two, at the least — were made for this end. In November, 1780, it was said in London that Commodore Johnstone had received a letter from Rodney asserting that André had twice safely met Arnold, and had even acted as his *valet-de-chambre:* and that the miscarriage was due to Clinton's hesitation to acquiesce in and instantly follow out the plans then arranged. There seems little foundation for this tale.

Rodney arrived at New York on the 14th September and, taking command of that station, readily listened to Sir Henry's desires : —

" At this period, Sir George Rodney arrived with a fleet at New York, which made it highly probable, that Washington would lay aside all thoughts against this place. It became therefore proper for me no longer to defer the execution of a project, which would lead to such considerable advantages, nor to lose so fair an opportunity as was presented, and under so good a mask as the expedition to the Chesapeake, which everybody imagined would of course take place. Under this feint I prepared for a movement up the North River. I laid my plan before Sir George Rodney and General Knyphausen, when Sir George, with that zeal for his Majesty's service, which marks his character, most handsomely promised to give me every naval assistance in his power.

"It became necessary at this instant, that the secret correspondence under feigned names, which had so long been carried on, should be rendered into certainty, both as to the person being General Arnold commanding at West Point, and that in the manner in which he was to surrender himself, the forts, and troops to me, it should be so conducted under a concerted plan between us, as that the king's troops sent upon this expedition should be under no risk of surprise or counterplot; and I was determined not to make the attempt but under such particular security.

"I knew the ground on which the forts were placed, and the contiguous country, tolerably well, having been there in 1777; and I had received many hints respecting both from General Arnold. But it was certainly necessary that a meeting should be held with that officer for settling the whole plan. My reasons, as I have described them, will, I trust, prove the propriety of such a measure on my part. General Arnold had also his reasons, which must be so very obvious, as to make it unnecessary for me to explain them.

"Many projects for a meeting were formed, and consequently several attempts made, in all of which General Arnold seemed extremely desirous, that some person, who had my particular confidence, might be sent to him; some man, as he described it in writing, *of his own mensuration*.

"I had thought of a person under this important description, who would gladly have undertaken it, but that his peculiar situation at the time, from which I could not release him, prevented him from engaging in it. General Arnold finally insisted, that the person sent to confer with him should be Adjutant-General Major André, who indeed had been the person on my part, who managed and carried on the secret correspondence." *

It was Arnold's wish that André, disguised as John Anderson, a bearer of intelligence from New York, should meet him at a cavalry outpost between Salem and North Castle, on the west side of the Hudson; and he notified Sheldon, its commander, that he hoped to encounter in this manner a valuable emissary. Of this too André was informed on the 3rd of September. But it was no part of the latter's plan to enter our lines in disguise, and so much of the arrangement as contemplated his doing so was at once thrown aside. On the strength of Arnold's letter, however, he wrote to Sheldon that he would come with a flag to the American outposts.

ANDERSON TO SHELDON.

New York, 7 *Sept.* 1780. — Sir: I am told my name is made known to you, and that I may hope your indulgence in permitting me to meet a friend near your outposts. I will endeavour to obtain permission to go out with a flag which will be sent to Dobb's Ferry on Sunday next the 11th at 12 o'clock, when I shall be happy to meet Mr. G. Should I not be allowed to go, the officer who is to command the escort, between whom and myself no distinction need be made, can speak on the affair.

Let me entreat you, Sir, to favour a matter so interesting to the parties concerned, and which is of so private a nature that the public on neither side can be injured by it.

I shall be happy on my part of doing any act of kindness to you in a family or a property concern, of a similar nature.

I trust I shall not be detained but should any old grudge be a cause for it, I should rather risk that than neglect

---

* Clinton to Lord G. Germain. — Spark's Arnold, 168.

the business in question or assume a mysterious character to carry on an innocent affair and as friends have advised get to your lines by stealth. I am with all regard Yr. most humble sert. JOHN ANDERSON.

This letter rather surprised Sheldon, to whom Anderson's name had not before been mentioned; but it answered its object of putting Arnold on the lookout, for it was at once transmitted to him. He artfully stated a case to disarm any suspicion, and directed that if Anderson should come to Sheldon's post, notice should be sent him by express and the supposed intelligencer escorted to his head-quarters. At the same time, on the allegation of business connected with his post, he resolved to seek Clinton's agent at the appointed time and place. He set out from West Point in his barge on the afternoon of the 10th; passed the night at Joshua Smith's house; and on the morning of the 11th descended nineteen miles to Dobb's Ferry, where André waited with Robinson to receive him.

Beverly Robinson was a gentleman of high standing. His father, speaker of the Virginia legislature, was an early friend to Washington, whose modesty and valor he complimented in language that is yet remembered. The son was married to a great heiress of the day, the daughter of Frederic Philipse, and with her acquired large estates on the Hudson. At his house Washington had met and sought to win the younger sister and co-heiress. His country-seat in the Highlands, two miles from West Point but on the east side of the river, was a large and handsome building surrounded by pleasant orchards and gardens and environed by sublime scenery. The American generals, considering it public property since its owner was in arms for the crown, were wont to use it as their own: it was now Arnold's, and some time Washington's head-quarters. There is a pleasant anecdote of an entertainment given at Paris by Marbois to La Fayette not long before his death. Americans and others were pres ent who had served in our war. At supper, the guests were led into a strange, large, low apartment, like a farmhouse kitchen, with one window and many small doors. On a rough table were arrayed large dishes of meat and pastry, bottles, glasses, silver mugs, &c. They gazed in surprise, and memory faintly struggled to recall the scene, till La Fayette suddenly cried out, " Ah, the seven doors and one window, and the silver camp-goblets such as the Marshals of France used in my youth! We are at Washington's head-quarters on the Hudson, fifty years ago!"

Robinson's circumspect and cautious character were thought needful to check the buoyancy of his comrade, and he was likewise fully acquainted with the pending negotiations. Indeed it was probably through him that Arnold's first overtures were made. But the large acquaintance and interests he had in the region, and his knowledge of the country, made his presence additionally desirable.

The interview was to occur on the east side of the river, at Dobb's Ferry; but as Arnold drew near, one of those circumstances which the pious man calls providence and the profane calls luck, prevented an encounter that must in all human probability have resulted in the consummation of the plot. Some British gun-boats were stationed at the place, which opened such a fire on the American barge that Arnold, though twice he strove hard to get on board, was put in deadly peril of his life and obliged to fall back. How this came to pass without Robinson's intervention we cannot imagine; for it is impossible but that an intimation from him would have caused the firing to cease. Or had he repaired with André and his flag to meet the solitary barge that evidently belonged to an officer of rank, an interview might at once have been effected in the most plausible manner in the world. The circumstances of the case would have rendered it easy for Arnold to publicly say that he would, since they were thus thrown together, waive the prerogative of rank that otherwise might have induced him to refer the enemy's flag to an officer of an equal grade, and to grant an interview on shore. The condition of Robinson's estate was a ready pretext for even a private reception; and there was no obstacle to André's being of the party. In the hope of being thus followed, Arnold retired to an American post on the west shore, above the ferry, where he remained till sundown: but no flag came. It is scarcely possible that the statement attributed to Rodney could have had an actual foundation here. At all events, he went back that night to West Point, and his coadjutor returned to New York. The failure of the meeting can only be accounted for by supposing that the English messengers were on the east bank of the ferry when Arnold was fired at, and could not interfere in season. They could hardly have been on the Vulture, since its boat was lowered to pursue the American barge, which it did so far and so vigorously as to have nearly captured it.

Hitherto, these transactions had been conducted with comparative freedom, for neither Washington or any other officer of very high rank being on the spot, Arnold was under no control but a regard to appearances; and he had plausible reasons to give for every step he had taken. But a new meeting must now be arranged at a moment when it was known the Chief would be in the neigborhood on his route to meet Rochambeau at Hartford. On the 13th, therefore, he instructed Tallmadge at North Castle to bring Anderson directly to him, should he present himself there. The caution was needless. André had no idea of meeting him elsewhere than on neutral ground or on a British deck. According to Marbois (who is not, however, confirmed by any authorities known to me), Clinton about this period warned Arnold that unless the engaged surrender was speedily made, circumstances might prevent its fulfilment; and called at the same time for plans and papers needful for his guidance. Arnold replied to this effect:—

"Notre maitre quitte le logis le 17 de ce mois. Il sera absent pendant cinq à six jours: profitons pour arranger nos affaires du temps qu'il nous laisse. Venez, sans delai, me trouver aux lignes, et nous réglerons définitivement les risques et les profits de la société. Tout sera prêt; mais cette entrevue est indispensable, et doit précéder l'expédition de notre navire."*

Hardly, however, had the discomfited and disappointed André returned to New York when events took a new turn. There was no longer room for doubt that the negotiation would be speedily and thoroughly effected. The chosen few to whom the secret was known were elate with anxious joy; and even they who knew not the cause could not but reflect in their countenances the satisfaction of their leaders, and the belief that at length irreparable injury was to fall on the American cause. "Let the Whigs enjoy their temporary triumph," wrote one of the best-informed loyalists about Clinton; "I would have them indulged in, as I really think it is one of the last they will enjoy." Tradition relates that there were not a few who believed that André was engaged in an affair that was about to ripen to a head, and from which, if

---

* Complot d'Arnold, &c. 91. Marbois was in 1780 secretary here to Luzerne's legation, and for long after French Consul-General, and Chargé. He was of studious and reflective habits and sound parts. John Adams thought him one of the best informed men in France. Gen. Cass says no foreigner ever understood us so well, and few Americans better. His opportunities were good; his intimacy with the leading men of the day gave him knowledge of their views about Arnold, whose business was constantly discussed by the allies. All of Arnold's papers too were seized, both at West Point and Philadelphia, and apparently scattered in various hands. Perhaps he may thus have had access to information or documents now unknown. Certainly some of his statements are not easily reconciled with the current history of the time; but it is incredible that he should give, with quotation-marks, translations of letters that had no existence but in his own imagination. "Marbois writes tittle-tattle and I believe does mischief," wrote Jay from the French court in 1783. The speeches that he puts in the mouths of some of the chief actors under circumstances that render it impossible they should have been reported, has license in long established historical usage. Every author of a certain school feels at liberty to use his hero's tongue as freely as Homer used those of Greeks and Trojans. "Ces coquins," said Condé to De Retz, "nous font parler et agir comme ils auroient fait eux-mêmes à notre place."

successful, he was to reap honors and reward. A baronetcy and a brigadiership were with good show of probability reckoned among his prospective gains.

There was nothing in the occurrences of the last moments which André spent in New York to warn him of his nearly impending fate. No boding friend or weeping mistress presaged evil to his plans; and the times were vanished when sagacious attendants brought such provident advices as Sir Gyron le Courtois received from his faithful squire:—"Sire, know that my heart tells me sooth that if you proceed farther you never will return; that you will either perish there, or you will remain in prison." So far from gloomy thoughts possessing his soul, he appears to have in these parting scenes entered even more freely than usual into the pleasures of the place. Madame de Riedesel chronicles briefly the visit she received from Clinton and himself on the day before his departure. Nor was this a solitary example. Where now in New York is the unalluring and crowded neighborhood of 2nd Avenue and 34th Street, stood in 1780 the ancient *bowerie* or country-seat of Jacobus Kip. Built in 1641 of bricks brought from Holland, encompassed by pleasant trees and in easy view of the sparkling waters of Kip's Bay on the East River, the mansion remained even to our own times in possession of its founder's line. Here spread the same smiling meadows whose appearance had so expanded the heart of Oloffe the Dreamer in the fabulous ages of the colony; here still nodded the groves that had echoed back the thunder of Hendrick Kip's musketoon, when that mighty warrior left his name to the surrounding waves. When Washington was in the neighborhood, Kip's house had been his quarters; when Howe crossed from Long Island on Sunday, Sept. 15th, 1776, he debarked at the rocky point hard by, and his skirmishers drove our people from their position behind the dwelling. Since then it had known many guests. Howe, Clinton, Knyphausen, Percy, were sheltered by its roof. The aged owner with his wife and daughters remained, but they had always an officer of distinction quartered with them; and if a part of the family were in arms for Congress, as is alleged, it is certain that others were active for the crown. Jacobus Kip of Kipsburgh led a cavalry troop of his own tenantry with great gallantry in De Lancy's regiment; and despite severe wounds survived long after the war, a heavy pecuniary sufferer by the cause which with most of the landed gentry of New York he had espoused.

On September 19th Colonel Williams of the 80th, then billeted here, gave a dinner to Clinton and his staff as a parting compliment to André. How brilliant soever the company, how cheerful the repast, its memory must have ever been fraught with sadness to both host and guests. It was the last occasion of André's meeting his comrades in life. Four short days gone, the hands then clasped by friendship were fettered with hostile bonds; yet nine days more, and the darling of the army, the youthful hero of the hour, had dangled from a gibbet.

It was recollected with peculiar interest that when at this banquet the song came to his turn, André gave the favorite military chanson attributed to Wolfe, who sung it on the eve of the battle where he died.

> "Why, soldiers, why
> Should we be melancholy, boys?
> Why, soldiers, why,
> Whose business 'tis to die!
> For should next campaign
> Send us to him who made us, boys,
> We're free from pain:
> But should we remain,
> A bottle and kind landlady
> Makes all well again."

CHAPTER XIV.

Robinson sent to Communicate with Arnold. — Correspondence. — André goes to the Vulture. — Correspondence with Clinton and Arnold.—Joshua Hett Smith selected as Arnold's Messenger.

THE arrival of Rodney on the 14th of September had been followed by the receipt of fresh communications from Arnold. On the 16th, Robinson was again sent up the river on the Vulture, and that for the future there should be no untimely interruptions from this vessel, its commander was measurably instructed in what was going on. If any omen might be derived from names, the Vulture was a fortunate ship for the enterprise. She herself had been very successful against our privateers; and thirty-five years before we find a band of prisoners, some of them detained as spies, (comprising not only the celebrated Home, in whose tragedy André had delighted to bear a character, but Witherspoon, now active for the Congress, and Barrow, in arms for the king,) had escaped from Charles Edward's hands, and flying from Doune castle by Tullyallan, were received on board the sloop-of-war Vulture, Captain Falconer.

At Teller's Point, about fourteen miles as the crow flies from Arnold's quarters, but of course more by way of the river, the Vulture came to anchor within easy view of King's Ferry and scarcely six miles from the works of Verplanck's and Stony Points. Hence Robinson on the 17th dexterously conveyed information by a flag to Arnold of his presence, and his readiness to aid the negotiation. His letter was received at Verplanck's by Livingston, and forwarded to head-quarters several miles above.

As Livingston played an important though an unwitting

part in the ruin of the plot, he may briefly be noticed here. He was the same officer who under Montgomery had borne so active share in the capture of André's regiment at Chambly; an amiable, well-informed young man, perfectly familiar with the French tongue. He now commanded the chief outpost of West Point, a work of unusual construction, planned by Gouvion, and hardly to be reduced without time, trouble, and heavy artillery. Hither he was ordered with his regiment on August 4th; the next day after Arnold, under whose command he was placed, had been sent to West Point. Chastellux remarks on a breakfast the Colonel gave him of beefsteaks, tea, and grog: his larder being as illy supplied as his men's wardrobe, who were sent in because they were the worst clad troops in the army, "so that one may form some idea of their dress."

Several persons were dining with Arnold when Robinson's letter was brought in. Carelessly glancing over it, he put it in his pocket, and without secrecy mentioned its contents which nominally were to ask an interview. Among the guests was Colonel Lamb, the second in command, who also had taken part in André's capture at St. Johns, and whose jaw was broken by a musket ball with Arnold before Quebec. He was too a good French linguist, and of much professional skill, but of restless genius and a bad temper, said Montgomery; brave, active, and intelligent, but very turbulent and quarrelsome. He now urged solid reasons for refusing Robinson's request, pointing out to Arnold the occasion such an interview would give for suspecting improper communications; and not resting satisfied with a promise to consult Washington on the matter till he had ascertained from both parties that the question was made and answered. Arnold, however, showed Robinson's letter to Washington on the evening of the 18th, as they crossed together at King's Ferry; and great must have been his chagrin at the positive terms in which he was advised of the impropriety of the chief commander of a post meeting any one himself.

He might send a trusty hand if he thought proper, but it was better to have nothing to do with business that pertained to the civil authorities. "I had no more suspicion of Arnold than I had of myself," said the chief in relating this. This discourse being in the presence of others discouraged him from a step so plainly disapproved of by his superior.

There were several circumstances in this brief voyage, noticed without suspicion at the moment, that were afterwards recalled with fearful significancy. One was Arnold's uneasiness when, after carefully examining for some moments the position of the Vulture, Washington closed his glass and in a low tone gave an order or made a remark to those nearest him. His words were inaudible to the traitor, whose heart must have quaked lest his guilt should be their subject. Still more palpable was his confusion when La Fayette turned to him and said — "General Arnold, since you have a correspondence with the enemy, you must ascertain as soon as possible what has become of Guichen!" The observation had a natural origin in matters that had already passed between himself and the company; but now to his disturbed conscience it was pregnant with cause for fear. In a confused and hasty manner, he abruptly demanded what La Fayette meant by his remark; but in a moment recovering himself, he subsided into silence. Ere the week was out, the witnesses of the scene came to the conclusion that for the instant he thought all was known and his arrest to occur on the spot.

But no such thing was dreamed of. Washington and his suite passed tranquilly on their way; Arnold accompanying them as far as Peekskill, where he had provided for their reception and where he and they passed the night of Monday, September 18th. The next morning they parted betimes, each on his own course — the one to Hartford, the other back to West Point. This was the last occasion of Arnold's meeting the man who had discerned his merit when it was denied and obscured by his first employer, Massachusetts; who had placed him high on the ladder of preferment, and had steadily recognized, despite the clamor of Congress and his subordinates, the existence of shining qualities, essential indeed to a general but not of universal occurrence in our army; who had supported firmly his lawful pretensions against the injustice of their common masters; and to whose unwearied integrity he owed not only his rank but his command. On Arnold's part it is but fair to say that I have seen nothing save his treason to induce me to believe him one of Washington's enemies and maligners; we know who some of these were, and that Arnold was not their friend.* But human ingratitude could hardly go beyond this sacrifice he was now bent on of all the chief held dear to his own baser interests. Washington "went on his way, and he saw him no more;" and with him went happiness, honor, and fame.

On the 15th, Arnold under the usual disguise had written to André, but there was probably a delay in the letter's transmission. Indeed the manner in which the correspondence was all along conveyed is not yet known; though at the time Arnold took command Moody, the well-known partisan and spy, was in duress at West Point, and his condition seems to have excited the general's attention. If relations existed between these two, there would be no difficulty in sending messages to any quarter. When he answered Robinson's letter on the 19th, however, and in general terms declined receiving any communications except of a public nature, he concealed within the folds of his ostensible note two others of a very different tendency. Each of these documents is erroneously dated as of the 18th.

ARNOLD TO ROBINSON.

September 18*th*, 1780. — Sir: I parted with his Excellency General Washington this morning, who advised me to

---

* In Rivington's Gazette, Dec. 19th, 1778, is an assertion that Arnold was engaged at that time with Mifflin, St. Clair, and Thompson, in an intrigue to remove Washington; but Rivington's unsupported authority in such a matter is of little value.

avoid seeing you, as it would occasion suspicions in the minds of some people, which might operate to my injury. His reasons appear to me to be well founded; but, if I were of a different opinion, I could not with propriety see you at present. I shall send a person to Dobb's Ferry, or on board the Vulture, Wednesday night the 20th instant, and furnish him with a boat and a flag of truce. You may depend on his secrecy and honor, and that your business of whatever nature shall be kept a profound secret; and, if it is a matter in which I can officially act, I will do every thing in my power to oblige you consistently with my duty. To avoid censure, this matter must be conducted with the greatest secrecy. I think it will be advisable for the Vulture to remain where she is until the time appointed. I have enclosed a letter for a gentleman in New York from one in the country on private business, which I beg the favor of you to forward, and make no doubt he will be particular to come at the time appointed. I am, &c.

P. S. I expect General Washington to lodge here on Saturday night next, and will lay before him any matter you may wish to communicate.

GUSTAVUS TO JOHN ANDERSON.

September 15*th.* — SIR: On the 11th at noon, agreeably to your request, I attempted to go to Dobb's Ferry, but was prevented by the armed boats of the enemy, which fired upon us; and I continued opposite the Ferry till sunset.

The foregoing letter was written to caution you not to mention your business to Colonel Sheldon, or any other person. I have no confidant. I have made one too many already, who has prevented some profitable speculations.

I will send a person in whom you can confide by water to meet you at Dobb's Ferry at the landing on the east side, on

Wednesday the 20th instant, who will conduct you to a place of safety, where I will meet you. It will be necessary for you to be disguised, and, if the enemy's boats are there, it will favor my plan, as the person is not suspected by them. If I do not hear from you before, you may depend on the person's being punctual at the place above mentioned.

My partner, of whom I hinted in a former letter, has about ten thousand pounds cash in hand ready for a speculation if any should offer, which appears profitable. I have also one thousand pounds on hand, and can collect fifteen hundred more in two or three days. Add to this I have some credit. From these hints you may judge of the purchase that can be made. I cannot be more explicit at present. Meet me if possible. You may rest assured, that, if there is no danger in passing your lines, you will be perfectly safe where I propose a meeting, of which you shall be informed on Wednesday evening, if you think proper to be at Dobb's Ferry. Adieu, and be assured of the friendship of GUSTAVUS.

September 18*th.* — The foregoing I found means to send by a very honest fellow, who went to Kingsbridge on the 16th, and I have no doubt you have received it. But as there is a possibility of its miscarriage, I send a copy, and am fully persuaded that the method I have pointed out to meet you is the best and safest, provided you can obtain leave to come out.*

---

* See Sparks's Wash. vii. 527; and "The Case of Major John André, Adjutant-General to the British Army, Who was put to Death by the Rebels, October 2, 1780, Candidly Represented: with Remarks on the said Case. 'If there were no other Brand upon this odious and accursed Civil War, than that single Loss, it must be most infamous and execrable to all Posterity.' — Lord Clarendon." New York, Rivington, 1780. 4to. pp. 27. This rare tract was apparently drawn up with Clinton's knowledge, but probably never published. The only copy I have seen is made up of the printer's proofs. The above letter differs from that given by Mr. Sparks in containing the words *by water* in the third section, and all in the fourth after *Adieu*. The fourth section omits also all to the word *Meet*. The preface to the tract is dated Nov. 28, 1780.

In his formal reply to Arnold's public letter, Robinson enclosed the assurance that he would remain on board and hoped that Anderson would come up. Meantime, those received were forwarded to New York; and Rodney as it would seem was now, on the night of the 19th, called into counsel on their consideration. To his active ready-witted mind, there could have appeared little difficulty in pushing the business through: and with some reluctance Clinton, whose various capacities of statesman, general, and diplomatist combined to tinge with procrastination all he undertook, consented that André should go with a flag to Dobb's Ferry. But all parties appear to have forgotten that adoption of the Admiral's advice involved regard to his habits of action; and it is very certain that he would never have suffered the envoy to go on shore without a reasonable assurance of his getting back again.

Arrangements were speedily made. André wrote to Robinson and Captain Sutherland of the Vulture, bidding them fall down to the Ferry, and was in the end the bearer of his own letters. Clinton gave him his parting orders, enjoining everything that prudence could suggest, and especially charging him to preserve his uniform and to avoid receiving papers. On this last point indeed Sir Henry was ever precise. In the spring of 1779, when a commissary was going from New York to the Convention prisoners at Charlottesville, he was commissioned with details for Phillips of the manœuvres at Monmouth. As he related them, Clinton sketched some hasty plans of the various evolutions of the day; but recollecting himself, said — "Clark, you must not take these, for if the Americans find them on you, they'll certainly hang you; therefore only tell General Phillips, *that on that day I fought upon velvet:* he will fully understand me." In fact, so far as can be judged, no papers from Arnold were needed. His letter just given states clearly enough his own effective force and Washington's: conversation could have settled the plan of attack; and Robinson and his loyal dependents must have furnished guides to every gorge in the neighborhood of his ancient home.

Marbois gives a highly colored account of the scene between Clinton and André on this occasion; and whether imagination or memory supplied its facts, there is a consistency in this part of his story which commands our attention, if it does not receive our faith. The interview, he says, was insisted on by Arnold as a condition precedent to any further action. So far all had prospered to his wish. There were heard none of those vague, sinister rumors that usually attend the explosion of a conspiracy: never had a design so prodigious more happily approached its appointed term. This profound secrecy was owing to Arnold's care that the matter should remain concealed in his own bosom and those of Robinson and André; and this was one of his motives for wishing to place in no other hands the information needful to bring matters to a head. But on the other part, he continues, Clinton saw more danger than practical advantage in the rendezvous. He had previously refused to sanction it with his permission, and he now feared lest so many precautionary measures should serve only to bring an unlucky end to an enterprise that hitherto had progressed so smoothly, but in so much danger. André, however, to whom great share of the glory of success must ensue, burned with impatience to play his part. He had even, says our chronicler, conceived a hope more ambitious by far than the seizure of the forts. He thought now to fix the surrender on the very day of Washington's return to West Point, and thus to crown his achievements with the capture of our main stay and chief. But apprehending that Clinton would not view this idea with favor, he contented himself with the request to meet Arnold for the purposes already discussed. The English general at length consented; and Marbois pretends to give (in translation, of course) the very words he spoke.

"Mon enfant," lui dit-il, "ton entreprise exige encore plus de sagesse que d'audace, conduis-la suivant ton desir jusqu'à ce qu'elle soit consommée ; va trouver Arnold, puisque tu crois la chose nécessaire. Je connois ton courage, et, si ta prudence y répond, je suis assuré du succès. Va, mon ami, finis d'un seul coup cette guerre ; ta famille est maintenant Anglaise. Tu seras donc compté parmi les héros de notre pays, et célèbre chez tous les peuples et dans tous les siècles."

Early on the 20th, André started for Dobb's Ferry, whence he proposed to send his letters to the ship. The tide was with him, and he determined to push on to where the Vulture lay, rather than thwart Arnold's expressed wish by altering her position. About seven P. M. he got on board in Haverstraw Bay, a little above Teller's Point ; and the night was passed in anxious expectation of the appearance of his confederate. But no signal or message came ; and morning found him bitterly disappointed. He feared too that his absence would be noted at New York ; and that — which does not appear to have been the case — he had himself missed Arnold by coming to the ship, instead of waiting at the Ferry. Unwilling, however, to lose the last chance, he made an excuse to Clinton for his prolonged stay in a note that might be safely read by any of the staff.

ANDRÉ TO CLINTON.

On board the Vulture, 21 *Sept.* 1780. — SIR: As the tide was favorable on my arrival at the sloop yesterday, I determined to be myself the bearer of your Excellency's letters as far as the Vulture. I have suffered for it, having caught a very bad cold, and had so violent a return of a disorder in my stomach, which had attacked me a few days ago, that Capt. Sutherland and Col. Robinson insist on my remaining on board until I am better. I hope to-morrow to get down again. I have the honor, &c.

With this, which was received by Sir Henry on the day of its date, was another and more important communication.

ANDRÉ TO CLINTON.

On board the Vulture, 21 *September*, 1780.—Sir: I got on board the Vulture at about 7 o'clock last night; and after considering upon the letters and the answer given by Colonel Robinson, "that he would remain on board, and hoped I should be up," we thought it most natural to expect *the Man I sent into the Country* here, and therefore did not think of going to the Ferry.

Nobody has appeared. This is the second excursion I have made without an ostensible reason, and Colonel Robinson both times of the party. A third would infallibly fire suspicions. I have therefore thought it best to remain here on pretence of sickness, as my inclosed letter will feign, and try further expedients. Yesterday the pretence of a flag of truce was made to draw people from the Vulture on shore. The boat was fired upon in violation of the customs of war. Capt. Sutherland with great propriety means to send a flag to complain of this to General Arnold. A boat from the Vulture had very nearly taken him on the 11th. He was pursued close to the float. I shall favor him with a newspaper containing the Carolina news, which I brought with me from New York for Anderson, to whom it is addressed, on board the Vulture. I have the honor, &c.*

André had boarded the Vulture in the highest spirits, confident of success; nor was even the cautious and circumspect Robinson disposed to believe in a failure. In fact Robinson was placed in his present position because, among other reasons, his character for clear-headedness stood as high as his reputation for probity and honor; and it was intended that should the negotiation be consummated by André rather than himself, he should at least exercise a wholesome check over his coadjutor's buoyancy. At this moment, neither of them seem to have dreamed of leaving the ship; they thought on

---

* MS.—Sir H. Clinton's Narr.

the contrary that Arnold would come on board, and but for one of those unexpected occurrences which, happening from time to time to mock the wisdom of the wise and the valor of the brave, it is probable that André would have returned to New York unsuccessful but unscathed. It is by such means that we are led oftentimes to ponder the saying of the wise Fabius: — *eventus stultorum magister.*

Traditional history relates that on the 20th of September, some young men with their guns came to a farmer who was pressing cider, and called for a draught from the mill. Perhaps to get rid of them, they were told that the Vulture was anchored in the stream hard by. They went on to the shore, and finding it even so, concealed themselves behind the rocks while a white flag, or its semblance, was so displayed on the strand as to invite the attention of the ship. A boat with a responsive ensign was dispatched — doubtless through Robinson's mediation, and in hope of communication with Arnold — to see what was wanted. So soon as it was within range it was fired on by the ambuscade that had adopted this treacherous mode of assailing the enemy, and which was enabled by its position to fly to places of security on the first sign of pursuit. It is occasion of shame to an American to be compelled to relate how treason was thus blindly fought by treason: since it was through this unjustifiable affair that the interview between André and Arnold was induced, and their consequent detection occasioned. For besides the device of the newspaper, a complaint of the wrong, signed indeed by Sutherland but countersigned by John Anderson, secretary, and in his handwriting, was sent with a flag to Arnold on the morning of the 21st.

SUTHERLAND TO ARNOLD.

Vulture, off Teller's Point, 21 *September.* — SIR: I consider it a duty to complain of any violation of the laws of arms, and I am satisfied that I now do it where I cannot fail to meet redress. It is therefore with reluctance I give you the concern to know, that, a flag of truce having been yesterday shown on Teller's Point, I sent a boat towards the shore, presuming some communication was thereby solicited. The boat's crew on approaching received a fire from several armed men, who till then had been concealed. Fortunately none of my people were hurt, but the treacherous intentions of those who fired are not vindicated from that circumstance. I have the honor to be, &c.

Let us now turn to Arnold, and see what were his plans for those communications that he had not dared to trust on paper.

Two miles and a half below Stony Point, in a square, two-storied stone house that still stands on the Haverstraw Road, dwelt a man of substance named Joshua Hett Smith. His general reputation was that of a warm whig, but Lamb, whose wife was a connection, seems to have set him down as a disaffected person, and forbade any intimacy between the households. In truth he appears to have been one of that class who run with the hare and hunt with the hounds. His brother the Chief-Justice, now a warm loyalist in New York, was said by his fellows to have hung back till the conquest of America was deemed certain. Another brother at London was charged with seditious practices there. He himself, however, was a man of education and intelligence ; and probably was chiefly careful to keep on good terms with whomsoever was uppermost, while in heart he preferred a reconciliation with Britain on the terms then offered, to a continuance of the war for Independence. He was withal a timorous, yet a prying, bustling sort of character ; delighted to have a hand in weighty affairs, but devoid of the nerve to carry him with good assurance through their implications.

Familiar in his social habits, well acquainted with the country and its inhabitants, and a landholder of some consequence, Smith had been usefully employed by the American general Howe to bring intelligence to West Point, and it was very natural Arnold should, on taking command, be soon brought into relations with him. He was not long in sounding the character of the man, and resolving to make of him a convenient tool. For though it is altogether likely that enough of the affair was confided to let Smith perceive he was engaging in an intrigue detrimental to Congress and Independence, it is incredible that the whole of the portentous secret should be committed to such a shallow vessel. But in the friendly intercourse that arose, Arnold conveyed to Smith the intention of employing him as a go-between to bring a British agent within the American lines. With no other evidence than his own, it is difficult to say how far the revelations to Smith were carried: but the conflicting statements of his Trial and his Narrative may be accounted for by the fact that in the one case his life was at stake, and he sought to make the best story he could for the Americans; in the other, he endeavored to vindicate his reputation with the English. With these lights, we may grope a little less blindly in the maze of his contradictions.

Thus it would seem that Arnold had already disclosed the ground he wished to stand on. He inveighed against the French alliance, and dilated on the unnatural union between a despotic monarch and an insurgent people fighting for freedom. He expatiated on the reasonableness of the terms proposed by the Commissioners of 1778, which he averred were proffered in all sincerity and good faith, and were fully acceptable to the great mass of Americans. He insinuated that Robinson was the bearer of propositions even more favorable, and such as could not but deserve and receive acceptance. He owned his desire for peace and his weariness of a war in which he had to contend not only against the arms of the enemy, but the persecution of the Pennsylvania government and the entire ingratitude of Congress. "Smith," said he, "here am I now, after having fought the battles of my country, and find myself with a ruined constitution and this limb" (holding up his wounded leg) "now rendered useless to me. At the termination of this war, where can I seek for compensation for such damages as I have sustained?" It is impossible not to recognize in this language that deep resentment of real and of fancied wrongs which had first bent Arnold's mind to his present course.

Having resolved that his interview with the British messenger should be within the American lines, he fixed on Smith's house for the stage, and its owner to conduct him thither. By Smith's own account, this arrangement was made about the 19th or 20th September; but the more probable theory of Mr. Sparks carries it back to the 14th or 15th, when Arnold met his wife there on her arrival and escorted her up to his quarters. However this may be, the upshot of the matter was that Smith consented to all that was asked. He took his family to Fishkill, thirty miles from his residence and about eighteen from head-quarters, that the house might be empty; and returning as directed to Robinson's House on the 19th, received, says Mr. Sparks, the necessary papers to pass to Dobb's Ferry or the Vulture on the evening of the 20th, and bring away the expected agent. Smith indeed asserts that Arnold himself brought them to his house at Haverstraw: but the point is of little consequence. For want of a boat or of boatmen, he did not fulfil his commission, nor indeed was he very ardent to do so; but he notified his employer of the omission by an express during the night. It must then have been Arnold's scheme to have passed the day with Robinson or André at Smith's house, and to have sent him back on the next night; for Smith's note found him in bed at head-quarters. It would appear that he had rather wished Smith to find boatmen among his own tenantry than to employ such as pertained to the regular service; and had also arranged for him a protection and a password by means of which he might at any time traverse our lines on land or water without hindrance. Riding down, however, after breakfast to Verplanck's Point, and finding that an order on the quartermaster to supply a light boat was unfulfilled, he directed that his own or a barge he had sent for should be carried into the creek by Smith's house as soon as it arrived. At the same time he received from Livingston the letter that had just been brought from the Vulture to inform him of André's being on board. In the afternoon he crossed over to Smith's and prepared for the adventures of the night.

On the preceding day Arnold had given Smith a pass:

Head-Quarters, Robinson House, September 20, 1780. — Permission is given to Joshua Smith, Esquire, a gentleman, Mr. John Anderson, who is with him, and his two servants, to pass and repass the guards near King's Ferry at all times. B. ARNOLD, M. Genl.

This was intended doubtless for his voyage to the Vulture. On the morning of the 21st, when he learned that the excursion had not been made, he conceived it possible that he might yet have to send to Dobb's Ferry: wherefore an additional pass was given: —

Head-Quarters, Robinson House, September 21, 1780. — Permission is given to Joshua Smith, Esq., to go to Dobb's Ferry with three Men and a Boy with a Flag to carry some Letters of a private Nature for Gentlemen in New York and to return immediately. B. ARNOLD, M. Genl.

N. B. He has permission to go at such hours and times as the tide and his business suits. B. A.

Smith had relied for boatmen on a couple of his tenants, Samuel and Joseph Colquhoun: simple, honest men, he says, accustomed to the water, and possessing his confidence. It required, however, considerable expostulation, and the promise of a handsome reward for compliance as well as threats of punishment if they refused, ere they yielded to his wishes and Arnold's. They were wearied already, and they distrusted a night-voyage to the enemy. The watchword *Congress* was given, which would secure them from interruption by our guard-boats; and both Smith and themselves were assured that the business was well understood by the British officers and the American, but that it was necessary for certain reasons to keep the matter from the tongues of the vulgar. At last they yielded, and towards midnight of the 21st, the boat pushed from the creek towards the Hudson. No flag was displayed from its bow; but the oarsmen as well as their passenger testify that they were told by Arnold and actually considered it was a flag-boat to the Vulture. How far the fact that it was now an hour when a flag could not have been seen if exhibited, and the passes just given, together with the ensuing letter, go to justify this assertion, the military reader must decide. Both Arnold and Smith charged the men to have nothing to say to the crew, — an injunction that was probably entirely disregarded. In returning, the boat was to make for a place at low-water mark on the west bank of the Hudson, between King's Ferry and the ship, being the foot of a mountain called the Long Clove. This spot is about five miles from Smith's house, and two below Haverstraw; and hither Arnold proceeded on horseback attended by Smith's negro servant also mounted. The letter sent to Robinson was as follows: —

ARNOLD TO ROBINSON.

September 21, 1780. — SIR: — This will be delivered to you by Mr. Smith who will conduct you to a place of Safety. Neither Mr. Smith or any other person shall be made acquainted with your proposals. If they (which I doubt not) are of such a nature that I can officially take notice of them, I shall do it with pleasure. If not, you shall be permitted to return immediately. I take it for granted Colonel Robinson will not propose anything that is not for the interest of the United States as well as himself. I am, sir, &c.

The art of this letter will be observed. Had it been intercepted, its writer might have been condemned for imprudence, but hardly compromised further. It would be easy for him to allege a conviction that Robinson was prepared to regain his estate at the cost of his honor.

Their oars carefully muffled with sheepskins, the voyagers passed noiselessly from the creek into the river. It was the tail of ebb as they glided softly and unnoticed under the shadow of the shore into full view of the works of Stony Point; and as their boat silently speeded along with a favoring tide, they drew fresh energy from the consciousness of uninterruption. The sky was serene and clear, and everything hushed and still. Little was said on the way. The twelve miles between King's Ferry and Teller's Point were soon overpassed, and the spars of the Vulture rose in view indistinct through the gloom. As they came near, they were hailed from the ship, and brought to by her side. By this time the tide was young flood, and the three men stood up in the boat fending off from the Vulture till Smith was ordered to come on board. Some rude salutations were passed by the officer of the deck; and in a moment a ship-boy appeared, and bade the visitor descend to the captain's cabin.

CHAPTER XV.

André leaves the Vulture. — Interview with Arnold and its Results. — Plans for Return. — Sets out with Smith by Land.

On entering the cabin Smith was politely received by his old acquaintance Robinson who, in full regimentals, was probably awaiting Arnold's arrival. He was presented to Sutherland, who lay ill in his berth; and offered a seat. Robinson then proceeded to the perusal of the letter; after which, apologizing for a momentary absence and ordering refreshments to be brought, he left the room. During the fifteen or twenty minutes that elapsed, Smith says he took the opportunity of commenting on his rough reception on deck. The captain's politeness made him amends, and the conversation then turned on indifferent subjects.

Meanwhile, Robinson and André (who was at the time in bed) were pondering on Arnold's letter. As the former was not named in the pass he declined, and probably did not wish, to go himself to the shore; and Marbois says that he earnestly urged André not to go. For his own part, he positively refused to leave the ship; but I find no evidence that he questioned the lawfulness of his companion's doing so. The letter and passes were examined by the three British officers; and they all thought that André at least might under them seek the shore without derogation to the customs of war. Nor did the feigned name by which he went alter the case in their opinion, since it was assumed by request of the general issuing the safe-conduct, whose authority to grant such documents was in this district supreme and unquestionable. André was therefore not to be balked, nor willing to risk the loss of so valuable a prize by refusing the last chance of coming to terms with the American leader. During the night of the 20th, and all through the 21st, he had anxiously anticipated the expected flag, and was full of fear lest some misadventure had occurred; and on the moment of Smith's arrival, he hurried from his bed and was impatient to be gone. He evidently considered himself exposed to no other risk than that of being perhaps detained by Arnold or by some other American; certainly he was careful to refuse anything that might prevent his claiming from an enemy the privileges of his quality. Sutherland suggested that he might wish to lay off his regimental coat, and offered him other apparel; but the proposal was not accepted. He had Clinton's orders, he said, to go in his uniform, and by no means to relinquish his character; and added that he had not the least fear for his safety, and was ready to attend Arnold's messenger, when and where he pleased. It would certainly appear as though he at least had contemplated all along the plan of going to Arnold if Arnold would not come to him.

When therefore Robinson reëntered the cabin he was accompanied by André, whom Smith had not yet seen and to whom, as Anderson, he was now introduced by Robinson with the remark that he himself should not go on shore, but that this person was authorized by Arnold to take his place. André was evidently equipped for the journey. Over his uniform was a large blue watch-coat, such as might appropriately be worn in a September night upon the water; and his large boots were visible below. Whether this surtout altogether hid the clothing beneath from the boatmen may be doubted; it did not from Smith, and it is evident they all knew themselves engaged in a business that was not without suspicion, though at the future investigation they declared the most entire ignorance of everything that was not already in proof. Before leaving the ship, moreover, Smith says he told the captain of the size of his boat and the probable difficulty of returning, and asked for the loan of two oarsmen from the crew: which request was denied. I much question whether, at the distance of time when this statement was published, its exact purport may not have become a little obscured. If the demand was made it would probably have been complied with, for André must have expected to return that night; and when as they were about to start, Robinson suggested that so large a boat with but two oars would be long on the way, and urged that the Vulture should send her yawl to tow them as far as convenient, Smith declined the offer lest a water-patrol should encounter them, and consider the presence of the English an infringement of the flag. In the former case, to be sure, the two new men would have been nominally covered by the pass; but in either, as it turned out, it had been well for the British to have carried out the suggestion. No guard-boat was in the way; the Vulture's armed barge might have safely come and gone; and two of her seamen in Smith's boat would have brought André back unharmed and undiscovered. But all parties on board seem to have considered it certain that Arnold's pass protected him from danger, and that he was sure to be returned as he went; else, says Sutherland, measures for bringing him off whenever he chose by the Vulture's boats could have been easily concerted and accomplished. It is indeed a marvel that on such an errand a man should venture into the lion's den, without taking every precaution to ensure a safe retreat. Had the ship's boat followed Smith's at a guarded distance, remained under the shore a few hundred yards off, and approached in due season, no suspicion would have been excited or discovery ensued. It was known that the tide would be strongly against a return, and it is not likely that Smith did not name the conspicuous place whither he was now to steer: a place far below the American lines. The lateness of the night with these other circumstances would have almost compelled an astute officer to insist that his own boat should appear with a sufficient crew at a concerted place and time. Happily for America this was not so arranged, and it is far from improbable that the chief actors were too much excited and confused to give sufficient heed to the remoter emergencies of their undertaking.

Several of the crew who had dropped into the boat to chat with the Colquhouns were now ordered out; and taking the helm Smith pushed away. Little was said, and that but about the tide and the weather, as he conveyed André to the Long Clove. He indeed alleges that he had mentioned that he was to bring his companion to his own house, and that a horse was provided at the shore for this end; but it is probable Arnold had nevertheless some notion of settling all the business at the water-side, though he provided for another contingency. When the boat reached the strand Smith left it, and picking his way through the darkness found Arnold at an appointed place higher up the bank in the concealment of the trees: "he was hid among firs," says Smith with emphasis. When told of the result of the mission and that Robinson's delegate, whose youth and gentleness had not argued the possession of a weighty trust, was in waiting below, he exhibited great agitation and expressed a regret that Robinson himself had not come; but bade the stranger to be led to him. This done, Smith was requested to retire to the boat and leave them together. The wearied oarsmen sank into slumber while their landlord, his vanity evidently chafing at his exclusion from the conversation, and his body trembling with ague, uneasily awaited on the shingle the termination of the interview. When the night began to wane he at last went back and warned the conspirators that it was time to be moving. He indeed declares that both Arnold and André joined with him in importuning the boatmen to return once more to the Vulture; and that they refused not only because of their fatigue, but because daybreak would overtake them on the way, and arrangements had been made to cannonade the vessel as soon as it was light. "You can reach the ship, and be far enough," said André, by Smith's account, "before that can happen; and the same flag that carried you to the ship will make you safe on your return to General Arnold's command." This indeed may have been said by or to Smith himself; but the boatmen testified that they saw nothing of Arnold or of André after the landing: that a noise in the thicket was all they heard; and that Smith's persuasions for them to go back were very languid.

It is clear that the arrangements were not yet finished, or else that Smith was ignorant of the momentous nature of the affair he was now involved in. His influence might undoubtedly have compelled the men to return; and had he fully perceived the importance of so doing, he surely would have exercised it. Even were the trip concluded in daylight, it would have been safer for him, had he known all, to have had the men detained with the boat on the Vulture till a week had elapsed and the plot fulfilled. Perhaps he was a little sullen at the cavalier treatment he had received, and indifferent to André's concern for retreat. But Mr. Sparks is of opinion that the true reason for André's not going back this night was the unfinished condition of the business. I take it, however, that it was just one of those cases in which men are governed by the circumstances of the moment: that were the Colquhouns willing André had been sent back; but as they were not so, and as there were motives for prolonging the interview, Arnold did not press them. For though he might have here given André the papers afterwards found upon him, and the principal details of the manœuvres to be executed by Clinton, it was impossible in the darkness to thoroughly explain the details. He had brought from head-quarters on the morning of the 21st the large official plans of the general works at West Point and of each particular work, that were prepared by the engineer Duportail. It was hardly possible, even with a dark lantern, to examine these in the place where he was. He might have had them with him to give to André if he returned to the Vulture: more probably they were left at Smith's house to be exhibited and explained at greater leisure. As matters now stood, therefore, Smith and his men took the boat back towards their starting-place, while the horse his negro servant had ridden was mounted by André, who in company with Arnold hastened to the house, three or four miles distant.

As they passed from the woods by the water into the main road, the sky was still dark with that peculiar gloom which precedes the dawn. Midway on their path lay the little hamlet of Haverstraw. It must be remembered that, as we have every reason to believe, it was André's wish and stipulation that he should not be taken within any of our posts. Now, as he entered Haverstraw, the hoarse challenge of the sentry was the first intimation he had that his design was to this extent thwarted. Mr. Cooper (by what authority unless La Fayette's I know not) says André confessed afterwards that on this interruption he thought himself lost. La Fayette forty years later seems to have stated as an opinion current in the army at the time, that Arnold had posted guards here where none for some time were before, to give color to the declaration, should he be detected, that his only motive was to decoy and secure an enemy; and Hamilton refers to the existence of the same notion. This theory, if carried beyond a very narrow bound, is confuted by the other facts of the case. Marbois remarks also on André's displeasure at this encounter: but it was now too late to complain. Smothering his resentment he followed Arnold to Smith's house, where they arrived in the gray of the morning of the 22nd. Some little space after, the owner of the mansion appeared.

The unusual occurrence of an enemy's ship lingering so long in their neighborhood had roused the fears and the anger of the inhabitants and the troops at Verplanck's. Her position was accurately reported to the commander. She was moored under Teller's Point, a large tongue of land which projects from the eastern shore into the Hudson on the north side of the mouth of the Croton River; and so near to the bank that she touched bottom at low water. Livingston therefore had applied to Arnold for two heavy guns, with which he was confident he could sink her; but the request was evasively denied. He then on his own responsibility carried a four-pounder to a lesser promontory of Teller's, known as Gallows Point; and at daylight of the 22nd, taking advantage of the moment of low tide, commenced such an incessant discharge on the vessel that for a time she "appeared to be set on fire"; and had she not floated off with the flood and dropped down beyond range, she probably would have been taken. Attracted by the noise, André repaired to a window which commanded a view of the Vulture, and gazed painfully at her as she passed down the stream. He did not attempt to hide from his companions his annoyance at her change of place: but breakfast being served, the three sat down together with a show of tranquillity. The conversation turned on Arbuthnot and the fleet; the royal army and its condition; nothing of a particular nature was said on any side. After breakfast, Arnold and André retired to an upper chamber where, secure from interruption, they were closeted for hours arranging the details of their affair.

Without a certain knowledge of what transpired, we are still enabled to follow with comparative confidence the line of engagements entered into. On the one hand, Arnold was perfectly aware of the value of what he was to give up, and expected to be paid handsomely. Clinton was as willing to buy as he to sell: he was, in his own words, ready to conclude the bargain "at every risk and at any cost." Long-time had circumstances separated these currents "which mounting, viewed each other from •afar and strove in vain to meet"; and now when the parties were at last in contact, it is impossible that the terms of union were not agreed on. Marbois says Arnold's success was to have been rewarded with £30,000 and the preservation of his rank; and that in his excess of caution he even wished the money put within his control in advance.

The plan of attack and defence was also settled. With an eye to this contingency Arnold had more than once declared his intention in case of assault to receive the enemy in the defiles that led to the works, and repulse them ere they approached the walls. Dearborn, Livingston, and his other subordinates who had heard not with perfect conviction this resolution, would thus be prepared to obey on occasion without suspicion. Washington seems to have been imbued with his ideas: at all events, he directed him in case of serious demonstration to abandon the posts at King's Ferry and concentrate everything at West Point. Nothing could have suited him better: for Verplanck's at least was designed and adapted to detain for some days a foe's progress up the stream. And with a general of Arnold's character, such a line of defence had its apparent advantages; the more, since his people could always fall back into the works. But that these should be as little useful as possible, he had, by dismounting the heaviest guns, throwing down parts of the masonry, &c., in various ways and under the fairest pretences of adding to its strength, put the fortress into such a state as even with a faithful commander it might have been insecure. A breach was made in the walls of Fort Putnam through which a section could march abreast; and nothing but a few loose boards closed the aperture. No covering was provided for the troops in the redoubts. A place of debarcation, known as Kosciusko's Landing, was left entirely unprotected by any of our works; and so defective were the police arrangements that it was by no means difficult for a stranger to enter the post itself, or an enemy's boat to pass undetected up the river.*

Matters being thus prepared, it was settled that André was to return directly to New York, and forthwith come again with Clinton and Rodney, who should advance against

---

* *MS. — St. Clair to Greene; Oct. 8th,* 1780. Returns of the same date preserved in the Heath MSS. show 125 pieces of ordnance of all calibres in the works at that period, together with 1817 muskets and numerous other military stores. The largest guns were twenty-four pounders.

West Point by land and water. The route, the place of debarcation, all was agreed upon: and while our men should be detached in various bodies to remote and separated gorges, the English through the unguarded passes were to fall on them in front and in rear, and so dispose of their bands as to encompass and capture in detail our betrayed soldiery. Hemmed in on every side by rugged acclivities or superior forces, there would be no alternative but to yield or be mowed down. The very guns and other signals to announce Clinton's progress were prescribed. That no misunderstanding should occur, the large and elaborate official plans of the forts and the surrounding country were spread before the negotiators; and there were plenty of men in the royal camp who were competent guides to every mountain path and defile. Indeed Clinton himself was well acquainted with the ground as far as King's Ferry, and, as we are told, had visited West Point itself in 1777, ere yet the works were erected. That Rodney's flotilla might meet with no difficulty, Arnold had taken a most secure precaution. A mighty chain, each link of which weighed 240 pounds, was carried by anchors and huge buoys across the stream to obstruct the passage of a hostile fleet; and water-batteries were so placed as to crush any attempts to destroy or remove it. Under pretence of necessary repairs, he had a link withdrawn, which was not to be replaced for some days: and meantime a slight knot, that would yield to almost any concussion, was the only bond that held the boom together and preserved the false semblance of a real impediment. Marbois tells us that when Clinton should be within three miles of the place, two of his officers in American uniforms were to come at full gallop to Arnold's quarters, receive his final words, and hasten back to Rodney. Then the Americans remaining in the works were to be stationed in positions that should not be attacked; for it must be borne in mind that West Point was so constructed that the possession of its superior fortresses gave command of all the others. He also alleges that the 25th or 26th September was assigned for the consummation of the conspiracy; and seems to connect this with a proposal urged by André but resisted by Arnold for the seizure of Washington and his suite, who would then be on return from Hartford. Washington and Hamilton however concur in thinking this scheme was not planned. A British subaltern gives the version of the notions entertained at the time in the best unofficial circles of the king's army :— "The plan, had not Major André been discovered, was that Sir Hy. Clinton on a certain day agreed upon between him and Genl. Arnold was to lay siege to Ft. Defiance. Genl. Arnold was immediately to send to Washington for a reinforcement, and before that could arrive to surrender the place. Sir Henry was then to make a disposition to surprise the reinforcement, which probably would have been commanded by Genl. Washington in person. Had this succeeded, it must have put an end to the war."* However this be it is very certain, as Heath remarks, that André's capture was in a very critical moment and prevented the most serious consequences to our cause.

We now come to the most extraordinary part of the whole transaction; the committal by Arnold, who had hitherto been so very wary, of those papers to André which, discovered, blasted the entire affair. These were not of a nature to be of absolute service to Clinton. They were not plans of the country or of the forts. They contained nothing that might not have been carried in their bearer's memory. A syllabus of their most important contents might have been conveyed in a memorandum of two lines innocent in purport or unintelligible to any but its maker. But they were documents that could not have come from any hand but Arnold's own, and their possession would enable Clinton to compel a fulfilment of his engagements. My theory therefore is that they were either tendered by Arnold or exacted by André as a pledge of fidelity. Perhaps André was already distrustful by reason of his inveiglement into our lines; perhaps he

* Mathew MS.

dreaded in the hour of performance a betrayal of the plot such as was witnessed at Seaton-Niddrie in the Douglass Wars; but evidently the papers he now took in hand against his general's orders were not necessary for his general's instruction. They were six in number.

(1.) An Estimate of the forces at West Point and its dependencies, Sept. 13th, 1780: showing a total of 3086 men of all sorts.

(2.) An Estimate of the number of men necessary to man the works at West Point and its vicinity, showing a total, exclusive of the artillery corps, of 2438 troops.

(3.) Artillery Orders issued by Major Bauman, Sept. 5th, 1780, showing the disposition of that corps in an alarm.

(4.) Major Bauman's return of the Ordnance in the different forts, batteries, &c. at West Point and its dependencies, Sept. 5, 1780: showing the distribution of 100 pieces.

(5.) Copy of a statement of the condition of affairs submitted by Washington to a Council of War, Sept. 6th, 1780.

(6.) "Remarks on Works at Wt. Point, a Copy to be transmitted to his Excell'y General Washington, Sep'r 1780.

Fort Arnold is built of Dry Fascines and Wood, is in a ruinous condition, incompleat, and subject to take Fire from Shells or Carcasses.

Fort Putnam, Stone, Wanting great repairs, the wall on the East side broke down, and rebuilding From the Foundation; at the West and South side have been a Chevaux-de-Frise, on the West side broke in many Places. The East side open; two Bomb Proofs and Provision Magazine in the Fort, and Slight Wooden Barrack. — A commanding piece of ground 500 yards West, between the Fort and No. 4 — or Rocky Hill.

Fort Webb, built of Fascines and Wood, a slight Work, very dry, and liable to be set on fire, as the approaches are very easy, without defenses, save a slight Abattis.

Fort Wyllys, built of stone 5 feet high, the Work above

plank filled with Earth, the stone work 15 feet, the Earth 9 feet thick. — No Bomb Proofs, the Batteries without the Fort.

Redoubt No. 1. On the South side wood 9 feet thick, the Wt. North and East sides 4 feet thick, no cannon in the works, a slight and single Abattis, no ditch or Pickett. Cannon on two Batteries. No Bomb Proofs.

Redoubt No. 2. The same as No. 1. No Bomb Proofs.

Redoubt No. 3, a slight Wood Work 3 Feet thick, very Dry, no Bomb Proofs, a single Abattis, the work easily set on fire — no cannon.

Redoubt No. 4, a Wooden work about 10 feet high and fore or five feet thick, the West side faced with a stone wall 8 feet high and four thick. No Bomb Proof, two six-pounders, a slight Abattis, a commanding piece of ground 500 yards Wt.

The North Redoubt, on the East side, built of stone 4 feet high; above the Stone, wood filled in with Earth, very Dry, no Ditch, a Bomb Proof, three Batteries without the Fort, a poor Abattis, a Rising piece of ground 500 yards So., the approaches Under Cover to within 20 yards. — The Work easily fired with Faggots diptd in Pitch, &c.

South Redoubt, much the same as the North, a Commanding piece of ground 500 yards due East — 3 Batteries without the Fort."

These were all in Arnold's writing save the fourth, and the sixth alone was of sufficient moment to warrant more than the briefest syllabus of its contents; and even this last, one would think, might have been digested into a compact note, incomprehensible without a clue. To his having the originals, however, André owed his detection. But when he took them, it would seem he had expected to return by water as he came; and to Arnold's warning to destroy them should accident befall the bearer he replied that such "of course would be the case, as when he went into the boat he should have them tied about with a string and a stone." Meantime

Arnold made André take off his boots, and conceal three of the documents between each stocking and the sole of his foot. It is not likely these dangerous testimonials would have been received had their bearer not still believed himself destined to go to the Vulture, which was now returned to the vicinity of her former position. Before ten A. M. of the 22nd, Arnold took his farewell and set off in his barge for head-quarters. "Before we parted," says André, "some mention had been made of my crossing the river and going another route; but I objected much against it, and thought it was settled that in the way I came I was to return." But that it was not definitely so arranged appears from Arnold's injunction that if he went by land he should exchange his uniform coat for another to be supplied by Smith. To this, though pressed peremptorily, André yielded a reluctant consent. "I was induced to put on this wretched coat!" said he afterwards, touching the sleeve of his disguise. The following safe-conducts were also calculated for either passage:—

Head Quarters, Robinson's House, Sep'r 22d, 1780.— Joshua Smith has permission to pass with a boat and three hands and a flag to Dobb's Ferry, on public business, and to return immediately.   B. ARNOLD, M. Gen.

Head Quarters, Robinson's House, Sep'r 22d, 1780.— Joshua Smith has permission to pass the guards to the White Plains, and to return; he being on public business by my direction.   B. ARNOLD, M. Gen.

Head Quarters, Robinson's House, Sep'r 22d, 1780.— Permit Mr. John Anderson to pass the guards to the White Plains, or below, if he chuses. He being on Public Business by my Direction.   B. ARNOLD, M. Gen.

When Arnold was gone, André passed the anxious day in waiting for Smith to take him off. His host's whole account of the affair is so shuffling and evasive, and so contradicted by the evidence of his own Trial, that we are compelled to suppose him from first to last conscious of unlawful designs on Arnold's part. Neither to his American judges nor to the English public did he tell the whole truth. There were apparently things in his conduct that he dared not afterwards avow. He is said, however, to have consumed part of the day in a fruitless effort to get possession of an American uniform belonging to Lieut. John Webb, that was left at Mrs. Beekman's house on the Croton. The lady suspected his want of authority to receive it and would not deliver it up to him. As Webb and André were much of the same size, the former's uniform would have been of much service in the disguised progress through our lines; but of course nothing of this sort was suspected at the time. Nevertheless there appears in Smith's Narrative an occasional touch of nature that carries conviction with it. He unsuccessfully sought to worm the secret of his guest's business, whom nothing interested but the prospect of departure and the difficulty of rejoining the vessel on which he wistfully gazed. "Never can my memory cease to record the impassioned language of his countenance, and the energy with which he expressed his wish to be on board the Vulture, when viewing that ship from an upper window of my house."

Smith had three courses to pursue. If he was a sincere whig, and distrusted Arnold, he should have sought counsel of some of the neighboring officers. If he was willing to go through with his undertaking, he should have started at once by land with André; or he should have prepared to carry him by water in the coming night. He did neither. He made no attempt to again engage the boatmen, nor did he set off by the land route till the day was spent. It must be stated that he made no secret to all whom he met of his connection with Mr. Anderson, a person employed by Arnold to get intelligence from New York: but at the same time he omitted no opportunity of producing an impression that their course was to be up the river to head-quarters, rather than down towards the city. As for the tale that he was imposed on by Arnold to believe that his guest was a young tradesman from New York who in vanity had borrowed a British uniform, it is effectually contradicted by his half-admission that he saw him in the coat upon the Vulture, and the fact that Robinson and Sutherland were in his company when he left the vessel in this very gear. But about the ague, that rendered a night on the water injurious to his comfort and health, there is less room for cavil; and though there is no doubt that he might, had he strongly wished it, have found means to convey André on board, he had at least a fair show of reasoning for preferring to escort him by the shore.

Mounted on a horse furnished by Arnold and accompanied by Smith and his negro, André at length started for New York. Had he been possessed of more knowledge of the habits and customs of all classes in this country, or had greater confidence existed between his host and himself, there were a thousand chances to one that the black fellow could have served his turn better than any man that had been thought of. Every one knows how apt at clandestine practices is the black domestic servant of America. If a negro would go to a nocturnal frolic twenty miles from his master's home, the choicest steed in the stable will be found dripping in his stall on the ensuing morning, nor can any one discover the cause. If a piece of household gossip that occurs at bedtime is known ere daybreak to half the kitchens in the community, the informant is surely a negro. To an obstinate perverseness which often rises into almost chivalric fidelity of disposition is united in the negro's character a certain spice of his savage origin that not only tells him bread eaten in secret is sweet and stolen waters pleasant; but which leads him in a manner to outwit the cunning of nature. The shortest and surest path through a swamp; the most secluded nook or narrowest channel among a thousand islets of the coast is sure to be known to the wanderer in darkness as well as his own fireside. Had André and Smith at this moment interested their attendant with a dram, a promise of a half-joe, and an injunction of perfect secrecy, I have no doubt that the next daybreak would have found the Englishman on the deck of the Vulture. If the servant himself was not competent to the undertaking, he had beyond question scores of friends who were; and a canoe or skiff with an experienced navigator would have brought André to the ship's side ere the sentry heard the dip of the paddle.

It was upon a Friday afternoon that this expedition was begun; and if any ill-omen was to be drawn from the day, André perhaps, like the gentle cavalier of old, might profess his confidence in the power that made the sun to rise rather than in the day's name that it rose on. Or if he took any heed of omens in the satisfaction at being released from his condition of inert and perilous suspense, the glorious words of Homer should have dispelled every painful thought: — the best omen of all is to strike for your country.

CHAPTER XVI.

André's Journey. — Westchester County. — Skinners and Cow-boys. — André's Capture. — Various Accounts of its Circumstances.

THE evening twilight was setting in when the travellers crossed the Hudson at King's Ferry, about two miles northwest of Smith's house. To his acquaintance on the road and to the officers of Verplanck's, Smith professed his destination to be Robinson's house; but while he paused to chat and drink, his companion eschewed all conversation or delay and passed slowly on. André's dress at this moment was a purple or crimson coat with vellum-bound button-holes and garnished with threadbare gold-lace, which, with a tarnished beaver hat, he had obtained from his guide. The remainder of his apparel was his military undress; nankin small-clothes and handsome white-topped boots. Over all was his well-worn watch-coat with its heavy cape, buttoned closely about his neck. From Verplanck's the road, with its ancient guide-post, *Dishe his di Roode toe de Kshing's Farry*, led northwesterly for fourteen miles towards Salem; intersected however at three miles distance by the direct highway from Peekskill through Tarrytown to New York, that follows the river and crosses the neck of Teller's Point. This would perhaps have been the best course for André to have pursued, had not Smith's false answers made it dangerous to have turned so soon down the river instead of up. By it the distance from Verplanck's to Dobb's Ferry, where were probably at this moment British gun-boats, was but about twenty-two miles; and to Tarrytown but about nineteen. Five and a half miles from Verplanck's another road from Peekskill intersects that to Salem, and bending away through

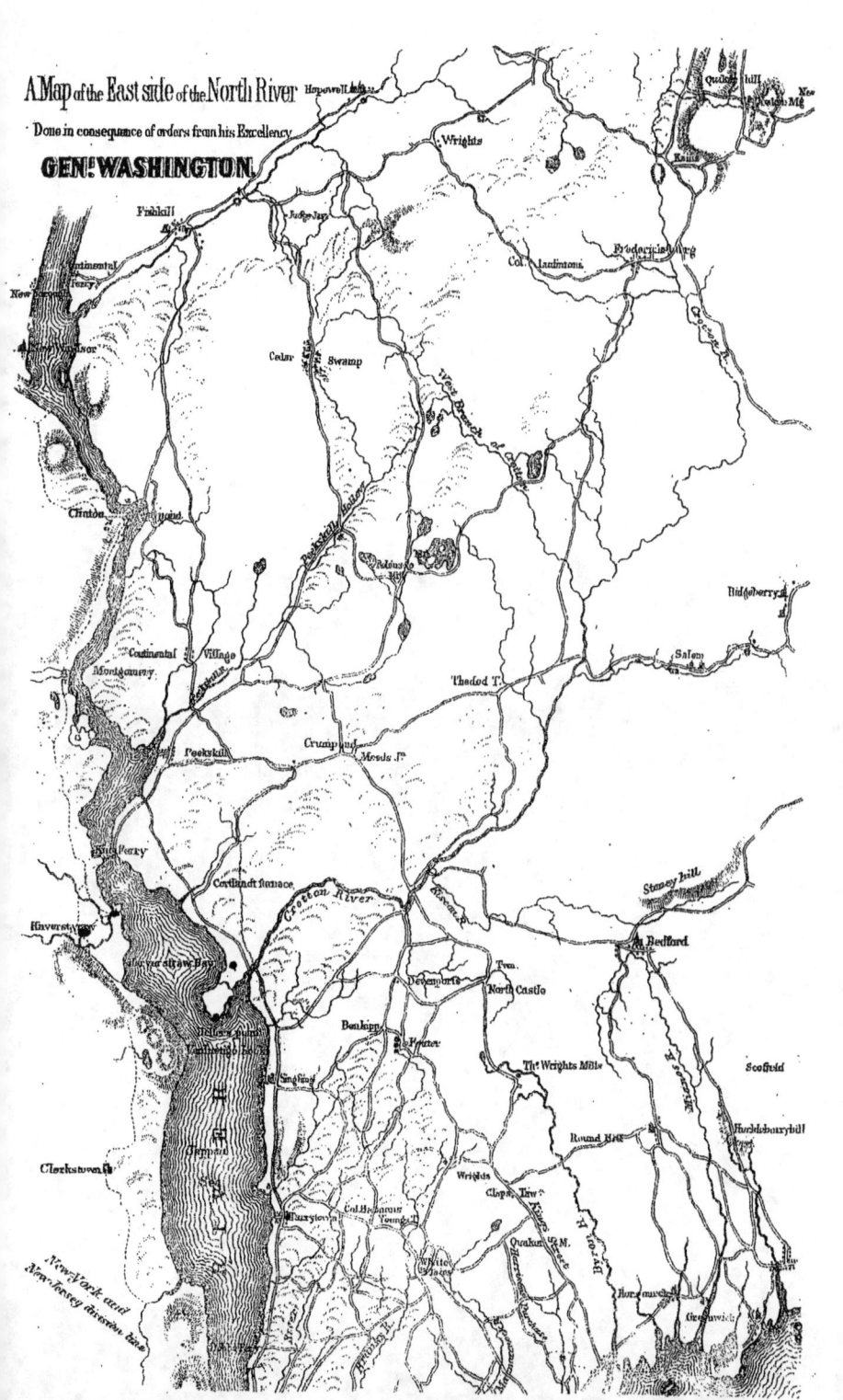

the interior crosses the Croton at Pine's Bridge and makes the distance by it to Tarrytown, as André eventually travelled, fully twenty-five miles. By cross-roads either route was about equally direct to White Plains.

Just before dark Smith overtook his companion and the servant, and the party now hastened onwards. Every attempt to bring André into conversation about the affairs of 1779 at Stony Point and the vicinity was fruitless. He was reluctant to talk, and anxious only to get on. Between eight and nine P. M. they stumbled across an American patrol under Captain Boyd, who compelled them to exhibit their pass and declare their errand. Smith had no hesitation in uttering his tale that they were on their way to get intelligence for Arnold; and Boyd, who seems to have been of a very inquisitive yet communicative disposition, overwhelmed him with questions and with advice. He was positive that their best route was by North Castle; the Tarrytown Road was infested with Cow-boys; and there was no propriety in their proceeding further that night. André was not a little disconcerted at all this, and privately urged Smith to push forward in despite of Boyd's advice; but his guide was fearful of exciting displeasure or suspicion and insisted on going no further. But instead of the house recommended to them for a lodging, he sought some miles back the dwelling of a loyal Scot who did not scruple to avow, much to André's contentment, his longings for the restoration of the king's authority. Here they procured admittance; but such was the distrust of the times that the farmer would not himself retire till he had seen his two guests ensconced in one bed. He had been lately harried of all his cattle: nevertheless he would take no pay for his humble accommodations.

André passed a restless night, tossing and sighing till he robbed Smith of that repose which he could not himself enjoy; and with the first glimpse of dawn was up and stirring, eager to get away. He sought the negro and bade him bring out the horses; and without waiting for breakfast, the party set forth betimes. When the horses appeared, the haggard countenance which betrayed a sleepless couch, lightened up with pleasure; and a serener expression supplanted its unmistakable dejection while the journey lessened under their feet. As the fear of detection subsided, his spirits rose proportionally to their late depression. He was filled with the sense of the awful dangers he had fallen into; of the imminent prospect of his extrication from an unforeseen whirlpool that had involved his life and his fame; and of the prodigious results that would ensue his deliverance. Behind lay death and shame; before him, glory, happiness, and renown. Unable to reveal to his companion the secret cause of his swelling satisfaction, he gave it vent through another channel, and burst into a flood of animated discourse. Everything that fell from his lips partook of the bright hues of his mind; and the delighted listener was fain to note the change from his previous reticence and gloom.

"I now found him highly entertaining: he was not only well informed in general history, but well acquainted with that of America, particularly New York, which he termed the residuary legatee of the British government, (for it took all the remaining lands not granted to the proprietary and chartered provinces). He had consulted the Muses as well as Mars, for he conversed freely on the belles-lettres: music, painting, and poetry, seemed to be his delight. He displayed a judicious taste in the choice of the authors he had read, professed great elegance of sentiment, and a most pleasing manner of conveying his ideas, by adopting the flowery colouring of poetical imagery. He lamented the causes which gave birth to and continued the war, and said if there was a corresponding temper on the part of the Americans, with the prevailing spirit of the British ministry, peace was an event not far distant; he intimated that measures were then in agitation for the accomplishment of that desirable object, before France could accomplish her perfidious designs. He sincerely wished the fate of the war could alone be determined in the fair, open field contest, between as many British in number as those under the command of Count Rochambeau at Rhode Island, whose effective force he seemed clearly to understand; he descanted on the richness of the scenery around us, and particularly admired, from every eminence, the grandeur of the Highland mountains, bathing their lofty summits in the clouds from their seeming watery base at the north extremity of Haverstraw Bay. The pleasantry of converse, and the mildness of the weather, so insensibly beguiled the time, that we at length found ourselves at the Bridge before I thought we had got half the way; and I now had reason to think my fellow-traveller a very different person from the character I had at first formed of him." *

As they approached Pine's Bridge, which crosses the Croton about twelve miles by their course from Verplanck's, they paused to bait their horses and to seek food at a wayside cottage, whose mistress had but the night before been robbed by the Skinners or Cow-boys of all she possessed save a little meal and a single cow.† The good woman's hospitality, however, was not measured by her larder. From her milk and her meal she prepared a sort of humble porridge or *soupaun* that the travellers, fasting since yesterday's dinner, did ample justice to without regard to the contemptuous sport which one of them had so lately bestowed on it in The Cow-Chase.

During breakfast Smith informed his companion of his intention to part. His understanding with Arnold was to continue to White Plains: and had he fulfilled it, André would have been saved. For Smith was known by and himself knew personally most of the people of this region; and had he been stopped by the captors there is little question that he

---

* Smith's Narr. 44.

† Smith says this was at the residence of an old Dutch *frau*, two and a half miles before coming to the bridge. Bolton (Westchester Co. i. 210) says it was at Mrs. Underhill's of Yorktown, whose grandson still possesses the house.

would have carried the matter through and without hesitation. In truth, he was probably afraid of compromising himself by a longer stay with one who evidently was not what he seemed: or he may have dreaded encountering the Cowboys below Pine's Bridge; for the Croton was regarded as the boundary between the English and Americans of the debatable land, or, in the language of the day, the Neutral Ground. André had no means of opposing this determination; nor was he perhaps sorry, now that he was almost out of danger, to be quit of his comrade. While Smith was paying for the breakfast, however, he mentioned his own condition as to funds, and borrowed one-half of the stock of paper-money in his guide's wallet. At parting, says Smith, he betrayed some emotion. He charged himself with a message to his own acquaintance and Smith's brother, the Chief-justice, and vainly urged the acceptance of his gold watch, as a keepsake, on his guide. With mutual good wishes they separated; and Smith hastened with his servant up the road; dined at head-quarters with Arnold, whom he represents as satisfied with his conduct; and supped on the next evening at Fishkill with Washington and his suite.

Westchester County, through which André now pursued his solitary way, was in the beginning of the contest signalized by its loyalty. Throngs of its people not only publicly avowed their intention to stand by the king and to shoot down any who came in the name of Congress to disarm them, but even put a measurable restraint upon the whigs; and retorted in kind many of those rude monitions of popular displeasure that in other places the tories were subjected to. If a prominent whig found his fences thrown down, or the manes and tails of his choicest horses disfigured by the clipping-shears, he knew it was a political enemy that had done this. Much of the soil, particularly towards the Hudson, was vested in large proprietors, — the Philipses, Coldens, De Lanceys, and Van Cortlandts, — and by them cultivated or leased out in small farms; so that in its extent of thirty miles, it had presented one of the most prosperous rural districts of America. The course of war, however, changed all this. The majority of the gentry sided with the crown, and took refuge in New York. Their dependents, and the agricultural populace generally whatever their political views, lost heart in an employment that rival armies alone profited by. Many who leased or owned farms were subjected to losses which drove them to desperation; and that class of the people who had nothing to lose and to whom honest labor was often denied, seem to have become thoroughly imbued with a spirit of spoil and robbery. Nominally, such as participated in these habits were divided into two orders: the Cow-boys robbed and cried "God save the King"; the Skinners stole for the sake of Congress. Of course each side pretended to confine its outrages to the enemies of its own political creed; but in point of fact it pillaged indifferently friend and foe who had a cow or a pig to be carried off, or a purse of gold to be yielded. These scoundrelly partisans were often personal acquaintances; they were more often in league, and playing into each other's hands. The Cow-boys were generally refugees who had been expelled from their homes and driven to reside within the British lines. The Skinners, though abiding in our bounds and professing attachment to our cause, were in reality, says Mr. Sparks, "more unprincipled, perfidious, and inhuman than the Cow-boys themselves: for these latter exhibited some symptoms of fellow-feeling for their friends, whereas the Skinners committed their depredations equally upon friend and foe." An idea of their comparative merits may be obtained from their respective titles: the Cow-boys were so called from their practice of harrying the cattle of whig farmers, and bringing them into New York; the Skinners got their name by reason of their stripping their victim of every thing he had in the world down to the merest trifle; not scrupling, if they thought money was to be extorted by the operation, to deprive his flesh of its nearest and most primitive covering. In this course, as

Mr. Sparks says, they had no more hesitation in visiting a wealthy whig than a tory; and so great was the appetite for villany, that no orders, nor even the presence of a commissioned officer could restrain them. If an American foraging party went out from the lines, as many volunteers from the country side as could join themselves to it attended and disgraced its progress: and they would return rich with horses, cattle, bed-stuffs, clothing, and whatever portable effects they could bear away to divide at their leisure. "The militia volunteers excelled in this business," said Aaron Burr. A crowd of the best whigs in the land would follow at their heels, hoping, and sometimes obtaining the restoration of their property, but not often the punishment of their robbers. When the protection of a regular party was wanting to these skulking thieves, they would maraud by night through the country round, and concert with their kindred the Cow-boys to take off their hands the plunder they could neither keep themselves nor sell within American jurisdiction. Then a meeting would occur, and the cows and sheep of the whig farmer be bartered for dry goods and gold brought by the Cow-boys from New York. A mock skirmish closed the scene of iniquity, and with pockets well lined and tongues loud in lying praise of their own bravery, the Skinners would return laden with booty which they pretended they had captured from a smuggling party of the enemy. Well might this state of affairs be styled a most "formidable conspiracy against the rights and claims of humanity!" *

To the armies on either side, rather than to any exertion of the civil authorities, is due the praise for any attempt to suppress these banditti. The continental officers on the lines

---

* "The Militia and Cow-boys are very busy in driving, and it is out of my power to prevent them. If I send the troops down below to prevent the Cow-boys the Militia are driving off in the rear, and if I have the troops above, the lower party are driving downwards, and the inhabitants are left destitute without any prospect of redress." — *MS. Jameson to Heath, Oct. 18th, 1780.*

were constantly instructed to prevent and repress them. Yet the task was difficult. The whig legislature of New York had enacted the confiscation of every man's property who refused the oath of allegiance : supplies of war intended for the enemy were also declared lawful prize ; and under these pretences, the sturdy rustic, who at sunset would bear down an inquisitive officer with protestations of his utter aversion to such practices, would ere morning justify his pillage of any neighbor's cattle-yard or sheepfold as a legitimate spoiling of the Egyptian. There is an undoubted rule of war in such cases, the seasonable application of which will always save many lives in the end. Its principles were published and practised by Napoleon and maintained by Wellington. When rival armies are in the field, it is lawful for any inhabitant to enlist under the flag of his country. If captured, he is a prisoner entitled to honorable treatment. But where peasantry refuse to enlist, yet secretly resist, — to-day peacefully working in their fields, to-night assaulting a picket-guard, — the general of the adversary is entirely justifiable in burning their habitations and hanging the men to the nearest tree. The army that can maintain its position in a hostile land has for the time being a right to the open opposition or the passive obedience of the inhabitants within its range.

At this very period we know how Westchester county, once such a scene of rural affluence and peace, appeared to a foraging party that bore off hundreds of loads of its hay and grain. The land was in ruins. Most of the farm-holders had fled, and such as remained were not permitted to reap where they had sown. The fields were covered with the tangled harvest-growths that decayed ungathered on the ground, and in the neglected orchards the fruit rotted in great heaps beneath the trees. The sturdy American who describes the scene attributes all the devastation to the enemy : for he considered Cow-boys and Skinners as renegades alike, and all villanous tories. He recites the tortures they employed to extort from the inhabitants the revelation of hoards which perhaps did not exist. The wretch would be hanged till he became insensible; then cut down and revived, and again hanged. The case of an aged Quaker makes it probable these ruffians were nominally whigs; for the Quakers were generally loyal. This poor old man had given up all his money, but more was required. To be sure that he was secreting nothing from them, his captors first inflicted the torment of *scorching:* they stripped him naked, immersed him in hot ashes, and roasted him as one would a potato, till the blistered skin rose from his flesh. Then he was thrice hung and cut down; nor did his oppressors leave him while life appeared to remain. When Burr commanded the advanced lines in this county, his indignation at all he witnessed first inspired him, he says, with a wish for arbitrary power. "I could gibbet half-a-dozen *good whigs*, with all the venom of an inveterate tory."

Through such a region, where none were safe with aught to lose and not force to defend it, André was now to go. After leaving Pine's Bridge, he was not long in resolving to abandon the route he was on and, striking to the right, to take the Tarrytown Road. It was shorter; and if, as Boyd had warned him, he might find the Cow-boys upon it, he probably esteemed them less perilous opponents than the Skinners. It was a bright pleasant morning on Saturday, the 23rd of September; and he looked forward to being ere sunset once more with his friends. Few incidents for a while interrupted his solitude. At the house of Mr. Staats Hammond he paused to ask for water, and the little children who brought it him from the well bore in mind their vision of a mounted man closely wrapt in his light-blue swan-skin cloak, with high military boots and round brimmed hat, who leisurely walked his bay horse to their door. The incongruous appearance of such a good-looking steed, with its handsome double snaffle bridle and its tail and mane filled with burrs, was not lost on them. The lad held the rein while the stranger drank.

"How far is it to Tarrytown?" he inquired. Four miles, replied the boy. "I did not think it was so far," said André, and resumed his way. At Chappequa, near Underhill's Tavern, he again questioned some Quakers whom he met as to the road, and whether troops were out below. At the foot of the Chappequa roads he took that leading to the river; and came into the Albany post-road near the village of Sparta. As he approached what is now called the André Brook, he had gone over nearly eleven miles of neutral ground.

He was now hard by Tarrytown, and even by his own showing, had been very lucky in his journey. "Nothing," he said to one of our officers, "occurred to disturb him in his route until he arrived at the last place, excepting at Crampon; he told me his hair stood erect, and his heart was in his mouth, on meeting Col. Samuel B. Webb, of our army—an acquaintance of his. He said the Colonel stared at him, and he thought he was gone; but they kept moving, and soon passed each other. He then thought himself past all danger. Whilst ruminating on his good luck and hairbreadth escape, he was assailed by three bushmen near Tarrytown, who ordered him to stand."

On the west of the road flowed the river; on the east rose the Greenburgh Hills, in whose bosom lies the world-renowned vale of Sleepy Hollow, with its old church, founded by the Philipse family, and the ancient bell with its legend *Si Deus pro nobis, quis contra nos*. Indeed on every hand stretched far and wide around him the fair manors of his friends the De Lanceys and those of the Philipses in which his coadjutor Robinson was so largely interested. Before him, scarce half a mile north of Tarrytown, a rivulet flowing from the hills crossed the road through a marshy ravine dark with shade, then known as Wiley's Swamp; and by a south-west course soon mingled its waters with that part of the neighboring Hudson which bears the name of the Tappaan Zee. "A few rough logs," says the venerable Knickerbocker, "laid side by side, served for a bridge over this stream. On that side of the road where the brook entered the wood, a group of oaks and chestnuts, matted thick with wild grape-vines, threw a cavernous gloom over it." Here, on the south or lower side of the bridge and on the west side of the path, were secreted among the bushes John Paulding, Isaac Van Wart, and David Williams, whose presence on this occasion saved America from a mortal blow.*

On the preceding day seven young men, mostly natives of or well acquainted with the neighborhood, had agreed to waylay the road in quest of spoil. The ravages of war had deprived them of all profitable and peaceful employment, and by their own account they were in hopes of wresting from some of the returning confederates of the Cow-boys, who had just forayed the country, a part of their ill-gotten gains. That they should have cared to encounter an armed force of any size is contradicted by the smallness and disposition of their own band; three of whom kept the ambush, while four watched from a hill-top lest the Light-horse should come on them unawares. For as they acted under no commission nor were detached from either the continental or militia organizations, it might have fared badly with them to have been interrupted by the American or the English authorities. It has been indeed said that the enterprise was permitted by the commanding officer at Salem; yet Tallmadge, the second officer and the efficient spirit of the dragoons, declared its character was such that had he fallen upon it he would have arrested its members as readily as André himself. It is fortunate therefore that they escaped the notice of this active and well-informed soldier.

Through all this part of our narrative, a fatal combination of circumstances was working against André. Had he pursued any other road, or had he arrived here two hours earlier, he would have escaped scot-free. The party had been but little more than an hour on the ground when, between eight

* See Appendix, No. II.

and nine A. M., one of them looking up from the game of cards in which they had engaged, discovered his approach. His boots, a valuable prize in those days, seem to have at once attracted the eyes of all.* "There comes a trader going to New York," said one. "There comes a gentleman-like looking man," said another to Paulding, "who appears to be well dressed and has boots on, whom you had better step out and stop, if you don't know him." As his horse's tramp clattered over the bridge they sprang to their feet, and Paulding, the master-spirit of the party, advanced with presented musket and bade him stand, and announce his destination. "My lads," he replied, "I hope you belong to our party." They asked which party he meant. "The lower party," he answered; and on their saying that they did, he seems to have betrayed an exultation that was unmistakable. "Thank God, I am once more among friends!" he

* The want of manufactured domestic articles was severely felt by our people during the war; and in the hottest pursuit of British cavalry an American trooper has been seen to peril his life for just such boots as André wore: leaping from his horse to strip a pair from the corpse of a royal officer, and escaping almost under the upraised swords of the enemy. We may all remember the ludicrous scene in a book, the terror of our childhood — Schinderhannes, the Robber of the Rhine — where forty or fifty Jews, amid protestations of entire poverty, are made to remove their boots, shoes, and stockings, and display the treasures they had there concealed; and how, each being told to resume his own articles, a furious fight was at once waged — first for the boots, next for the shoes. The date of this scene is in the close of the eighteenth century. The large horseman's boots which André wore were very different articles from those which common acceptation has received. I have seen a sign-board, commemorating the capture, that stood for many years in Philadelphia, and which erroneously displayed a pair of genuine comedy top-boots in lieu of the originals. Three months previous to André's detection, a letter was published which purported to have been written by our Gen. Maxwell to Mr. Caldwell, in which the writer explicitly states that till he receives a pair of boots he cannot appear in public. The events of the capture as given above are described in three forms, according to the version given by the captors themselves; by André; and by tradition. It is impossible to entirely reconcile all of them; so the reader shall have an opportunity of comparing them together, and with Appendix, No. II., where the captors themselves are more particularly noticed.

cried, as he recognized a royal uniform on Paulding's back. "I am glad to see you. I am a British officer out of the country, on particular business, and I hope you won't detain me a minute;" and in proof of his assertion he exhibited the gold watch, which was an article then seldom possessed by the gentlemen of our service. On this they told him he was their prisoner; that they were Americans, and he must dismount. He laughed, unconcernedly producing Arnold's pass and remarking, "My God, I must do anything to get along!" None but Paulding were able to read or write; and he treated the safe-conduct with little respect, after the previous avowal. "Had he pulled out General Arnold's pass first, I should have let him go."

They now led him aside to a gigantic whitewood or tulip-tree, twenty-six feet in girth, that stood like a landmark a little southward of the stream.

"Its limbs were gnarled and fantastic, large enough to form trunks for ordinary trees, twisting down almost to the earth, and rising again into the air. It was connected with the tragical story of the unfortunate André, who had been taken prisoner hard by; and was universally known by the name of Major André's Tree. The common people regarded it with a mixture of respect and superstition, partly out of sympathy for the fate of its illstarred namesake, and partly from the tale of strange sights and doleful lamentations told concerning it."

Under this tree, which by a strange chance was scathed with lightning on the very day that the news of his execution came to Tarrytown, André was searched. He warned his captors of Arnold's displeasure at this proceeding, and protested he had no letters; but nothing would satisfy them but an examination of his person. "My lads," said he, "you will bring yourselves into trouble":—but they vowed they did not fear it, and while by their compulsion he threw off his clothing, piece by piece, Williams was deputed to the examination. Nothing appeared, however, till one boot was removed; then it was evident that something was concealed in the stocking. "By ——," cried Paulding — "here it is!" — and seizing the foot while Williams withdrew the stocking, three folded half-sheets of paper enclosed in a fourth indorsed West Point were revealed. The other foot was found similarly furnished. "By ——," repeated Paulding, "he is a spy!"

They questioned him as to where he obtained these papers; but of course his replies were evasive. They asked him whether he would engage to pay them handsomely if they would release him, and he eagerly assented. He would surrender all he had with him, and would engage to pay a hundred guineas or more, and any quantity of dry goods, if he were permitted to communicate with New York. Dry goods, it will be remembered, was the general term for articles peculiarly precious to our people. Paulding peremptorily stopped this conversation; swearing determinedly that not ten thousand guineas should release him. Williams again asked him if he would not escape, if an opportunity offered. "Yes, I would," said André. "I do not intend that you shall," was the rejoinder; whereon the prisoner to all further interrogatories prayed them to lead him to an American post, and to question him no more. They now set forth towards their comrades on the hill, Paulding leading the horse on which the captive was mounted. As the parties drew together, the guide informed Yerks, the chief man of the remaining four, of their prize, making him at the same time descend and produce his watch in verification of his quality. "He then asked him for his watch," says Yerks, "at the same time warning him not to make any attempt at escape, for if he did he was a dead man." Presently the course was resumed across the country to North Castle; avoiding roads and "each taking their turns at the bridle, some marching on either side, the remainder bringing up the rear." André was taciturn, only speaking to answer questions, and then but shortly. As they paused at the house of one of the party, Paulding went in advance to its proprietor (perhaps his comrade's father) and said: — "Be careful how you talk; I believe we have got a British officer." Here they tarried a little, and one of the women of the family pressed André to eat. "No, I thank you," he answered in sadness, "I have no appetite to take anything." Soon resuming the march in such wise as before, they at length accomplished the twelve miles that brought them to Jameson's quarters, and delivered their prisoner into his hands.

We must now hear another and less pleasing narration of some of these transactions; and particularly, so far as may be, obtain André's own account of the affair. The late General King, of Ridgefield, Connecticut, then a lieutenant in Sheldon's dragoons, who had custody of him within a few hours of his arrival, relates the story André told, and which he himself implicitly received and always upheld as nothing but the truth. It must be premised that it was not altogether unusual for persons near the British lines to kidnap an officer riding out when none of our troops were near the city, and detain him till he promised to pay a ransom. This practice was at length in a measure checked by the officers themselves, who not only paid the extorted gold, but caused the recipient to be imprisoned or flogged. King says, then, that André in the course of his revelations (which are otherwise partly sustained by what we now know) told how he was challenged near Tarrytown by three bushmen.

"He says to them, I hope, gentlemen, you belong to the lower party. We do, says one. So do I, says he, and by the token of this ring and key you will let me pass.* I am a British officer on business of importance, and must not be detained. One of them took his watch from him, and ordered him to dismount. The moment this was done, he said he found he was mistaken, and he must shift his tone. He says, I am happy, gentlemen, to find I am mistaken.

---

* This is probably another version of the production of the prisoner's watch.

You belong to the upper party, and so do I. A man must make use of any shift to get along, and to convince you of it, here is General Arnold's pass, handing it to them, and I am in his service. Damn Arnold's pass, says they. You said you was a British officer, and no money, says they. Let's search him. They did so, but found none. Says one, he has got money in his boots, let's have them off and see. They took off his boots, and there they found his papers, but no money. They then examined his saddle, but found none. He said, he saw they had such a thirst for money, he could put them in a way to get it, if they would be directed by him. He asked them for to name their sum for to deliver him at King's Bridge. They answered him in this way. If we deliver you at King's Bridge, we shall be sent to the Sugar House, and you will save your money. He says to them, if you will not trust my honor, two of you may stay with me, and one shall go with a letter which I shall write. Name your sum. The sum was agreed upon, but I cannot recollect whether it was five hundred or a thousand guineas — the latter I think was the sum. They held a consultation a considerable time, and finally they told him, if he wrote, a party would be sent out and take them, and then they all should be prisoners. They said they had concluded to take him to the commanding officer on the lines."

That André actually made this statement, or at least gave in his own language its essential facts, none can doubt, we are told, who knew King either personally or by reputation. Circumstantial evidence also testifies to the fact. Captain Samuel Bowman of the Massachusetts line (whose character is faithfully represented in that of his sons) records that for the twenty-four hours preceding the execution he was constantly with the prisoner, and of course the conversation turned on the occasion of his confinement. His story is given here as he told it.

"To this gentleman André himself related, that he was passing down a hill, at the foot of which, under a tree playing cards, were the three men who took him. They were close by the road side, and he had approached very near them before either party discovered the other: upon seeing him, they instantly rose and seized their rifles. They approached him, and demanded who he was? He immediately answered that he was a British officer; supposing, from their being so near the British lines, that they belonged to that party. They then seized him, robbed him of the few guineas which he had with him, and the two watches which he then wore, one of gold and the other of silver. He offered to reward them if they would take him to New York; they hesitated; and in his (André's) opinion, the reason why they did not do so was the impossibility on his part to secure to them the performance of the promise."

To all this must be superadded the conviction of Tallmadge, to whom the character of both captive and captors was more or less known, that the same story, which he also heard from his prisoner, was true. He most publicly avowed his belief that André's boots were taken off in pursuit of plunder, not of the proofs of treason; and that had he been in condition to hand over the price demanded, he would not have been detained or discovered. The sagacity and the probity of a very distinguished soldier cannot be too highly estimated in considering the authority this declaration of his bears with it.

Thus we have before us the story as told respectively by André and by the captors themselves. What tradition relates may be distrusted but not suppressed. It says that the captors were in wait for men of their acquaintance who had gone into New York with cattle to sell to the British, a share of whose money they hoped to win or otherwise get from them as they returned. They were stretched on the ground playing cards when André was discovered advancing slowly, and studying his route on a paper in his hand. As he drew near, apparently suspecting the danger that might lurk in such a covert, he quickened his pace, thrusting the paper into the boot of his off leg — a very convenient receptacle for any light, loose article. One of the three observed to the others: "Here comes a fellow with *boots;* let us stop him." They did so, and speedily asked him what was that paper he had thrust in his boot. The road which he travelled was much frequented, and several spectators soon gathered to the scene, and by their presence prevented the conclusion of a bargain to which both parties were equally well inclined.

Tradition in this case has little value save as a matter of curiosity; but from the other and more respectable authorities it is difficult to avoid at least the inference that but for the strong energetic spirit of Paulding, there is a probability that André would have got off. It is evident that his captors were of wild, unsettled dispositions, engaged now on an expedition that was certainly unsanctioned by the laws and practices of the American army. That they despoiled their prisoner is also established: and but for the papers on his person the matter might have ended there. The resolution and sagacity of Paulding are testified by the course pursued on this discovery; and while we can easily see how young men in their position delighted in enterprises that had a zest in their very risks and unlawfulness, it is as plain that when love of plunder and love of country were conspicuously balanced before their eyes, the former kicked the beam. Their service to America was so great as to completely cover up the circumstances that enabled them to render it. It was charged that some of them at least were of that large class who, changeable as motes in sunbeams, were to be found by chance arrayed with either side that prevailed in the Neutral Ground: —

> "Commutare viam, retroque repulsa reverti
> Nunc huc, nunc illuc, in cunctas denique partes."

If this be so they are not the first whose night's exploit at Gadshill is a little gilded over by the day's service at Shrewsbury.

Washington, Hamilton, and the world have marvelled at the failure in this critical moment of André's usual address and presence of mind. Has it ever been considered possible that matters might have been so ordered that nothing but force could have got him through? He avowed himself British: so did his captors, and seized him. There was more probability to a stranger of their being British, than himself. They were near the royal lines, and one of them in a royal jacket. He next produced Arnold's pass. This was thrown aside; though there was nothing but his previous assertion, which was founded on their own stratagem, to warrant the suspicion that it was not valid. That they thought him a spy when they searched him is more than I believe. General Heath says they knew not what he was; nor he, whether his captors were Americans, British, or refugees. It is, however, proper to say that on every subsequent occasion they solemnly and steadily professed the entire purity of their conduct and motives in all this transaction.

CHAPTER XVII.

André a Prisoner in our Lines. — Intercourse with American Officers. — Letters to Washington. — Arnold's Escape.

RETAINING André's horse, watch, and other effects as lawful prize to be sold for the benefit of the seven, the captors handed him over to Lieut.-Col. John Jameson who, in command of Sheldon's Dragoons and some Connecticut militia, was now at North Castle. Jameson was a Virginian; an approved soldier, of gentle manners and unstained integrity. His manly person, comely face, dark eyes and hair, and polite bearing are commemorated by the ladies of his time; and he was wounded in a service at Valley Forge which received Washington's especial thanks. To him the prisoner was still John Anderson; and a careful scrutiny of the mysterious papers threw no light on the business. Pure himself he suspected least of all things the guilt of his general; and though the pass was a puzzle to him, he thought the whole affair was a device of the enemy to injure Arnold and plant distrust and dissension in our camp. So Washington pronounced of his conduct, when calm reflection had dispelled the effect of the angry disappointment in which he dropped words that stigmatized it with bewilderment and egregious folly. To the conclusions that Jameson now came, André's language perhaps aided; for well he knew that to but one man in our army could he look for relief. If he might meet Arnold ere the affair leaked out, both might escape together. He therefore uttered not a syllable that would betray the secret; and with intense satisfaction heard he was to be sent to West Point. He already had desired that Arnold might be instructed that John Anderson was arrested with a pass signed by the general; and Jameson thought the simplest plan would be to send the prisoner himself to head-quarters. It was his duty under ordinary circumstances to report the transaction to Arnold; and accordingly in a brief note he related what was done, and dispatched Lieutenant Allen and four of the Connecticut militia with the letter and captive to West Point. The papers he transmitted by express to Washington. By these means he had discharged his duty, and at the same time given such warning of the business that but for the Vulture, of whose position he was not aware, and for the unexpected delay in his enclosures reaching the chief, Arnold really could not have escaped. When Jameson therefore is accused of imbecility on this occasion, it is well to recall his actual conduct, and to reflect on the insubordination he would have been charged with, had Arnold been innocent, in daring to report directly to the commander-in-chief, without regard to his lawful superior, to whom all details of duty should ordinarily be submitted.

André was already advanced some distance towards West Point when, late in the day, Major Tallmadge returned to North Castle from a temporary service on which he had been detached. Tallmadge was no ordinary man; and though now but twenty-six years of age he possessed a remarkably matured judgment. His education was liberal, and ere entering the army he had taught a public school in Connecticut. To the knowledge of mankind, and particularly of that portion of it who inhabited this part of the country, was added the especial acquirements his peculiar service involved: for from early in 1778 to the end of the war he was employed by Washington to carry on the secret correspondence with our spies in New York, and in guarding Westchester county from the depredations of Cow-boys, Skinners, and De Lancy's Refugee corps. The general character of every inhabitant was a necessary part of such an officer's knowledge, and to deal with a spy a duty of his every-day life. He had moreover a laudable pride in his profession; and now that accoutrements came in from France, his troop in Sheldon's dragoons, mounted all on dapple-gray horses, with their black bearskin holsters and straps, and helmets crowned with horse-tail plumes, presented an effect not often seen at the period in our ranks.

Had Tallmadge returned sooner, or not at all, André would not have been hung. In the one case, Arnold would have been seized on; in the other, both would have got away together. For no sooner had Jameson related what had transpired, than coupling the letter Arnold had written him respecting this very Anderson with the treacherous documents and pass, he was convinced of his General's treason. He warmly represented the inconsistency of Jameson's course, and offered to take on himself all blame if permission might be accorded to prevent any notice going to Arnold of the capture. Convinced of Arnold's innocence, Jameson was not the less disturbed by his Major's suggestions; and undecided on any persistent course he consented to detain André while the letter still went to Arnold. An express was hurried off with these instructions, and the prisoner's journey interrupted. During the part of the night that remained, Jameson and Tallmadge took a deliberate survey of their captive. Despite his wayworn air and rusty apparel, there was a gentleness and refinement in all he did that bespoke no ordinary man; and the manner of his walk as in gloomy meditation he paced the chamber-floor, and the precise military mode in which he turned upon his heel, convinced both that he was no civilian. Early on the morrow he was sent over to South or Lower Salem, to the head-quarters of Sheldon's regiment.

About eight A. M., then, on September 24th, André was brought to the Gilbert farm-house, and committed to the custody of Lieut. King of the Dragoons, who has left us this account of what ensued.

"He looked somewhat like a reduced gentleman. His small-clothes were nankeen, with handsome white-top boots

— in fact, his undress military clothes. His coat purple, with gold-lace, worn somewhat threadbare, with a small-brimmed tarnished beaver on his head. He wore his hair in a queue, with long black beard, and his clothes somewhat dirty. In this garb I took charge of him. After breakfast my barber came in to dress me, after which I requested him to go through the same operation, which he did. When the ribbon was taken from his hair I observed it full of powder; this circumstance, with others that occurred, induced me to believe I had no ordinary person in charge. He requested permission to take the bed whilst his shirt and small-clothes could be washed. I told him that was needless, for a shirt was at his service, which he accepted. We were close pent up in a bedroom, with a vidette at the door and window. There was a spacious yard before the door, which he desired he might be permitted to walk in with me. I accordingly disposed of my guard in such a manner as to prevent an escape. While walking together he observed he must make a confidant of somebody, and he knew not a more proper person than myself, as I had appeared to befriend a stranger in distress. After settling the point between ourselves, he told me who he was, and gave me a short account of himself, from the time he was taken in St. Johns in 1775 to that time."

Returning to the house, writing materials were supplied him, and since he was informed that his papers were sent to Washington, whose orders, and not Arnold's, should decide his condition, he immediately wrote to our commander.

ANDRÉ TO WASHINGTON.

Salem, the 24th Sept. 1780. — SIR: What I have as yet said concerning myself was in the justifiable attempt to be extricated; I am too little accustomed to duplicity to have succeeded.

I beg your Excellency will be persuaded that no alteration

in the temper of my mind, or apprehension for my safety, induces me to take the step of addressing you, but that it is to rescue myself from an imputation of having assumed a mean character for treacherous purposes or self-interest, a conduct incompatible with the principles that actuate me, as well as with my condition in life. It is to vindicate my fame that I speak and not to solicit security. The Person in your possession is Major John André, Adjutant General to the British Army.

The influence of one Commander in the army of his adversary is an advantage taken in war. A correspondence for this purpose I held; as confidential, in the present instance, with His Excellency Sir Henry Clinton.

To favor it I agreed to meet upon ground not within posts of either army a person who was to give me intelligence; I came up in the Vulture M. of War for this effect and was fetched by a boat from the shore to the beach; being there I was told that the approach of day would prevent my return and that I must be concealed until the next night. I was in my Regimentals and had fairly risked my person.

Against my stipulation my intention and without my knowledge before hand I was conducted within one of your posts. Your Excellency may conceive my sensation on this occasion & will imagine how much more I must have been affected, by a refusal to reconduct me back the next night as I had been brought. Thus become prisoner I had to concert my escape. I quitted my uniform & was passed another way in the night without the American posts to neutral ground, and informed I was beyond all armed parties and left to press for New-York. I was taken at Tarry Town by some volunteers. Thus as I have had the honour to relate was I betrayed (being Adjutant General of the B. Army) into the vile condition of an enemy in disguise within your posts.

Having avowed myself a British Officer, I have nothing to

reveal but what relates to myself which is true on the honour of an officer and a Gentleman. The request I have to make to your Excellency and I am conscious I address myself well, is that in any rigor policy may dictate, a decency of conduct towards me [may] mark that tho' unfortunate I am branded with nothing dishonorable as no motive could be mine but the service of my King and as I was involuntarily an impostor.

Another request is, that I may be permitted to write an open letter to Sir Henry Clinton, and another to a friend, for cloaths and linnen.

I take the liberty to mention the condition of some gentlemen at Charlestown who being either on parole or under protection were ingaged in a Conspiracy against us. Tho' their situation is not exactly similar, they are objects who may be set in exchange for me, or are persons whom the treatment I receive might affect.

It is no less Sir in a confidence in the generosity of your mind, than on account of your superior station that I have chosen to importune you with this letter. I have the honor to be with great respect, Sir, your Excellency's most obedient & most humble servant,   JOHN ANDRÉ, Adj. Genl.

His Excy. Gen. Washington.

This letter written, a load was lifted from André's mind. He was no longer compelled to associate with gentlemen under a false name and guise. Despite Tallmadge's previous suspicions, its contents amazed him when it was given him to read: but neither he, nor King, Bronson, and the other officers at the post, could remain unmoved by the refinement and amiability of their guest. His other arts came in aid of his conversational powers, and with ready hand and easy light-heartedness of manner, he sketched his own progress under the rude escort of militia to their quarters. "This," said he to Bronson, " will give you an idea of the style in which I have had the honor to be conducted to my present abode."

With similar pleasantries he passed away the morning as unconcernedly as though he were in no danger whatever.

Let us now follow the letters to Washington and Arnold. As the first had taken the lower road to Hartford through Peekskill and Danbury, he was expected to return by the same route; and Jameson's messenger came nearly to Danbury in hope to meet him. From prudential or other motives, however, Washington had followed the way that struck the Hudson higher up. He passed through Providence, where eager throngs with torches and loud acclamations welcomed his appearance. "We may be beaten by the English," he said, pressing the hand of Dumas; "it is the fortune of war, but behold an army which they can never conquer." On the afternoon of the 24th he reached Fishkill, eighteen miles above Robinson's House, and after a brief halt, set forth again in design to spend the night with Arnold. Scarce had he ridden three miles, however, when unexpectedly he encountered the French envoy, M. de Luzerne, on his way also to Rochambeau. There was much to be said on both sides; the day was advanced, and the minister was urgent that Washington should turn back to the nearest public house. He returned thus to Fishkill and here, as has been observed, at an entertainment provided by General Scott for the distinguished visitors, he sat at board with Joshua Smith, each little dreaming of what had transpired since the yesterday morning, or of the blow that averted from the one should so shortly fall on the other. On the 25th, his baggage was forwarded betimes to Robinson's House, with intimation that Washington and his suite would be there to breakfast.

Winding through rugged hills that Chastellux describes as the proper abodes of bears, the main road approached the Hudson but a little above West Point; and here Washington turned his horse into a country path which descended to the stream. La Fayette remonstrated at the diversion: they were already late, and their hostess expected them. "Ah," said Washington, "I know you young men are all in love with Mrs. Arnold, and wish to get where she is as soon as possible. You may go and take your breakfast with her, and tell her not to wait for me. I must ride down and examine the redoubts on this side of the river, and will be there in a short time." But his suite remained also, save two aides who rode on with the message.*

Breakfast was served without delay on their arrival at Robinson's House, and with Arnold's family and Burnet and some other officers they sat down in the low-ceiled room that still remains unchanged. Heavy beams extend above; and wainscotting protects a fireplace without a mantelpiece. Opening into this was another room used by Arnold as an office. While at table, a letter was delivered to the General. It was Jameson's of the 23rd, now brought by Allen, that told him of André's capture, of his detention, and of the transmission to Washington of the papers that he bore. Burnet, McHenry, and others afterwards remarked on the tranquillity with which he received the terrible tidings this scroll conveyed. Some little embarrassment he indeed betrayed, but nothing in his manner or words indicated its momentous nature or cause. He retained his place for several minutes, joining in the general conversation: then pleading business, he begged his guests to make themselves at home while he was for a little absent from them. For he well knew that he had not a minute to lose. It was now two full days since André was taken, and Washington might in any instant come upon him in full possession of his guilty secret. To the Aides he said that he was compelled to cross to West Point without delay, and bade them tell their chief on arriving that he would speedily return.

But his wife's experienced eye had already detected an agitation in her husband's manner which escaped those less observant: and while he made his apologies to his guests, she had

---

* Whether these were Hamilton and McHenry or Shaw and McHenry, I am not clear. See Hamilton Hist. Rep. ii. 54. Cooper's Trav. Bach. i. 211. Penn. Packet, Oct. 3, 1780. Thacher, 263.

also risen from the board, and followed him from the apartment. Peremptorily ordering Allen to mention to no one that he had brought a letter from Jameson, he bade the coxswain of his barge be summoned and a horse prepared. "Any horse," he cried, — "even a wagon-horse!" Then he repaired to Mrs. Arnold's chamber and with stern brevity apprised her that they must at once part, and perhaps forever: that his life depended on his instant flight. The panic-struck woman screamed loudly while he, bidding the maid whom the outcry had already alarmed to attend her mistress, pressed her swooning form to his breast, gave a hasty kiss to his unconscious child, and passed again to the breakfast-room to mention the lady's unexpected illness. At the door he leaped on the horse of one of his aides, and without other attendance than that of Larvey, his coxswain, who followed on foot, dashed down the path which in half a mile brought him to the water-side; Larvey shouting to the bargemen as he descended to hasten to their places. Seizing the holsters from his saddlebow, Arnold sprang into the boat, and in his eagerness to be gone would have had the bowman push off ere all the men were mustered. In a moment they were in the stream; and with nervous anxiety, but apparently resolute not to be taken alive, he reprimed his pistols, and retaining them in his hands kept cocking and half-cocking them along all the way. He sat it would seem in the prow; and when the bow-oarsman answering told him that in their haste the crew had brought no weapons save two swords, his vexation was not concealed. However, the tide was in his favor, and he hurried them on. He bore a flag, he said, to the Vulture, seventeen or eighteen miles below, and must reach her in all haste, to return to meet Washington at his quarters; when two gallons of rum should reward their labor. The oarsmen, observes Washington, "were very clever fellows, and some of the better class of soldiery." Quickened by their general's words, they bent to their work and the barge spun through the waters.

Well might Arnold be in haste, for behind him and on either side was danger. As he neared King's Ferry, the ship came broadly into view, riding at anchor a little below the mooring where André left her and still waiting his return. Gliding between Verplanck's and Stony Points, Livingston from the shore in amazement recognized his commander waving as a white flag the handkerchief he had bound to the end of his walking-stick: and with no suspicion of the plot was nevertheless so surprised at the scene that he would fain have manned a guard-boat and come alongside of Arnold to know the meaning of such anomalous procedures. But the crews were dispersed on shore, and ere anything could be done the barge was under the Vulture's batteries. Livingston afterwards thought his presence in this juncture would have so disturbed the traitor that his secret would have escaped, and his person probably seized; but it is questionable whether anything could now have shaken Arnold's composure, and whether on the first attempt at restraint he would not have blown out Livingston's brains.

Alongside of the ship, Arnold unbound his handkerchief and wiped from his brow the great beads which hung there. Hastening on board, he explained to Sutherland and Robinson the position of affairs, and calling up the bargemen, endeavored to allure them into the king's service under threats of retaining them else as prisoners. The coxswain Larvey sturdily refused. "If General Arnold likes the king of England let him serve him," quoth he; "*we* love our country, and intend to live or die in support of her cause": and so said his six comrades. Sutherland, though indignant, would not interfere with Arnold's orders. He bade Larvey go with his flag to shore and procure some necessaries for the party; and when they reached New York Clinton at once gave them their parole: an unusual favor to private men. Two of them, English deserters, had wept bitterly on the ship at the prospect of going to New York to be identified and hanged: once there, they slipped on board a letter of marque just ready to sail, and got away undiscovered. The remainder were released with a parting word and some money from Arnold, and were soon again with their friends.*

There was nothing to keep the Vulture longer, after a flag had been sent to Verplanck's with letters to Washington from Arnold and Robinson. The first, with an enclosed letter to his wife and assurances of her innocence and entreaties for her protection, contained also some protestations of integrity. The last is as follows: —

ROBINSON TO WASHINGTON.

Vulture off Sinsink, Sept. 25th, 1780. — SIR : I am this moment informed that Major André, Adjutant Genl. of His Majesty's Army in America, is detained as a prisoner by the army under your command. It is therefore incumbent on me to inform you of the manner of his falling into your hands : He went up with a flag, at the request of General Arnold, on publick business with him, and had his permit to return by land to New-York; under these circumstances Major André cannot be detained by you, without the greatest violation of flags, and contrary to the custom and usage of all nations, and as I imagine you will see this matter in the same point of view as I do, I must desire you will order him to be set at liberty, and allowed to return immediately; every step Major André took was by the advice and direction of General Arnold, even that of taking a feigned name, and of course not liable to censure for it. I am, Sir, not forgetting our former acquaintance, your very H. Sert.

BEV. ROBINSON, Colo.

---

* Heath says, when Larvey was offered a commission in the British service, he swore he would be —— before he fought on both sides· but that discontented at not receiving from the Americans what the enemy had proposed, he sought and got his discharge from our army. That Arnold also gave the crew their choice of going ashore or of enlisting with him: that one or two stayed, and the rest were sent ashore with Larvey, is also asserted by Heath, whose authority here is very good indeed.

The anchor was weighed, and on the flag's return the ship made sail that afternoon, and reached New York the next morning.

Meanwhile Jameson's courier in quest of Washington had passed through South Salem and probably received there André's letter of the 24th. He came to Robinson's House after the chief had crossed the river. For when he heard on arrival near noon, and a full hour after Arnold's departure, what that officer had said and done, Washington thought there was no better time for examining the works at West Point than when its commander was on the spot. After a hurried breakfast, he hastened away to be back ere dinner-time; followed by La Fayette and all his suite save Hamilton. As they crossed the river, overhung with lofty crags and hills, Washington listened for the thirteen great guns that should salute his approach. The echoing thunders of cannon here reverberating from the opposite banks had acquired a sort of celebrity. But no bustle of preparation greeted his coming, nor was there any exhibition of the formal pomp and ceremony of war. The party were permitted to land with no acknowledgment of its quality, and the commanding officer had barely time to hurry down the path to receive it.

To a character of Washington's punctilio this manner of reception was not agreeable. Lamb in some confusion apologized for it by stating the unexpected nature of the visit. "How!" said the Chief, "is not General Arnold here?" "No, sir, we have not seen him on this side of the river to-day." Washington said afterwards that on this he was struck with the impropriety of Arnold's conduct, and had some misgivings; but he never for a moment suspected the real cause. The party climbed the hill, and after an hour or two of general inspection and the tardy salute of thirteen guns being at last rendered, it returned to the other shore.

As they drew near Robinson's House, Hamilton was seen excitedly pacing the court-yard with a parcel of papers in his

THE TREASON DISCOVERED. 333

hands. These were Jameson's enclosures that had arrived about 2 P. M., and which in virtue of his post the secretary had opened in his chief's absence. Retiring together to their examination, they soon possessed Arnold's secret. It was at once resolved to arrest him if possible, and Hamilton and McHenry were despatched at full gallop to Verplanck's for this end. But it was 4 P. M. when they started in pursuit of a man who had left at 10 A. M.; who, ere their feet were in the stirrups, must have been under the Vulture's guns. By 7 P. M., notice that the Vulture was gone with Arnold to New York came with Robinson's and the traitor's letters to headquarters.

Washington had not noised the treason. He saw Mrs. Arnold, whose hysterical passion satisfied all about her that she could communicate nothing in regard to the business; and to La Fayette and Knox, with eyes suffused, he had privately revealed the affair. "Arnold is a traitor and has fled to the British," said he. "Whom can we trust now?" But the gravity of the risk was not lost on him: the very day had doubtless arrived that had originally been fixed on for the execution of the design; and as the wind was favorable for an ascending fleet, there was no knowing but what an attack might be made that very night. Brief space sufficed to show that every thing possible had been done to facilitate it. The works were found neglected; the troops dispersed. Forthwith the garrison was armed to the teeth, and the lines manned. Couriers were now sent in every direction, bringing up detachments of the garrison; warning officers to stand on their guard; and rousing with the alarm the camp at Tappaan from its midnight slumbers. When he perceived the condition of his hostess, Washington with entire calmness bade the guests sit down without ceremony, since her illness and Arnold's absence left no other alternative: and no stranger would have conjectured from his manner that he was in possession of the fatal secret.

Ere the cloth was removed, the affair began to leak out

in whispers among the guests; and it was not until the 26th or 27th that it was buzzed openly abroad. But when Arnold's letter came in, the rage which Washington had so far kept down seemed about to obtain full sway; and they who were accustomed to note his every change of mood or countenance saw, or thought they saw, according to La Fayette, the bursting of a mighty storm of wrath. But every angry word was suppressed. "Go," he said to an aide, " to Mrs. Arnold, and inform her that though my duty required no means should be neglected to arrest General Arnold, I have great pleasure in acquainting *her* that he is now safe on board a British vessel of war." *

As may be supposed, where no one knew how far the treason had extended or by what means it had been carried on, the wildest rumors flew from mouth to mouth; some tolerably true, many intolerably unfounded. Chief among these was the still repeated tale that André had penetrated our works at West Point, when in truth he had been no nearer to them than the outside of the forts at King's Ferry, many miles below. The bargemen were lately and may yet be living in the full belief that they had carried Arnold and André up from Smith's house to head-quarters; and described

---

* Trav. Bach. i. 216. In this work Mr. Cooper gives several particulars of Arnold's treason, that possess a particular value from the authorities which supplied them. He heard not only La Fayette's recollections declared forty-five years later on the very ground, but also had "Arnold's own statement from a British officer, who was present when the latter related his escape at a dinner given in New York, with an impudence that was scarcely less remarkable than his surprising self-possession." That details so valuable are so little referred to proceeds perhaps from the exceeding dulness of the book: but La Fayette's evidence, given from recollections that in the outset were tinged with great excitement, must be cautiously received. Thus to Mr. Cooper he said that when McHenry entered the chamber where he was dressing for dinner, and carried off his pistols to pursue Arnold, not a word was said of the plot; nor was it apparently communicated to him till he and Knox learned it together from Washington. In his Memoirs, however, the marquis distinctly asserts that "General Washington and I" discovered the conspiracy. It is possible that Marbois may have derived from this source some of his information.

the occasion with a minuteness that extends to every article of the supposed spy's apparel. Letters of the period from our army reported that disguised as Smith's serving-man he had gone all through our camp; that he was recognized and betrayed by a British deserter, and brought in with his arms pinioned; and that Washington and La Fayette were to have slept that night at Smith's house, where in the dead of darkness Robinson with a picked party was to seize them; on which Arnold should yield West Point. The marquis himself conceived that both he and Luzerne would on the day of Arnold's flight have been prisoners, but for André's detection. The best British contemporary gossip says that he was betrayed by Smith, whose hanging was demanded by many people in New York; that on his third return from a clandestine meeting with Arnold, he was stopped by some Americans who at first dismissed but afterward pursued and stripped him of his watch and money: whereon he advised them to let him go, since if they took him to their officers, the spoil would be forfeited: that he did not offer them these things when they seized him: that to Washington he confessed nothing but that he was a spy, until some of our own spies identified him, two of whom had long resided in New York as loyalists: that it was Arnold's disapproval which prevented his return by a flag; and that he would give no explanation of the papers he bore or of the connections he had formed in our army. These accounts, mixed with much error, shadow forth certain facts and undoubtedly came from André's near friends.

CHAPTER XVIII.

André brought to West Point. — Sent to Tappaan. — His Case submitted to a Court of Enquiry. — Its Decision approved by Washington.

It has been reported that Arnold bade his wife burn all his papers. This she did not do; and they were of course now seized, and eventually scattered to the four winds of heaven. From these, and from information of his recent movements, a ray of light began to penetrate the mystery. Orders were already sent that André should be brought up; at 7 p. m. of the 25th, these were repeated, with injunctions to guard against his escape. "I would not wish Mr. André to be treated with insult," wrote Washington; "but he does not appear to stand upon the footing of a common prisoner of war, and therefore he is not entitled to the usual indulgences which they receive, and is to be most closely and narrowly watched." The first courier reached Sheldon's post at midnight. André was in bed at the time, but he arose and prepared to obey the orders. A more dismal night for so dismal a journey could not have been found. The rain fell heavily and the skies were dark and scowling, when he parted with companions to whom he avowed so many obligations, and among whom, he said, whatever happened to him he could never thenceforward recognize a foe. The strong escort that guarded him was led by King; and when it came to North Salem meeting-house, he met the second express, who bade him change his route. On the way, probably as a further precaution, Tallmadge and two other officers joined the party that, marching all night, came to Robinson's House on the morning of Tuesday, the 26th September. Smith, who had already been brought there a prisoner, gives a very particular but unluckily not very probable account of André's arrival. There may be some truth in his story of his own reception, for both Hamilton and Harrison state under oath that Washington spoke warmly on the occasion, and used strong language to wring forth a confession of his guilty dealings.

"I answered that no part of my conduct could justify the charge, as General Arnold if present would prove; that what I had done of a public nature was by the direction of that general, and if wrong he was amenable; not me, for acting agreeably to his orders. He immediately replied, ' Sir, do you know that General Arnold has fled, and that Mr. Anderson whom you have piloted through our lines, proves to be Major John André, the adjutant general of the British army, now our prisoner? I expect him here, under a guard of one hundred horse, to meet his fate as a spy, and unless you confess who were your accomplices, I shall suspend you *both* on yonder tree,' pointing to a tree before the door. He then ordered the guards to take me away."

About two hours later, he continues, he heard the tramp of horses, and soon after the voice of André blended with those of Washington and his suite. Their conversation was conducted in an adjoining apartment, and he does not pretend to repeat it: but he intimates that its tendency was rather to soothe than to intimidate the prisoner, and to procure from him further information of the conspiracy. But Smith, like Marbois, must always be received distrustfully; and if he means here that André was personally examined by Washington, he is utterly wrong. Washington saw Tallmadge indeed and asked him many questions; but he declined having the prisoner brought before him: and Tallmadge always believed that, incredible as it may seem, he never saw André in all his confinement.

In fact, however, I suppose there can be little question that while every honest man in the army was enraged at this nefarious attempt to defraud him of his liberty and to win by guile what the sword could not accomplish, Washington and some of his nearest generals had peculiar cause for indignation. The patron and the supporters of Arnold knew too well the deadly hostility of many powerful civilians to doubt now the handle that might be made of this transaction. St. Clair and Schuyler had already suffered under the calumnious suspicions of the people they defended; and the ridiculously false but industriously propagated story, that the evacuation of Ticonderoga was purchased by Burgoyne with silver balls which, cast into our lines, were collected by St. Clair and divided between Schuyler and himself, was not discountenanced by the action of Congress. Schuyler indeed, a gentleman by birth, education, and habit, had refused longer to hold a commission which subjected him to unmerited ignominy; but St. Clair's fortune was scanty, and though even now he was unjustly suspected of corrupt dealings with the enemy, he continued to serve in the field with unabated zeal. Nor was Washington himself, long distrusted by many in Congress, unconscious of the motive that caused his army to be attended by a permanent committee of that body; and his earnest and fruitful confidence in Arnold gave additional vigor to his resentment at the reward his confidence had received. "Whom can we trust now?"—he well might ask; and in the extremity of his anger, there can be no doubt as to what his favorite's fate would have been, had the fortunes of war brought him into American hands. In after life, even in the most unrestrained hours of social ease, he could not refer to the absconding officer without the most unmitigated terms of contempt: and at the existing moment he seems evidently to have shared in the universal sentiment of the army, that by every means in their power, a dreadful punishment should be inflicted on the prisoners in his hands who stood nearest to the original offence. His letters written prior to the report of the Board of Officers show very clearly the conviction that André was a spy, and that Smith was equally worthy of death. To the President of Congress he comments (Sept.

26th) on André's letter of the 24th as "endeavoring to show that he did not come under the description of a spy." On the same date a writer from the camp expresses the belief that both prisoners " will grace a gallows this day." On the 30th, the press controlled by the party that had so stoutly opposed Arnold in Philadelphia, the seat of Congress, loudly directed public opinion to those who as senators or in social life were his friends, as the sharers of his guilt; and pointed to Mrs. Arnold as an accomplice. On the same day, with Arnold's effigy those of André and Smith were borne through the streets, hanging from a gallows: "The Adjutant-General of the British Army and Joe Smith; the first hanged as a spy and the other as a traitor to his country." Truly, both yet lived, and one was never hanged at all: but this exhibition of political feeling shows very clearly how bitter might have been the heats had no punishment been inflicted on any offender.* Even in the higher grades of the army, there was a yearning for vengeance, mingled with abhorrence of the wrong and discontent with the friends of its author. Over every other consideration, however, there prevailed in the breasts of these brave and good men unutterable loathing and supreme hatred for every development of the crime that would have bartered away themselves and their constituents as though they had been beasts of the field.†

* There is no means of ascertaining whether the debates in Congress involved at this time the character for integrity of Arnold's previous supporters; but a letter from Washington to Reed (Oct. 18, 1780) shows that the promulgation of Arnold's private correspondence had occasioned Reed to inquire into the Chief's sympathy with the latter in his troubles at Philadelphia, and to inveigh against Schuyler. Washington's reply cleared his own skirts from any unfair preference for Arnold, and discredits the imputations on Schuyler's character. As Reed's letter is not given, its nature can only be inferred from the reply to it; for which see Reed's Reed, ii. 277.

† " Your infamous Arnold has abandoned himself to an eternal infamy! What demon impelled him to take this detestable step? Is his wife the cause or only the occasion of the crime? Is —— mixed with this horrible affair? Is Smith hanged? Cannot André be hanged? I am very curious to hear all the details of this atrocity; be kind enough to give them to me. Arnold is not the only man whom I blame; he who once has made the

On the evening of the 26th, the prisoners were transported from Robinson's House across the river and securely bestowed at West Point. On the 27th, Washington, having probably resolved on the course eventually pursued, sent secret orders to Greene that he should receive them in camp on the ensuing day.

"They will be under an escort of horse, and I wish you to have separate houses in camp ready for their reception, in which they may be kept perfectly secure; and also strong, trusty guards trebly officered, that a part may be constantly in the room with them. They have not been permitted to be together, and must still be kept apart. I would wish the room for Mr. André to be a decent one, and that he may be treated with civility; but that he may be so guarded as to preclude a possibility of his escaping, which he will most certainly attempt to effect, if it shall seem practicable in the most distant degree."

Accordingly on the morning of the 28th, they were brought down to the landing-place; when, says Smith, "I saw the amiable André near me, amongst a crowd of officers. On stretching my hand out and preparing to address him, I was told by Major Tallmadge sternly that no conversation must take place between us." Each was seated in a barge well-manned, and with a favoring tide was soon at Stony Point. Here at the King's Ferry landing, a detachment of the 2nd Light Dragoons was in waiting. Tallmadge took the command and, with André in the rear and his companion in the van, they rode away through Haverstraw towards Tappaan (or Orangetown, as it was often called), where lay the main army. A march of ten miles brought them to the house of Mr. John Coe where, while Tallmadge vigilantly posted videttes and sentinels, the party dined. They resumed their journey after dinner and by a circuitous route reached Tap-

---

country suspicious of his virtue is not the most culpable, when the blind and criminal confidence that is put in him makes him a traitor. That's between you and me." — Col. Louis de Fleury to Steuben, Oct. 6, 1780. *Kapp's Steuben.* 625.

paan about dusk. The squadron was paraded before the church in which Smith was confined for the night; and quarters were provided for André at the house of a Mr. Mabie, which, though altered within, still stands as the '76 Tavern. Here every attention that circumstances admitted was rendered him. But for a fuller account of this day's proceedings we are indebted to the recollections of Tallmadge. Seated side by side in the boat that bore them down the Hudson, the conversation between the two soldiers was free and unreserved. The one was as anxious to listen as the other was ready to communicate; for though professional foes on the field, they were both kind-hearted gentlemen. André unhesitatingly pointed out the spot on the west bank where it was arranged that, in the event of the conspiracy's success, he was to have debarked at the head of a picked corps, and passed unopposed up the steep to the rear of Fort Putnam. The acquisition of this key to all the works would, as Tallmadge observes, in every probability have given to André a very large part of the praises sure to follow in the train of Clinton's triumph; and the narrator's animation, as he painted the means by which he should have conducted his detachment, was not disturbed by an inquiry as to the rewards in store for him. Military glory was all he sought, was his reply: the applause of his king and his country would overpay his services; perhaps a brigadiership might be bestowed. In all this passage, he seems to have been free from apprehensions as to his ultimate prospects. It was not until he had taken horse for the Clove that he interrogated his companion and keeper in regard to the treatment he was likely to receive from our hands. Tallmadge candidly reminded him of the fate of his own classmate and friend, Nathan Hale. "Yes, he was hanged as a spy," quoth André: "but surely you do not consider his case and mine alike?" "They are precisely similar, and similar will be your fate," was the answer. It shook the prisoner's fortitude, and his lively discourse was chilled. The friendly offer of the American to conceal the deficiencies of his toilet by the loan of a dragoon cloak was declined, although it had been suggested by André's own comments upon the shabby apparel he was wearing; but Tallmadge's urgency at length procured its acceptance. Enveloped in its folds, he came into our quarters.*

We may gather from Tallmadge's reminiscences that till he drew near Tappaan, André had little doubt that the Americans, though exasperated at what had occurred, could not fail to view him as at the most but a spy in appearance and involuntarily; that beyond some personal discomforts, he had nothing to fear. The ominous warning of Tallmadge was confirmed by the general order issued by Greene on the 26th, when, as senior officer in Washington's absence, he promulged to the army the explanation of the alarm which had resounded through the camp.

"*Headquarters, Orange Town, Sept.* 26, 1780. — Treason of the blackest dye was yesterday discovered. General Arnold, who commanded at West Point, lost to every sentiment of honour, of private and public obligation, was about to deliver that important post into the hands of the enemy. Such an event must have given the American cause a deadly wound, if not a fatal stab. Happily the Treason has been timely discovered to prevent the fatal misfortune. The Providential train of circumstances which led to it affords the most convincing proofs that the Liberties of America are the objects of Divine Protection. At the same time that the Treason is to be regretted, the General cannot help congratulating the army in the happy discovery. Our enemies despairing of carrying their point by force, are practising every base art to effect, by bribery and corruption, what they cannot accomplish in a manly way. Great honour is due to the American army that this is the first instance of Treason of the kind, where many were to be expected from the nature of the dispute. And nothing is so bright an ornament

* See also Tallmadge's Letter in Appendix No. IV.

in the character of the American Soldiers as their having been proof against all the arts and seductions of an insidious enemy.

Arnold has made his escape to the enemy, but Major André, the Adjutant General of the British Army, who came out as a spy to negotiate the business, is our prisoner. His Excellency the Commander-in-Chief has arrived at West Point from Hartford, and is no doubt taking proper measures to unravel fully so hellish a plot.

This language was doubtless communicated to André by some of his American companions, and must have shocked his anticipations of a more lenient interpretation of his character. Meanwhile, however, his friends were acting with promptitude in the line their sense of duty dictated. Arnold's letter of the 25th to Washington had not touched on André's condition, though it averred the innocence of his aides and of Smith. It is perhaps therefore not unfair to infer that at the moment he did not consider the prisoner in peril of life. Robinson at the same time had assured Washington that André was so covered with flags and safe-conducts that even to arrest him was a violation of the laws of war. On their report, Clinton at once reclaimed his Adjutant-General, enclosing Arnold's statement of the case.

CLINTON TO WASHINGTON.

New York, Sept. 26, 1780. — SIR: Being informed that the King's Adjutant Genl. in America has been stopped under Major Genl. Arnold's passports, and is detained a prisoner in your Excellency's army, I have the honor to inform you, Sir, that I permitted Major André to go to Major General Arnold, at the particular request of that General Officer; You will perceive, Sir, by the enclosed paper, that a Flag of Truce was sent to receive Major André, and passports granted for his return. I therefore can have no doubt but your Excellency will immediately direct that this officer has permission to return to my orders in New York. I have the honor to be, &c.

ARNOLD TO CLINTON.

New York, 26 *September*, 1780. — Sir: In answer to your Excellency's message, respecting your adjutant-general, Major André, and desiring my idea of the reasons why he is detained, being under my passports, I have the honor to inform you, Sir, that I apprehend a few hours must restore Major André to your Excellency's orders, as that officer is assuredly under the protection of a flag of truce sent by me to him for the purpose of a conversation, which I requested to hold with him relating to myself, and which I wished to communicate through that officer to your Excellency. I commanded at the time at West Point, had an undoubted right to send my flag of truce for Major André, who came to me under that protection, and, having held my conversation with him, I delivered him confidential papers in my own handwriting to deliver to your Excellency; thinking it much properer he should return by land, I directed him to make use of the feigned name of John Anderson, under which he had, by my direction, come on shore, and gave him my passports to go to the White Plains on his way to New York. This officer therefore cannot fail of being immediately sent to New York, as he was invited to a conversation with me, for which I sent him a flag of truce, and finally gave him passports for his safe return to your Excellency; all of which I had then a right to do, being in the actual service of America, under the orders of General Washington, and commanding general at West Point and its dependencies. I have the honor to be, &c.

To these communications no answer was at present given. Washington was not perhaps sorry to keep the enemy in such suspense concerning André's fate, as would afford ample opportunity of preparing for a vigorous defence of West Point ere any movement against it should be undertaken. He also probably wished to obtain the opinion of his generals before he replied. Accordingly, having on the evening of the 28th repaired to camp, he caused a board of every general officer present with the army to be convened.* Smith declares the general impression to have been that its object was rather to determine once for all the limits within which a flag should protect its bearer — for there had been some previous difficulties on this point — rather than to decide on André's immediate fate. This assertion is manifestly absurd. There is every reason to believe that nothing less was designed than what is proved by the record: and besides, it must not be forgotten that from the beginning Washington had apparently made up his own mind respecting the prisoner's character. His own judgment we may believe would have given him to death; but with the caution and wisdom that always characterized the commander-in-chief, he refrained from acting in so serious a matter until he had heard the best opinions at his disposal. This was a course of which justice must approve. That his anger should now be fearfully roused can hardly be questioned. The very applause which was bestowed on its restraint shows its force and strength. Long after his death, one who had studied him narrowly observed that Washington's "temper was naturally irritable and high-toned, but reflection and resolution had obtained a firm and habitual ascendency over it. If ever, however, it broke its bounds, he was most tremendous in his wrath." It should be added that the storm seldom rose without good cause; and never was there greater provocation than here. The thought that he so long warmed in his

---

* So it is authoritatively stated: yet where were Wayne and Irvine? Perhaps a laudable delicacy restrained these gentlemen from deciding on the fate of an enemy whose satire had so lately been personally aimed at themselves in *The Cow-Chase*.

bosom the serpent that had turned to sting him; the disagreeable uncertainty of the plot's extent; the public danger, and the damage his own prestige and that of the cause might receive in Congress and with the French; everything combined to incense him.* That he should resolve therefore, if the measure accorded as well with the sense of justice of others as with his own, to make such an example in this case as would effectually prevent any further tampering with his subordinates, is as natural as probable. His position warrants the idea. He had hazarded everything — life, fortune, reputation, domestic happiness — on the risk of success; and now after five years of battling it out with the public enemy and with his own, at a moment when America could hardly stagger along, when all his soul was bent on maintaining matters, to have the prize snatched at in this underhand manner was too much for human endurance. Had he not himself deemed André a spy he would not, in my opinion, have summoned the board. And indeed there is good reason to believe that even before they came together, some of our principal generals had learned enough of the facts of the case to satisfy them of the improbability of their arriving at any other conclusion than that the prisoner was an undoubted spy.†

On Friday then, the 29th September, just one week since he had started from Smith's house for New York, André was brought before the tribunal. It was assembled in an old Dutch church at Tappaan, now pulled down, and con-

---

* The correspondence between M. de Ternay and the Count de Vergennes shows how seriously, even in its lopped and mutilated state, the plot affected the opinions and estimates of our allies. The party-heats of Congress were unusually violent at this period, and its committee that attended the camp was falling into an unpopularity by reason of the tincture of "army principles" it had imbibed. See Sparks's Wash. vii. 226, 241.

† "He has a great antipathy to spies, although he employs them himself, and an utter aversion to all Indians," was written of Washington in the beginning of 1780.

sisted of fourteen officers, of whom Greene was president. The authority of the meeting was first read.

Head-Quarters, Tappan, Sept. 29th, 1780. — GENTLEMEN: Major André, Adjutant General to the British army will be brought before you for your examination. He came within our lines in the night on an interview with Major General Arnold, and in an assumed character; and was taken within our lines, in a disguised habit, with a pass under a feigned name, and with the enclosed papers concealed upon him. After a careful examination, you will be pleased, as speedily as possible, to report a precise state of his case, together with your opinion of the light, in which he ought to be considered, and the punishment that ought to be inflicted. The Judge Advocate will attend to assist in the examination, who has sundry other papers, relative to this matter, which he will lay before the Board. I have the honor to be Gentlemen, Your most obedient and humble servant,

G. WASHINGTON.

The Board of General Officers convened at Tappan.

It is to be regretted that the task of composing this letter should have fallen on Hamilton, between whom and the prisoner an intercourse almost confidential was growing up; and who, says La Fayette, "was daily searching some way to save him." And whether its nature was that of an indictment or of a simple statement of facts, every reader will remark that its opening charge that André entered our lines in the night in an assumed character was putting a very strong construction on his own voluntary admissions, which were all the evidence on the point. He landed without our lines as Anderson: here his rank and real name became known to Arnold; and in his uniform, over which was a surtout or watchcoat, he was unwittingly brought by Arnold within the lines. No one else but the sentry who challenged his approach seems to have seen him from the time of his leaving the boat to his arrival at Smith's house: and Arnold here took all the responsibility of reply. Therefore technically at least André might have urged that in so full uniform as officers generally wear by night, and with his name and quality fully known to the American commander, and the only American officer with whom he had thus far to do, he entered our lines. Neither does it seem that he was taken within our lines, as is alleged in the letter. Tarrytown was nearer to the British post at Kingsbridge than to any of ours. The remaining statements of the letter are exactly and literally true.*

The prisoner was now called to listen to the names of the officers who composed the board. These were Major-Generals Greene, Stirling, St. Clair, La Fayette, Howe, and Steuben; Brigadiers Parsons, Clinton, Knox, Glover, Patterson, Hand, Huntington, and Starke. Greene was president, and John Lawrence the Judge-advocate-general. This officer's share in the proceedings was limited to the preparation of

* The chief authorities for the Trial are the Proceedings of the Board in the original manuscript, and also as published by Congress; and a letter from Hamilton to Sears. The first was sent by Washington to Congress, Oct. 7, 1780, with a view to publication: and in pamphlet form was immediately and widely diffused. In this country the observation, appended by Congress, that all the circumstances of the case show that the proceedings "were not guided by passion or resentment" met with general approval. In England, the Gentleman's Magazine, by no means a ministerial journal, expressed the feelings of a very large class in a notice of the publication. "The above account, having been published by Congress, it may without any very violent strain of probability be conjectured that they thought Gen. Washington's severity to André stood in need of some apology. How far the Congress account justifies Gen. Washington's conduct towards the brave André the public will judge for themselves." It was however at Washington's own desire that the account was printed.

Hamilton wrote not only to Sears, but to Miss Schuyler and to Laurens, and the details he gives of André's deportment during the trial and in his confinement are very interesting. One at least of these letters seems intended for a demi-publicity. La Fayette describes it as "a masterpiece of literary talents and amiable sensibility." I have verified the Account as given by Congress by comparison with the original MSS. preserved at Washington, and have corrected some of its errors.

the case on behalf of government, and eliciting the facts before the court. He was a native of Cornwall in England, and by admission of all a man of humanity and sensibility. His age was about André's own, and his whole conduct evinced his sympathy with the prisoner, whom he warned of the peril in which he stood, and exhorted to preserve his presence of mind; to be cool and deliberate in his answers; and to except freely to any interrogatory that he thought ambiguous. He promised in advance that any such should have its form fairly and justly altered. Greene also advised him that he was free to answer or stand mute to the questions to be proposed, and cautioned him to weigh well what he said. He was asked if he confessed or denied the statements of Washington's letter to the board. In reply, he acknowledged as his own the letter to Washington of September 24th which the Judge-advocate had put in evidence, and furthermore submitted this additional paper that he had drawn up.

ANDRÉ'S STATEMENT.

On the 20th of September, I left New York to get on board the Vulture, in order (as I thought) to meet General Arnold there in the night. No boat, however, came off, and I waited on board until the night of the 21st. During the day, a flag of truce was sent from the Vulture to complain of the violation of a military rule in the instance of a boat having been decoyed on shore by a flag, and fired upon. The letter was addressed to General Arnold, signed by Captain Sutherland, but written in my hand and countersigned "J. Anderson, Secretary." Its intent was to indicate my presence on board the Vulture. In the night of the 21st a boat with Mr. —— and two hands came on board, in order to fetch Mr. Anderson on shore, and if too late to bring me back, to lodge me until the next night in a place of safety. I went into the boat, landed, and spoke with Arnold. I got on horseback with him to proceed to —— house, and in the way passed a guard I did not expect to see, having Sir Henry Clinton's directions not to go within an enemy's post, or to quit my own dress.

In the morning A. quitted me, having himself made me put the papers I bore between my stockings and feet. Whilst he did it, he expressed a wish that in case of any accident befalling me, that they should be destroyed, which I said, of course would be the case, as when I went into the boat I should have them tied about with a string and a stone. Before we parted, some mention had been made of my crossing the river, and going by another route; but, I objected much against it, and thought it was settled that in the way I came I was also to return.

Mr. —— to my great mortification persisted in his determination of carrying me by the other route; and, at the decline of the sun, I set out on horseback, passed King's Ferry, and came to Crompond, where a party of militia stopped us and advised we should remain. In the morning I came with —— as far as within two miles and a half of Pine's Bridge, where he said he must part with me, as the Cow-boys infested the road thenceforward. I was now near thirty miles from Kingsbridge, and left to the chance of passing that space undiscovered. I got to the neighbourhood of Tarrytown, which was far beyond the points described as dangerous, when I was taken by three volunteers, who, not satisfied with my pass, rifled me, and, finding papers, made me a prisoner.

I have omitted mentioning, that, when I found myself within an enemy's posts, I changed my dress.

The Proceedings as published by Congress, being rather a manifesto than a report of the trial, makes no mention of this Statement. It gives however what is doubtless designed for an abstract of its contents and of his oral replies to interrogations. The italics are from the pamphlet.

— " That he came on shore from the Vulture sloop-of-war in *the night* of the 21st September inst., somewhere under the Haverstraw mountain. That the boat he came on shore in carried *no flag*, and that he had on a surtout coat over his regimentals, and that he wore his surtout coat when he was taken. That he met Gen. Arnold on the shore, and had an interview with him there. He also said that when he left the Vulture sloop-of-war, it was understood that he was to return that night; but it was then doubted, and if he could not return he was promised to be *concealed on* shore, in a place of safety, until the next *night*, when he was to return in the same manner he came on shore; and when the next day came he was solicitous to get back, and made enquiries in the course of the day, how he should return, when he was informed he could not return that way, and must take the rout he did afterwards. He also said that the first notice he had of his being within any *of our outposts* was, being challenged by the sentry, which was the first night he was on shore. He also said, that the evening of the 22d of September inst., he passed *King's Ferry, between our posts of Stony and Verplanck's Points,* in the *dress he is at present in, and which he said is not his regimentals,* and which dress he procured after he landed from the Vulture, and when he was within *our posts,* and that he was proceeding to New-York, but was taken on his way, at Tarry-town, as he has mentioned in his letter, on Saturday the 23d of September inst. about nine o'clock in the morning."

The six papers from Arnold being produced, he acknowledged they were found in his boots: the pass to John Anderson was also owned, and the fact that he had assumed that name. Anderson's letter to Sheldon of September 7th (*ante,* page 262) was also read. He avowed himself its author; but though it went to prove his intention not to enter our lines, he observed that it could not affect the present case, as he wrote it in New York under Clinton's orders.

"The Board having interrogated Major André about his conception of his coming on shore under the sanction of a flag, *he said, That it was impossible for him to suppose he came on shore under that sanction,* and added, That if he came on shore under that sanction, he certainly might have returned under it.

"Major André having acknowledged the preceding facts, and being asked whether he had anything to say respecting them, answered, He left them to operate with the Board."

It was probably in connection with this point of a flag that Greene asked the question: — " When you came on shore from the Vulture, Major André, and met General Arnold, did you consider yourself acting as a private individual, or as a British officer?" "I wore my uniform," was the reply, "and undoubtedly esteemed myself to be what indeed I was, a British officer." It will be recollected that it was not as an officer he was acting and clad when he was arrested.*

His personal examination was now concluded, and the prisoner being remanded into custody, the board considered Arnold's and Robinson's letters of the 25th, and Clinton's (with Arnold's statement enclosed) of the 26th September to Washington. Of their contents — or indeed of their existence — it does not appear that André was apprised: nor was it necessary that he should be. No other testimony was presented, nor indeed was there any more in the power of the board to adduce save that of Smith and the boatmen. The first was in custody; and as his preliminary examination by Washington was in the presence of La Fayette and Knox, who were of the board, as well as of Hamilton and Harrison who were not, they knew what he could say respecting André's coming ashore from the Vulture. By their evidence afterwards, on his own trial, this briefly amounted to the asseveration that he went to the Vulture by Arnold's direction with a flag which, despite the darkness of the night, he thought a sufficient protection; that he brought away André in his uniform, which was not laid aside till the next day; and that the

* I have this anecdote from Mr. Sparks, who received it from La Fayette himself.

prisoner came to land under the assumed name of Anderson. The boatmen could only say that they were under the impression they were asked beforehand to go with a flag. This testimony is not of much importance, though it shows that some persons at that day considered a safe-conduct and a flag identical.

To these details of what passed before and in the board, but a passage or two more can be added. It is recorded that André was profoundly sensible of the liberal and polite behavior that he met with from the Court, and warmly avowed his sense of their generous treatment. "I flatter myself," he said when the examination was over, "that I have never been illiberal, but if there were any remains of prejudice in my mind, my present experience must obliterate them." On the other hand, his own deportment was composed and dignified; his answers open, clear, and to the point, and free from all argumentative insinuation. Their frank ingenuousness is testified to by Hamilton, who says his confession was so full that the board condemned him on it without calling a witness. His only reserve was in regard to others; in all that he said, he avowed his carefulness to avoid everything that could involve any one else, even shunning to mention names. Thus when Greene referred to his meeting Arnold at Smith's house — "I said a house, sir, but I did not say whose house!" exclaimed André. "True," replied Greene; "nor have we any right to demand this of you after the conditions we have allowed."

Though there is nothing in the published Proceedings to show that the prisoner endeavored to prove himself not a spy, we cannot doubt that he took that ground before the board. Smith's affirmation that he did may be passed by; his comment on his own letter to Sheldon and the tone of his written statements lead to the belief that he upheld himself to have been involuntarily, and without anything beyond apparent guilt, forced into that category.

When all the evidence before them was put in and consid

ered, the board proceeded to collect its voices. La Fayette is authority for pronouncing the decision unanimous; and though Smith alleges that neither Steuben nor Howe approved it, there is good reason to believe him as incorrect here as in other places. It is probable, let us hope, that La Fayette himself was equally astray when, on the 4th of July, 1825, at his mansion in Paris, he assured the son of an officer who had been peculiarly associated with André's closing scenes, in reference to the action of the board, — " that it was a painful duty, in consideration of the gallantry and accomplishments of that officer, but the court was impelled not only by the rules of war but by the example of the British army itself, in the execution of Captain Hale on Long Island for a similar offence, to pass a like judgment." This consideration I cannot believe at all influenced the determination of the board; nor will I willingly admit that La Fayette himself was governed by it in giving his vote. Their enemies have indeed said, doubtless untruly, that he and Greene being personally hostile to Arnold were the warmest advocates for André's condemnation: and it is not unlikely that his companions were not all as prompt as himself in coming to a conclusion. "Some of the American generals too," he wrote to his wife, "*lamented*, while they kept twisting the rope that was to hang him." But a moment's reflection will show how great a wrong is worked to the character of our leaders by the imputation of such a motive. Hale was a man whose disposition and whose fate indeed resembled André's; but whose case in its characteristics was widely dissimilar. In fulfilment of Washington's desires and with the purest intentions of serving his country, he premeditatedly entered the British lines as a spy, and was detected. His own kinsman betrayed him, and he was arrested while yet the embers smouldered of the great fire of the 21st of September, 1776, and in the height of the excitement that this unjustifiable conflagration occasioned among the British. He was instantly hanged by order of Sir William Howe; and the circumstances of his execution reflect disgrace upon the English arms. But even had his case in every particular been parallel with André's, it will be borne in mind that fully four years had elapsed since its occurrence. The English were now under another chief who, as was well known, had carefully avoided putting to death those over whose lives the laws of war gave him control; and who but recently had given up an acknowledged spy to Washington's intercessions. And in any case it is certain that our people had hanged persons of that character in sufficient numbers since Hale's death to satisfy every demand of retaliation.* Had the *lex talionis* therefore at all been presented for a principle of action to our generals, it would undoubtedly have at once been set aside. That there was anger in their hearts is not improbable; that their verdict was consciously influenced by it or any other motive than a simple disposition to decide the case before them on its individual merits should not be questioned. They may indeed have felt, when they looked on the prisoner, what the great Pharaoh in the Arabian tale expresses:—"men are not to be reckoned as we reckon animals; one camel is worth no more than another, but the man who is before me is worth an army." But this very reflection could only warn them to more scrupulously mete no other sentence than the law awarded. This sentence appears in the concluding paragraph of the report, which was signed by every member of the board.

"The Board having considered the letter from his Excellency General Washington respecting Major André, Adjutant

---

* In hurriedly glancing over Thacher's Military Journal, I see recorded in this single volume the executions of no less than eight British spies between the dates of Hale's death and André's. The fate of one who was reclaimed by Tryon, is characteristically set forth in Putnam's reply. — " Sir: Nathan Palmer, a lieutenant in your king's service, was taken in my camp as a *spy*, — he was tried as a *spy*, — he was condemned as a *spy*, — and you may rest assured, Sir, that he shall be hanged as a *spy*. I have the honor to be, &c., *Israel Putnam*. P. S. Afternoon, he is hanged."

General to the British army, the Confession of Major André, and the papers produced to them, REPORT to His Excellency the Commander in Chief the following facts which appear to them concerning Major André.

"*First*, That he came on shore from the Vulture sloop of war, in the *night* of the 21st of September inst. on an interview with General Arnold, *in a private and secret manner.*

"*Secondly*, That *he changed his dress within our lines, and under a feigned name, and in a disguised habit*, passed our works at *Stoney and Verplank's Points* the evening of the 22d of September inst. and was taken the morning of the 23d of September inst. *at Tarry Town, in a disguised habit*, being then on his way to New-York, and, *when taken*, he had in his possession several papers, which contained *intelligence for the enemy.*

"The Board having maturely considered these facts, DO ALSO REPORT to His Excellency General Washington, that Major André, Adjutant General to the British Army, ought to be considered as a Spy from the enemy; and that, agreeable to the law and usage of nations, it is their opinion he ought to suffer death."

The day was probably well advanced ere this report was prepared. On the next, it received Washington's sanction.

Head Quarters, September 30th, 1780. — The Commander in Chief approves of the opinion of the Board of General Officers, respecting Major André, and orders that the execution of Major André take place to-morrow, at five o'clock, P. M.

CHAPTER XIX.

André's Deportment after the Death-Warrant. — Letters to Clinton, and between Washington and the British Generals. — Plans for substituting Arnold for André. — The Execution delayed.

As yet it would seem that an answer had been given neither to André's request of the 24th September for permission to apply for necessary apparel and linen and to forward an open letter to Clinton, nor to that general's communication of the 26th. The latter delay was probably occasioned by a wish to obtain the decision of the Court of Enquiry, and, perhaps, to ascertain the inclinations of Congress. Greene had swiftly transmitted the first intelligence of Arnold's conduct: and on the 30th, Washington's letter of the 26th was received by that body. Marbois says that the Chief privately sought its desires in the present contingency, and that although there was no public debate, it was informally determined not to interfere with the judgment of the military tribunal.

The interest and even attachment which the prisoner's condition and character had already inspired in the feelings of many of our officers has been previously noticed. Among those whose rank more nearly approaching his own rendered intercourse less restrained and embarrassing, Hamilton stood first. He was then but about twenty-three years of age, and his grade and disposition, and his relations to the American leader, were not unlike those that André had filled in another sphere. In laudable ambition, too, and in natural gifts as well as accomplishments, there was much in common between the two; and the very jests that one had offered at the other's expense were an additional incitement to personal kindnesses that should wipe away the inconsiderate levity of The Cow-Chase. From the moment that the captive was brought in, there was a constant exercise of Hamilton's good-offices. On a former occasion his friend, Major William Jackson, had received much civility from André; and to him Hamilton repaired. "Major Jackson," he said, " I have learned that André was very kind to you when you were a prisoner. Will you not now visit him?" The suggestion was unnecessary, for no man was better endowed than Jackson with those kindly feelings which not less than the sterner traits characterize an accomplished soldier; but the story shows the zeal with which Hamilton in befriending André, while he sought to direct indignation against Arnold was careful to provoke compassion towards his unfortunate co-adjutor. Nor is it strange that he who esteemed Julius Cæsar as the greatest of humankind, was drawn towards a man whose character also exhibited "the commanding superiority of soul, the generous clemency, and the various genius which could reconcile and unite the love of pleasure, the thirst of knowledge, and the fire of ambition." Such we are told were Cæsar's qualities: such in a minor scale were André's. Nor was Jackson's a solitary case: there were several in our army who had in confinement received substantial proof's of André's goodness: and these were not now wanting in showing him civilities.

During the brief hours of life that remained, Hamilton was in constant intercourse with him: and it was apparently immediately on his being withdrawn from the presence of the board that he endeavored to procure through the influence of his friend, what he had himself asked for some days before. His doom was indeed not yet pronounced, but he must have perceived the tendency of the current that was flowing so strongly towards the grave; and in the very tenderness of his treatment by those in whose guard he slept and waked, he could not but have recognized the impulse to make his remaining hours as easy as possible, since they were to be so very few and full of trouble. But the attachment between Clinton and himself was firm and reciprocal. Sir Henry avowed, years afterward, that he had not forgotten nor could ever cease to lament his fate and his worth; and André during his imprisonment spoke of his patron as a child might speak of a tender father.* Now, when the prospect of death was imminent, he thought of a possible future pang that might occur to his friend, and he sought to avert it by a renewal of the petition which on his own score merely, his wounded sensibilities would perhaps have not again permitted him to advert to. He repeated to Hamilton his desire to write to his commander.

" In one of the visits I made to him, (and I saw him several times during his confinement,) he begged me to be the bearer of a request to the general, for permission to send an open letter to Sir Henry Clinton. 'I foresee my fate, (said he,) and though I pretend not to play the hero, or to be indifferent about life, yet I am reconciled to whatever may happen, conscious that misfortune, not guilt, will have brought it upon me. There is only one thing that disturbs my tranquillity. Sir Henry Clinton has been too good to me; he has been lavish of his kindness. I am bound to him by too many obligations, and love him too well, to bear the thought that he should reproach himself, or that others should reproach him, on a supposition that I had conceived myself bound by his instructions to run the risk I did. I would not for the world leave a sting that should embitter his future days.' He could scarce finish the sentence, bursting into tears in spite of his efforts to suppress them, and with difficulty col-

---

* Mr. Cooper says, "It is certain he always spoke of Sir Henry Clinton (the English commander-in-chief) with the affection and confidence of a child, until he received his last letter, which he read in much agitation, thrust into his pocket, and never afterwards mentioned his general's name." — *Trav. Bach.* i. 221. This is the only intimation that exists of his receiving any letter from Sir Henry during his confinement: and I do not believe one word of that part of the anecdote. It is probable, if Mr. Cooper got it from La Fayette (which is not declared) that the latter was forgetful.

lected himself enough afterwards to add, 'I wish to be permitted to assure him I did not act under this impression, but submitted to a necessity imposed upon me, as contrary to my own inclination as to his orders.'"

Hamilton found little difficulty now in obtaining the required permission; and the letter was at once written. It must have been sent unsealed to head-quarters, and copied ere it left our camp: its contents were known through the army before the author was hanged. This was certainly in ill-taste. It was just that precautions should be used to prevent communications with the enemy prejudicial to our interests; but worded as it was, the language of the document should never have passed the walls of the general's marquee. It was enough to satisfy justice that the writer's body should swing from a gibbet: there was no necessity of exposing to the gloating eye of all the world the secret agonies of his soul.

ANDRÉ TO CLINTON.

TAPPAN, 29 *September*, 1780.

SIR, — Your Excellency is doubtless already apprized of the manner in which I was taken, and possibly of the serious light in which my conduct is considered, and the rigorous determination that is impending.

Under these circumstances, I have obtained General Washington's permission to send you this letter; the object of which is, to remove from your breast any suspicion that I could imagine I was bound by your Excellency's orders to expose myself to what has happened. The events of coming within an enemy's posts, and of changing my dress, which led me to my present situation, were contrary to my own intentions, as they were to your orders; and the circuitous route, which I took to return, was imposed (perhaps unavoidably) without alternative upon me.

I am perfectly tranquil in mind, and prepared for any

fate, to which an honest zeal for my King's service may have devoted me.

In addressing myself to your Excellency on this occasion, the force of all my obligations to you, and of the attachment and gratitude I bear you, recurs to me. With all the warmth of my heart, I give you thanks for your Excellency's profuse kindness to me; and I send you the most earnest wishes for your welfare, which a faithful, affectionate, and respectful attendant can frame.

I have a mother and three sisters, to whom the value of my commission would be an object, as the loss of Granada has much affected their income. It is needless to be more explicit on this subject; I am persuaded of your Excellency's goodness.

I receive the greatest attention from his Excellency General Washington, and from every person under whose charge I happen to be placed. I have the honour to be, With the most respectful attachment, Your Excellency's most obedient, and most humble servant,

JOHN ANDRÉ, Adjutant-General.

His Excellency General Sir Henry Clinton, K. B. &c. &c. &c.

On the same day General Robertson had addressed a letter to our camp, reiterating the reclamation of André.

ROBERTSON TO WASHINGTON.

New York, 29 *September*, 1780. — SIR: Persuaded that you are inclined rather to promote than prevent the civilities and acts of humanity, which the rules of war permit between civilized nations, I find no difficulty in representing to you, that several letters and messages sent from hence have been disregarded, are unanswered, and the flags of truce that carried them detained. As I ever have treated all flags of truce with civility and respect, I have a right to hope that you will order my complaint to be immediately redressed.

Major André, who visited an officer commanding in a district, at his own desire, and acted in every circumstance agreeably to his direction, I find is detained a prisoner. My friendship for him leads me to fear he may suffer some inconvenience for want of necessaries. I wish to be allowed to send him a few, and shall take it as a favor if you will be pleased to permit his servant to deliver them. In Sir Henry Clinton's absence it becomes a part of my duty to make this representation and request. I am, Sir, &c.

This letter must have arrived early on the 30th, and with it came the servant, Peter Laune, bringing the much wanted necessaries of the toilet. Washington with his aides and some guards being on the spot when the flag landed, saw the luggage searched, and then bade a soldier conduct the man to his master; whom he found "confined in a room, but not in fetters, under a strong guard, with double centinels, and two rebel officers in the room on duty." The returning flag bore back this reply: —

WASHINGTON TO ROBERTSON.

Tappan, Sept. 30, 1780. — Sir : I have just received your letter of the 29th instant. Any delay which may have attended your flags, has proceeded from accident and the peculiar circumstances of the occasion; not from intentional neglect or violation. The letter, which admitted of an answer, has received one as early as it could be given with propriety, transmitted by a flag this morning. As to messages, I am uninformed of any that have been sent. The necessaries for Major André will be delivered to him agreeable to your request. I am, Sir, &c.

André's condition was not yet so desperate as to shut out

every hope of saving him. Mr. Sparks says that Washington was very anxious to do so: but a victim — and an eminent one — was demanded. The magnitude of the affront called for a commensurate expiation, and there was but one person who could be substituted in the prisoner's stead. The unanimous approval bestowed by the army and the nation on André's execution, though accompanied with unrepressed regret for its cruel necessity, arose from this conviction. None could tell where the treason was to end: and though as it turned out no others were involved, yet at the moment, so far from being assured upon that point, the army's confidence was shaken in various quarters, and Washington himself is seen privately investigating the suspicions that pointed to the uppermost grades of the Court of Inquiry itself. The only security was to act promptly and with such decision as should effectually deter others from a like offence. We all recollect Robinson Crusoe's dealings with the birds in his cornfield. He might drive them away as often as he would; but no sooner was his back turned than their plundering was resumed: "I could easily see the thieves sitting upon all the trees about me, as if they only waited till I was gone away, and the event proved it to be so." But when he hung a few of the marauders in chains and left them dangling *in terrorem*, it so disgusted their surviving comrades that ever after they shunned the spot in holy horror. So it was now with our troops, who feared that the next attempt at seduction or betrayal would terminate less fortunately. But there is no question that Arnold's death would have been more grateful than André's; though as Laurens justly suggested, "example will derive new force from his conspicuous character." Hamilton, soon after the latter's execution, summed up the dilemma: "There was in truth no way of saving him. Arnold or he must have been the victim; the former was out of our power."

There were two ways of getting possession of Arnold; by seizure, or by exchange. Both were tried, but the last only made any progress during André's life. It was sought to induce him to apply in his own name to Clinton for the exchange. A gentleman, surmising that Arnold had been prepared from the first to sacrifice André to his own security, and that on this score Sir Henry might be willing to give him up, opened the matter to the condemned man, who declined the expedient. Tradition has named Hamilton as having made the overture. "If Arnold could —" he began. "Stop," peremptorily interposed the captive: "such a proposition can never come from *me!*" * But Hamilton himself, on the very day of the execution, has thus addressed his betrothed: —

"It was proposed to me to suggest to him the idea of an exchange for Arnold; but I knew I should have forfeited his esteem by doing it, and therefore declined it. As a man of honor, he could not but reject it; and I would not for the world have proposed to him a thing which must have placed me in the unamiable light of supposing him capable of a meanness, or of not feeling myself the impropriety of the measure. I confess to you, I had the weakness to value the esteem of a dying man, because I reverenced his merit."

The idea was nevertheless cherished at head-quarters. Greene, it will be seen, suggested it to Robertson; and Washington without committing himself ostensibly to the proposal, indirectly brought it before Clinton. Simcoe declares that among the letters between the generals, a paper was slipped in unsigned, but in Hamilton's writing, saying "that the only way to save André was to give up Arnold." The occasion of this must have been when Washington wrote to Clinton, on the 30th September, enclosing André's open letter of the 29th.

WASHINGTON TO CLINTON.

Head-Quarters, Sept. 30, 1780. — Sir: In answer to

* Cooper, apparently *ex rel.* La Fayette. *Trav. Bach.* i. 221.

your Excellency's letter of the 26th instant, which I had the honor to receive, I am to inform you that Major André was taken under such circumstances as would have justified the most rigorous proceedings against him. I determined, however, to refer his case to the examination and decision of a Board of General Officers, who have reported, on his free and voluntary confession and letters: —

"First, that he came on shore, from the Vulture sloop-of-war, in the night of the 21st of September instant, on an interview with General Arnold, in a private and secret manner.

"Secondly, That he changed his dress within our lines; and, under a feigned name, and in a disguised habit, passed our works at Stony and Verplanck's Points, the evening of the 22d of September instant, and was taken the morning of the 23d of September instant, at Tarrytown, in a disguised habit, being then on his way to New York; and, when taken, he had in his possession several papers, which contained intelligence for the enemy."

From these proceedings it is evident, that Major André was employed in the execution of measures very foreign to the objects of flags of truce, and such as they were never meant to authorize or countenance in the most distant degree; and this gentleman confessed, with the greatest candor, in the course of his examination, " that it was impossible for him to suppose, that he came on shore under the sanction of a flag." I have the honor to be, &c.*

---

* "The closing part of the report of the board of officers was not quoted in the letter to Sir Henry Clinton. It was in the following words: — 'The Board, having maturely considered these facts, do also report to his Excellency General Washington, that Major André, adjutant-general to the British army, ought to be considered as a spy from the enemy, and that, agreeably to the law and usage of nations, it is their opinion he ought to suffer death.'" *Sparks's Wash.* vii. 539. The *Case of Major André* however gives the letter as in my text, but probably took it and other matter from the publication of Congress. Yet this last work printed the letter of Washington in such a manner as to lead to the inference that the omission

Captain Aaron Ogden of New Jersey was one of the most distinguished soldiers of his grade in our ranks. He was of good birth, unblemished integrity, and approved courage; and had been pierced by a bayonet in one of the characteristic night-marches of André's first patron, General Grey. Though his kinsman of the same name had followed Arnold to the gates of Quebec, it is probable that this gentleman held him in no great liking, since Maxwell, his own former leader, perfectly hated him. Ogden had now a company in La Fayette's Light Infantry division; a *corps d'élite*, picked from the whole army.

On the evening of the 29th, when the Board had finished its deliberations, Ogden was commanded to wait upon Washington the next day at eight A. M. precisely. The chief alone met him at the door, and privately gave him his orders. He was to select twenty-five choice dragoons, reliable men and of good appearance, and procuring for himself the best horse he could find, to carry a flag and deliver a packet for Clinton to the commander of the nearest British post. Further, before departing he was to call for additional instructions on La Fayette, who lay with his brigade in advance of the main army and nearer to New York. The orders he received from La Fayette were that he "should if possible get within the British post at Powles Hook, and continue there during the night; and that he should privately assure the commanding officer there, without taking him aside for the purpose, that he, Captain Ogden, was instructed to say that if Sir Henry Clinton would in any way suffer Washington to get General Arnold within his power, that Major André should be immediately released." Ogden therefore so contrived his march, that it was the evening of the 30th when he came to the British outpost.

of the concluding paragraph was intentional: and indeed, if Clinton could have at all been brought to surrender Arnold, it was desirable that he should be afforded a pretence of ignorance that he was remanding him to the gallows.

He was told that he might remain while his despatch was sent in; but he replied that he had peremptory directions to give it up to no one but the officer commanding the post. The circumstances of the case — for it must have been evident that his papers had some connection with André — provoked a suspension of the usual customs, and he was permitted to pass in and deliver them as he was bidden. He was received with great politeness and, the evening now being advanced, was offered quarters for the night. No opportunity however occurred for the fulfilment of his secret duties until supper was served, when, in courtesy to a stranger, he was seated by the commandant. In the course of conversation he was asked of André's probable fate, and promptly answered that he would be hung. Was there no means, exclaimed the Englishman, of saving him? There was certainly a means, whispered Ogden in reply: let Arnold be surrendered, and he was prepared to say, though with no formal assurance from Washington to the effect, that André would be yielded up. The officer at once carried this important communication to his General. On his return he gave Ogden the only reply that any soldier should have expected. The suggested course was totally inadmissible, and Clinton would not even consider it. At daybreak everything was prepared for Ogden's departure; and it was not till this moment that he found out that his chosen sergeant had deserted to the enemy. This evasion however was performed in obedience to Washington's own and secret arrangements, concealed for the time from Ogden himself, and directed with a view to procure a sure and unsuspected spy in the British lines, as well as an intelligent watchman over Arnold and his every motion.

Meanwhile, intelligence of the finding of the court and of his fate were communicated to André through two officers from Greene, one of whom was his aide, Major Burnet. The sentence was listened to with a composure that his informants vainly strove to emulate. The prisoner had steeled himself to encounter death: "I avow no guilt," he said, "but I am resigned to my fate." Yet he shrunk from the idea of the halter. "Since it was his lot to die," he said, "there was still a choice in the mode which would make a material difference to his feelings; and he would be happy, if possible, to be indulged with a professional death"; and he seems to have at once verbally petitioned, probably through Hamilton, that Washington would consent to his being shot. Probably anticipating no refusal to this request, he retained for some time a tranquillity of spirit approaching even to cheerfulness. The arrival of his servant had enabled him to discard the slovenly raiment that had previously embarrassed him, and he was now as neat and comely in his appearance as though he were doing duty before his sovereign at Windsor Castle instead of languishing in a condemned cell. Still looking for his execution on the day originally assigned, he busied himself in farewell communications to his friends. To Captain Crosbie he wrote that "the manner in which he was to die had at first given him some slight uneasiness, but he instantly recollected that it was the crime alone that made any mode of punishment ignominious, and that he could not think an attempt to put an end to a civil war, and to stop the effusion of human blood, a crime. — He should therefore meet death with the spirit becoming a British officer, and neither disgrace his friends nor his country." These letters he confided to his servant, to be delivered when he returned to New York.

In fact, every authority testifies to the composure and dignity preserved by this unfortunate man while he was in our hands. "All of the court that inquired into his case," says La Fayette, "were filled with sentiments of admiration and compassion for him." "He behaved with so much frankness, courage, and delicacy, that I could not help lamenting his unhappy fate," continues the marquis. "It is impossible to express too much respect or too deep regret for Major André." Heath wrote that his behavior "was becoming an officer and a gentleman, and such in his last moments as drew tears from many eyes. But it must be remembered that he who consents to become a spy when he sets out has by allusion a halter put round his neck, and that by the usage of armies if he be taken the other end of the halter is speedily made fast to the gallows." Tallmadge observes "that from the few days of intimate intercourse I had with him, which was from the time of his being remanded to the period of his execution, I became so deeply attached to Major André, that I could remember no instance where my affections were so fully absorbed by any man. When I saw him swing under the gibbet, it seemed for a time utterly insupportable: all were overwhelmed with the affecting spectacle, and the eyes of many were suffused with tears. There did not appear to be one hardened or indifferent spectator in all the multitude assembled on that solemn occasion." Thacher, Hamilton, Washington himself, bear witness that his whole conduct to the last breath of life was that of the accomplished man and gallant officer. The test applied to his character was a severe one: for neither by day nor night was he without an American officer at his side; nor, unless when busied with his pen, or buying peaches from the country people of the neighborhood, had he any other means of employing his thoughts than in such society. Any lapse from the most lofty propriety would have been instantly detected and remarked on.

The morning orders of Sunday, October 1st, published to the army the finding of the Board of Officers, and concluded with this paragraph: —

"The Commander-in-chief directs the execution of the above sentence in the usual way, this afternoon, at five o'clock, precisely."

We may suppose that this intelligence was not long in coming to the prisoner, and that he saw now a likelihood of his request to be shot being disregarded. It was believed in our camp that Washington himself was not disinclined to grant it, but that the advice of his generals deterred him.

Greene, it was said, was clear that André was a spy and should die the death of a spy: that were he not hanged, the notion that there were grounds for this extent of leniency would be twisted into a belief that his death was entirely uncalled for. The public good, he thought, required the use of the rope. And Greene's biographer and kinsman seems to believe that this general was positive on the point, though "it was with a trembling hand and eyes dimmed with tears that he signed the fatal decree." Burnet declares that Washington was convinced he could not consistently with the customs of war alter the manner of death "without subjecting himself to the charge of instability or want of nerve." But André resolved on a direct appeal; and we gather from Hamilton's language but a brief moment before the fatal hour that it did not fail for lack of his mediation with Washington:—

"Poor André suffers to-day;— everything that is amiable in virtue, in fortitude, in delicate sentiment, and accomplished manners, pleads for him; but hard-hearted policy calls for a sacrifice. He must die——. I send you my account of Arnold's affair; and to justify myself to your sentiments, I must inform you, that I urged a compliance with André's request to be shot, and I do not think it would have had an ill effect; but some people are only sensible to motives of policy, and, sometimes, from a narrow disposition, mistake it.

"When André's tale comes to be told, and present resentment is over,— the refusing him the privilege of choosing the manner of his death will be branded with too much obstinacy."

On the morning of October 1st, André amused himself with some last reminiscences of that art whose pleasant exercise had so constantly attended his life. A pen-and-ink likeness of himself, drawn on this occasion without the aid of a mirror, was sketched by him in the presence of Mr. Tomlinson, an officer of the attendant guard, to whom he gave it as a memorial. It is still preserved in the Trumbull gallery at Yale College. He was wont to make such portraits for his friends; and from the writing materials, &c., displayed on the table, we may conjecture that this was produced when his last letter to Washington was written. At this period his air was serene, though his thoughts must have been agonizing: for say or do what he would, he could not brook the idea of a felon's death. But like the savage warrior at the stake, he felt that there was no moment, sleeping or waking, when he might privately give vent to the effusions of natural emotion; and his composure was steadfastly preserved. His servant was not so calm; and on this morning, which there was no reason to believe was not André's last on earth, Laune entered the chamber with his face bathed in tears. His master noticed it, and tranquilly dismissed him: "Leave me," said he, "till you can show yourself more manly."

The day was passing away and the hour at hand that was prescribed for the execution. The gibbet was erected, the grave dug, and the coffin provided; and throngs of spectators crowded to the appointed spot. Captain Ebenezer Smith, of the Massachusetts Line, was in waiting at André's side as commandant of the guard appointed to escort him to the gallows. He describes the prisoner's manners on this trying occasion as highly pleasing, and his conversation intelligent: but the mental agony which convulsed his whole frame as the moment of doom came near was too much for the honest-hearted gentleman to stomach. It seemed to him, he said in terse and nervous phrase, as though the very flesh was crawling upon André's bones as he paced the floor. Captain Smith faced all the perils, all the privations of our revolutionary contest,—and he probably had his share of pleasure and of comfort in the ensuing years,—but he ever avowed that the respite which relieved him from his melancholy charge made this Sunday to be reckoned among the happiest days of his life. The occasion of the interruption was the intelligence brought by Ogden from Clinton. He had arrived in camp that morning; but for some reason the postponement of the execution does not appear to have been announced until late in the afternoon. Clinton's letter was as follows:

CLINTON TO WASHINGTON.

New York, Sept. 30, 1780.—SIR: From your Excellency's letter of this date, I am persuaded the Board of General Officers, to whom you referred the case of Major André, can't have been rightly informed of all the circumstances on which a judgment ought to be formed. I think it of the highest moment to humanity, that your Excellency should be perfectly apprized of the state of the matter, before you proceed to put that judgment in execution.

For this reason, I shall send his Excellency Lieutenant-General Robertson, and two other gentlemen, to give you a true state of facts, and to declare to you my sentiments and resolutions. They will set out to-morrow as early as the wind and tide will permit, and will wait near Dobb's Ferry for your permission and safe-conduct, to meet your Excellency, or such persons as you may appoint, to converse with them on the subject. I have the honor to be, &c.

P. S. The Honorable Andrew Elliot, Esq., Lieutenant-Governor, and the Honorable William Smith, Esq., Chief-Justice of this Province, will attend his Excellency Lieutenant-General Robertson.

CHAPTER XX.

Expedients of the British to procure André's Liberation. — Their Failure — Correspondence in the Case.

POWLES HOOK was only separated from New York by the Hudson, and was almost opposite Clinton's head-quarters. The papers brought by Ogden were therefore not long in coming to his hand; and he at once summoned Mr. Smith the king's chief-justice of New York, Mr. John Tabor Kempe the attorney-general, and other civilians, to meet in consultation with his general officers. Having stated the circumstances of the case and submitted Washington's letter, Sir Henry asked Smith whether in his opinion the Americans could hang André as a spy. The chief-justice said that a reference to the authorities on the question led him to believe they could not; and in this opinion the officers concurred. But Kempe preserving a silence, one of them put the same query to him. Without going into the law of the matter he curtly answered, " I think they will hang him." The querist turned away in disgust, and the attorney-general presently retired. The conclusion arrived at by the council, however, was that as the American board could not have been possessed of full evidence in the business, a deputation should proceed forthwith to our lines, armed with satisfactory proofs of André's innocence : and that Washington should be notified by return of his own flag of the coming envoys.

So soon as André's imprisonment was known, Simcoe had put himself in readiness to recapture him ; and begged of Clinton that in any attempt of that nature his regiment should have the honor of its charge. Thinking the prisoner might perhaps be sent on to Congress, his scouts vigilantly watched the route between our camp and Philadelphia, to give timely warning of any chance to fall on the escort. Henry Lee and himself, being particular enemies on public grounds, were very good friends in private; and he lost no time in asking an interview with our partisan leader, of which the real object was to speak about André. Lee replied on the 2nd October, writing perhaps under the impression that prevailed in La Fayette's camp of the success of Ogden's negotiation for Clinton's consent to the surrender of Arnold: "I am happy in telling you that there is a probability of Major André's being restored to his country, and the customs of war being fully satisfied." But before the letter was sealed Lee had better intelligence, and he concludes in this wise: — "Since writing the foregoing, I find that Sir Henry Clinton's offers have not come up to what was expected, and that this hour is fixed for the execution of the sentence. How cold the friendship of those high in power!"*

It would indeed have been the extreme of baseness in Clinton, under all the circumstances, to have given Arnold up in exchange for André; and though the full details of what had gone before could not have been known in our camp, it is

* Simcoe comments that no offers were made by Clinton. In this he is right; for the proffered exchanges of American prisoners for André were not such offers as Lee meant. Simcoe was, either for book-learning about his profession or conduct on the field, one of the best soldiers of his day: and the extreme language he uses in his reply to Lee must therefore have interest, as showing the feeling of the enemy in regard to the execution: — "I am at a loss to express myself on the latter paragraphs of your letter; I have long accustomed myself to be silent, or to speak the language of the heart. The useless murder of Major André, would almost, was it possible, annihilate the wish which, consentaneous to the ideas of our sovereign and the government of Great Britain, has ever operated on the officers of the British army, the wish of a reconciliation with their revolted fellow subjects in America. Sir Henry Clinton has the warmest feelings for those under his command, and was ready to have granted for Major André's exchange, whatever ought to have been asked. Though every desire I had formed to think, in some instances, favourably of those who could urge or of him who could permit the murder of this most virtuous and accomplished gentleman, be now totally eradicated; I must still subscribe myself with great personal respect, sir, your most obedient and obliged servant, J. G. Simcoe." — *Simcoe's Mil. Jour.* 293.

evident that there was sufficient cause to prevent the proposal being made to him in other than a covert manner. That it should be unhesitatingly refused is not to be wondered at. But there is some reason to suppose that in this juncture Arnold may himself have made an overture perfectly in keeping with his reckless intrepidity of character. In the beginning of 1782, he was assailed at London with a public charge of having basely left André to die that his own life might be saved. On this a British officer, who appears to have enjoyed the friendship of military men of the highest social rank, came forward with a statement for the truth of which he appealed to the gentlemen who were in the fall of 1780 members of Clinton's family. He declared that he was with the English army when André was captured and Arnold came in; that it was currently reported and believed in the lines that Arnold himself proposed to Sir Henry that he might be permitted to go out and surrender himself, in exchange for André; and that the reply was — " Your proposal, sir, does you great honour; but if André was my own brother, I could not agree to it." This anecdote is not devoid of support from what we know of the man's nature; and it is certain that both to himself and the world, his certain death under circumstances such as these would have worn a very different aspect from that which would have followed a discovery and arrest ere his flight was made good.*

Whether simply in decent respect to Clinton's communication of September 30th, or, as Lee intimates, in hope that he might consent to yield Arnold, André's execution had been respited until noon of October 2nd. This postponement was thus entered in the orderly book of a Connecticut regiment on the 1st: — "*Evening Orders.* Major André is to be executed tomorrow, at twelve o'clock precisely. A battalion of eighty files from each wing to attend the execution. Fourteen general officers of the most honorable and unimpeachable character constituted the court martial," *etc.*†

* See Appendix, No. I. † Here follow their names.

Leaving New York betimes, the Greyhound flag-of-truce schooner had a speedy passage to Dobb's Ferry, within four miles of Tappaan, bringing with her the deputation before named, and Beverly Robinson who it was supposed would be admitted to give a statement of the manner in which André went ashore. This fact goes to discredit the stories that prevail and have already been referred to of Robinson's distrust of the security under which his companion left the Vulture. The character of the gentlemen whom he now accompanied was proportionate to the importance of their mission. Smith, the brother of André's guide, was of high legal attainments, and passed from the chief-justiceship of New York under the crown to that of Canada. His historical writings are valuable. Eliot was "a tall, thin, Scots gentleman with a pimply face," father-in-law of André's friend Cathcart, and long known and respected both in Philadelphia and New York, in which last city he said in 1774 that he had for ten years as Collector of Customs lived happily among the inhabitants and to the satisfaction of his superiors. His wife was of one of the chief Philadelphia families, and he had borne the circumstance in mind when chance gave an opportunity of befriending an American prisoner from her own town. But the strength of the embassy lay in Robertson, whose persuasive powers were so well known that the tories loudly declared he would, had he been allowed an interview, indubitably have put the affair in such a way to Washington as to compel at least a reconsideration of André's case. He was a canny Scot from the kingdom of Fife; by nationality sagacious and brave, and by education skilled in the nature of his kind. If we may believe tradition, he wrought with other silver than what lay on his tongue; and when his eloquence failed was as ready to conquer with gold as with steel. Bred to arms, the peace of 1763 found him resident at New York with his regiment: and when the revolution broke out he was not only perfectly familiar with the general character of the people of New York and New England, but was on terms of easy intercourse with many of the chief characters on the continent. He was shut up in 1775 in Boston, as appears by his letter of July 20th to Captain Montague, thanking him for a present from the seas: "two turtles, at a time when a bit of beef or mutton is a rare feast, command my gratitude." Later, he was commandant under Howe at New York; and passing on occasion to England, returned in 1780 much trusted by ministers, and in the double capacity of governor of the province and general third in rank of the king's forces on the continent. "He is an arch-fiend," wrote Gates at this time to Reed, "and knows how to make use of every knave in his government, and you and I know and believe there are as rank knaves and traitors in that government as in any in the Union. Whigs, take care!" He had set on foot secret intelligences with men of good standing in our army and in New England very soon after he had been sworn into his civil office on the 22nd March, by Tryon's sick-bedside; and while large parts of the heavy importations of specie that England made into New York in this epoch were constantly sent out of the lines, he is charged by the anonymous translator of Chastellux with a device that took even toll of the cash ere it reached American pockets. Not an English guinea or Portuguese moidore was suffered, says he, to pass the British lines, till it was duly clipped or sweated. Thus depreciated, it was more acceptable to our people than their own paper currency, which, like the enchanted coins of old, might have ever so fair appearance at first, but soon shrivelled up into a heap of worthless leaves. The diminished pieces were known as *Robertsons*. Divided into halves, fourths, and eighth parts, the mutilated gold, under the apt name of *sharp-shinned* money, found ready circulation.

It was settled that the delegates should not meet Washington, and that Robertson alone should come ashore. Eliot and Smith were civilians: Robinson was not named in Clinton's letter. Accordingly Greene, not in an official capacity but as a private gentleman, was deputed to receive the English lieutenant-general. Their conversation endured through the afternoon to near nightfall: and Robertson thus describes it to his superior.

ROBERTSON TO CLINTON.

Off Dobb's Ferry, 1*st October*, 1780. — SIR : On coming to anchor here, I sent Murray on shore, who soon returned with notice that General Green was ready to meet me, but would not admit a conference with the other gentlemen.

I paid my compliments to his character, and expressed the satisfaction I had in treating with him on the cause of my friend, the two armies, and humanity. He said, he could not treat with me as an officer; that Mr. Washington had permitted him to meet me as a gentleman, but the case of an acknowledged spy admitted no official discussion. I said that a knowledge of facts was necessary to direct a General's judgment; that in whatever character I was called, I hoped he would represent what I said candidly to Mr. Washington.

I laid before him the facts, and Arnold's assertions of Mr. André's being under a flag of truce, and disguised by his order. He showed me a low-spirited letter of André's, saying that he had not landed under a flag of truce, and lamenting his being taken in a mean disguise. He expresses this in language that admits it to be criminal. I told him that André stated facts with truth, but reasoned ill upon them; that whether a flag was flying or not, was of no moment. He landed and acted as directed by their General. He said they would believe André in preference to Arnold. This argument held long. I told him you had ever shown a merciful disposition, and an attention to Mr. Washington's requests; that in the instance of my namesake, you had given up a man evidently a spy, when he signified his wish;*

---

* Here Robertson could take strong ground ; for Washington himself had so late as the 26th July, 1780, in writing to Clinton, expressly complimented the enemy's general upon the kindness with which he had treated his American prisoners. This fact by the way ought in itself to discredit the idea that our leaders felt a necessity of retaliating Hale's execution.

that I courted an intercourse and a return of good offices; that André had your friendship and good wishes, and that Mr. Washington's humanity to him would be productive of acts of the same kind on our part; that if Green had a friend, or Mr. Washington was desirous of the release of any man, if he would let me carry home André, I would engage to send such a man out. He said there was no treating about spies. I said no military casuist in Europe would call André a spy, and would suffer death myself, if Monsieur Rochambault, or General Knyphausen, would call him by that name. I added, that I depended upon General Green's candour and humanity to put the facts I had stated, and the arguments I had used in their fairest light, to Mr. Washington; that I would stay on board all night, and hoped to carry Mr. André, or at least Mr. Washington's word for his safety, along with me the next morning.

Green now with a blush, that showed the task was imposed, and did not proceed from his own thought, told me that the army must be satisfied by seeing spies executed. But there was one thing that would satisfy them — they expected if André was set free, Arnold should be given up. This I answered with a look only, which threw Green into confusion. I am persuaded André will not be hurt. Believe me, Sir, &c.

Beyond what is here stated, Robertson is said to have intimated that under the circumstances any harsh treatment to André would be retaliated on persons in New York and in Charleston, where Mr. Gadsden and several other distinguished prisoners of war were accused of engaging in a correspondence with Gates while on parole within the British lines. Greene replied that such language could neither be listened to nor understood. The gossip of the English camp reported that these gentlemen were offered for André; and that even the release of Mr. Laurens was suggested without effect. The American version, as collected by Marbois, agrees with Robertson's account so far as it goes; grounding the proposed reference to Rochambeau and Knyphausen on the plea of their impartiality as strangers. He says also that Greene took the position that the finding of the court was not to be opened, and that Robertson's suggestion of an appeal to Congress was inadmissible. He concludes with an extravagant anecdote of Greene's reading in contemptuous silence the open letter of Arnold that was handed to him, and casting it at Robertson's feet when with no other word he broke up the interview.*

Greene promised to repeat to Washington as well as he could bear it in mind, what Robertson had said: and the latter returned to his friends on the Greyhound well satisfied that things were now in a prosperous train. They anxiously waited a reply till the following morning, when this note was delivered.

GREENE TO ROBERTSON.

Camp, Tappan, 2 October, 1780. — Sir: Agreeably to

---

* It is barely possible that there may be some groundwork of truth in this anecdote, and that an aversion to Greene and a reluctance to shorten the confinement of the President of Congress, hence grew up in Cornwallis's mind. A note in his Correspondence (i. 75), characterizes Greene as "coarse in his manners and harsh in his conduct": and I have before me a curious MS. letter from a loyalist of high character written at London, Feb. 6, 1782, which says: — "Lord Cornwallis has not yet appear'd either in the House or at Court; it is confidently reported that a proposal which was made to him at the time of his capture, and which he rejected with the sullen dignity of a British peer, will now be accepted at the instance of the ministry; and that an exchange between him and Laurens will take place. The latter is returned from Bath, and tho' not yet able to use his limbs is much visited and caressed by the minority. It is added that, after the exchange effected, his Lordship will be sent to replace the discountenanced and disgraced Sir Harry. If so, Mr. Galloway has been writing to very little purpose, and I am afraid the friends to government out of the lines will not rejoice. But the people of England, caught by brilliant actions and too indolent for close reflection, are so prepossessed in favor of Lord Cornwallis, that it will not be an easy task to convince them of his incapacity or disaffection."

your request I communicated to General Washington the substance of your conversation in all the particulars, so far as my memory served me. It made no alteration in his opinion and determination. I need say no more, after what you have already been informed. I have the honor to be, &c.

These tidings, after his previous conclusions, must have been astounding to Robertson; who forthwith addressed Washington directly.

ROBERTSON TO WASHINGTON.

Greyhound Schooner, Flag of Truce, Dobb's Ferry, 2 October, 1780. — SIR: A note I had from General Greene leaves me in doubt if his memory had served him to relate to you with exactness the substance of the conversation that had passed between him and myself on the subject of Major André. In an affair of so much consequence to my friend, the two armies, and humanity, I would leave no possibility of a misunderstanding, and therefore take the liberty to put in writing the substance of what I said to General Greene.

I offered to prove, by the evidence of Colonel Robinson and the officers of the Vulture, that Major André went on shore at General Arnold's desire, in a boat sent for him with a flag of truce; that he not only came ashore with the knowledge and under the protection of the general who commanded in the district, but that he took no step while on shore, but by the direction of General Arnold, as will appear by the enclosed letter from him to your Excellency. Under these circumstances, I could not, and hoped you would not, consider Major André as a spy, for any improper phrase in his letter to you.

The facts he relates correspond with the evidence I offer, but he admits a conclusion that does not follow. The change of clothes and name was ordered by General Arnold, under whose directions he necessarily was, while within his command. As General Greene and I did not agree in opinion, I wished that disinterested gentlemen of knowledge of the law of war and of nations might be asked their opinion on the subject, and mentioned Monsieur Knyphausen and General Rochambeau.

I related that a Captain Robinson had been delivered to Sir Henry Clinton as a spy, and undoubtedly was such; but that, it being signified to him that you were desirous that the man should be exchanged, he had ordered him to be exchanged. I wished that an intercourse of such civilities as the rules of war admit of, might take off many of its horrors. I admitted that Major André had a great share of Sir Henry Clinton's esteem, and that he would be infinitely obliged by his liberation; and that if he was permitted to return with me, I would engage you would have any person you would be pleased to name set at liberty. I added, that Sir Henry Clinton had never put any person to death for a breach of the rules of war, though he had, and now has, many in his power. Under the present circumstances, much good may arise from humanity, much ill from the want of it. If that could give any weight, I beg leave to add that your favorable treatment of Major André will be a favor I should ever be intent to return to any you hold dear.

My memory does not retain with the exactness I could wish the words of the letter, which General Greene showed me, from Major André to your Excellency. For Sir Henry Clinton's satisfaction, I beg you will order a copy of it to be sent to me at New York. I have the honor to be, &c.

Robertson had brought two letters from Arnold to Washington; one was a resignation of his commission; the other was enclosed in the communication just printed, and was as follows:—

ARNOLD TO WASHINGTON.

New York, 1 *October*, 1780. — SIR: The polite attention shown by your Excellency and the gentlemen of your family to Mrs. Arnold, when in distress, demand my grateful acknowledgment and thanks, which I beg leave to present.

From your Excellency's letter to Sir Henry Clinton, I find a board of general officers have given it as their opinion, that Major André comes under the description of a spy. My good opinion of the candor and justice of those gentlemen leads me to believe that, if they had been made fully acquainted with every circumstance respecting Major André, they would by no means have considered him in the light of a spy, or even of a prisoner. In justice to him, I think it my duty to declare that he came from on board the Vulture at my particular request, by a flag sent on purpose for him by Joshua Smith, Esq., who had permission to go to Dobb's Ferry to carry letters, and for other purposes, and to return. This was done as a blind to the spy-boats. Mr. Smith at the same time had my private directions to go on board the Vulture, and bring on shore Colonel Robinson, or Mr. John Anderson, which was the name I had requested Major André to assume. At the same time I desired Mr. Smith to inform him that he should have my protection, and a safe passport to return in the same boat as soon as our business was completed. As several accidents intervened to prevent his being sent on board, I gave him my passport to return by land. Major André came on shore in his uniform (without disguise), which, with much reluctance, at my particular and pressing instance, he exchanged for another coat. I furnished him with a horse and saddle, and pointed out the route by which he was to return. And, as commanding officer in the department, I had an undoubted right to transact all these matters; which, if wrong, Major André ought by no means to suffer for them.

But if, after this just and candid representation of Major

André's case, the board of general officers adhere to their former opinion, I shall suppose it dictated by passion and resentment; and if that gentleman should suffer the severity of their sentence, I shall think myself bound by every tie of duty and honor to retaliate on such unhappy persons of your army as may fall within my power, that the respect due to flags, and to the laws of nations, may be better understood and preserved.

I have further to observe that forty of the principal inhabitants of South Carolina have justly forfeited their lives, which have hitherto been spared by the clemency of his Excellency Sir Henry Clinton, who cannot in justice extend his mercy to them any longer, if Major André suffers, which, in all probability, will open a scene of blood at which humanity will revolt.

Suffer me then to entreat your Excellency, for your own and the honor of humanity, and the love you have of justice, that you suffer not an unjust sentence to touch the life of Major André. But if this warning should be disregarded, I call Heaven and earth to witness that your Excellency will be justly answerable for the torrent of blood that may be spilt in consequence. I have the honor to be, &c.

It was proper enough that Arnold should state the circumstances under which André had come and gone — for indeed who other could have recounted all of them — but beyond that he had no right to go. His threats of retaliation were simply impertinent to both Clinton and Washington, and well fitted to provoke the indignation of our people. But I have no doubt that Washington, if he received the letter in time, gave due consideration to the facts it contained, albeit there was little in the way they were put that could alleviate his anger. He was not the man to punish André for Arnold's "consummate effrontery." But it is probable that André was hanged before the communication came to Washington's hand: for Robertson, we are told, when he had forwarded it, set out about noon to return to New York; and this was just the hour of the execution. It does not appear that particular information of the impending event was given to him; and Clinton continued anxiously to wait further intelligence from our camp and a reply to this last letter. None coming, he again prepared to address Washington, and at the same time called on Sutherland for a statement of what, as would seem, he intended him to declare had the commissioners been permitted to open the case. Neither letter was sent, however; for after Clinton's, but before Sutherland's was written, the news arrived of André's death. To preserve the connection, however, both are given here.*

CLINTON TO WASHINGTON.

New York, October 4th, 1780. — SIR: I conceived I could not better or more fully explain my sentiments in answer to your Excellency's letter of the 30th September, respecting Major André, than by sending Lieut. Gen. Robertson to converse, if possible, with you, Sir; or at least with some confidential officer from you. I cannot think Lieut. Gen. Robertson's conversation with General Green has entirely answered the purposes for which I wished the meeting. General Green's letter of the 2d instant to General Robertson, expresses that he had reported to you, Sir, as far as memory served, the discourse that had passed between them, and that it had not produced any alteration in your opinion or determination concerning Major André.

I have, Sir, most carefully reperused your letter of September 30th, which contains, indeed, an opinion of a Board of your General Officers, but in no respect any opinion or determination of your Excellency. I must remain, therefore, altogether at a loss what they may be, until you are so

---

* MS. Narrative of Correspondence respecting General Arnold: in Sir H. Clinton's of the 11th Oct. 1780. State Paper Office, America and W. Inds. vol. 126.

good to inform me, which I make no doubt of your Excellency's doing immediately. I will, Sir, in the mean time, very freely declare my sentiments upon this occasion, which positively are, that under no description, Major André can be considered as a Spy; nor by any usage of nations at war, or the customs of armies, can he be treated as such. That officer went at Major General Arnold's request from me to him, at that time in the American Service, and Commanding Officer at West-Point. A flag of truce was sent to receive Major André, with which he went on shore, and met General Arnold. To this period he was acting under my immediate orders as a military man. What happened after, was from the entire direction and positive orders of Major General Arnold, your officer commanding at West-Point: And Major André travelled in his way to New-York, with passports from that American General Officer, who had an undoubted right to grant them. And here it may be necessary to observe, that Major André was stopped upon the road, and on neutral ground, and made a prisoner two days prior to Major General Arnold's quitting the American service at West-Point. From all which I have a right to assert, that Major André can merely be considered as a Messenger, and not as a Spy. He visited no Posts, made no Plans, held no conversation with any person save Major General Arnold; and the papers found upon him were written in that General Officer's own hand-writing, who directed Major André to receive and deliver them to me. From these circumstances, I have no doubt but you, Sir, will see this matter in the same point of view with me, and will be extremely cautious of producing a precedent which may render the future progress of this unfortunate war liable to a want of that humanity, which I am willing to believe your Excellency possesses, and which I have always pursued. I trust, Sir, to your good sense, and to your liberality, for a speedy release of Major André, who, I am free to own, is an Officer I extremely value, and a Gentleman I very sincerely regard.

I enclose to you, Sir, a list of persons, among whom is a Gentleman who acted as the American Lieutenant Governor of South-Carolina. A discovered conspiracy and correspondence with General Gates's army have been a reason for removing these persons from Charlestown to St. Augustine. Being desirous to promote the release of Major André upon any reasonable terms, I offer to you, Sir, this Lieut. Governor, Mr. Gadson, for my Adjutant General; or will make a military exchange for him, should you, Sir, prefer it. Lieut. Gen. Robertson, in his report to me, mentions his having requested from your Excellency a copy of Major André's letter to you, Sir, upon which seems to be grounded great matter of charge against him — given, as if that letter might be considered as a confession of his guilt as a spy. I have waited until this evening with some impatience for the copy of the Letter I mention, not doubting but your Excellency will send it to me. I have now to request you will, Sir, do so, and I shall pay to it every due consideration, and give your Excellency my answer upon it immediately. I have the honor to be, &c.

SUTHERLAND TO CLINTON.

Vulture, off Spiken Devil, October 5th, 1780. — SIR: The account Col. Robinson has given your Excellency of our transactions, during our late excursion, is so full and just in all its particulars, that there is very little left for me to add. But as they have been attended with such fatal consequences to Major André, I hope it will not be held improper if I beg leave to submit my own observations on the subject: — at least so far as they relate to his leaving the Vulture, and the light I then saw him in.

Your Excellency has already been informed, that on the night of the 21st Sept., a Mr. Smith came on board with a flag of truce. The substance of his order was, for himself and two servants to pass to Dobb's Ferry and back again.

He likewise had a written permission to bring up with him a Mr. John Anderson and boy, and a letter addressed to Col. Robinson : all of these papers signed B. Arnold.

Most of these circumstances I had been previously taught to expect; and I had also been informed that Major André was the person understood by John Anderson, and that he was to go on shore under that name, to hold a conference with General Arnold. Mr. Smith's powers appeared to me of sufficient authority ; and as Major André's going under a fictitious name was at the particular request of the officer from whom they were derived, I saw no reason for supposing he, from that circumstance, forfeited his claim to the protection they must otherwise have afforded him. Clear I am that the matter must have appeared in the same light to him; for had it not, measures might have been concerted for taking him off whenever he pleased, which he very well knew I, at any time, was enabled to accomplish. I am likewise persuaded that Mr. Smith's ideas perfectly coincided with ours ; —for when on the point of setting off, Col. Robinson observed, that as they had but two men in a large boat, they would find some difficulty in getting on shore — and proposed that one of our's should tow them some part of the way : to which he objected, as it might, in case of falling in with any of their guard-boats, be deemed an infringement of the flag.

On my first learning from Major André, that he did not intend going on shore in his own name, it immediately occurred to me, that an alteration of dress might likewise be necessary ; and I offered him a plain blue coat of mine for that purpose, which he declined accepting, as he said he had the Commander in Chief's direction to go in his uniform, and by no means to give up his character; adding, at the same time, that he had not the smallest apprehension on the occasion, and that he was ready to attend General Arnold's summons when and where he pleased.

The night the flag was first expected, he expressed much anxiety for its arrival ; and all next day was full of fear lest anything should have happened to prevent its coming. The instant it arrived on the ensuing night, he started out of bed, and discovered the greatest impatience to be gone; nor did he in any instance betray the least doubt of his safety or success.

I own I was equally confident. Nor can I now, on the most mature consideration of circumstances, find the least reason for altering my opinion. What, therefore, could possibly have given rise to so tragical an event as has unhappily befallen Major André, is matter of the utmost surprise and concern to me. I have the honour to be, &c.

A. SUTHERLAND.

His Excellency Sir Henry Clinton.

CHAPTER XXI.

André applies to be Shot. — His Request denied. — He is hanged. — Various Accounts of the Execution. — Honors bestowed on his Memory. — His Remains removed to Westminster Abbey.

THE first sentence of death passed in our army was, I believe, during the Quebec expedition of 1775: the culprit was respited by Arnold at the gallows, and sent back to Washington. The earliest military execution seems to have been that of one of the body-guards, who plotted with Tryon to seize our General and deliver him to Howe. The most interesting was not unlike this in many of its circumstances.

On the morning of the day originally fixed for his death, André made a moving appeal for a change of its mode.

ANDRÉ TO WASHINGTON.

Tappan, 1 *October*, 1780. — SIR: Buoy'd above the terror of death by the consciousness of a life devoted to honorable pursuits and stained with no action that can give me remorse, I trust that the request I make to your Excellency, at this serious period, and which is to soften my last moments, will not be rejected.

Sympathy towards a soldier will surely induce your Excellency and a military tribunal to adapt the mode of my death to the feelings of a man of honor. Let me hope, Sir, that if ought in my character impresses you with esteem towards me, if ought in my misfortunes marks me the victim of policy and not of resentment, I shall experience the operation of those feelings in your heart, by being informed that I am not to die on a gibbet.

I have the honor to be your Excellency's most obedient and most humble servant,

JOHN ANDRÉ, Adj. Genl. to the British Army.*

There are few, I would fain believe, who can read these noble lines, in which decent self-respect contends with wounded sensibility, without regretting that the same policy that

---

* I believe that this was the second and last letter written by André to Washington; to neither of which did our chief reply. What then must we think of this language of Miss Seward to her friend Miss Ponsonby? I give the passage at length to show what tricks memory will sometimes play with us: —

"No, dear madam, I was not, as you suppose, favoured with a letter from Gen. Washington expressly addressed to myself; but a few years after peace was signed between this country and America, an officer introduced himself, commissioned from Gen. Washington to call upon me, and assure me, from the general himself, that no circumstance of his life had been so mortifying as to be censured in the monody on André as the pitiless author of his ignominious fate: that he had labored to save him — that he requested my attention to papers on the subject, which he had sent by this officer for my perusal. In examining them, I found they entirely acquitted the general. They filled me with contrition for the rash injustice of my censure. With a copy of the proceedings of the court-martial that determined André's condemnation, there was a copy of a letter from Gen. Washington to General Clinton, offering to give up André in exchange for Arnold, who had fled to the British camp, observing the reason there was to believe that the apostate general had exposed the gallant English officer to unnecessary danger, to facilitate his own escape: copy of another letter of Gen. Washington to Major André, adjuring him to state to the commander in chief his unavoidable conviction of the selfish perfidy of Arnold, in suggesting that plan of disguise which exposed André, if taken, to certain condemnation as a spy, when, if he had come openly in his regimentals, and under a flag of truce, to the then unsuspecting American general, he would have been perfectly safe; copy of André's high-souled answer, thanking General Washington for the interest he took in his destiny: but observing, that, even under conviction of General Arnold's inattention to his safety, he could not suggest to General Clinton anything which might influence him to save his less important life by such an exchange. These, madam, are the circumstances, as faithfully as I can recall them at such a distance of time, of the interview with General Washington's friend, which I slightly mentioned to yourself and Lady Eleanor, when I had the happiness of being with you last summer."

The American officer referred to is supposed to have been Colonel Humphreys.

exacted the sacrifice prescribed the most rigorous fulfilment of its harshest details. The request was pronounced inadmissible by Washington's counsellors: and since assent was out of his power, he was unwilling to wound the writer by a refusal. No reply was therefore made.

Letters of farewell to his mother and his nearest friends were written: and the condemned man's calmness was still evinced in the exercise of his pen. On this same evening he sketched from memory, as a memento for a friend in New York, the striking view of the North River that had presented itself to him as he looked from the window of Smith's house, and figured the position of the Vulture as she rode at anchor beyond his reach. Tradition also assigns to this occasion the composition of some last verses, that were long cherished on the lips of the common people.* The morning of Tuesday, October the 2d, 1780, found him with his mortal duties all performed and not afraid to die.

The prisoner's board was supplied from Washington's own table: on this day his breakfast was sent him, as usual, from the General's quarters. He ate with entire composure, and then proceeded to shave and to dress with particular care. He was fully arrayed in the habits of his rank and profession, with the exception of sash and spurs, sword and gorget. The toilet completed, he laid his hat on the table and cheerfully said to the guard-officers deputed to lead him forth, "I am ready at any moment, gentlemen, to wait on you." Though his face was of deadly paleness, its features were tranquil and calm; his beauty shone with an unnatural distinctness that awed the hearts of the vulgar, and his manners and air were as easy as though he was going to a ball-room rather than the grave.

The spot fixed for the closing scene was in an open field belonging to the owner of the house wherein he was detained, and on an eminence that commands an extended view. It was within a mile, and in open sight of Washington's quar-

* See Appendix, No. III.

ters. Here the lofty gibbet was erected, and the shallow grave of three or four feet depth was digged. The office of hangman, always an odious employment, was perhaps on this occasion more than usually so. None of our soldiers undertook it. One Strickland, a tory of Ramapo Valley, was in our hands at the time. His threatened fate may have been hard: his years were not many; and by the price of freedom he was procured to take on himself the necessary but revolting character. Under an elaborate disguise, he probably hoped to go through the scene, if not unnoticed, at least unknown.

Besides the officers that were always in the chamber, six sentinels kept watch by night and by day over every aperture of the building; and if hope of escape ever rose in André's breast, it could not have developed into even the vaguest expectation. To the idea of suicide as a means of avoiding his doom he never descended. The noon of this day was the hour appointed for the execution; and at half an hour before, the cortége set forth. André walked arm-in-arm between two subalterns; each, it is said, with a drawn sword in the opposite hand. A captain's command of thirty or forty men marched immediately about these, while an outer guard of five hundred infantry environed the whole and formed a hollow square around the gibbet within which no one save the officers on duty and the provost-marshal's men were suffered to enter. An immense multitude was however assembled on all sides to witness the spectacle, and every house along the way was thronged with eager gazers; that only of Washington excepted. Here the shutters were drawn, and no man was visible but the two sentries that paced to and fro before the door. Neither the Chief himself nor his staff were present with the troops; a circumstance which was declared by our people and assented to by André as evincing a laudable decorum. But almost every field officer in our army with Greene at their head led the procession on horseback: and a number followed the prisoner on foot, while the outer guard, stretching in single file on either side and in front and rear, prevented the concourse from crowding in. In addition to all those who came in from the country-side, it is unlikely that many of the army who could contrive to be present missed the sight. Every eye was fixed on the prisoner; and every face wore such an aspect of melancholy and gloom that the impression produced on some of our officers was not only affecting but awful.

Keeping pace with the melancholy notes of the dead-march, the procession passed along: no member of it apparently less troubled than he whose conduct was its cause and whose death was its object.* In the beautiful Orientalism of Sir William Jones, he dying only smiled while around him grieved. His heart told him that a life honorably spent in the pursuit of glory would not leave his name to be enrolled among those of the ignoble or guilty many: and his face bespoke the serenity of an approving and undismayed conscience. From time to time, as he caught the eye of an acquaintance,— and especially to the officers of the Court of Enquiry,— he tendered the customary civilities of recognition, and received their acknowledgments with composure and grace. It seems that up to this moment he was persuaded that he was not to be hanged, but to be shot to death: and the inner guard in attendance he took to be the firing party detailed for the occasion. Not until the troops turned suddenly, at a right angle with the course they had hitherto followed, and the gallows rose high before him, was he undeceived. In the very moment of wheeling with his escort, his eye rested on the ill-omened tree; and he recoiled and paused. "Why this emotion, sir?" asked Smith, who held one of his arms. "I am reconciled to my fate,"— said André, clenching his fist and convulsively moving his arm,— "but not to

---

* Benjamin Abbot, a drum-major, who beat the dead-march on this occasion, died at Nashua, N. H., in 1851, aged 92. Peter Besançon who followed La Fayette hither from France, and who died at Warsaw, New York, in 1855, was probably the last surviving spectator.

THE EXECUTION. 395

the mode of it!" "It is unavoidable, sir," was the reply. He beckoned Tallmadge, and inquired anxiously if he was not to be shot:—"must I then die in this manner?" Being told that it was so ordered—"How hard is my fate!" he cried; "but it will soon be over."

Ascending the hill-side, the prisoner was brought to the gibbet, while the outer guard secured the ceremony from interruption. During the brief preparations, his manner was nervous and restless—uneasily rolling a pebble to and fro beneath the ball of his foot, and the gland of his throat sinking and swelling as though he choked with emotion. His servant who had followed him to this point now burst forth with loud weeping and lamentation, and André for a little turned aside and privately conversed with him. He shook hands with Tallmadge, who withdrew. A baggage wagon was driven beneath the cross-tree, into which he leaped lightly, but with visible loathing; and throwing his hat aside, removed his stock, opened his shirt-collar, and snatching the rope from the clumsy hangman, himself adjusted it about his neck. He could not conceal his disgust at these features of his fate: but it was expressed in manner rather than in language. Then he bound his handkerchief over his eyes.

The order of execution was loudly and impressively read by our Adjutant-General Scammel, who at its conclusion informed André he might now speak, if he had anything to say. Lifting the bandage for a moment from his eyes, he bowed courteously to Greene and the attending officers, and said with firmness and dignity:—"All I request of you, gentlemen, is that you will bear witness to the world that I die like a brave man." His last words murmured in an undertone were,—"It will be but a momentary pang!"

Everything seemed now ready, when the commanding officer on duty suddenly cried out,—

"His arms must be tied!"

The hangman with a piece of cord laid hold of him to perform this order: but recoiling from his touch André vehemently struck away the man's hand, and drew another handkerchief from his pocket with which the elbows were loosely pinioned behind his back. The signal was given; the wagon rolled swiftly away; and almost in the same instant he ceased to exist. The height of the gibbet, the length of the cord, and the sudden shock as he was jerked from the coffin-lid on which he stood, produced immediate death.

A minute account of the scene is given by a soldier who was present on the occasion.*

"I was at that time an artificer in Colonel Jeduthan Baldwin's regiment, a part of which was stationed within a short distance of the spot where André suffered. One of our men (I believe his name was Armstrong) being one of the oldest and best workmen at his trade in the regiment, was selected to make his coffin, which he performed, and painted black, agreeably to the custom in those times. At this time André was confined in what was called a Dutch Church, a small stone building with only one door, and closely guarded by six sentinels. When the hour appointed for his execution arrived, which I believe was two o'clock P. M., a guard of three hundred men were paraded at the place of his confinement. A kind of procession was formed, by placing a guard in single file on each side of the road. In front were a large number of American officers of high rank on horseback. These were followed by a wagon containing André's coffin; then a large number of officers on foot, with André in their midst. The procession moved slowly up a moderately rising

---

* Barber and Howe: Hist. Coll. N. J. p. 77. This story is told in a simple and probable form: but it contains some inaccuracies that might reasonably be looked for in the tale of a private soldier whose knowledge of all save what he saw came from the hearsay of the camp.

The preceding sketch of the execution is collated from the accounts of Thacher, Tallmadge, and Russell, eye-witnesses of the scene; and as nearly as possible is given in their own words. Thacher, 274: N. E. Mag. vi. 363. Sparks's Arn. 255: Irving's Wash. iv. 149, 157: MS. Mem. of Russell's account: Vind. Capt. p. 26.

hill, I should think about a fourth of a mile to the west. On the top was a field without any enclosure. In this was a very high gallows, made by setting up two poles, or crotches, and laying a pole on the top. The wagon that contained the coffin was drawn directly under the gallows. In a short time André stepped into the hind end of the wagon; then on his coffin — took off his hat, and laid it down — then placed his hands upon his hips, and walked very uprightly back and forth, as far as the length of his coffin would permit; at the same time casting his eyes upon the pole over his head, and the whole scenery by which he was surrounded. He was dressed in what I should call a complete British uniform; his coat was of the brightest scarlet, faced or trimmed with the most beautiful green. His under-clothes, or vest and breeches, were bright buff, very similar to those worn by military officers in Connecticut at the present day. He had a long and beautiful head of hair; which, agreeably to the fashion, was wound with a black ribband, and hung down his back. All eyes were upon him; and it is not believed that any officer of the British army, placed in his situation, would have appeared better than this unfortunate man. Not many minutes after he took his stand upon the coffin, the executioner stepped into the wagon, with a halter in his hand, which he attempted to put over the head and around the neck of André; but by a sudden movement of his hand this was prevented. André took off the handkerchief from his neck, unpinned his shirt-collar, and deliberately took the end of the halter, put it over his head, and placed the knot directly under his right ear, and drew it very snugly to his neck. He then took from his coat-pocket a handkerchief, and tied it over his eyes. This done the officer that commanded (his name I have forgotten) spoke in rather a loud voice, and said that his arms must be tied. André at once pulled down the handkerchief he had just tied over his eyes, and drew from his pocket a second one, and gave it to the executioner; and then replaced his handkerchief. His arms were tied just above the elbows, and behind the back. The rope was then made fast to the pole over head. The wagon was very suddenly drawn from under the gallows, which together with the length of the rope gave him a most tremendous swing back and forth; but in a few minutes he hung entirely still. During the whole transaction, he appeared as little daunted as Mr. John Rogers is said to have been, when he was about to be burnt at the stake; but his countenance was rather pale. He remained hanging, I should think, from twenty to thirty minutes; and during that time the chambers of death were never stiller than the multitude by which he was surrounded. Orders were given to cut the rope, and take him down, without letting him fall. This was done, and his body carefully laid on the ground. Shortly after, the guard was withdrawn, and spectators were permitted to come forward and view the corpse; but the crowd was so great, that it was some time before I could get an opportunity. When I was able to do this, his coat, vest, and breeches, were taken off, and his body laid in the coffin, covered by some under-clothes. The top of the coffin was not put on. I viewed the corpse more carefully than I had ever done that of any human being before. His head was very much on one side, in consequence of the manner in which the halter drew upon his neck. His face appeared to be greatly swollen, and very black, much resembling a high degree of mortification. It was indeed a shocking sight to behold. There were at this time standing at the foot of the coffin, two young men, of uncommon short stature. I should think not more than four feet high. Their dress was the most gaudy that I ever beheld. One of them had the clothes, just taken from André, hanging on his arm. I took particular pains to learn who they were; and was informed that they were his servants, sent up from New York to take his clothes; but what other business I did not learn.

"I now turned to take a view of the executioner, who was still standing by one of the posts of the gallows. I walked nigh enough to him to have laid my hand upon his shoulder, and looked him directly in the face. He appeared to be about twenty-five years of age, his beard of two or three weeks' growth, and his whole face covered with what appeared to me to be blacking taken from the outside of a greasy pot. A more frightful-looking being I never beheld; his whole countenance bespoke him to be a fit instrument for the business he had been doing. Wishing to see the closing of the whole business, I remained upon the spot until scarce twenty persons were left, but the coffin was still beside the grave, which had previously been dug. I now returned to my tent, with my mind deeply imbued with the shocking scene I had been called to witness."

Every authentic account that we have shows how much our officers regretted the necessity of André's death, and how amply they fulfilled his parting adjuration. The tears of thousands, says Thacher, fell on the spot where he lay; and no one refrained from proclaiming his sympathy.* Many wept openly as he died; among whom it is recorded (apparently on the testimony of Laune) was La Fayette. Certainly the marquis bore witness to the infinite regret with which the fate of such a noble and magnanimous character inspired him. It was believed in the army that Washington's soul revolted at the task, and that he could scarcely command the pen when he subscribed the fatal warrant. An American officer who was present and who brought the news to Burgoyne's troops detained at Winchester, asserted that our General shed tears on the execution, and would fain have changed its mode. Without depending entirely on anecdotes which, though of contemporaneous origin, are not

* While these pages are going through the press, one of our most distinguished historical students and writers has obliged me with a communication respecting André's death:—" I have met revolutionary men who were with him as sentinels on the day of his execution. One, Enos Reynolds, told me more than once the sad story, as tears ran down his cheeks. 'He was the handsomest man I ever laid my eyes on,' was one of his phrases: and he said the men all around him were weeping when he met his fate."

supported by direct evidence, it is very certain that no little sorrow was felt on the occasion by both friends and foes. Bronson for instance, whose association with the prisoner continued from his arrest to the gallows-foot, never recurred willingly to the event, nor without hearty regret and emotion. The highest testimony is that of Washington. "André has met his fate," wrote he, "and with that fortitude which was to be expected from an accomplished man and gallant officer:" and again — "The circumstances under which he was taken justified it, and policy required a sacrifice; but as he was more unfortunate than criminal, and as there was much in his character to interest, while we yielded to the necessity of rigor, we could not but lament it." This was said a few days after André's death. In after-years, though he once indeed at his own table went over the details of Arnold's defection, Washington is reported by his confidential attendants to have never, even by his own fireside, alluded to André's trial or fate.

Others were not so guarded, and of course a thousand wild rumors, distorted from the truth by political bias, went flying over the land. The English reports must have originated in part with the servant Laune, for they are early and in part correct. André's dying words are given in palpable error. "Remember that I die as becomes a British officer, while the manner of my death must reflect disgrace on your commander." Another account says that before signing to the hangman to proceed he thus addressed our officers: "As I suffer for the service of my country, I must consider this hour as the most glorious of my life. Remember, that I die as becomes a British officer, while the manner of my death must reflect disgrace on your commander." We can understand how a bewildered and grief-stricken valet may have confused together the incorrect recollections of what private consolatory remarks his master may have made to him, and what he said publicly: but there was less excuse for the ostentatious manner in which the Pennsylvania Packet of

Oct. 31, 1780, made André exclaim to our army: "Be my witnesses, while I acknowledge the propriety of my sentence, that I die like a brave man." If he protested not against it, it is certain he never acknowledged the justice of his fate. The same journal however at other times gave more reasonable accounts; and thus gratified its ancient partisan feelings in a comment upon Clinton's bad bargain:—

> 'Twas Arnold's post Sir Harry sought;
> Arnold ne'er entered in his thought.
> How ends the bargain? let us see;
> The fort is safe as safe can be:
> His favorite perforce must die:
> His view's laid bare to ev'ry eye:
> His money's gone—and lo, he gains
> One scoundrel more for all his pains.
> André was gen'rous, true, and brave—
> And in his place he buys a knave.
> 'Tis sure ordain'd that Arnold cheats
> All those of course with whom he treats.
> Now let the Devil suspect a bite,
> Or Arnold cheats *him* of his right.

The sorrow and indignation of André's friends gave occasion to other unfounded charges. At Southampton, where his family connections extended, it was reported that Clinton solicited " as a singular favor, after his dear friend and companion should be hung, the body might be sent to him — but Washington refused. Clinton then sent again, that since the sentence was to bury the body under the gallows, it might be taken up and brought to New York, there to be interred with the military honors due to so brave and accomplished a young man. This Washington also refused."

This silly tale is sufficiently exposed by Sir Henry's own statement that he knew not of his Adjutant's being hanged till the arrival of Laune with his master's baggage told him all was over. When the burial at the gibbet's foot was about to be made, the man had demanded André's uniform, which was accordingly removed and given him. The corpse was then laid in earth, and no monument but the usual cairn, such as rose over the spot where Gustavus fell at Lutzen "for liberty of conscience," marked the solitary grave. The surrounding field was cultivated, but the plough still shunned the place: for it was customary in this region for the laborers in their tillage to spare the soil that covered a soldier; and as early as 1778 the fields of Long Island were noticed to be checkered over with patches of wild growth that showed where men lay who were slain in the battle there.

With generous sensibility Colonel William S. Smith of our army embraced the opportunity of purchasing the watch that the captors had taken. It was sold for their benefit for thirty guineas. He bought it; and mindful of the tender affection with which André had been heard to speak of his mother and sisters in England, sent it in to Robertson to be transmitted to these ladies. The unfortunate man's Will testifies with what regard his whole domestic circle was held. It was sworn to before Carey Ludlow, Surrogate of New York, and admitted to probate October 12th, 1780.

"The following is my last will and testament, and I appoint as executors thereto Mary Louisa André, my mother; David André, my uncle; Andrew Girardot, my uncle; John Lewis André, my uncle. To each of the above executors I give fifty pounds. I give to Mary Hannah André, my sister, seven hundred pounds. I give to Louisa Catharine André, my sister, seven hundred pounds. I give to William Lewis André, my brother, seven hundred pounds. But the condition on which I give the above-mentioned sums to my aforesaid brother and sisters are that each of them shall pay to Mary Louisa André, my mother, the sum of ten pounds yearly during her life. I give to Walter Ewer, Jr., of Dyers Court, Aldermanbury, one hundred pounds. I give to John Ewer, Jr., of Lincoln's Inn, one hundred pounds. I desire a ring, value fifty pounds, to be given to my friend, Peter Boissier, of the 11th Dragoons. I desire that Walter Ewer, Jr., of Dyers Court, Aldermanbury, have the inspection of my papers, letters, manuscripts. I mean that he have the first inspection of them, with liberty to destroy or detain whatever he thinks proper; and I desire my watch to be given to him. And I lastly give and bequeath to my brother John Lewis André the residue of all my effects whatsoever. Witness my hand and seal, Staten Island, in the province of New York, North America, 7th June, 1777.

JOHN ANDRÉ.
Captain in the 26th Regiment of Foot.

N. B. The currency alluded to in this my will is sterling money of Great Britain. I desire nothing more than my wearing apparel to be sold by public auction."

It may well be supposed that the news of the execution was received at New York in sorrow and in anger. Joshua Smith says: "No language can describe the mingled sensations of horror, grief, sympathy, and revenge, that agitated the whole garrison; a silent gloom overspread the general countenance; the whole army, and citizens of the first distinction, went into mourning." Miss Seward also mentions the signs of grief the troops displayed in their apparel; and in November a London account censures Clinton for not employing the heated animosity of his men to strike an avenging blow. "The troops at New York on hearing of his execution raised such an outcry for vengeance, and to be led to the attack of Washington's camp, that the Commander-in-Chief could hardly keep them within the bounds of discipline: and many letters mention, that as Sir Henry had an army at least equal to Washington's, he ought to have indulged them: for the determined spirit with which they were actuated would have made them invincible against any superiority. On this account the military critics say he has given another convincing proof that he is a general who does not know when to act. After this, few rebel prisoners will be taken. The universal cry of the soldiers at New York is, REMEMBER ANDRÉ!"

But if Clinton would not expose his men to a doubtful enterprise, he was not unmindful either of the fame or the last wishes of his friend. By public orders his memory was released from any imputation that might arise from the manner of his death.

Head-Quarters, New York, 8 *Oct.* 1780. The Commander in Chief does with infinite regret inform the Army of the death of the Adjutant General Major André.

The unfortunate fate of this Officer calls upon the Commander in Chief to declare his opinion that he ever considered Major André as a Gentleman, as well as in the line of his military profession, of the highest integrity and honor, and incapable of any base action or unworthy conduct.

Major André's death is very severely felt by the Commander in Chief, as it assuredly will be by the Army; and must prove a real loss to his Country and to His Majesty's service.

How far the army felt their loss may be gathered from Simcoe's orders to his own regiment, by the officers and men of which André was personally known. He commanded them to wear for the future black and white feathers as mourning for a soldier "whose superior integrity and uncommon ability did honour to his country and to human nature. The Queen's Rangers will never sully their glory in the field by any undue severity: they will, as they have ever done, consider those to be under their protection who are in their power, and will strike with reluctance at their unhappy fellow-subjects, who, by a series of the basest artifices, have been seduced from their allegiance; but it is the Lt. Colonel's most ardent hope, that on the close of some decisive victory, it will be the regiment's fortune to secure the murderers of Major André, for the vengeance due to an injured nation and an insulted army." *

In England, the feeling was bitter and lasting. Despite the isolated and private protests of unimpassioned reason or political prejudice, panegyric was lavishly bestowed on "the English Mutius"; and execration as liberally wasted on his slayers. Revenge was freely spoken of, and it was even supposed in some quarters that the authorities would not hesitate to strain a point to come by it. "The Ministry will be glad to have vengeance for Major André," quoth Lutterloh (a character who earned a dirty subsistence by betraying all who trusted him, whether English or French), as he rattled the blood-money for which he had just sworn away the life of the Baron de la Motte, a French spy at London. But government was belied by such language.

Trumbull the artist was at the time studying his profession at London, whither he had come after a failure to negotiate some Connecticut public securities on the continent. Considering that his father was the governor of his native state and an active whig through all the war; and that he himself had but recently resigned from the army, his proceeding was suspicious in the extreme. Like André, he had been aide to the commander-in-chief, and also deputy-adjutant general:

* Simcoe's Mil. Jour. 152. A gentleman of distinction thus wrote at the time in relation to the universal topic of conversation: — "I never heard that Mr. André was to be married to Miss K——. Two lovers she has undoubtedly had since her reign; Mr. D——, and the young officer who fell at Germantown. Since that the world has never left her idle. The first time I saw her, I was told she would soon be married to Lord Drummond, and so I entered it in my book: soon afterwards, to an officer in the N. Y. volunteers, whom I forget: to two or three, after that: — but she still remains in 'single blessedness.' I never heard of André's letter to his mother, nor of the picture. One picture was certainly found in his luggage, which his mind had been sufficiently at ease to perform: a striking view up the North River. The ladies here went into mourning on his death: his character was delineated and his fate lamented in general orders: an unaffected gloom hung over the army for some days; and never was Mr. W—— so execrated, as for being accessory to his unmerited execution." — MS. Letter, New York, Nov. 8, 1780.

and it was thought he would make a capital *pendant* to the Englishman. He was at once arrested on a charge of treasonable practices and thrown into gaol. By his own account he was treated with humanity, and Mr. West represented his case to the king. "I pity him from my soul," said the monarch. — "But, West, go to Mr. Trumbull immediately, and pledge to him my royal promise that in the worst possible event of the law his life shall be safe." Really Trumbull had committed no offence since his arrival: but as he had no right to be in England at all save as a prisoner, it was seven months ere he was released on surety to leave the kingdom and not return. And in October, 1782, a travelling American, awakened as he slumbered in his carriage by the shouts of a party of armed horsemen who swore to hang some object of their wrath, avows that his first impression was that he, though in no way connected with André's death, was now to expiate it by his own. It is to the pervading interest that attached itself to André's story, and the romantic character of his career, that the origin of the ghost-stories about him may be attributed. There is yet another connected with him:

"Miss H. B. was on a visit to Miss André, and being very intimate with the latter, shared her bed. One night she was awakened by the violent sobs of her companion, and upon entreating to know the cause, she said, 'I have seen my dear brother, and he has been taken prisoner.' It is scarcely necessary to inform the reader that Maj. André was then with the British army, during the heat of the American war. Miss B. soothed her friend, and both fell asleep, when Miss André once more started up, exclaiming, 'They are trying him as a spy,' and she described the nature of the court, the proceedings of the judge and prisoner, with the greatest minuteness. Once more the poor sister's terrors were calmed by her friend's tender representations, but a third time she awoke screaming that they were hanging him as a spy on a tree and in his regimentals, with many other circumstances! — There was no more sleep for the friends; they got up and entered each in her own pocket-book the particulars stated by the terror-stricken sister, with the dates; both agreed to keep the source of their own presentiment and fears from the poor mother, fondly hoping they were built on the fabric of a vision. But, alas! as soon as news, in those days, could cross the Atlantic, the fatal tidings came, and to the deep awe as well as sad grief of the young ladies, every circumstance was exactly imparted to them as had been shadowed forth in the fond sister's sleeping fancy, and had happened on the very day preceding the night of her dream! The writer thinks this anecdote has not been related by Miss Seward, Dr. Darwin, or the Edgeworths, father and daughter, who have all given to the public many interesting events in the brilliant but brief career of Major André."

It is creditable to the British government that in consideration of the magnitude of André's attempted service, and the disastrous fate with which his efforts were crowned, nothing was wanting to testify either its care for his fame or its respect for his wishes. On the 13th November Captain St. George, Clinton's aide, delivered that general's despatches of the 12th October to Lord George Germain.

"The unexpected and melancholy turn, which my negotiation with General Arnold took with respect to my Adjutant General, has filled my mind with the deepest concern. He was an active, intelligent, and useful officer; and a young gentleman of the most promising hopes. Therefore, as he has unfortunately fallen a sacrifice to his great zeal for the King's service, I judged it right to consent to his wish, intimated to me in his letter of the 29th Sept., of which I have the honor to inclose your lordship a copy, that his Company which he purchased should be sold for the benefit of his mother and sisters. But I trust, my lord, that your lordship will think Major André's misfortune still calls for some farther support to his family, and I beg leave to make it my humble request, that you will have the goodness to recommend them in the strongest manner to the King, for some beneficial and distinguishing mark of His Majesty's favor." *

What was asked was granted. The king is said to have instantly ordered a thousand guineas from the privy purse to be sent to Mrs. André, and an annual pension of £300 to be settled on her for life with reversion to her children or the survivor of them: and after knighthood was proffered, on the 24th March, 1781, in memory of his brother's services, the dignity of a baronetcy of Great Britain was conferred upon Captain William Lewis André of the 26th Foot, and his heirs male forever.† A stately cenotaph in Westminster Abbey also preserved the remembrance of the life and death of Major André. Hither Arnold was once observed to lead his wife and to peruse with her the inscription that referred to the most important scenes in his own career.

Forty years later, the pomp and ceremony with which the remains of the brave Montgomery were publicly brought from Canada to New York, called the attention of the British consul at that city to the fact that the dust of another who too had borne the king's commission, and whose first captivity had graced Montgomery's first triumph, still filled an unhonored grave in a foreign land. He communicated with the Duke of York, Commander of the Forces, and it was

* MS. Sir H. Clinton to Lord G. Germain (Separate) New York, 12 Oct. 1780, S. P. O. On the 11th, Clinton wrote the general story of his dealings with Arnold. "The particulars respecting the ill-fated ending of this serious, I may say great affair, shall be detailed in a Narrative — wherein all papers and letters connected with it shall be inserted." This Narrative has not been printed, but I have freely used all its facts in the text of this work.

† A tombstone in Bathhampton church-yard, near Bath, has this inscription: "Sacred to the Memory of Louisa Catharine André, late of the Circus, Bath: Obit. Dec. 25, 1835, aged 81. Also of Mary Hannah André, her sister, who died March 3, 1845, aged 93 years." Sir William Lewis André, the brother, married: and surviving his son of the same name, who was a director of the London Assurance Company, died at Dean's Leaze, Hants, 11th Nov. 1802, when the title became extinct.

decided to remove André's corpse to England. The Rev. Mr. Demarat who now owned the ground, gave ready assent to the consul's proposals. "His intentions had become known," says an American writer — "some human brute — some Christian dog — had sought to purchase or to rent the field of Mr. Demarat, for the purpose of extorting money for permission to remove these relics. But the good man and true rejected the base proposal, and offered every facility in his power." On Friday, August 10th, 1821, at eleven A. M., the work was commenced not without fear that it would be in vain: for vague whispers went around that, years before, the grave was despoiled. At the depth of three feet, the spade struck the coffin-lid, and the perfect skeleton was soon exposed to view. Nothing tangible remained but the bones and a few locks of the once beautiful hair, together with the leather cord that had bound the queue, and which was sent by Mr. Buchanan to the sisters of the deceased. An attentive crowd of both sexes, some of whom had probably beheld the execution, was present.

"The farmers who came to witness the interesting ceremony generally evinced the most respectful tenderness for the memory of the unfortunate dead, and many of the children wept. A few idlers, educated by militia training and Fourth of July declamation, began to murmur that the memory of General Washington was insulted by any respect shown to the remains of André; but the offer of a treat lured them to the tavern, where they soon became too drunk to guard the character of Washington. It was a beautiful day, and these disturbing spirits being removed, the impressive ceremony proceeded in solemn silence." *

If this anecdote is true, these ruffling swaggerers were all who did not cheerfully encourage the proceedings. Ladies

---

* So repeats Mrs. Childs (Letters from New York), who brought to the scene a solemn conviction that André's death was a "cool, deliberate murder," and whose account of what she saw and heard is tinctured with this feeling.

sent garlands to decorate the bier: even the old woman who kept the turnpike-gate threw it open free to all that went and came on this errand; and six young women of New York united in a poetical address that accompanied the myrtle-tree they sent with the body to England.

The bones were carefully uplifted, and placed in a costly sarcophagus of mahogany, richly decorated with gold and hung with black and crimson velvet; and so borne to New York to be placed on board the Phaeton frigate which, by a happy significancy, so far as her name was concerned, had been selected for their transportation to England. Two cedars that grew hard by, and a peach-tree bestowed by some kind woman's hand to mark the grave, (the roots of which had pierced the coffin and turned themselves in a fibrous network about the dead man's skull,) were also taken up. The latter was replanted in the King's Gardens, behind Carlton House.

In his account of the exhumation the consul in warm phrase expressed his conviction that the body had been robbed of its clothing by our people. It was reasonable that he should think so: for Thacher, an eye-witness and minute chronicler of the transaction, believed positively that André was buried in his uniform; of which not a vestige, not a solitary button, was found when the grave was opened. But there is abundant contemporaneous proof, American and English, that Laune obtained his master's regimentals after he was put in the shell, but before he was laid in earth. In correcting his own error, Thacher set Buchanan right. In gratitude for what was done, the Duke of York caused a gold-mounted snuff-box of the wood of one of the cedars that grew at the grave to be sent to Mr. Demarat; to whom the Misses André also presented a silver goblet, and to Mr. Buchanan a silver standish.

A withered tree, a heap of stones, mark the spot where the plough never enters and whence André's remains were removed. The sarcophagus came safely across the sea, and forty-one years and more after they had been laid by the Hudson its contents were reinterred in a very private manner hard by the monument in Westminster Abbey. The Dean of Westminster superintended the religious offices, while Major-General Sir Herbert Taylor appeared for the Duke of York, and Mr. Locker, Secretary to Greenwich Hospital, for the sisters of the deceased.

In the south aisle of the Abbey wherein sleeps so much of the greatness and the glory of England stands André's monument. It is of statuary marble carved by Van Gelder. It presents a sarcophagus on a moulded panelled base and plinth; the panel of which is thus inscribed : " Sacred to the memory of Major John André, who, raised by his merit, at an early period of life, to the rank of Adjutant-General of the British forces in America, and, employed in an important but hazardous enterprise, fell a sacrifice to his zeal for his King and Country, on the 2d of October, 1780, aged twenty-nine, universally beloved and esteemed by the army in which he served, and lamented even by his foes. His gracious Sovereign, King George III., has caused this monument to be erected."

On the plinth these words are added : " The remains of Major John André were, on the 10th of August, 1821, removed from Tappan by James Buchanan, Esq., his majesty's consul at New York, under instructions from his Royal Highness the Duke of York, and with permission of the Dean and Chapter, finally deposited in a grave contiguous to this monument, on the 28th of November, 1821."

The monument stands seven and a half feet high in relief against the wall, beneath the sixth window of the south aisle. The projecting figures of the sarcophagus represent a group in which Washington and André are conspicuous: the former in the act of receiving from a flag of truce a letter which is variously said to signify that in which the prisoner petitioned to be shot, and more reasonably, the demand of Clinton for his release. Britannia with a very lugubrious lion reposes on the top of the cenotaph. On the whole, the work is not a triumph of the sculptor's art.

Hard by the spot are the monuments of Roger Townshend and of Howe, whose lives were lost in the same scenes where André first lost his liberty: and those of Sir Cloudesley Shovel, Wolfe, Warren, Stuart, and other British warriors whose history is interwoven with that of America, rise under the same roof. The covert sneer with which Addison refers to many of the tombs in this Abbey can have no just relation to the funeral honors of such characters as these. "They put me in mind of several persons mentioned in battles of heroic poems, who have sounding names given them for no other reason but that they may be killed, and are celebrated for nothing but being knocked on the head." A man can hardly do more or better than die for his country.

CHAPTER XXII.

Considerations upon the Justice of André's Sentence. — Conflicting Opinions. — Character of our Generals. — Reflections on André's Fate.

WAS the condemnation of André in accordance with the principles of the laws of war? was his execution justifiable? are questions that fourscore years have left where they were at the beginning. English authors have acquiesced in the propriety of the sentence; an American writer has pronounced it a deliberate murder; yet most of these appear to have known very inaccurately the facts of a case upon which they have, sometimes with much elegance and vigor expressed a decided opinion. Winterbotham an English clergyman, Hinton a painstaking annalist, are satisfied that all was done lawfully. Coke was an officer of the 45th; yet he publishes the belief that the rules of war were not infringed. Romilly's opinion, though that of a young man not yet admitted to the bar, is of more weight: he wrote while the heat occasioned by the first intelligence was at its height, and with good information; but he justifies the sentence on the plea that, though André was taken on neutral ground, he had nevertheless been in our lines in disguise, and the safe-conduct with which he was armed was issued by one whom he knew to be a traitor, for no other end than to bring that treason to a successful conclusion. Mackinnon, of the Coldstreams, is also clear that André was a spy and entitled to his fate: and this gentleman's rank, and the summary of facts on which he gives his judgment, add additional consequence to his language. Locker's decision is particularly interesting. He was the personal friend of André's sisters, and represented them at the reinterment in Westminster

Abbey. He had therefore peculiar opportunities of hearing evidence in favor of André. Immediately after the ceremony, he published his conviction that André's conduct had undoubtedly fixed on him the character and exposed him to the punishment of a spy. He also justified Washington's inflexibility by the circumstances of the case, and the absolute necessity to the American cause of a terrible example. Other critics of less note subscribe to these general sentiments, or modify their decrees to the idea of Charles Lamb, when he speaks of "the amiable spy, Major André." And the books of Miss Seward and Mrs. Childs, published on opposite sides of the ocean, fully justify Tallmadge's declaration, that had the verdict been left to a jury of ladies the prisoner was sure of an acquittal.

In America there has been but one leading opinion expressed on the subject. The action of its authorities has never been impugned save in the instance adverted to above. It is true that the majority of writers have not investigated the point: but their inferences entirely coincide with those of Marshall, Sparks, Biddle, and Irving, who were competent as any in the land to arrive at just conclusions. And it is to be remarked that the Englishmen who, by the course of events or their own application, have attained a degree of information on the question commensurate with that possessed by our own chief historical authorities, are not less decided, albeit widely differing in their determinations. Let us first look at the views of such as by convenience of time and place got their impressions, as it were, at the fountain-head.

Of the conclusions of the leaders of our own army, little need be said. The finding of the court of inquiry and its confirmation by Washington sufficiently indicate the sense of our generals. That of the enemy was diametrically opposite; although from Clinton's omission to publicly impute unsoundness of judgment or improper motives to his adversaries, it was inferred in this country that he acquiesced in the justice of the sentence. I must confess that Sir Henry's general orders of Oct. 8th, 1780, would prevent such a conclusion in my mind: and Lord Mahon, by an extract from Clinton's MS. Memoirs, has undoubtedly refuted any deduction that "the opinions of Sir Henry Clinton on this subject were essentially the same as those of General Washington." Though it was little known in our own days, it must have been a familiar fact to all who lived in Clinton's intimacy that in no wise nor at any time did he conceive Washington's course justifiable. When Stedman, a royal officer in our Revolution, published his history of the war and half admitted André's guilt by protestations of the absence of every intention that could have drawn him into the position of a spy, Sir Henry affixed this brief manuscript comment to the paragraph — " Ignorance of whole transaction — too tender a subject to explain upon now. See blank leaves at the end." Accordingly a written statement was afterwards inserted by Clinton at the conclusion of the book, which, though essentially the same with that given from his MSS. by Lord Mahon, may well be published here. It is entitled in the writings before me,—

SIR HENRY CLINTON'S ACCOUNT OF ARNOLD'S AFFAIR.

(From his MS. History of the War, Vol. II. p. 43.)

September, 1780. About eighteen Months before the present period, Mr. Arnold (a major General in the American Service) had found means to intimate to me, that having cause to be dissatisfied with many late Proceedings of the American Congress, particularly their alliance with France, he was desirous of quitting them and joining the cause of Great Britain, could he be certain of personal security and indemnification for whatever loss of property he might thereby sustain. An overture of that sort coming from an officer of Mr. Arnold's ability and fame could not but attract my attention; and as I thought it possible that like another General, Monk, he might have repented of the part he had taken, and wish to make atonement for the injuries he had done his Country by rendering her some signal and adequate benefit, I was of course liberal in making him such offers and promises as I judged most likely to encourage him in his present temper. A correspondence was after this opened between us under feigned names; in the course of which he from time to time transmitted to me most material intelligence; and, with a view (as I supposed) of rendering us still more essential service, he obtained in July, 1780, the command of all the Enemy's forts in the Highlands, then garrisoned by about 4000 men. The local importance of these posts has been already very fully described in the last Volume of this History; it is therefore scarcely necessary to observe here that the obtaining possession of them at the present critical period would have been a most desirable circumstance; and that the advantages to be drawn from Mr. Arnold's having the command of them struck me with full force the instant I heard of his appointment. But the arrival of the French armament, the consequent expedition to Rhode Island, and the weakness of my own force together with the then daily increase of Mr. Washington's, obliged me to wait for some more favourable opportunity before I attempted to put that gentleman's sincerity to the proof.

In the mean time wishing to reduce to an absolute certainty whether the person I had so long corresponded with was actually Major General Arnold commanding at West Point, I acceded to a proposal he made me to permit some officer in my confidence to have a personal conference with him, when every thing might be more explicitly settled between us than it was possible to do by letter, and as he required that my Adjutant General, Major André, who had chiefly conducted the correspondence with him under the signature of John Anderson, should meet him for this purpose on Neutral Ground, I was induced to consent to his doing so from my great confidence in that officer's prudence and address. Some attempts towards a meeting had been accordingly made before Sir George Rodney's arrival. But though the plan had been well laid, they were constantly frustrated by some untoward accident or other; one of which had very nearly cost Mr. Arnold his life. These disappointments made him of course cautious: and as I now became anxious to forward the execution of my project while I could have that naval chief's assistance, and under so good a mask as the Expedition to the Chesapeak which enabled me to make every requisite preparation without being suspected, I consented to another proposal from General Arnold for Major André to go to him by water from Dobb's ferry in a boat which he would himself send for him under a Flag of Truce. For I could have no reason to suspect that any bad consequence could possibly result to Major André from such a mode, as I had given it in charge to him *not to change his dress or name on any account*, or possess himself of writings by which the nature of his Embassy might be traced, and I understood that after his Business was finished he was to be sent back in the same way. But unhappily none of these precautions were observed; on the contrary, General Arnold for reasons which he judged important, or perhaps (which is the most probable) losing at the moment his usual presence of mind, thought proper to drop the design of sending Major André back by water, and prevailed upon him, or rather compelled him as would appear by that unfortunate Officer's letter to me, to part with his uniform, and under a borrowed disguise to take a circuitous route to New York through the Posts of the Enemy under the sanction of his passport. The consequence was (as might be expected) that he was stopped at Tarrytown and searched, and certain papers being found about him concealed, he was (notwithstanding his passport) carried prisoner before Mr. Washington, to whom he candidly acknowledged his name and quality. Measures were of course immediately taken upon this to seize General Arnold; but that officer being fortunate enough to receive timely notice of Major André's fate effected his escape to a King's Sloop lying off Taller's Point, and came the next day to New York.

I was exceedingly shocked by this unexpected accident, which not only ruined a most important project, which had all the appearance of being in a happy train of success, but involved in danger and distress a confidential friend, for whom I had (very deservedly) the warmest esteem. Not immediately knowing however the full extent of the misfortune, I did not then imagine the Enemy could have any motive for pushing matters to extremity, as the bare detention of so valuable an officer's person might have given him a great power and advantage over me; and I was accordingly in hopes that an official demand from me for his immediate release, as having been under the sanction of a Flag of Truce when he landed within his posts, might shorten his captivity, or at least stop his proceeding with rigour against him. But the cruel and unfortunate catastrophe convinced me that I was much mistaken in my opinion of both his policy and humanity. For delivering himself up (it should seem) to the rancour excited by the near accomplishment of a plan which might effectually have restored the King's Authority and tumbled him from his present exalted situation, he burnt with a desire of wreaking his vengeance on the principal actors in it; and consequently regardless of the acknowledged worth and abilities of the amiable young man, who had thus fallen into his hands, and in opposition to every principle of policy and call of humanity he without remorse put him to a most ignominious death; and this at a moment when one of his Generals was by his own appointment in actual Conference with Commissioners whom I had sent to treat to him for Major André's release.

The manner in which Major André was drawn to the Enemy's Shore (manifestly at the instance and under the sanction of the General Officer who had the command of the district) and his being avowedly compelled by that officer to change his dress and name and return under his passport by land, were circumstances which, as they certainly much lessen the imputed criminality of his offence, ought at least to have softened the severity of the Council of War's Opinion respecting it, notwithstanding his imprudence of having possessed himself of the papers which they found on him. Which, though they led to a discovery of the nature of the business that drew him to a conference with General Arnold, were not wanted (as they must have known) for my information. For they were not ignorant that I had myself been over every part of the ground on which the Forts stood, and had of course made myself perfectly acquainted with everything necessary for facilitating an attack of them. Mr. Washington ought also to have remembered that I had never in any one instance punished the disaffected Colonists (within my power) with Death, but on the contrary had in several shewn the most humane attention to his intercession even in favour of avowed spies. His acting therefore in so cruel a manner in opposition to my earnest solicitations could not but excite in me the greatest surprise; especially as no advantage whatever could be possibly expected to his Cause from putting the object of them to death. Nor could he be insensible (had he the smallest spark of honour in his own breast) that the example, though ever so terrible and ignominious, would never deter a British Officer from treading in the same steps, whenever the service of his Country would require his exposing himself to the like danger in such a War. But the subject affects me too deeply to proceed — nor can my heart cease to bleed whenever I reflect on the very unworthy fate of this most amiable and valuable young man, who was adorned with the rarest endowments of Education and Nature, and (had he lived) could not but have attained to the highest honours of his profession !!! ——

The Marquis Cornwallis was not at New York when the

catastrophe occurred, nor does he seem to have been one of Clinton's admirers or Arnold's supporters in the royal service: but he was undoubtedly well informed of the facts of the case, of which he expresses himself thus:—

"The sad episode of Major André took place in this year. The details need not be given, but it may be observed that, among the members of the court by which he was tried, were two foreigners, ignorant of the English language, and several of the coarsest and most illiterate of the American generals. Doubts have been entertained whether Washington had timely information of the requests and remonstrances made by Sir Henry Clinton, who, had he been disposed to retaliate, could easily have selected among his prisoners Americans deserving the name of spy much more justly than Major André. In any case the execution of that officer leaves an indelible blot on the character of Washington." *

Whether or not Beverly Robinson, as is said, distrusted the safety of André's leaving the Vulture, it is clear from his letter and Sutherland's that these officers considered him unlawfully detained, and, of consequence, unlawfully done to death. Robertson's emphatic assertion of the erroneous finding of the court of inquiry will also be borne in mind; and his proffer to die himself if Knyphausen and Rochambeau would not agree with him. What the first might have thought we do not know: the tendency of the last may be guessed from his own recorded words. André deserved a better fate, he thought, but the severity of the laws and the necessity of an example enforced his condemnation. His Aide, Count Mathieu Dumas, afterwards lieutenant-general, is more explicit. He says André having come to Arnold in a peasant's disguise was justly condemned and executed as a spy.

* Corr. Corn. i. 78. In 1791 the marquis, as governor-general of India, exchanged official compliments with our President; though "he himself continued in troubled waters," he said, he wished "for General Washington a long enjoyment of tranquillity and happiness." Wash. in Dom. Life, 57.

This language would lead us to suppose that the question of flags and safe-conducts was not raised in the French camp.

In reciting the opinions of such of the enemy as were acquainted with the facts of the case, that of Simcoe must not be ignored. This distinguished man was not only thoroughly a practical soldier, but, what was more rare then than in these days, was well versed in the learning, ancient and modern, of his profession. His language is strong and bitter; yet entirely repugnant as it is to some of my own convictions, I think it only fair to present it at length. On one point he seems to have hit a more correct view than some of his fellows: he attributes to Washington a full knowledge of all the circumstances of the affair. The undercurrent of his thoughts seem to indicate a theory that one motive for rigorous proceedings was to prevent distrust on the part of the French auxiliaries; who certainly would have been in a very awkward position had Arnold's designs succeeded. This is very questionable: as has been said, I believe André's case was decided on its merits, though policy undoubtedly had to do with the fulfilment of the sentence. Simcoe declares, however, that he "had certain and satisfactory intelligence that the French party in general, and M. Fayette in particular who sat upon his trial, urged Mr. Washington to the unnecessary deed." One might well ask how he got this "certain intelligence:" but let us see how he speaks of the conduct of our chiefs:—

"Major André was murdered upon private not public considerations. It bore not with it the stamp of justice; for there was not an officer in the British army whose duty it would not have been, had any of the American Generals offered to quit the service of Congress, to have negotiated to receive them; so that this execution could not, by example, have prevented the repetition of the same offence. It may appear, that from his change of dress, &c., he came under the description of a spy; but when it shall be considered 'against his stipulation, intention, and knowledge,' he became absolutely a prisoner, and was forced to change his dress for self-preservation, it may safely be asserted that no European general would on this pretext have had his blood upon his head. He fell a victim to that which was expedient, not to that which was just: what was supposed to be useful superceded what would have been generous; and though, by imprudently carrying papers about him, he gave a colour to those, who endeavoured to separate Great Britain from America, to press for his death, yet an open and elevated mind would have found greater satisfaction in the obligations it might have laid on the army of his opponents, than in carrying into execution a useless and unnecessary vengeance.

"It has been said, that not only the French party from their customary policy, but Mr. Washington's personal enemies urged him on, contrary to his inclinations, to render him unpopular if he executed Major André, or suspected if he pardoned him. In the length of the war, for what one generous action has Mr. Washington been celebrated? what honourable sentiment ever fell from his lips which can invalidate the belief, that surrounded with difficulties and ignorant in whom to confide, he meanly sheltered himself under the opinions of his officers and the Congress, in perpetrating his own previous determination? and, in perfect conformity to his interested ambition, which crowned with success beyond all human calculation in 1783, to use his own expression, 'bid a last farewell to the cares of office, and all the employments of public life,' to resume them at this moment (1787) as President of the American Convention? Had Sir Henry Clinton, whose whole behaviour in his public disappointment, and most afflicting of private dispensations, united the sensibility of the Friend, with the magnanimity of the General, had he possessed a particle of the malignity which, in this transaction, was exhibited by the American, many of the principal inhabitants of Carolina then in confinement, on the clearest proof for the violation of the law of nations, would have been adjudged to the death they had merited. The papers which Congress published, relative to Major André's death, will remain an eternal monument of the principles of that heroic officer; and, when fortune shall no longer gloss over her fading panegyric, will enable posterity to pass judgment on the character of Washington." *

Though clothed in language painful to our ears, we cannot deny that, so far as we know, the opinions of these English officers familiar with the facts were opposed to those of our own generals. Lord Rawdon hardly forms the exception. Under these circumstances it has been said that the British sentiment, by reason of the superior military knowledge of its exponents, was more likely to be accurate; and that their education had not sufficiently instructed the American leaders in the principles of international law. It should seem that at this day the question ought to be rather as to the correctness of their decision than their fitness to make it: but it may be as well to glance hastily at the circumstances attending the composition of the court. Good or bad, it was certainly the best we had in an army of which Chastellux testifies the generals were distinguished for their military appearance and behavior, and even the subalterns manifested a union of capacity and good-breeding.

As president of the board and reputedly one of the firmest in promoting André's death, Greene is the head and front of those who offended by their unprofessional breeding and limited education. Born in 1740, Greene had been a blacksmith: he was a blacksmith when he marched to Boston, and was raised from the ranks of a militia company to a colonial major-generalcy. The case is not singular. It was

* Mil. Journ. 152, 294. As governor of Upper Canada Simcoe in 1795 is described by Rochefoucault-Liancourt as just, enlightened, frank, and brave: but unswerving in his aversion to the United States and constantly speculating on a campaign that should lead him to Philadelphia. If he did not instigate he certainly did not discourage the Indian wars of the northwest, in which St. Clair was so terribly cut to pieces.

a smith that led the Turks from the slavery of the Altai Mountains to royal greatness; and for centuries the exercise of anvil and sledge preserved the memory of the deeds that changed the forge for the throne. The abrupt translation of the stuttering Michael from the cinders of his smithy to the porphyry palaces of the Eastern Empire furnishes history with one of its most glaring illustrations of the mutability of fortune and the blindness of the popular will. The blacksmith's apron that commemorated the imperial origin long led the Persians to victory, until the jewels with which it continued to be embroidered entirely hid the leather from view. Greene's was one of those cases in which promotion was born of merit, and the general's worth obscures his unprofessional origin. Though self-educated, the advisers of his studies were President Stiles and Lindley Murray. His reading was thorough rather than large. His military textbooks were Cæsar's Commentaries, Plutarch, Turenne's Memoirs, and Sharpe's Military Guide: but he was familiar with Blackstone and with Ferguson's Civil Society, and I am able to state positively had carefully read over Vattel. To his capacity in the field Tarleton bears ample testimony; and it is odd that the beginning and the ending of his campaignings should involve the idea of a spy. To procure arms to use against the English, in 1774 or 1775 he slipped into Boston, watched the discipline of the troops at their morning and evening parades, and when he smuggled out a musket and accoutrements he brought a deserter along as a drillmaster to the militia corps with which he served. In Carolina, he employed a young lady on secret services of the greatest danger without scruple; and after the evacuation of Charleston towards the end of the war, when the whig governor arrested Captain Ker and his crew who had come with a flag to Greene, he called a council of officers and with their concurrence enforced the flag-party's release by an armed demonstration on the place. This circumstance tends to show that Greene understood the nature of his present business, and also that no seeking after the applause of the civil powers was likely to bend him from the path of professional integrity: and indeed at the time of André's sentence he was out of favor with Congress. He was a calm, circumspect man: fond of general principles; his mind clear, comprehensive, and logical. Unwearied in collecting premises, he was immovable in his conclusions. It is probable enough that however accurate and reasonable were his mental operations, his manners may have savored of his youthful associations: but such as they were, he abided with them. It is recorded that even after both had left the army, he continued to refuse satisfaction to a brother officer whom he did not think the proprieties of martial life entitled to demand it.*

If Greene was of humble birth and self-taught, Stirling, born in 1726, was directly the reverse. He was of noble blood and had ineffectually sued for the earldom that he always claimed as his rightful inheritance. His education was liberal: he was versed in the classics and proficient in the severe sciences. In 1754, he aided in founding the New York Society Library: and in the ensuing war, was a member of the military family of Shirley, the king's chief general here. Thacher tells an idle camp-fire story of his punctilious adhesiveness to the dignity of his rank, but adds: — "In his personal appearance his lordship is venerable and dignified; in his deportment, gentlemanly and graceful; in conversation, pleasing and interesting." His convivial habits were specially satirized by André in The Cowchase. Chastellux mentions the same infirmity, but

---

* It may be added that Greene was noted for the prompt severity with which he checked the disorders of his command: and more than one execution proves how firm he was in preserving the legitimate discipline of war. A good idea of the military capacity of our generals may be got from their proposed emendations of the Articles of War, Oct. 1775. On this occasion, Greene demanded a Provost-marshal, and desired that treason in the army against the United States should be clearly defined, and the penalty prescribed.

says he was very brave, zealous, sensible, and of information; though without capacity, old, and dull. He certainly was sincere and steady in his devotion to our cause.

St. Clair, born in Scotland in 1734, had a thoroughly liberal education at one of the best Scottish universities. He was intended for medicine, but his taste being for arms he obtained a commission through the influence of his elevated connections, and came to America with Boscawen in 1755. He was a lieutenant under Wolfe and esteemed a very meritorious officer, capable of reaching great military distinction. He was appointed to the command of Fort Ligonier in Pennsylvania; and retiring from the army after the Peace of 1763, filled some important civil offices in that province. In March, 1774, Governor John Penn wrote to Lord Dunmore: — "Mr. St. Clair is a gentleman who for a long time had the honour of serving his Majesty in the regulars with reputation, and in every station of life has preserved the character of a very honest man."*

La Fayette, born in 1757, is too well known to ask many words here. His education, civil and military, was as good as his years would permit. He was brave and intelligent, and covetous of popular applause. In 1787, Jefferson wrote that he had an undue love of popularity. This, and his hatred to England, led him into such escapades as his challenge to Lord Carlisle for language used regarding

---

* St. Clair's fate was a hard one and unmerited. After having served in almost every American siege or action of consequence in the Seven Years' War, and abandoning an estate in Scotland to take up arms in our Revolution, his honour was wofully impugned. He was court-martialled by Congress for neglect of duty, cowardice, treachery, &c.; and though of course acquitted (being entirely innocent) his feelings were naturally stung. Sullivan, too, published a letter, Aug. 6, 1777, which seemed to question his fidelity, until he disavowed any such meaning, Aug. 30. St. Clair earned and kept Washington's esteem; but in after-life he was stripped of his appointments by government, defrauded of his rights, and lived in old age for several years "in the most abject poverty." Pennsylvania then granted him a pension of $650 yearly, on which he wore out his few remaining days.

France in his quality of Commissioner; but they did him no harm with the multitude. The sword of honor that Congress gave him in 1779, "I am proud," said he, "to carry into the heart of England." Like Simon of Montfort, our people rejoiced that a Frenchman and foreigner, himself the subject of a despotism, should be so penetrated with their oppressions as to lead them to liberty in a civil war. He was liberal of his person and his purse in our cause, and his name was beloved by our nation, even when it was proscribed by his own. For, after active efforts, having succeeded in setting a constitutional reform in motion, the storm that rose in France bore down the best of those who had aided the movement. The National Assembly declared him a traitor to his country, and flying from arrest to the enemy, he was closely immured at Olmütz. Efforts were made to procure the intercession of England in his behalf; but there was little reason to expect that England should espouse his cause. Pitt set his face against it; and when a lord bewailed his unhappy state to George III. in hope of exciting the royal sympathy, the king is said to have cut the speaker short with two pregnant words — "Remember André." *

* Anal. Mag. ii. 172. In the Commons, March 17, 1794, Gen. Fitzpatrick moved that the king be besought to intercede with the court of Berlin for La Fayette and his companions. Burke vehemently replied in most denunciatory terms against La Fayette, whom he considered the author and origin of innumerable outrages in France. The only precedent, he said, for the interference of one power with another in behalf of the subject of a third was "the case of the interposition of the late court of France, which was now so frequently denominated despotic and tyrannical, in favour of Sir Charles Asgill, an interposition which was chiefly rendered effectual by the exertions of the late unfortunate queen." France, he continued, claimed La Fayette as a traitor, whom the rabble he had been instrumental in elevating to power, were desirous of sacrificing. He had volunteered for America and against England before any hostilities between England and France, and had rebelled against his own lawful sovereign. After citations of his alleged participation in some popular violences in his own country, Burke concluded: "I would not debauch my humanity by supporting an application like the present in behalf of such a horrid ruffian." The motion was lost: 46 against 153; but the episode is a curious one in La Fayette's life. It is not often Americans have heard him called by such names.

Of Robert Howe not a great deal is known. He was probably an Englishman: at all events he was in the English service before the war; was settled in North Carolina; and had commanded (I think) Fort Johnston, where a garrison of ten men was kept up in time of peace. He was an early and active whig, representing Brunswick county; and in 1775, was proclaimed against by Gov. Martin as " Robert *Howes,* alias Howe." In 1776 Clinton debarked on his plantation; and specially excepted him from grace. He is described by Smith as a good officer and a superior engineer: and I have other reasons for believing that here Smith is right. Irvine and others however distrusted his general capacity in a serious emergency. It is probable that Howe had all the book-learning of his trade. His years were doubtless well advanced at this time, and Chastellux pronounces him fond of music, the arts, and pleasure, and of cultivated mind. In August, 1785, he was appointed by Congress to treat with the Western Indians.

Steuben, born in 1730, had served at the age of fourteen; but he does not appear to have held higher than regimental rank in the Prussian army. The idea of his having been a favorite general of the great Frederick's is all a delusion. He was an honest old soldier of fortune, and a singularly accomplished disciplinarian.* His review of a brigade would

---

* An incident at Yorktown shows his perfect acquaintance with the laws of war, in opposition to La Fayette's. He commanded in the trenches when a flag came out with proposals of capitulation. While the negotiation went on, La Fayette's tour of duty arrived; as it was of course a point of honor to plant our flag on the enemy's fortress, there was a competition for the command that would give the right. Steuben asserted that having received the flag, he was entitled to retain his place till the negotiation was closed either by surrender or renewed hostilities. La Fayette denied this, and marched with his division to relieve the German: who would not be relieved. La Fayette appealed to Washington: the case was carried to Rochambeau and his chiefs, and it was decided that the baron was right, and must retain the command. The matter does not seem to have ended here. Ensign Denny (apparently of La Fayette's division) was detailed to erect our standard when the troops entered York-

extend to every arm and accoutrement of every officer and private; blaming or praising as the case required. The surgeon's list would be examined, the disorders of the patients inquired into, and their treatment. These inspections are sometimes the subject of precise narration, yet no annalist mentions any difficulty of language in comprehending or satisfying the baron. On the contrary we are expressly told that though never perfectly its master, he had like La Fayette a sufficiently correct knowledge of our tongue. He was not however on friendly terms with La Fayette; and in America would boast of having been in the battle of Rossbach where he made the Frenchmen run. Steuben was beloved by his troops, to whom, like Trajan or Hadrian of old, he would not scruple to give himself manual instruction. Simcoe distinguishes his capacity as superior to that of his fellows; and esteemed him an expert soldier, well-skilled in adapting the science of war to the character of his followers and the nature of the country. There is no earthly reason to suppose that he did not perfectly comprehend the circumstances of André's case, whose fate he commiserated. "It is impossible to save him," wrote the baron. "He put us to no proof, but in an open, manly manner confessed everything but a premeditated design to deceive. Would to God the wretch who drew him to death could have suffered in his place!" *

town, and was in the act of planting it on the parapet before the three armies when Steuben galloped up, took the flag, and planted it himself. Ill blood existed on both sides, and a challenge from Butler of Wayne's brigade went to Steuben, which it required all the influence of Washington on one side and Rochambeau on the other to hush up. *Mems. Hist. Soc. Penn.* vii. 214, 486.

* Kapp's Steuben, 290, 477. Thacher, 195, 517. The baron never failed to speak loudly of Arnold's misconduct after his desertion. While inspecting Sheldon's Dragoons, the hated name struck his ear on the roster. He called the bearer to the front, and found his equipments in capital order. "Change your name, brother soldier, you are too respectable to bear the name of a traitor." "What name shall I take, general?" "Take any other name. Mine is at your service." The trooper's name was thenceforth Steuben: and after the war, he settled on land bestowed by

Parsons was a Connecticut lawyer before the war, and a graduate of Harvard in 1756. He was of a good Massachusetts family, and in 1780 was probably about forty years of age. In 1775 he was settled in the tenth colonelcy of the continental army by Washington, albeit he had headed a remonstrance of the Connecticut line to its legislature against the action of Congress that gave precedence to Putnam over Spencer. They "had no objection to the appointment of Generals Washington and Lee," but apprehended danger to the morals and discipline of the line by Putnam's superiority. Memorials of this kind Washington had in wise aversion. Parsons was a man of parts.

Clinton, born in 1737, was perhaps of the same blood with Sir Henry, in resisting whom he had been severely wounded. He displayed an early fondness for military life, and served in the Seven Years' War. He excelled in the exact sciences, and was father of De Witt Clinton. In 1775, he was with Montgomery, and his name heads the apology by which that general was persuaded to resume the command that the insubordination of some of his officers had provoked him to throw up.*

---

his new godfather. "I am well settled, general," quoth he, "and have a wife and son. I have called my son after you, Sir." "I thank you, my friend; what name have you given the boy?" "I called him Baron," was the answer; — "what else could I call him!"

If Steuben's after-life was for a time clouded by pecuniary distress, it is grateful to know that his services at last commanded a substantial acknowledgment from America which made his old age comfortable.

* In 1777, one Daniel Taylor, deceived by the British uniforms which a party of our troops wore, and by the name of General Clinton, did not discover his position till he was led before our general. He then swallowed a silver bullet, but an emetic bringing it back, it was found to unscrew and contain this note: — "To GENERAL BURGOYNE: — *Fort Montgomery, Oct. 8th,* 1777. Nous voici — and nothing between us but *Gates.* I sincerely hope this *little* success of ours may facilitate your operations. In answer to your letter of the 28th of September by C. C. I shall only say, I cannot presume to order, or even advise, for reasons obvious. I heartily wish you success. Faithfully yours, H. CLINTON." — Taylor was hanged: "Out of thine own mouth shalt thou be condemned," said the American officer.

Knox, born in 1750, had a good though not a collegiate education, and in youth was so fond of military pursuits that at eighteen he was chosen captain of a volunteer company of grenadiers. He was a bookseller, and acquainted with the French language; and though his talents were unknown to Samuel Adams, they were at once discovered in our army. The aged and incapable Gridley was ousted from the command of the artillery department, and under direction of Knox a system of fortifications were thrown up before Boston, whose strength Howe owned at sight, without venturing to a practical test. Mrs. Warren attributes his advancement to personal rather than military considerations; though she confesses he made an excellent officer. The testimony of Washington, of Rochambeau, of Dumas, and of Rawdon to his great military qualifications, added to that of Chastellux as to his understanding and information, are sufficient to establish the real worth of his character.

Glover, born about 1735, was, I believe, of a wealthy family of Marblehead. He took an early share in the contest. Diminutive in person, he was active in habit and a good soldier. He had probably been a ship-owner before the war, and the regiment that he raised in 1775 was mainly composed of seafaring men. It was one of the first filled up in Massachusetts, and when taken into continental pay still preserved its efficiency. The roster of officers, with its Williams and Thomases, offers a contrast to the Jedidiahs, Abels, and Abijahs, the Penuels, Melatiahs, and Amoses, who at that time so often made a New England regimental list to savor of "a catalogue of Praise-God Barebones's parliament or the roll of one of old Noll's evangelical armies." In service it was especially exempted from the sweeping contempt that was visited on the shortcomings of some of its countrymen by the middle and southern soldiery. "The only exception I recollect to have seen to these miserably constituted bands from New England was the regiment of Glover from Marblehead. There was an appearance of discipline in this corps; the officers seemed to have mixed with the world, and to understand what belonged to their stations. Though deficient, perhaps, in polish, it possessed an apparent aptitude for the purpose of its institution, and gave a confidence that myriads of its meek and lowly brethren were incompetent to inspire. But even in this regiment there were a number of negroes, which, to persons unaccustomed to such associations, had a disagreeable, degrading effect." * Glover's command led the advance in the passage of the Delaware at Trenton, and its commander was never found remiss.

Of Patterson I find nothing beyond Thacher's record of a visit to his quarters in 1781, when "the general humorously apologized that he could afford us nothing better than a miserable glass of whiskey grog."

Hand, born in Ireland in 1744, came hither as surgeon's mate to the 18th or Royal Irish in 1774, and resigning his commission, practised medicine. He had applied for the post of Hospital Director when Washington (Oct. 12, 1775) wrote to Congress that he was ignorant of the merits of the respective candidates. He was named second lieutenant-colonel of our army (Nov. 2, 1775) in Thompson's Pennsylvania regiment, whose courage before Boston, when others behaved with backwardness, was specially noticed a week later in

---

* Graydon, 148. "These were the lads that might do something!" cried the spectators, as, 500 strong, it came along after the defeat of Long Island. A passage in the citation above may render it necessary to remark that negroes were hardly thought worthy to share in the struggle for Independence. The Massachusetts Provincial Congress (Oct. 1774), being requested in its efforts to preserve its constituents from slavery, to consider the state and circumstances of the Negro Slaves in the province, refused to entertain the question, and voted that "the matter now subside." Accordingly, at a Council of War, Oct. 8, 1775, present Washington, Ward, Lee, Putnam, Thomas, Spencer, Heath, Sullivan, Greene, and Gates, it was unanimously resolved to reject all slaves from enlistment, and, by a great majority, to reject negroes altogether. At a conference of a Committee from Congress and the civil authorities of all New England with Washington in the same month, it was agreed that negroes should be altogether rejected from enlistment in our army.—*Am. Arch. 4th ser.* iii. 1040, 1161.

General Orders. He was now brigadier of La Fayette's *corps d'élite.*

Huntington, born in 1743 and a graduate of Harvard in 1763, was a merchant of good estate and ancient family at Norwich, and was son-in-law of Governor Trumbull. His manners were cold, but he had acknowledged sense and information; and his virtues must have been remarkable, since through the terms of four different occupants of the presidential chair he retained the collectorship of customs at New London from 1789 until he was removed by death in 1815.

Stark, born in 1728, seems to have had but a rural education. But war had a charm for him, and what military knowledge could be acquired by command of a partisan company in the Seven Years' War, he doubtless possessed. The assumption of superiority by the young British officers drove him to resign; though his qualities had gained him the confidence of Abercrombie, nephew of the commanding general, and of the young Lord Howe. He was a hardy, honest, self-willed man, impatient of subordination where he did not think it due. Difficulties on this point sprung up as soon as he joined our army in 1775: and later, he resigned in discontent with being overslaughed in promotions. He only resumed arms in the service of New Hampshire on the express condition of exemption from obedience to the orders of Congress. The public confidence in him was so great that John Langdon gave his money, his plate, and his merchandise, to set on foot Stark's opposition to Burgoyne: and the Bennington victory was of such moment that he was forthwith made a continental brigadier. He felt the hardship of the case, but united with his brethren in the judgment that André was a spy, and should be put to death: and not long after, in his own command, hung Lovelace for a like offence. He ran a saw-mill when the war broke out; and is described by Thacher as joining to an unspotted character and great private worth, neither the habits nor the appearance of an officer.

Such was the constitution of the board that pronounced on André's case. If some of its members may be found

Wise without learning, plain and good,

the greater part by far must be confessed to have been of sufficient education and of military training.* Of Washington nothing need be said: but can we suppose that if he and St. Clair, Stirling, Clinton, Howe, and Stark, had continued to hold the king's commission from the Seven Years' War, and now sat in a court called by royal authority, their decision would not have been received in England as authoritative, especially when confirmed by the concurrent voices of Steuben and La Fayette? That the English leaders sincerely thought it erroneous in principle and colored with passion or policy may not be questioned; and their public and private respectability enforces our attention to their views. But what reason is there to suppose that prejudice or excitement should sway one party less than the other? Indeed the case appears to have admitted at least of such nice distinctions that we cannot refuse the attribute of perfect sincerity to both: for even within the last few years, the patient investigation of two calm and vigorous minds on either side has left the question exactly where it was before. Lord Mahon is satisfied that the Americans were wrong. Major Biddle, whose own military antecedents give weight to his conclusions, is convinced they were eminently right. It might seem presumptuous for me to declare positively that either side is in error; since after all the case was one not covered by any prescription of the text-books on the laws of nations or of war; and therefore was apparently to be governed by the deductions of a military tribunal from the great

---

* My friend Major Charles J. Biddle has already so satisfactorily gone over this ground, as well as much more relative to the subject of this book, that an apology is almost necessary for my treating of it at all.

general principles therein laid down. For it is not evident that André entered our lines in disguise, which is one of the first requisites to a spy from the enemy: and the suborning of a hostile general, though protested against by Vattel as incompatible with personal purity, is allowed to be in accordance with international law: and much more so, he says, is it fair to merely accept the proposals of a traitor. The romantic interest that has always been attached to André's character has in a measure clouded the judgment that men would arrive at as to his fate: it will be well therefore to give a summary here of the facts as they are drawn from the story of not one, but all sides.

Arnold volunteered to surrender West Point on sufficient assurance that he should lose neither in pocket nor in rank by so doing. He demanded that an agent should meet him to settle the preliminaries. By Clinton's order, André went in a king's ship for this end, expecting the interview would occur on board, or at least under a flag of truce and not in our lines. Arnold's emissary brought him from the Vulture in his uniform and with a safe-conduct from that general, but under a feigned name, by night, and with a watch-coat covering his person. There is little doubt here that Smith saw him in uniform, and that he had no intention of exposing himself to any other risk than of becoming a prisoner of war. He came ashore at a place very near to but not within our lines. Here Arnold met him, and well knowing his name and quality, under the plea that he could not possibly return to the ship that night, led him unawares and against his stipulation within our picket though not into any of our works. André still was attired as when he landed. He remained concealed for nearly a day, making no plans or observations, but possessing himself of all the information Arnold had to give. For what end is not accurately known (though Arnold alleges it was his direction that they should be thus transmitted to Clinton) he took several important papers from the American general, and concealed them on his person. By the same orders he disguised himself, and abandoned his uniform; and acting in every respect by Arnold's direction, and under his safe-conduct passed through our lines into neutral ground, bearing an assumed character both in dress and in name. Here he was taken, having from before he entered until after he left our limits been known to and directed by our general there commanding.

In considering these facts, it must be remembered that by André's own avowal he was, though involuntarily, an impostor; and that the boat carried no flag, nor did he suppose he came ashore under that sanction. This last declaration may be balanced by the fact that he did not then believe he was to be brought anywhere but to neutral ground: but the after-incidents are not thus altered. The question then arises whether Arnold had lawfully the power to secure him, by the means employed, from the vengeance of the Americans? This is a point that military men must solve. Arnold had undoubtedly the right to issue safe-conducts that would protect their bearer from our troops, provided the business was fair to our country. Had he, so far as the bearer was concerned, the right to go further? How far does the fact that André was inveigled, as it were, into a position that left him no other means of extrication than such as Arnold prescribed affect the merits of his case? And above all, was or was not the safe-conduct given to him in a feigned name when he was to come ashore, equivalent to a flag?

The gist of the American opinion seems to be that a fraud of this nature taints everything it touches; and the parties to it, if at all they are compassed by the letter of the law, are justly amenable to punishment. Whether André therefore left the Vulture under sufficient protection is an important question. Had he openly borne a flag of truce sent either from his own party or by the Americans, he could unquestionably have passed back under it at any season. A flag gives its bearer the sanctity of an ambassador; the violation of whose safe-conduct has from the most polished nations of antiquity been the received signal for rancorous war. "Men of Tarentum," said the Roman legate to the Greeks that mocked at his defiled garments; "it will take not a little blood to wash this gown." Even the wild Arabs of the desert respected the safety of the envoy that brought them the most insulting missives; and beyond making him swallow the scroll, ventured on no personal aggression: and the red Indian esteems himself in perfect security when he advances with the calumet in hand. In fact, a flag of truce is the substitute for the ancient herald. In the first stages of our war, "a trumpeter or flag of truce" were correlative terms. Passing in the face of danger, they courted publicity by appeals to eye and ear. In Canada, Montgomery and Prescott employed a flag and drum: and that his flag-officer was twice fired on from the walls of Quebec Arnold regarded as a most infamous infraction of civilized warfare. So at Boston in 1775, Howe tartly intimated to Washington that our people so constantly fired upon his officers returning from parleys applied for by ourselves, that he desired no intercourse between the two armies should continue, except where Washington would send his own letters in by a drummer: and in the turmoil before Yorktown, the flag that proposed surrender was accompanied by a drum beating a parley. The after-passage of flags without a drum was especially commented on. But the drum and trumpet were lawfully hushed when armies were not met face to face: and then it is possible that a safe-conduct may have been equivalent to a flag of truce. Robertson took this view: but it does not clearly appear whether Greene denied it *in toto*, or merely held that André did not come ashore with anything in the form of a protection.

To my mind it is clear that as his errand was of a nature directly opposed to the end for which flags are designed, and as he was detected in an appearance of guilt, it would require a very strong case to exonerate André from punishment. The reader must decide whether such a case was made out by his friends. If he was within our lines under a flag, why did he not return under its protection? If he was not thus guarded, in what capacity was he there? The tendency of some writers to suppose that the moment a man becomes a spy he puts himself out of humanity's reach has probably warped many judgments on this matter. In point of fact, there is nothing in the history of ancient or modern warfare to warrant such a theory. That in the abstract the proceeding is no more defensible than manslaying, cannot be denied: but it is with the customs of this world, not with sublimated abstractions, that we have to do. We will pass over the examples of the Jews, because this people's ways in war or in peace were almost peculiar to themselves.* But "in the most high and palmy state of Rome" we find spies and deserters constantly encouraged. The Spaniard Balbus, the friend alike of Pompey and of Cæsar, acquired unprecedented honors through such secret service in a civil war: and his name is immortalized by the eloquence of Cicero. Constantine, the upholder of our faith, esteemed it no degradation to seduce his opponent's followers: and another Cæsar did not think the imperial purple was sullied by entering the Persian camp as a spy, and following up his explorations with a prodigious rout. By such means Alfred drove the Danes from England. Nor need we rest upon the dusty records of by-gone ages: the annals of modern warfare furnish abundant and far more valuable examples of the light in which the character and services of a spy are held. In the Peninsular War they were freely employed by all

---

* Though Joshua indeed sent his spies down into the promised land, we do not want examples of the manner in which the Old Testament has taught people to deal with such characters. The Calvinist minister who urged the Rochellois to slay the king's trumpeter bringing proposals to the revolted city found a text for even further proceedings. "If any one entice thee secretly to go and worship other gods, thou shalt surely kill him; thine hand shall be first upon him to put him to death, and afterwards the hand of all the people." — *Mérimée: Charles IX.* c. 25.

parties, and were not necessarily thought base. Wellington had a legion of them in the French lines, from the haughty grandee who boasted a *sang azul* noble as the king's, to the little cobbler on the bridge of Irun, who sat on his bench and from one year's end to another kept tale of every French soldier that entered Spain. British officers also notably acted in the field as spies: and where double treason was not wrought Napier says all these characters were highly meritorious. Carrara did not scruple to offer honors and wealth to Ney if he would desert his standard: and Napoleon himself, not only by allurements but more unjustifiably by severities, sought to bring to his own aid the professional services of persons over whom the fortunes of war gave him power.*
There is one case in particular however in these times that strongly reminds us of André's.

In 1809, the imperial ambition of Bonaparte excited the republican officers to look to St. Cyr or Ney as a leader in its repression. John Viana, the son of an Oporto merchant, brought proposals from the French plotters to Marshal Beresford, asking that an English officer should meet them to arrange the plan of action, which involved the seizure and surrender of Soult, their leader. "This was a detestable

---

* Captain Colquhoun Grant was the most famous English spy in the Peninsular War, though he always kept his uniform. Being employed by Wellington to ascertain Marmont's route, and thus his purpose, he got in front of the French and after a hard chase was run down. Marmont received him kindly, for he was overjoyed at the capture, and sat him down to dinner. "I would have shot him on the spot," he said, "had it not been for respect to something resembling a uniform that he wore when taken." But he took his parole not to be rescued by guerillas on the road (Wellington having offered $2000 reward for his recovery) and sent him to Bayonne with secret orders to the governor there to send him in irons to Paris. Grant wormed out this secret; and eloping at Bayonne, went himself to Paris and remained there unsuspected till he heard one day that an American sailor named Jonathan Buck had suddenly died, leaving his passport uncalled for at the Bureau. He at once claimed it, pretending to be Buck; hastened to the mouth of the Loire; got a clandestine passage on a vessel; and in four months from his original capture he was again playing around the skirts of the French in Spain.

project," says Napier, "for it is not in the field, and with a foreign enemy, that soldiers should concert the overthrow of their country's institutions. It would be idle and impertinent in a foreigner to say how much and how long men shall bear with what they deem an oppressive government; yet there is a distinct and especial loyalty due from a soldier to his general in the field; a compact of honor, which it is singularly base to violate, and so it has in all ages been considered." An English colonel in uniform reluctantly went by night to meet them on a lake behind the French outposts. They missed each other, and returning he found Viana and the French Adjutant-Major D'Argenton in the English lines. The latter boldly went on to Beresford at Lisbon, conceiving his backers too numerous and powerful for him to incur much danger in his own army. Wellesley did not give the plan very hearty encouragement; and when D'Argenton came back a second time (the first essay being unnoticed or unpunished) he gave him the good advice to avoid receiving an English safe-conduct. The warning was disregarded. D'Argenton was discovered and condemned: but the punishment was not executed, and he finally escaped. Others, French colonels, also conferred with Sir Arthur in his campaigns: nor must we forget Don Uran de la Rosa, whom the English thought a Spaniard, the Spanish an Italian, the French no one knows what, and the mystified Alava, Cagliostro or some such wizard: and who dined alternately in the opposing camps, carrying intelligence indifferently to either side. The case of the Frenchman Perron, who came over from Sindia in 1803 on overtures from Lord Lake, was not unlike Arnold's.

In our Revolution then we need not be surprised to find that the employment of spies was practised on the most extensive scale from the very outset. In the siege of Boston, John Carnes, a grocer, is commemorated as Washington's secret intelligencer; and by handbills sent in on the wind the troops were tempted to desert and to supply our own ranks. In 1775 also, by order of Congress two persons were privately sent by our general to Nova Scotia, to discover its strong places and to tamper with the people. In England we had a perfect corps of spies; some of them men of position. In New York, Washington maintained through the war, and particularly in 1779 and 1780, an organization that under the guise of zealous loyalists never failed to advise him instantly of any considerable movement. These kept their secret so well that at the evacuation he had to send Tallmadge in while yet Carleton held the town, to provide for the safety of his agents. One who had never been suspected was caught tempting soldiers to desert, and hanged at Brunswick. Another, whose observations perhaps on occasion saved Washington's life, was able by his connections with the West Indian house of Kortwright and Company, to unsuspectedly pick up much useful information for our army. Yet his character was so little affected by these transactions that he remained the valued friend of both Hamilton and Washington; and it was perhaps to set his patriotism straight in the popular view that our general on the final entrance into the city took his first breakfast at his house. Arnold had him seized and tried hard to hang him, when he came over; but there was not enough evidence.* It was believed when Clinton started to relieve Cornwallis, that by means of a white flag displayed on a roof in New York and answered by a gun about a mile from Paulus Hook, the expedition was betrayed to the Americans and the news telegraphed 600 miles on to Washington in forty-eight hours. Congress itself not only retained spies in that city, but through the war left no stone unturned to sap the fidelity

* Hamilton's Hist. Rep. i. 46, 527. It may have been to this person that Washington refers in his letter to Congress, Oct. 15, 1780: — "Unluckily the person in whom I have the greatest confidence is afraid to take any measure for communicating with me just at this time, as he is apprehensive that Arnold may possibly have some knowledge of the connection, and may have him watched. But as he is assured that Arnold has not the most distant hint of him, I expect soon to hear from him as usual."

of the enemy's army; offering particularly great pecuniary temptations to officers to desert with their commands. The English did the same; and both sides had some success. A regular spy association for the enemy ramified through Norwalk, Stratford, and other Connecticut towns; and our generals were pestered with more than one such a "sly, artful fellow" as McKeel, seducing the soldiers and getting recruits for the British. In fact, La Fayette and every other general hesitated not to use a spy; and the better the man the better was the intelligence. In the same year that André was hanged, Washington applied to Bowdoin and Heath for some draughtsmen of superior understanding, firmness, and fidelity, to clandestinely make plans for him of the enemy's works; and if he sometimes found his own secrets betrayed to Clinton, he did not scruple to mislead the go-betweens with false intelligence. Such courses are sanctioned by the customs of war, and if Rush's plan of sending a German baron into Howe's lines to seduce the Hessians found favor in American eyes, the British thought it as fair to seek to allure Sullivan, Moultrie, Ethan Allen, and others, to exchange their service and break their faith: a severe construction of the law might even have brought Franklin, Chase, and Carroll into an awkward predicament had their Canadian mission left them in Carleton's hands. Indeed the action of Arnold was for the moment fondly believed in England to have been shared by his fellows; and the names of Knox and Stirling, Howe, Sullivan, and Maxwell, were ridiculously bandied about as of fallers-off from the cause.

It may be as well to observe that our Congress had in 1778 clearly announced the rigor with which they would on necessity deal with any but an unimpeachable flag. Lieutanant Hele was sent from New York with a flag of truce to Philadelphia, bearing copies of the Commissioners' Manifesto addressed to Congress, the several legislatures, the clergy, the army, and the people at large. His vessel was wrecked, and after some suffering and loss of life the crew were rescued and brought to Philadelphia. Congress thereon resolved that the nature of Hele's mission was not to be protected by a flag, and threatened for some time to proceed to extremes with him. It is said, but with no evidence of truth, that during his prolonged detention Hele avenged himself, by seducing Arnold. But this and other instances plainly showed that Congress was not to be restrained on occasion from restricting the sanctity of flags to its narrowest limits.

The inflexibility with which Washington regarded André's case has been the subject of severe criticism. But the public weal was in my opinion the motive as well as the measure of his conduct. Emergences sometimes spring up in which it is difficult to decide whether the general good does or does not demand unshrinking severity: and it must be confessed that no offence so tends to shake the stern impartiality of the sovereign authority as that which seems to threaten the subversion of all its rights and powers. Yet had Brutus failed to doom his son to death, we are well advised that the unsettled liberties of Rome would have perished in their cradle. The necessities of the state is proverbially the tyrant's plea; but how often do we see its advantages practically illustrated in the increased welfare of the community. Every one recollects how many Sepoys in the late Indian rebellion were blown into fragments on this pretext; yet who will say that, with regard to humanity at large, real mercy did not here temper justice? No civilized nation hesitates to fulfil to the bitter end the rescripts of its tribunals, when national existence is threatened with destruction by lenity. We have Mr. Fox's authority (and better is not to be obtained) for saying that the brother of the king of France — l'Homme au Masque de Fer — was by state policy the inmate of a dungeon from his cradle to his bier. If we turn to English annals we find so late as 1815 the first jurists of the land — one might nearly say of the world — discussing the fate of Napoleon. Lord Ellenborough, Sir William Grant, the great Stowell, — whose interpretations of international law may almost be considered as its text, — the Chancellor Eldon — all were ranged, " a terrible show," in solemn conclave on the destiny of one whose fiat had lately made Europe tremble. A more lofty tribunal never judged a greater man; yet the diversity of opinion that arose sets the conflicting sentiments on André's case utterly in the background. This man was for giving him up to Louis XVIII. to be tried for treason; that, for setting him at perfect liberty; and the next, that he was a mere pirate — "*hostis humani generis* carrying about with him *caput lupinum*." The solution of the business was, in Eldon's common-sense view, — "that the case was not provided for by anything to be found in Grotius or Vattel, but that the law of self-preservation would justify the keeping of him under restraint in some distant region, where he should be treated with all indulgence compatible with the peace of mankind." Here principles supplied the want of precedent as perfectly as in André's case.

But when all is spoken, shall we pronounce André's an unhappy fate? Has not the great law of compensation gilded his name with a lustre that in life could never, with all his ardent longing for fame, have entered into his most sanguine hopes? If he perished by an ignominious means, he perished not ignominiously: if he died the death of a felon, it was with the tears, the regrets, the admiration of all that was worthy and good in the ranks alike of friend and of foe. The heartiest enemies of his nation joined with its chiefs in sounding his praises and lamenting his lot. If reputation was his goal, who of his compeers has surpassed him in the race? If we turn to his own army, we see some protracting an unnoted existence, some laid on the shelf and repining in obscurity, some haltingly keeping a place in the world's eye less by merit than by fortune. Abercrombie it is true died happily in the arms of victory; while Simcoe sunk at the moment when the pathway to the glory that none more coveted and that few were so capable to attain was fairly laid open to him. Despard, his social messmate and fellow-prisoner, succumbed to the laws of his own land. The generous Rawdon, his predecessor in the Adjutant-generalcy, born to a princely title and a princely estate, with talents and courage equal to the highest posts, frittered away fortune and existence in dependence on the selfish friendship of the Prince Regent; and after experiencing the disappointment of having the cup of power raised to his lips but to be snatched away, was dismissed into the "splendid banishment" of the Antipodes where the brave Mathew, a brother soldier in the American war, had already found a death so horrid that André's was an enviable fate. Nay, the very sovereign he served so faithfully and well, might have been glad to exchange conditions with him. Old, mad, and blind, with a soul as darkened as were his organs of sense, he lingered out his weary days in a secluded and guarded chamber under the control of keepers whom his few glimpses of returning understanding announced as men that had subjected his person to the indignity of the rod. And of the Americans with whom André had to do, how sad was often their career; where decrepitude and poverty came hand in hand, and the ingratitude of the empire they had cradled as it were in their bucklers and christened with their best blood, was at once their ruin and its shame.* The man among them who took the warmest interest in André's condition, whose efforts to save his life were equal to the affectionate praise that he gave his memory, was doomed to as hard a destiny. Four and twenty years after the execution at Tappaan the same river that flowed within view of the gibbet passed the shore where Alexander Hamilton, the foremost man in all this western world, was shot to death. Henry Lee, from whose intervention the amelioration of André's fate was so hoped

* The half-pay for life, pledged by Congress to the officers that held out in its cause, and the solitary dependence of many of them, is not paid to this day.

for, survived to fall into the most distressing poverty, and, after being brutally beaten by the American mob, to be "cast into a loathsome jail, and subjected to the combined persecution of political rancour, personal cupidity, and vulgar malice." And Washington himself lived to hear his countrymen deny to him the possession of either military or civil merit; to endure the necessity of relieving his character from the charge of official peculation; to be told that his misdeeds had polluted the presidential ermine to an extent almost irremediable; and to die not universally regretted by the American people. Surely there are as bitter crosses in the worthiest life as any which befell André.

In the fulfilment of an enterprise which as he fondly believed would, if successful, crown him with the honors due to the man who had restored harmony to a divided empire, extinguished the flames of civil war, and gilded with renewed lustre the arms of his country, André perished. His motives, inimical as they were to our cause, were eminently respectable, and no otherwise alloyed with personal ambition than is allowable to all human hands that seek to serve the state. He died in the morning of his life, before success had stained with envy the love that all who knew him bestowed upon his worth; ere his illusions of youth were dispelled, and while the wine was yet bright in his cup and the lees untasted. His dust is laid with that of kings and heroes; and his memory drawing as a jewel from its foil fresh brightness from his death —

> Of every royal virtue stands possess'd;
> Still dear to all the bravest and the best.
> His courage foes, his friends his truth proclaim,
> His loyalty the king, the world his fame!

APPENDIX No. I.

BENEDICT ARNOLD.

I SHALL refrain from lengthening this note by the insertion of some curious unpublished documents respecting Arnold's earlier career, and confine myself entirely to such matters as may not be generally known relative to his history after it became connected with André's. The reader will find in The Life of Arnold, by Mr. Sparks, an accurate and skilfully drawn account of his general history. Mr. Sabine, whose opportunities of procuring information about the Loyalists were very great, declares it certain that Arnold was in communication with Robinson before he went to West Point; and it is probable that the letter which Marbois says was found among his papers and was the first overture received from an agent of Clinton's was written by Robinson. It is retranslated here from the French version.

"Among the Americans who have joined the rebel standard, there are very many good citizens whose only object has been the happiness of their country. Such men will not be influenced by motives of private interest to abandon the cause they have espoused. They are now offered everything which can render the colonies really happy; and this is the only compensation worthy of their virtue.

"The American colonies shall have their parliament, composed of two chambers, with all its members of American birth. Those of the upper house shall have titles and rank similar to those of the house of peers in England. All their laws, and particularly such as relate to money matters, shall be the production of this assembly, with the concurrence of a viceroy. Commerce, in every part of the globe subject to British sway, shall be as free to the people of the thirteen colonies as to the English of Europe. They will enjoy, in every sense of the phrase, the blessings of good government. They shall be sustained, in time of need, by all the power necessary to uphold them, without being themselves exposed to the dangers or subjected to the expenses that are always inseparable from the condition of a State.

"Such are the terms proffered by England in the very moment when she is displaying extraordinary efforts to conquer the obedience of her colonies.

"Shall America remain without limitation of time a scene of desolation — or are you desirous of enjoying Peace and all the blessings of her train? Shall your provinces, as in former days, flourish under the protection of the most puissant nation of the world? Or will you forever pursue that shadow of liberty which still escapes from your hand even when in the act of grasping it? And how soon would that very liberty, once obtained, turn into licentiousness, if it be not under the safeguard of a great European power? Will you rely upon the guaranty of France? They among you whom she has seduced may assure you that her assistance will be generous and disinterested, and that she will never exact from you a servile obedience. They are frantic with joy at the alliance already established, and promise you that Spain will immediately follow the example of France. Are they ignorant that each of these States has an equal interest in keeping you under, and will combine to accomplish their end? Thousands of men have perished; immense resources have been exhausted; and yet, since that fatal alliance the dispute has become more embittered than ever. Everything urges us to put a conclusion to dissensions not less detrimental to the victors than to the vanquished: but desirable as peace is, it cannot be negotiated and agreed upon between us as between two independent powers; it is necessary that a decisive advantage should put Britain in a condition to dictate the terms of reconciliation. It is her interest as well as her policy to make these as advantageous to one side as the other; but it is at the same time advisable to arrive at it without an unnecessary waste of that blood of which we are already as sparing as though it were again our own.

"There is no one but General Arnold who can surmount obstacles so great as these. A man of so much courage will never despair of the republic, even when every door to a reconciliation seems sealed.

"Render then, brave general, this important service to your

country. The colonies cannot sustain much longer the unequal strife. Your troops are perishing in misery. They are badly armed, half naked, and crying for bread. The efforts of Congress are futile against the languor of the people. Your fields are untilled, trade languishes, learning dies. The neglected education of a whole generation is an irreparable loss to society. Your youth, torn by thousands from their rustic pursuits or useful employments, are mown down by war. Such as survive have lost the vigour of their prime, or are maimed in battle: the greater part bring back to their families the idleness and the corrupt manners of the camp. Let us put an end to so many calamities; you and ourselves have the same origin, the same language, the same laws. We are inaccessible in our island; and you, the masters of a vast and fertile territory, have no other neighbours than the people of our loyal colonies. We possess rich establishments in every quarter of the globe and reign over the fairest portions of Hindostan. The ocean is our home, and we pass across it as a monarch traversing his dominions. From the northern to the southern pole, from the east to the west, our vessels find everywhere a neighbouring harbor belonging to Great Britain. So many islands, so many countries acknowledging our sway, are all ruled by a uniform system that bears on every feature the stamp of liberty, yet is as well adapted to the genius of different nations and of various climes.

" While the Continental powers ruin themselves by war, and are exhausted in erecting the ramparts that separate them from each other, our bulwarks are our ships. They enrich us; they protect us; they provide us as readily with the means of invading our enemies as of succouring our friends.

" Beware then of breaking forever the links and ties of a friendship whose benefits are proven by the experience of a hundred and fifty years. Time gives to human institutions a strength which what is new can only attain, in its turn, by the lapse of ages. Royalty itself experiences the need of this useful prestige: and the race that has reigned over us for sixty years has been illustrious for ten centuries.

" United in equality we will rule the universe: we will hold it bound, not by arms and violence, but by the ties of commerce; the lightest and most gentle bands that humankind can wear."

By the kindness of Mr. Bancroft I am able to give the precise sum that Arnold received in satisfaction of his alleged losses through his defection. It was £6315; of which he remitted £5000 to London to be invested in stocks, and procured therefrom £7000 four per cent. consols. It must be recollected that such compensation was customary when an officer went over by previous arrangement from one standard to another. In the beginning of the war, when Lee's capacity was held of the chiefest importance to our cause, he refused to give up his British rank by entering our service till a committee of one from every colony in Congress had heard his statement of probable losses, and agreed to indemnify him therefor. Arnold also got a brigadiership from the English. "Had the scheme succeeded," wrote an officer of the Coldstreams, "no rank would have overpaid so important a service"; and I am told on good authority that the prevailing sentiment of the royal army esteemed his proceedings a proper return to right principles and conduct. The money he got however was a scoff to our friends. The banker's receipt of his remittance was found in a captured vessel, and Franklin wrote of it to La Fayette: "Judas sold only one man, Arnold three millions. Judas got for his one man thirty pieces of silver, Arnold not a halfpenny a head." Mr. Sparks says a pension was after the war given to each of Arnold's children; and in 1782, William Lee wrote to our Secretary for Foreign Affairs: — "The late British Ministry died as they had lived, for one of their last official acts was to give the traitor Arnold, by patent, one thousand pounds sterling pension per annum for his and his wife's lives."

Arnold was active enough in the British cause. It was reported, though apparently untruly, that he had fifty of the warmest Whigs in New York seized immediately on his arrival. On the 28th Oct. 1780, he wrote to Lord George Germain, advising England to assume the arrears of pay, at most £500,000, of our soldiers enlisted for the war, or to offer a bounty of fifteen or twenty guineas to every deserter, half down, the rest at the end of the contest. He thought the offer of a title to Washington would have a good effect: and if arms instead of seduction were to be pursued, pointed out how he might be brought to action and beaten. His own sacrifices swell the remainder of this letter. (MS. S. P. O. R. 30 Nov.) The hatred of the Americans, however, went far beyond the praise of the English. It reminds us of that of the

Persians for Omar: and if the caliph's name signified the devil, Arnold's became synonymous with everything that is bad in our political vocabulary. "May this arrow go to the heart of Omar!" said the Persians when they bent the bow: and no effort of our leaders was spared to get the defaulter in their hands, where short rope, short shrift would have been his doom. Washington set on foot a plan for his seizure: La Fayette ordered that he should, if captured, be expressly prevented from surrendering as a prisoner of war: Jefferson thought a bribe of 5000 guineas would ensure a successful kidnapping dash into his camp. Of Washington's enterprise, in which Harry Lee and sergeant Champe figure so romantically, little need be said here, since the story has already been well told and roundly criticized. Jefferson calls it an historical romance, but there is no doubt that its main facts are generally true; that Champe was induced to desert and enter the English service under Arnold, with the design of kidnapping him. A Mr. Baldwin of Newark was procured to see Champe daily in New York, and aid him in the project: for which he was to receive 100 guineas, 500 acres of land, and three slaves. The story was originally told by General Henry Lee himself. I was informed by the late Edward D. Ingraham, Esq., a most accomplished historical student and book-collector, that a Mr. Beresford, compositor and foreman in the printing-house where Lee's volumes were struck off, had told him that the materials for the book came to them in a very undigested form and that they were put into their public shape by one Lewis P. Francks, who was also employed in the office: in confirmation of which Beresford added that the *copy* was kept by them at their discretion, and that Francks and himself had still possession of many of its original letters of Washington, &c. As Gen. Lee was in duress when he sent his memoirs to press, this anecdote seems plausible enough; and Mr. Ingraham was inclined to believe that the discrepancies in Lee's account might thus be accounted for. However, all attempts were fruitless to get hold of Arnold; though he led daring and destructive forays to Connecticut and to Virginia.

It was at Philadelphia, where Congress sat and where political antagonism among the Whigs ran fiercest, that Arnold was most bitterly condemned. He was attainted as a traitor, and his effects forfeited and sold. He had formerly opposed the views of the party there in power: the state government had brought him before a court-martial; and on his trial he had imputed to President Reed, with whom he was on most angry terms, precisely the same intentions of defection that he then nursed in his own bosom. To the natural expression of hatred of his crime was now joined too open an opportunity to be lost of hitting his former friends and revenging political scores. The *Packet*, the organ of the dominant section of Whigs, was loud and bitter in its indignation. It called on Congress and on the public to offer a free pardon and £100,000 to any one that would deliver him up dead or alive. This it urged would make him distrust his companions, and "at least send Arnold sooner to the infernal regions." As we can hardly believe that had circumstances put it in his power, Arnold would have spared these his mortal foes, it is not surprising they pursued this course. When he marched through Montreal he passed a stately old mansion, with a stone dog and bone surmounting the door, and this legend that may have served him in stead in his hours of rage:

> Je suis le chien qui ronge l'os,
> Sans en perdre un seul morceau;
> Le temps viendra, qui n'est pas venu
> Je mordrai celui qui m'aura mordu.

Wounded pride and the prospect of revenge had doubtless much to do with his behavior. The journal went on however to denounce him, and to call attention to those who had once supported him: and his wife's share in his guilt was suggested. The state government, Sept. 27, 1780, seized his and her papers. There was nothing to criminate her; but there were letters found reflecting harshly on the French Minister. These were secured by a member of the government — a restless zealot, says Marbois, who to serve his own party scrupled at no rigor towards its opponents — and sent to the ambassador who magnanimously thrust them unread into the fire. The *Packet* alleged also an understanding to have existed between Charles Lee and Arnold when the first came back from captivity to Valley Forge, and in proof cited from a Cork newspaper of Jan. 14, 1779, a paragraph intimating that Lee was bribed by Clinton to annoy him as little as possible in the march by Monmouth and through Jersey. It is proper here to correct an error flagrantly made by Marbois, who had every opportunity of knowing better, and repeated by Lord Mahon, respecting the lenity bestowed on Mrs. Arnold. She received none at all, unless it was in refraining to attaint her without any forthcoming evidence. At camp indeed she was believed innocent, and permitted to choose her destination. She came to her father at Philadelphia, and was anxious to remain with him; offering security to write no letters to her husband during the war and to send all received from him at once to government. The civil authorities refused her appeal, and enforced their order of exile during the war. She was compelled to go to New York, where her distressed and dejected air was very observable for a time. When her spirits however were restored she shone, we are told, in society as " a star of the first magnitude," and expectation even in London was excited by the asseverations of Tarleton and other returning officers " that she was the handsomest woman in England."

On his own arrival, though well received at court where leaning on Carleton's arm he was presented by Sir Walter Stirling, and in the cabinet where he was consulted by Germain and regarded as a very sensible man, Arnold had some pretty hard raps to receive from the Opposition. In the Commons Lord Surrey is said to have sent word to him that he would move the house to be cleared unless he withdrew, and only consented to his remaining for that once because he was introduced by a member and promised never to come again. It is difficult to believe some of the anecdotes, pointed or pointless, that are told of his rebuffs. But it appears that he was once hissed at a playhouse: and that party raillery was not withheld from him. Burke and Fox protested against his employment; and it was rumored that the king had promised not to confide to him the charge of British troops. A noble satirist in 1777 had reproached him with the reports of his early misdeeds about horses:

> *One* Arnold too shall feel our ire;
> By horses torn, let him expire
> Amidst an Indian screech!
> Nor by his death let vengeance cease,
> The jockey's ghost can't rest in peace,
> If Burgoyne forge his speech!

" Mr. Arnold," quoth the writer, " is understood to have been originally a dealer in horses, and to have had his conduct *severely criticised*, as being the reverse of Saul, in respect to certain strayed asses; for instead of finding them before they were lost, he was unable to recover them after. (See 1st Sam. ix. 3.)" The same bard now again made him his theme.

AN ODE
ADDRESSED TO GENERAL ARNOLD.

Welcome, " one Arnold," to our shore!
Thy deeds on Fame's strong pinions bore
   Spread loyalty and reason:
O! had success thy projects crown'd,
Proud Washington had bit the ground,
   And Arnold punish'd treason.

Around you press the sacred band,
Germain will kneel to kiss your hand,
   Galloway his plaudits blend:
Sir Hugh will hug you to his heart;
The tear of joy from Twitcher start;
   And Cockburn hail his friend.

Since you the royal levees grace,
Joy breaks through Denbigh's dismal face,
   Sir Guy looks brisk, and capers;
Grave Amherst teems with brilliant jests:
The refugees are Stormont's guests;
   His wine's a cure for vapors.

Mild Abingdon shouts out your praise:
Burgoyne himself will tune his lays,
   To sing your skill in battle;
Greater than Han's, who scal'd the Alps,
Or Indian chief's, who brought him scalps
   Instead of Yankee cattle.

For camp or cabinet you're made:
A Jockey's half a courtier's trade,
   And you've instinctive art;
Although your outside's not so drest,
Bid Mansfield dive into your breast,
   And then report your heart.

What think you of this rapid war?
Perhaps you'll say we've march'd too far,

And spar'd when we should kill:
Was it by coursing to and fro
That Sackville beat the daring foe
Or bravely standing still?

Heroic Sackville, calm and meek —
Tho' Ferdinando smote his cheek,
He never shook his spear;
(That spear, in Gallic blood fresh dyed;)
But like Themistocles, he cryed,
Frappez, mon prince! — but hear.

As yet we've met with trifling crosses,
And prov'd our force e'en by our losses;
(Conquest or death's the word:)
Britons, strike home! Be this your boast,
After two gallant armies lost,
Sir Henry — has a third.

Worn out with toils and great designs,
Germain to you the seals resigns,
Your worth superior owns;
Would rev'rend Twitcher now retreat,
We still might keep a greater fleet
By bribing o'er Paul Jones.

O'er Twitcher's breast, and Germain's too,
Fix Edward's star and ribbon blue,
To ravish all beholders;
That when to heaven they get a call,
Their stars (like Eli's cloak) may fall
On Paul's and Arnold's shoulders.

Carmarthen, ope your sacred gates,
The gen'rous, valiant Germain waits,
Who held the Atlantic steerage:
(He'll shine a jewel in the crown)
When Arnold knocks all traitors down,
He too shall have a Peerage!

Should faithless Wedderburne decline
To rank his name, Germain, with thine,
This truth (unfee'd) I'll tell you;
Rise a Scotch Peer — right weel I ween,
You'll soon be chose — one of sixteen —
Dare Grafton then expel you?

APPENDIX.

A more interesting tirade, insomuch as it lets in more light on Arnold's history, was made by a Mr. Robert Morris, a Welshman, who had been Secretary to the Bill of Rights Society. Morris had been left in a confidential relation by Lord Baltimore to his natural daughter. The girl had property, and he married her while she was yet very young. In two years she separated from him. He published his transactions about Arnold in a pamphlet of which I know of but one copy. It is entitled "Morris, Arnold and Battersby. Account of the Attack I made on the character of General *Arnold*, and the dispute which ensued between me and Captain *Battersby*. *R. Morris.* London, 1782." 8vo. pp. 32.

The fray began by Morris publishing, Feb. 9, 1782, a letter in the General Advertiser, in which he says Arnold had been transported from England to America for horse-stealing and was thus exposed in both countries to be hanged. But he should not be averse to the rope, since he left André to be hung, to spare himself the risk of sending him back as he came. "He sent him off to run every hazard by himself, secure of his own flight in case André was stopt." The bribe was all he wanted: "£8000, which he was sure to touch, was a capital sum for such an original beggar." He is indignant at Arnold's reception at Court. "When Sir H. Clinton was trying every negotiation and manœuvre to save his Aid-de-Camp, when whole battalions were turning out to make an offer of their blood in one desperate attempt to rescue him from the midst of the American Army, this inglorious fellow, who had brought him into and left him in all this scrape, made no offer of the surrender of his person back to the Americans, which he knew was a sacrifice that would at once be accepted, and would be a sure preservation to Major André from his impending fate." He concludes with the wish that Arnold would resent his letter; but unfortunately, liberal as he is of assertion, he had made one here that did not serve his turn. A Captain James Battersby, of the 29th Foot, who had sailed from Chatham, Feb. 28, 1776, for the relief of Quebec, and was captured with Burgoyne and several years a prisoner, had returned to England in the summer of 1781. He wrote to the Morning Herald that he verily believed Arnold did offer to surrender himself. Morris's reply evaded this point, and generally abused Clinton and Arnold: on which Battersby wrote a sharp letter, suggesting that he had already offered to fight Morris and now repeats the challenge:

that Arnold will not notice such a low fellow : — " were he disposed to resent audacious and unprovoked insolence, there are a few braying asses of rank whom he would first chastise " : — but the captain has ordered one of his negro drum-boys to chastise his antagonist. Morris again writes in general invective against Arnold, and follows with an address to Battersby, in which he says he does not believe the story of Arnold's offer of surrender, because he never heard it from any one else : and that if it were true, Arnold should have gone off without Clinton's knowledge.

Morris now strove to get a meeting from Arnold while a friend looked after Battersby. " Captain Battersby," he gently observes, " I should have no objection to see killed by any other hand instead of my own, while there was any chance of General Arnold giving me the meeting." Volunteers came to his aid against *Anti-Yankey* (Captain Battersby): "I am your man," writes Mr. Thomas Halling, " against Anti-Yankey, or any other rascally refugee whatsoever.

> I'll fight him,
> I'll beat him,
> I'll roast him,
> I'll eat him ! "

At last, a duel was arranged. Major Stanhope (Lord Harrington's brother) was the captain's second ; but being prevented from acting, Governor Skeene took his place. Captain Bailie acted for Morris. A reconciliation however intervened and the dispute was accommodated : and since Arnold's courage at least was unquestionable, we must suppose there was some other reason for his not meeting his assailer. In truth Morris's publication was in very bad taste. He says Burgoyne remarked of the dispute between himself and Battersby and its occasion : " that it was just like two gentlemen quarreling for a common ——."

More valuable by far, though not of less singular rarity, is the *Remarks on the Travels of M. de Chastellux: London, Wilkie*, 1787 : 8vo. pp. ii. 80 ; — an anonymous work which I am more and more convinced was written or directed by Arnold's own hand. The translator of Chastellux had printed matters in his Notes peculiarly offensive to Arnold and of such a nature that the author would never have admitted many of them into his own pages, severe though they be in their reflections on the English and their recent acquisition. All that is said, however, by the writer of the Remarks in relation to the business of West Point is rather in vindication of Arnold's conduct than in explanation of its details.

"From the Translator we gather, that general Arnold received seven thousand pounds in the funds; and from the Author, that he was to deliver up West Point. The death of major André is universally known; and the rank that he bore of adjutant-general in the British army. From these inferences, admitting their truth, what deductions can we draw? Could Arnold alone give up West Point? Would an adjutant-general have visited him for what he alone could have accomplished? Would he have been hazarded for the completion of so small an object? Is there nothing in Arnold's asseverations? Gave he no reasons for his conduct? He did. Much of this extraordinary event will doubtless be ever concealed; and probably little more than what has already transpired will be known to the present generation. Arnold's assertions, that America in general was satisfied with the offers of the British nation, that it was averse to the French, and the continuation of the war, were true. It has been before observed, that Washington asserted, that he would never agree to independency; and though the Congress decreed that all their votes should be styled unanimous, it is well known that more than once a single voice or two has decided upon their most important resolutions. To a certain length Galloway acceded to the American cause, and in England, people at different periods desisted from their support of America as she receded from her connections with this country; this did the great and wise earl of Chatham, the first statesman of the age.

"The argument is not whether this change of sentiment proceeded from patriotic principles, or sinister passions; it is the fact that I insist on. In our own civil wars, Hyde and Essex, Falkland and Whitlock, and many others, furnished the precedent; and this conduct must arise from the nature of man, imperfect in himself, his judgments, and opinions; and actuated from events and effects originating from so imperfect a source. Was it not so, how could a war ever be terminated? A brave, but a divided people, under the influence of conscience, and a firm belief of the justice of their cause, would fight to their mutual destruction, 'and darkness be the burier of the dead.' History, when it points out to us the calamities of civil wars, uniformly delineates their termination, not so much in the destruction of mankind, as in their change of opinion. Had Lambert escaped from his pursuers, and the army revolted from Monk, what would have been Monk's fate? And in what light would posterity consider his memory? A republican, and therefore unconstitutional party, at present detract from his reputation, but he is venerated by Englishmen in general, as the restorer of the peace of his country. That general has been blamed for permitting the restoration of the king without compact: the time necessary for making such a *free, general,* and *English compact,* would have ruined his measures; secrecy alone could give success to his arduous undertaking. He trusted, and he trusted justly, that the spirit of the times would secure the liberty of the subject, against which it was visible the crown must contend in vain. Clarendon had wisdom sufficient to distinguish the momentary acclamations of all ranks of people, happy in the termination of their individual miseries, from the sober and collective voice of their judgment. If the house of Stuart, on the removal of that great man, forgot their own interests, and ungratefully invaded the liberties of the people, it certainly was contrary to the calculations of reason, and they lost the crown in consequence; the spirit of the people, as one man, rose up against them, and let it be remembered, the Revolution was effected without bloodshed. Had Arnold, and those who thought with him, given a severe blow, and without bloodshed, to Washington's army; had he broke the civil chains of the people, and restored the sword to their hands, had they accepted the more than independency which was offered to America by Great Britain; and had the empire by these means been restored to union, who would have enjoyed the blessings of this age, and been the favourite of posterity, the active, enterprising American Arnold, or the cool, designing, frenchified Washington? These terms are derived from the Marquis's Memoirs; his opinions, and the rejoicings of the Americans upon the failure of Arnold's attempt, establish its magnitude."

In other places, the *Remarks* give some information of affairs that would be valuable according to our absolute certainty of the communicator. Of the American army he says that it was made up of all nations, and only kept efficient by the severest discipline and the coöperation of the civil authorities, which punished severely all who did not profess devotion to America. The militia spread around the camp at least served to intercept deserters and prevent marauds. Many of the generals are roughly handled; La Fayette, Sullivan, Stirling, and Greene among the number. Wayne has some praise; "if he should ever read my account of the Marquis de la Fayette, he will enjoy it, and say it is true." Lee, Mifflin, and Gates are spoken of more kindly. Reed is spoken of with severity; and what are alleged to be particular facts in connection with the imputed defection that Arnold on his trial brought up against him are recited. Of Washington the writer observes: — "I have no resentment to that general; his virtues and his vices are now out of the question; and whether he continues a land-jobber in Virginia, or the president of Congress, is totally indifferent. The exposition of truth is all my design. Success animates a mercenary army; Mr. Washington had no hold on this chain of union. The capture of Lord Cornwallis's army was the effect of joint operation and French artillery. The surprise of Washington at Brandywine and defeat at Germantown, have not added to his reputation; and the terming his repulse at Monmouth a defeat of the British army, proved, that having assumed French politics, he was intoxicated with their manners. The Congress called it a victory, the army knew the term to be a 'dishonourable gasconade.'"

Arnold's affairs could not have been bad in England, but they were not good to his wish. In the spring of 1785, he was so disappointed at not getting a hearing before the Board on Loyalist Claims that he resolved to withdraw his suit and retire into the country. Later in the year, he proposed going into trade again. "General Arnold is gone out to America too," wrote Adams to Jay. "From this, some persons have conjectured that war is determined on, or at least thought not improbable. He went to Halifax in a vessel of his own, with a cargo of his own, upon a trading voyage, as is given out. This I can scarcely believe. It would hardly be permitted a general officer to go upon such a trade. He said himself he had a young family to provide for, and could not bear an idle life. This is likely enough. I rather think then, that he has obtained leave to go out and purchase himself a settlement in Nova Scotia or Canada, that he may be out of the way of feeling the neglect and contempt in which he is held by not only the army, but the world in general."

The same military spirit, the same intolerance of inactive subordination that marked his character in our service followed Arnold into that of the British. Great as were his crimes, he can neither be accused of a lack of personal intrepidity, nor of a cringing subservience that prized slothful prosperity above the hazards of the field. In 1780 an English writer, commenting on his general's neglecting or refusing to disturb our military arrangements, uses these words:—" General Arnold, in beseeching Clinton to march out and attack Washington and Rochambeau, and on his refusal offering to do it himself with 6000 or even 5000 men, must have ruined himself completely with Sir Henry. It would be much better now for General Arnold to be in London than at New York." It must not, however, be forgotten that his defection encountered from many quarters as severe censure in England as it had received in America. To the samples of this opinion already cited I will add but one other, which is curious as showing how André was by some still styled St. André.

ARNOLD: OR, A QUESTION ANSWERED.

Our troops by Arnold thoroughly were bang'd,
And poor St. André was by Arnold hang'd;
To George a rebel, to the Congress traitor,
Pray what can make the name of Arnold greater?
By one bold treason, more to gain his ends,
Let him betray his new adopted friends!

No. II.

THE CAPTORS.

THERE has been for some years a controversy about the character and motives of the men who arrested André. On the one hand is the contemporaneous eulogy bestowed on their conduct by Washington, and the sense in which it has generally been regarded by the public. New York gave each of them a farm. Congress ordered silver medals inscribed *Fidelity* and *Vincit Amor Patriæ* to be made for Paulding, Williams, and Van Wart; and also voted each a yearly pension of two hundred silver dollars for life. On the other is the assertion of several weighty evidences that they were marauders, whose object was simply spoil.

On the 13th January, 1817, Paulding's petition for an increased pension was debated in the House of Representatives. Tallmadge opposed the prayer earnestly, going with minuteness into the details of the event from which it arose. He said the captors only brought their prisoner in because they thought they would get more for his surrender than for his release: that he fully believed in André's assertions that their object was to rob him, and that they would have let him go if he could have satisfied their demands. They took off his boots in quest of plunder, not to detect treason; and were, he said, men of that suspicious class who passing between both armies were as often in one camp as the other; and whom he himself should probably have apprehended, as was always his custom, had he fallen on them. His wishes prevailed with the House, and the petition was rejected by a large majority: but out of doors his language was strongly criticised and his conduct condemned. Van Wart and Paulding came forth with affidavits declaring the imputations untrue: and a sort of autobiography of Williams confirms the statement that it was no idea of the captors to negotiate with their prisoner. Van Wart swears he had not, nor did he believe his comrades had, any intent of plundering André; while Paulding alleges they took everything he had. The testimony on Smith's trial in 1780 shows that the proposal of releasing André for money first came from Williams and was put a stop to by Paulding: but we may suppose the former to have been insincere in his proffer, though it was promptly accepted by the captive.

In support of Tallmadge's view, King, who had the earliest charge of André, suggests that the time and place where the arrest occurred made the character of the captors questionable. "The truth is, to the impudence of the men, and not to the patriotism of any one of them, is to be attributed the capture of Major André." Major Shaw too, Washington's aide, who was present in all the proceedings attendant on the discovery of the treason, calls them "militia, or rather a species of freebooters who live by the plunder they pick up between the lines." A distinguished English friend, whose father served at the time with Clinton, has favored me with what we may suppose was the opinion derived at New York from André's letters,— "I must frankly say that my father has repeatedly told me he was taken by some marauders lying, *as was commonly the case*, on the neutral ground for pillage. That they told him if he could make good his offers anywhere without going within the lines they would free him — but on recent occasions young officers had made promises and had handed the delinquents over to the Provost-Marshal on arriving. This, and the magnitude of his offers, led them to decide on turning north in lieu of south: — nothing else." Thus it is established that what the captors deny was maintained by André himself and by well-informed officers of our army. Now the reputation of Tallmadge, King, and Shaw is just as good in our eyes as that of Paulding, Van Wart, and Williams: and it certainly was a great deal better in their own day. The only reason why their declarations do not weigh down the others is that they were not eye-witnesses of the scene. It is fair therefore to look further into the antecedents of the Captors.

John Paulding their leader was a lusty youth, six feet high and just turned of manhood, and of active spirit. Twice had he already been taken to New York a prisoner, and each time escaped. He returned from his second captivity but four days before he stopped André. His grandfather Joseph Paulding was a tenant of the great landholder Philipse at the beginning of the war, and professing neutrality was not disturbed. His sons however are represented as whigs; though I take it that Joseph, the captor's father, was one of those who, April 11, 1775, protested their abhorrence of Congress and their devotion to "King and Constitution." The old man died: the farm was pillaged: the young men had nothing to do; and on Paulding's second escape in the dress of a German Yäger that he got in New York, he joined this party to waylay the road and intercept the returning Cowboys. The act of legislature of 24th June, 1780, made it lawful for any man to seize for his own use cattle going to the enemy: under this it is said they were sanctioned in their purpose. Whatever this plea may be worth, and even admitting a certain undisciplined wildness of youth, it seems from his own statements that Paulding was in his propensities decidedly a whig.

Isaac Van Wart in his old days most solemnly protested that he never held unlawful intercourse with the enemy or visited their camp. In opposition to this is the assertion of one of the tory Pines of Pine's Bridge that he knew Van Wart was a British militia-man, for he "had been told so by Van Wart himself."

There is also an ominous complaint preserved in Ohio among the family papers of General Putnam. "Mrs. Hannah Sniffen says that Gabriel, Joseph, and Abraham Riquard, David Hunt, Isaac Van Wart, and Pardon Burlingham, did, on the night of the 27th ult., take from Mr. James Sniffen, an inhabitant of White Plains, without civil or military authority, *three milch cows*, which they have converted to their own private use. Crom Pond, July 9th, 1780. *Hannah Sniffen, in behalf of her father.*"

David Williams tells us himself all we know of him: he served for six months with Montgomery at St. John's, and was till 1779 in the militia of Westchester county. He narrates the marauds he shared in while in this service. In the summer of 1780 being out of employ, he and his friends "worked for their board on *Johnnycake*"; and occasionally took their guns and went on the road. Van Wart was his cousin: and twice in the summer they made seizures of people and cattle. The American civil authorities interfered in both instances and compelled restitution. Then came the adventure with André. A monument on the spot commemorates this last event: nor are honorable memorials wanting to the several graves of the three captors.

Mr. Headley thinks Paulding alone was free from the charge of seeking to bargain with their prisoner. The public at large believe them pure alike, and honorable. I cannot for my own part but confess that there was at least colorable ground for the conclusion of Tallmadge; but the encouragement of Washington and Congress and their own solemn affidavits are two serious obstacles to an implicit faith in its truth.

No. III.

VERSES CONNECTED WITH ANDRÉ'S EXECUTION.

Whether or not André composed a sort of farewell song before he died, it is certain he has had the reputation of doing so. The doughty Sergeant Lamb of the Fusileers, in his *Journal of the American War* (p. 338), gives a hymn of nine verses as having been written by André in his confinement. The opening stanza will I fancy be sufficient:

> Hail, sovereign love, which first began
> The scheme to rescue fallen man!
> Hail matchless, free, eternal grace
> Which gave my soul a hiding place!

The philosopher of the kitchen, the accomplished Brillat-Savarin, evidently did not refer to this piece in his *Physiologie du Gout.* In October, 1794, he visited his friend Mr. Bulow, a revolutionary officer at Hartford, Connecticut; and was overjoyed at killing " une dinde sauvage." After the toils of the chase were ended, says he : — " Pour reposer la conversation, M. Bulow disait de temps à autre à sa fille aînée : ' Mariah ! give us a song.' Et elle nous chanta sans se faire prier, et avec un embarras charmant, la chanson nationale *Yankee dudde*, la complainte de la reine Marie et celle du major André, qui sont tout à fait populaires en ce pays." The words and music of these last two pieces are given in The American Musical Miscellany : Northampton, 1798. I find André's Lament also in a large collection of broadsides, made by the late Isaiah Thomas of Worcester and preserved in the American Antiquarian Society. It is entitled — " Major André · written while he was a prisoner in the American camp ; " and was " printed by Nathaniel Coverly, Jr., Milk-street, corner Theatre-Alley, Boston." A very rude and unmeaning woodcut adorns or disfigures the head of the sheet : and the lines are given here less as André's own than as a matter of curiosity.

> Ah, Delia ! see the fatal hour ! farewell, my soul's delight,
> But how can wretched Damon live, thus banish'd from thy sight ?
> To my fond heart no rival joy supplies the loss of thee;
> But who can tell if thou, my dear, will e'er remember me ?
>
> Yet while my restless, wand'ring tho'ts pursue their lost repose,
> Unwearied may they trace the path where'er my Delia goes ;
> Forever Damon shall be there attendant still on thee.
> But who can tell &c.
>
> Alone, thro' unfrequented wilds, with pensive steps I rove,
> I ask the rocks, I ask the trees, where dwells my distant love ?
> The silent eve, the rosy morn, my constant searches see.
> But who can tell &c.
>
> Oft I'll review the smiling scenes, each fav'rite brook and tree,
> Where gaily pass'd those happy hours, those hours I pass'd with thee.

APPENDIX.

What painful, fond memorials rise from every place I see!
Ah! who can tell &c.

How many rival votaries soon their soft address shall move;
Surround thee in thy new abode, and tempt thy soul to Love:
Ah, who can tell what sighing crowds their tender homage pay;
Ah, who can tell &c.

Think, Delia, with how deep a wound the sweetly painful dart,
Which thy remembrance leaves behind has pierc'd a hopeless heart:
Think on this fatal, sad adieu, which severs me from thee:
Ah! who can tell &c.

How can I speak the last farewell; what cares distress my mind;
How can I go to realms of bliss and leave my love behind!
When Angels wing me to the skies I'd fain return to thee:
But who can tell &c.

The concluding verse is not to be found in the version of the Repertory.

What André may have neglected himself, other hands supplied. *The Literary Miscellany* (Stourport: J. Nicholson; 1812), vol. vii., declares the lines to Delia beginning "Return, enraptured hours" were composed in his imprisonment. Others formed his praises into a Glee, wherewith to compose the souls of aldermen at corporation feasts.

A 4 VOC. PAXTON.*

Round the hapless André's urn
  Be the cypress foliage spread;
Fragrant spice profusely burn,
  Honours grateful to the dead:
Let a soldier's manly form
  Guard the vase his ashes bears;
Truth, in living sorrow warm,
  Pay a mourning nation's tears.
Fame, his praise upon thy wing,
  Through the world dispersing tell;
In the service of his King,
  In his Country's cause he fell!

But it was his friend Miss Seward who at greatest length and with most applause brought Poetry to lament André's fate. From the beginning to the end this lady was *au courant* as to the army in America; and I have heard that from her Scott got the premises

---

* Hobler's Glees, as sung at the Crown and Anchor Tavern: London, 1794.

of The Tapestried Chamber. She had for several years been accustomed to pour forth her verses among a party of poets of quality who thus amused themselves under the auspices of Lady Miller, and whose bantlings were printed in four volumes in 1781 as *Poetical Amusements at a Villa near Bath.* Walpole so inimitably describes the whole assembly that we will trespass a little to give their account in his own words: — " You must know, Madam that near Bath is erected a new Parnassus, composed of three laurels, a myrtle-tree, a weeping-willow, and a view of the Avon, which has been new-christened Helicon. Ten years ago there lived a Madam Riggs, an old rough humourist who passed for a wit; her daughter, who passed for nothing, married to a Captain Miller, full of good-natured officiousness. These good folks were friends of Miss Rich, who carried me to dine with them at Batheaston, now Pindus. They caught a little of what was then called taste, built and planted, and begot children, till the whole caravan were forced to go abroad to retrieve. Alas! Mrs. Miller is returned a beauty, a genius, a Sappho, a tenth Muse, as romantic as Mademoiselle Scuderi, and as unsophisticated as Mrs. Vesey. The Captain's fingers are loaded with cameos, his tongue runs over with *virtu*, and that both may contribute to the improvement of their own country, they have introduced *bouts-rimés* as a new discovery. They hold a Parnassus-fair every Thursday, give out rhymes and themes, and all the flux of quality at Bath contend for the prizes. A Roman vase dressed with pink ribbons and myrtles receives the poetry, which is drawn out every festival; six judges of these Olympic games retire and select the brightest compositions, which the respective successful acknowledge, kneel to Mrs. Calliope Miller, kiss her fair hand, and are crowned by it with myrtle, with —— I don't know what. You may think this is fiction, or exaggeration. Be dumb, unbelievers! The collection is printed, published. — Yes, on my faith, there are *bouts-rimés* on a buttered muffin, made by her Grace the Duchess of Northumberland; receipts to make them by Corydon the venerable, alias George Pitt; others very pretty by Lord Palmerston; some by Lord Carlisle; many by Mrs. Miller herself, that have no fault but wanting metre; and immortality promised to her without end or measure. In short, since folly which never ripens to madness but in this hot climate, ran distracted, there never was anything so entertaining or so dull — for you cannot read so long as I have been telling."

APPENDIX.

Under such friendly auspices Miss Seward wrote her Monody on André, a poem of considerable merit, which has possessed greater popularity than any other of her writings and has gone through numerous editions. Its objurgations of Washington were regarded as just censure by many of her admirers, who considered his reputation snuffed out like a candle by Miss Seward's eloquence:

> Thy pen, more potent than Ithuriel's spear
> Strips from the ruthless Chief his corselet's pride,
> And shews his heart of Nero's colour dy'd.

And indeed she herself esteemed it highly. To commemorate the death of Lady Miller, she invokes the same Muse that had then befriended her:—

> Ye, who essay'd to weave the golden thread,
> And gem with flow'rs the woof of high applause
> The pious veil o'er shroudless *André* spread,
> O'er *André*, murder'd in his country's cause.

That his memory might rest in literature like Garrick in the picture between the Tragic and the Comic Muse, James Smith has added his mite to Miss Seward's labors, in a pretended volume of letters from America called *Milk and Honey, or the Land of Promise:* Letter vii.; Mr. Richard Barrow to Mr. Robert Briggs.

> — Bob, Jonathan's *queer;* he is *mizzled* a ration,
> He does not half-stomach a late exhumation;
> Some *culls*, here, have taken to grubbing the clay
> That tucks up the body of Major André.
> With yon resurrectionists, that is not very
> Unusual, who dig up as fast as you bury,
> And charge iron coffins the devil's own fee —
> (Lord Stowel there buried the poor patentee,)
> But here, Bob, the *gabies* have not come to that.
> Would you fancy it? Jonathan's yet such a *flat*
> As to think, when a corpse has been waked by a train
> Of mourners, 'tis wicked to wake it again.
>
> Methinks you're for asking me who André was?
> (Book-learning and you, Bob, ain't cronies, that's pos.)
> I'll tell you, André, urged by arguments weighty,
> Went out to New York Anno Domini '80.
> He quitted the land of his fathers to bleed
> In war, all along of his love for Miss Sneyd;

But, finding his name not enroll'd in a high line
Of rank for promotion, he took to the *Spy-line.*
He sew'd in his stocking a letter from Arnold:
A sentinel *nabb'd* it — why didn't the darn hold?
Or why, when he stitch'd it up, didn't he put
The letter between his sole-leather and foot?
By mashing it, then, he had 'scap'd all disaster,
As Pipes mash'd the letter of Pickle, his master.
Within the lines taken, a prisoner brought off,
They troubled him with a line more than he thought of;
For, finding the young man's despatches not *trim,*
To shorten my story, Bob, they despatch'd him.

He long might have slept with the *ci-devant* crew,
As soundly as *here* other buried men do;
But fashion, as somebody says on the stage,
In words and in periwigs will have her rage.
The notion of bringing dead people away
Began upon Paine, and went on to André;
The Yankees thought Cobbett was digging for *dibs,*
But when out he trundled a thighbone and ribs,
They did not half-like it; and cried with a groan,
" Since poor Tom's a-cold, why not leave him alone?"

American writers have also made the story their fictitious theme. The tragedy of *Arnold,* that of *André,* and the verses of Mr. Willis and Mr. Miller have at various times been given to the public.

No. IV.

COLONEL BENJAMIN TALLMADGE TO GENERAL HEATH.

[From the Heath MSS.]

Pine's Bridge, Oct. 10*th,* 1780. — DEAR GENERAL: Since my return from Head Quarters a few days since, I have been honored with your agreeable favor of the 21st ult. with its enclosed from Mr. Broome, as also another of the 30th ult. I am much obliged to you for your kind attention in forwarding my letters to Mr. Broome as well as his Returns to me.

APPENDIX.

Before this reaches you, the information of *Major André's* execution must undoubtedly have been received. Thro' the course of his Tryal and Confinement (during which I had the charge of him a great part of the time) he behaved with that fortitude which did him great honor. He made every confession to the Court which was necessary to convict him of being a Spy, but said nothing of his accomplices. During his confinement I became intimately acquainted with him; and I must say (nor am I alone in the opinion) that he was one of the most accomplished young gentlemen I ever was acquainted with. Such ease and affability of manners, polite and genteel deportment, added to an enlarged understanding, made him the idol of General Clinton and the B. army. On the day of his execution he was most elegantly dressed in his full regimentals, and marched to the destined ground with as much ease and cheerfulness of countenance as if he had been going to an Assembly room. Tho' his fate was just, yet to see so promising a youth brought to the gallows drew a tear from almost every spectator. He seemed, while with me, to be almost unmindful of his fate, and only regretted his disappointment.

Since Arnold has been at New York, he has flung into the Provost many of our friends whom he will have punished if possible. I fear it will injure the chains of our intelligence, at least for a little time, till the present tumult is over. I am happy that he does not know even a single link in my chain. His Excellency General Washington has undoubtedly given you the particulars of the whole hellish plot, which was laid to have nearly overthrown the liberties of this country. So providential, I had almost said miraculous a detection of such deep-laid villany can hardly be found in the history of any people.

Joshua Smith, an accomplice with Arnold, was under arrest when I left Head Quarters a few days since, and will doubtless be punished capitally.

Oct. 11*th.* — I have this moment received information from my agents at New York, but no letters. The conduct of that infamous Arnold has been such since his arrival at New York that our friends, who were not even suspected, are too much agitated at the present juncture to favor us with intelligence as usual. I hope in a little time the storm will blow over. I have two accounts from New York, but neither thro' my old channel; one of which is that the enemy have embarked a considerable body of troops and were put to sea; another that their embarkation goes on very slowly.

The letter herewith sent please to forward to Mr. Broome. With compliments to the gentlemen of your family, I am, &c.

P. S. His Excellency General Washington, with the Light Infantry, the Pennsylvania, Connecticut, and Massachusetts Lines, has moved lower down New Jersey, near Posaick falls. General Green with the New Jersey, New York and New Hampshire Lines, has gone to West Point.

INDEX.

A

Adams, John, ecstacy of, over a Philadelphia dinner, 119.
American affairs desperate, but retrieved at Trenton and Princeton, 97.
American spies, cases of, 440–442.
Amherst, Lord, advice of, in event of the French alliance, 160.
Arbuthnot, Admiral, account of, 222.
Clinton's army carried south by fleet of, 224.
Army, British, defective organization of, 43.
Deserters from, become American drill-masters, 64.
Officers of, gross private conduct of, 64.
Pigtails uniform, but noses irregular in, 44.
André, Major John, ancestry of, 1, 2, 6.
Aide of General Grey, appointment of, 99.
American lines, effort to leave the, by, 302.
Answers, frank and ingenuous, of, 353.
Army, appointment in, and views thereof by Lord Mahon, Sparks, and Miss Seward, 39–41.
Arnold's capture necessary to save, 363.
Arnold's correspondence with, 220, 273
Arnold's offer to be exchanged for, 375.
Arnold, Mrs., letter to, by, 220.
Birth, education, and accomplishments of, 6, 7, 88.
Boots of, papers concealed in the, 296–298.
Business, aversion to, subdued by, 27.
Canada, on his way to, visit to Philadelphia of, 42–44.
Carlisle, at, imprisonment of, 90–92.
Charleston, letter from before, by, 225.
Clinton, Sir Henry, letters to, by, 277, 360.
Composure and firmness in his last moments of, 371.
Condemnation and order for the execution of, 356.
André, consultation of English officials on the case of, 373.
Cope, Caleb, correspondence with, by, 89–96.
Cornwallis, view by, of the fate of, 420.
Counting-house of his father, a clerk in, 9.
Courage and coolness of, 470.
Courtship of Miss Sneyd ended by, 29.
Cow-chase, the, by, 236, 249.
Death-sentence and manly conduct of, 368.
Deputation from Clinton to save, 371–378.
Despard, Colonel, a fellow-prisoner of, 91, 93, 95.
Dream of Cunningham, prophetic of the fate of, 42.
Dream of his sister foreshadowing the fate of, 406.
Dream written by, 213–217.
Dress in elegant regimentals at his execution, by, 470.
Drop-scene painted by, 154.
Duel of Howe and Gadsden, by, 203–205.
Edgeworth's view of the courtship by, 30.
Exchange of regiments by, 199.
Execution and preparation therefor, by, 392–399.
Execution of, postponement of the, 371.
Farewell letters, verses, and sketch by, 392.
Fate of, not altogether unhappy, 444–446.
Gage's camp at Boston visited by, 54.
Gentle and humane nature of, 233.
Germany visited by, 41.
Ghost-story prefiguring the fate of, 183.
Grief of Americans for fate of, 399, 400.
Hamilton obtains privilege of writing for, 359, 360.
Honora Sneyd courted by, 12–15.
Imprisonment, manner of the, of, 90, 362.

474   INDEX.

André, interview of, with Arnold prevented, 264.
Jameson, Lieutenant - Colonel, receives, 321.
Journal and memoir of the war by, 99.
Knox, General, adventure of, with, 85.
Lancaster, prisoner at, drawing taught by, 86–89.
Liberation by exchange of, 96.
Likeness of himself executed by, 370.
Mischianza, account of the, by, 167–177.
Ogden, Captain, mission of, and its failure to save, 366.
Paulding, Williams, and Van Wart, arrest and search, 312–315.
Pension to the family of, 408.
Personal appearance of, 150, 222.
Philadelphia visited by, perhaps to observe Congress, 44.
Piozzi, Mrs., and the uncle of, 2.
Prisoner, is taken, at Fort Chambly, 80.
Promotion and appreciation of the worth of, 199.
Remains removed to England, and burial in Westminster Abbey, of, 409–411.
Rewards for the success of, 267.
Sentence of, justice of the, considered by various authors, 413–444.
Seward, Miss Anna, letters to, by, 17–28.
Seward, Miss, the will of, and Honora's picture by, 84.
Sheldon, Colonel, letter to, by, 262.
Simcoe and Henry Lee attempt to save, 374.
Simcoe's opinion of the case of, 421.
Simcoe's order of mourning for, 404.
Smith, Joshua Hett, parts from, 305.
Spy at Charleston supposed to be, 228.
Statement of his case written by, 349.
Theatrical tastes of, 53.
Trial by court-martial of, 347–356.
Washington, letter to, avowing himself to be, 324–326.
Webb, Colonel Samuel B., met by, 311.
Whitman, Lieutenant, release of, by, 114.
Will of, 402.
Yankee Doodle's expedition in Rhode Island by, 195–197.
André, Captain William Lewis, created a baronet, 408.
Arnold, General Benedict, André's arrest, and flight to the Vulture, of,328, 329.
André's interview with, prevented, 264.
André, letter to, by, 259.
André, correspondence with, of, 220–273.
Chastellux, translation of, remarks in, supposed to be by, 458.
Clinton, Sir Henry, letter to, by, 344.
Clinton's narrative of the treason of, 415–419.
Arnold, concealment among the trees, of, 289.
England, reception in, of. 453.
Indignation, feeling of, against, 339.
Morris and Battersby, dispute of, about, 456, 457.
Ode in England addressed to, 454.
Passports for André and Smith given by, 283–298.
Philadelphia, feeling in, against, 451, 452.
Price paid for the treason of, 450.
Proposal, the first, to, 447–449.
Robinson, Beverly, letter to, by, 284.
Trading voyage by, 460.
Arnold, Mrs., appeal of, to remain in Philadelphia, rejected, 453.

B

Barren Hill, Lafayette at the battle of, 161.
Biddle, Charles J., and Lord Mahon, exponents of American and English opinion in case of André, 434.
Board of general officers to try André, 348.
Boots of André, a valuable prize, 313–315.
Boston, British forces at, 63–65.
Massacre, Warren's oration on the, at, 67.
Provisions, fresh, easily obtained in, 66.
South Church as a riding-school in, 63.
Bowman, Captain Samuel, statement of André's capture by, 317, 318.
Brandywine, battle of, 107, 108.
Burgoyne, General, surrender of, 105.
Burke, Edmund, denouncing Lafayette, 427.
Byron, Lord, description of Edgeworth by, 31.
Buchanan, British consul, removes André's remains to England, 408–410.

C

Cadwalader, General, anecdote of, 160.
Caldwell, Rev. James, wife of, shot, 247.
Canada, contentment of the people of, 73.
Captors of André, review of the character of the, 461–464.
Carleton, Sir Guy, prudent administration of the Canadas by, 72.
Cathcart, Lord, account of, 147.
Caucus brought in use by Adams and others, 60.
Chambly, Fort, surrendered by Major Stopford, 80.
Champe, Sergeant, discrepancies in adventure of, accounted for, 451.
Charleston, siege and fall of, 225–227.
Chastellux, remarks on statements in translation of, supposed to be by Arnold, 458, 459.
Chew's house, intrepid attack on, 114.
Clinton, General James, sketch of the character of, 430.

INDEX. 475

Clinton, Sir Henry, André charged to retain his uniform and not receive papers, by, 275.
Burgoyne failed to be relieved by, 102-105.
Germain, Lord George, despatch to, by, 407.
Howe's plans, remarks on, by, 98.
Howe, Sir William, succeeded by, 164.
Order, announcing death of André, of, 404.
Robertson's letter to, 378.
Washington, letters to, by, 372-385.
Congress fails to excite discontent in Canada—resentment therein, 73.
Congress, inclination of, as to André, 357.
Coudray plans the works at Red Bank, 130.
Court-martial on André, character of the officers composing the, 423-433.
Cow-boys and Skinners, attempt to repress the disorders of the, 309.
Division of the neutral ground and spoliation of both sides by, 307.
Napoleon and Wellington effectually repress such characters as, 309.
Crusoe, Robinson, hangs birds in chains with good effect, 363.

D

Day, Thomas, eccentric treatment of young ladies, and courtship of Honora Sneyd, by, 32, 33.
Dobb's Ferry, André meets Arnold at, 263.
Donop, Count, failure to take Red Bank, and death of, 129.
Drewy, instance of André's humanity, by, 233.

E

Easton, Colonel, is heartily kicked by Arnold, 75.
Edgeworth, Richard Lovell, marries Honora, and afterward, Elizabeth Sneyd, 36, 37.
England, false views in, and effect in the colonies, 50.

F

Fat and well-dressed officers, anecdote of, 144.
Franks, Miss, the celebrated and fascinating, 166.

G

Gage, General, the appointment and character of, 60, 61.
Galloway, Joseph, view of Howe's campaign, by, 135.
Germantown, battle of, 112-116.
Ghost-stories, André's fate foreshown by, 42, 183, 406.

Girardot, family-name of André's mother, 1.
Glover, General, character of, 431.
Granada, plunder of the Island of, 221.
Grant, Captain Colquhoun, the famous English spy, 439.
Greene, General, character of, 425.
General Order to the army on Arnold's treason, by, 342.
Robertson, letter to, by, 380.
Grey, General Sir Charles, Baron Grey de Howick, character of, 99, 100.
Gustavus, Arnold writes under the name of, 259.

H

Hale, Nathan, case of, executed as a spy, 341.
Hamilton, Alexander, aversion of, to a counting-house, 16.
Kindly feeling for André, of, 357, 358.
Urges shooting instead of hanging André, 370.
Hand, General Edward, character of, 432.
Harry and Lucy, Edgeworth's story of, 36.
Headless soldier, account of the, 253.
Heath, General, view of André's captors by, 320.
Hessians, English and American feeling against, 128.
Howe, General Robert, character of, 428.
Howe, Sir William, character of, 137-142.
Incompetency at Long Island, of, 96.
Howes, ancestry of the, 136.
Huntington, General Jedediah, character of, 433.

I

Independence, diversity of feeling in the colonies as to, 52.
Early feeling not for, 46.
Secret plans to secure, 47, 48.
Insubordination, and Schuyler will no longer coax, wheedle, or even lie, 79.
Iron mask, man of the, 443.

J

Jackson, Major William, good treatment of, by André, 358.
Jameson, Lieutenant-Colonel, prudent course of, on receiving André, 321, 322.
Jersey, New, strategy of Howe and Washington in, 101.

K

Kegs, battle of the, 158.
King, General, statement of André's capture by, 316, 317, 323.
Knights of the Mountain and the Rose, difference between the, 181.
Knox, General Henry, character of, 431.

L

Lafayette, character and English opinion of, 426, 427.
Lamb, Colonel, urges Arnold to refuse Robinson an interview, 270.
Lee, General Charles, at Monmouth, 188.
Lichfield, sketch of the society at, 11.
Livingston attacks and drives off the Vulture, 292.
Livingston, Miss Susannah, a writer, 248.

M

McLane, Colonel, patriotism and enterprise of, 116.
Magna Charta and the Iron Barons, 200.
Mahon, Lord, view of André's case by, 434.
Marbois, Barbé, entertainment of Lafayette by, 263, 264.
    Clinton urged Arnold to a speedy surrender of West Point, asserted by, 265.
Market people receive two hundred lashes, 159.
Massachusetts, bishops viewed with terror in, 59.
    Clergy, enormous influence of, in, 58.
    Congress of, Provincial, meets at Salem, in, 61.
    Earth and hell said to be combined against, 59.
    Indians of Stockbridge induced to fight by, 68, 69.
    Indians of other tribes decline the overtures of, 68, 69.
    Political and social condition of, 57.
    Popularity, the mode of securing, in, 58.
    Tar and feathers temper freedom of thought in, 63.
    Tories lead a devil of a life in, 62.
    Treatment of officials in, 61.
Meadows, General, reproaches Sir William Howe, 160.
Mischianza, fete of the, 165, 181.
Mob spirit, prevalence of, in New England, 55, 56.
Moody, the spy, at West Point, 272.
Montgomery, General, to Schuyler on the propensity of the soldiers to steal, 83.
Moses's Law, i. e., thirty-nine, frequently administered in New England, 77.
Munchausen, Captain Frederick, aid to General Howe, 146.
Mutiny of American troops, and general dissatisfaction of the people, 252, 254.

N

Negro, character and habits of the, 300, 301.
New England troops, Puritanical names among, 431, 432.

New York, André's execution, effect of, in, 403.
    Appearance in 1778, of, 206, 207.
    Boston, travel between, and, 55.
    Belles, the reigning, of, 210–212.
    Bowerie of Jacobus Kip in, 267.
    Dining by candle-light in, 210.
    Dinner to André at the Bowerie, in, 268.
    Elopements with British officers in, 211.
    Evacuation by the Americans, 1776, of, 184.
    Evacuation by the British, 1783, of, 139.
    Fortifications, the powerful, of, 207.
    Last hours of André in, 267.
    Lobsters at Hell-Gate destroyed by cannonading, 208.
    New-Year's calls in vogue in, 210.
    Philadelphia, travel between, and, 54.
    Refugees, American, in, 209.
    Sons of Liberty in, 55.
    Theatrical and other amusements in, 209.
    Watches, custom of wearing two, in, 209.
    Winter of unusual severity in, 230.
Neutral ground reached by André, 306.
Newport, investment of, 194–197.

O

Ogden, Captain Aaron, mission of, from Washington to save André, 366.

P

Paoli, night attack at, 110.
Parliament, discordant views in the British, 48.
    Personal feeling leads to intemperate statements in, 49, 50.
    Washington, by arms, refutes slanders uttered in, 49.
Parsons, General Samuel H., character of, 430.
Patriot, a true picture of the ardent, 123.
Patterson, General John, little known of, 432.
Paulding, John, account of, 463.
Penington, Edward, anecdote retained in family of, 181.
Philadelphia, amusements and pursuits of British officers in, 145–158.
    André's arrival at, 44.
    British army occupies, 111.
    Congress meets at Carpenter's Hall in, 46.
    Custom-house at, broken open, 53.
    Delegates to Congress, entertainment at the State-house to, by the local gentry of, 53.
    Evacuation by the British army in 1778, of, 185.

INDEX.

Philadelphia, false news of fighting, and its effect in, 52.
Feeling not hostile to England in, 46.
Fortifications and disposition of British troops in, 116-118.
Mischianza, account by André of the, in, 167-177.
Plundering by soldiers in, 124-126.
Prisoners, suffering of, in, 139.
Review of the British army in, 145.
Social life, ease and elegance of, in, 119-122.
Theatricals, amateur, in, 152.
Washington's army passes through, 107.
Poetry, the, on Major André, 464-469.
Portsmouth, fort at, captured, 71.
Praise-God Barebones style of names among Massachusetts troops, 431.
Prison-ships, horrors of the, 139.
Prisoners, treatment of, in America, 84.
Profanity at head-quarters complained of by a Connecticut captain, 78.
Punishment of soldiers, bloody and cruel, 252, 253.

R

Red Bank, Donop moves against, 127.
Robertson, the arch-fiend and coin-sweater, 377.
   Clinton, Sir Henry, letter to, by, 378.
   Washington, letters to, by, 361-381.
Robinson, Beverly, account of, 263.
   André goes to Dobb's Ferry with, 263.
   Arnold's letter to, 272.
   Breakfast of Washington at house of, 328.
   Washington, letter to, by, 331.
Rochambeau, strength of, at Newport, 231.
Romilly, Sir Samuel, opinion of, as to the case of André, 413.

S

Safe-conduct, as to validity of Arnold's, 486.
St. André, Nicholas, remarkable career of, 2-5.
St. Clair, General Arthur, sketch of the unfortunate, 426.
St. John's surrendered by Major Preston, 80.
Sanford and Merton, story of, by the eccentric Thomas Day, 37.
Seward, Miss Anna, and society at Lichfield, 10, 11.
   Letter to Miss Ponsonby about Washington and André's execution, by, 391.
Shippen, Edward, and his family, 151.
Simcoe, orders of, on death of André, 404.
Smith, Joshua Hett, character of, and the extent of his complicity with Arnold, 280, 284, 299.

Smith, J. Hett, André abandoned by, 305.
Smuggling not viewed with aversion in the colonies, 54.
Sneyd, Honora, meets André, and death of, 12-37.
Sneydborough, North Carolina, named by Edgeworth, 38.
Sons of Liberty in New York, and Gouverneur Morris thereon, 55.
Spies, instances of celebrated, 438-442.
   Treatment by Americans of, 355.
Stark, General John, character of, 433.
Steuben, Baron, character of, 428, 429.
Stirling, General Lord, character of, 425.
Stony Point, capture of, by Wayne, 219.
Suspicions, mean and unjust, entertained by Congressmen and others, 338.
Sutherland, Captain, of the Vulture, writes to Clinton, 387.

T

Tallmadge, Colonel, character of, 322.
   Heath, General, letter to, with account of André's last days, by, 469-471.
   Views of André's captors, of André, and of Arnold, by, 318-323.
Tarleton. Banastre, the cool and reckless, 148, 149.
Ticonderoga taken "with uncommon rancor," by Ethan Allen, 75.
Toft, Mary, the impostor, as a rabbit-breeder, 3.
Travel between Boston and Philadelphia, 54, 55.
Treason, price paid Arnold for his, 292.
Truce, flag of, fired upon, 279.
Trumbull, Colonel, imprisonment in England, of, 406.

V

Valley Forge, the American army at, 143, 144.
Van Wart, Isaac, account of, 463.
Vulture, André leaves the, with defective measures for his return, 286-290.
   Personages carried on the, 269.
   Return to New York, of the, 332.

W

War, Revolutionary, England's admirable condition for the, 50.
   American condition for the, 51.
Washington, André, desiring to be shot, writes to, 391.
   André never seen by, 337.
   Arnold, on the impropriety of his interview with Robinson, spoken to by, 270.
   Arnold, threatening retaliation, writes to, 388.
   Arnold, Mrs., informed that her husband was on the Vulture, by, 334.

INDEX.

Washington, Clinton, Sir Henry, letter to, by, 364.
    Return to West Point, of, 327.
    Robertson, reply to, by, 362.
    Salute neglected, and indignation of, 332.
    Smith, J. Hett, reception of, by, 337.
    Stealing repressed by flogging, by order of, 83.
    Treatment of André and Smith by direction of, 340.
    Wrath, tremendous, of, 345.
Wayne's attack on the wood-cutters, 235.
West Point, André brought prisoner to, 337.
    Arnold appointed to command of, 251.
    Clinton's hopes of the capture of, 256, 257.
    Considered an American Gibraltar, because of the strength of, 255.
    Defences made insecure by Arnold at, 293, 294.
    Garrison armed and defences repaired at, 333.
    Salute to Washington neglected at, 332.
West Point, Washington returns in time to save, 327.
Westchester County, condition of affairs in, 306-310.
Westminster Abbey, cenotaph to André in, 408-411.
Wharton, curious anecdote of Duke, 165.
Whitemarsh, General Howe fears to attack Washington at, 132.
Williams, David, account of, 464.

Y

Yale College, sketch of himself by André, preserved in, 370.
Yankee Doodle's expedition to Rhode Island, 195-197.

Z

Zedwitz, Colonel, treason of, to deliver West Point, 251.

THE END.

www.ingramcontent.com/pod-product-compliance
Lightning Source LLC
Chambersburg PA
CBHW051334230426
43668CB00010B/1255